ISBN 978-1-331-81320-0
PIBN 10238032

TRUE MEN
AS WE NEED THEM;

A BOOK OF INSTRUCTION FOR MEN IN THE WORLD.

BY

REV BERNARD O'REILLY, L.D.
(LAVAL.)

"EVERY BOY AND YOUTH IS, IN HIS MIND AND SENTIMENTS, A KNIGHT, AND ESSENTIALLY A SON OF CHIVALRY. NATURE IS FINE IN HIM. NOTHING BUT THE CIRCUMSTANCE OF A MOST SINGULAR AND UNHAPPY CONSTITUTION, AND THE MOST PERVERTED AND DEGRADING SYSTEM OF EDUCATION, CAN EVER TOTALLY DESTROY THE ACTION OF THIS GENERAL LAW." —KENELM HENRY DIGBY.

FOURTH EDITION.

P. J. KENEDY,
EXCELSIOR CATHOLIC PUBLISHING HOUSE,
5 BARCLAY STREET, NEW YORK.
1888.

TO

His Eminence,

JOHN, CARDINAL McCLOSKEY

ARCHBISHOP OF NEW YORK,

THIS BOOK

ON

TRUE MEN

IS HUMBLY AND AFFECTIONATELY

Dedicated

BY

THE AUTHOR.

ARCHBISHOPRICK OF NEW YORK.

218 MADISON AVE., NEW YORK,
Sept. 6th, 1878.

DEAR FATHER O'REILLY .

I am much pleased with your new work entitled "True Men as We Need Them."

It is full of instructive lessons and wise counsels presented in an attractive form and adapted to various classes of men as we find them around us in the world.

I hope it will receive a wide circulation and be productive of much good. I need not add that it has my cordial commendation.

Please accept my best wishes for your health and happiness, and believe me to remain,

Very sincerely your friend and servant,
JOHN CARD. McCLOSKEY,
Archbishop of New York.

REV. B. O'REILLY.

THE AUTHOR'S PREFACE.

THE hearty welcome given by the public to the MIRROR OF TRUE WOMANHOOD, encourages the author to send forth this volume as a companion to it. The same plan, so far as the subject-matter would permit, has been followed in both.

Much of the utility as well as of the success of the present work will depend on those who have so generously patronized its predecessor,—the True Women of America. Coming from their hand to husband, son, or brother, the book will prove acceptable and most precious. Its lessons too must derive much of their power to please and to instruct from the eloquent advocacy of the wives and mothers to whom we must owe the true men of the future.

Renewing his sincere thanks to publisher, printer, and engraver, for their zealous and kindly coöperation, the author now leaves his work to the judgment of the public, and beseeches on its readers the blessing of Him who is Himself both Very God and True Man,—the ever-blessed Model of all true nobility of life.

NEW YORK, 8th September, 1878.

TABLE OF CONTENTS.

CONTENTS.

TRUE MEN AS WE NEED THEM.

CHAPTER I.

INTRODUCTORY.

The Ideal of Manhood.

" The age of chivalry is gone ! " calmly observe the calculating sophists, who lead the mind of the moderns, and persuade them that the world is hastening, under their influence, to a period of increased light and civilization,—a most convenient maxim to establish from the declamation of an orator ! For that is as much as to hold, that there is no longer occasion for men to be generous and devoted, faithful and indifferent to their own selfish interest, full of high honor, not aiming to follow the erring multitude, but emulous of imitating the example and of joining the society of the celestial citizens : an assertion . . . characteristic of a class of men . . . with whom every age is gone but that of economists and calculators.—KENELM HENRY DIGBY.

THAT this book will be read by young men throughout the length and breadth of our land is a hope which its author must cherish fondly. For many years of his life he has labored in educating the youth of America ; he would fain devote its crowning work to repair the errors committed in this apostleship of education. A long and comforting experience has also taught him how much there is in the hearts of American youth as well as in those of its ripest manhood, of most precious resources for the prosperity of their common country and the honor of their ancestral faith : how, then, can he help being encouraged and thrilled by the thought of aiding, in his measure, toward forming

1   1

for the coming age the chivalrous patriots and the chival
rous Christians who are to enlighten and to save the world?

He would, then, ask every noble-hearted boy and every
high-souled man who reads this page, to trust himself in
the perusal of these chapters to the guidance of one who, in
leading them through the ancient paths and placing the
while before their eyes the illustrious examples of modern
excellence, aims only at firing their souls with a holy am-
bition and an emulation fruitful in great deeds.

It is, in very truth, the love of excellence in all that can
elevate man, perfect all the attributes of true manhood, and
thereby increase a hundred-fold his power for good, that is
inculcated throughout this book. Nor,—and we hasten to
affirm it at the very outset,—is the ideal which is here held
up for the imitation of both young and old, anything like
the high standard of moral perfection, according to which
the Christian Church for nineteen centuries has been wont
to judge the virtues of those we call Saints.

Who are the True Men described here?

We are writing for men of the world, not for the apostolic
men who have to keep alive and spread the Christian faith
by their ministrations and example, nor for those who
seclude themselves from the world to become Christlike by
the practice of self-denial and self-sacrifice. Our instruc-
tions are intended to benefit laymen of all classes, as dis-
tinguished from the priest, the monk, or the hermit.
Not that the manly virtues here inculcated and illustrated
are not necessary to all those who believe in the dread
responsibilities of human conduct and expect an eternal
reward for the excellence required of all God's servants,—
but that the perfection demanded of religious orders and
the consecrated ministers of God's word, is higher in degree
and differs in kind, in many respects, while the sterling
qualities of heart and soul demanded of true men of the
world are to be measured by the peculiar duties and exi-
gencies of their worldly position.

Moreover, the True Men whom we have here before our mind's eye,—and we have been blessed by acquaintance with many such,—combine in their lives so many heroic and Godlike features, that, although living in the turmoil of wordly affairs, they would be hailed as Saints by the holiest of priests or the most unworldly of ascetics.

The True Christian, the True Man.

Our True Men, to be sure, we conceive to be, before and above all else, true Christians, sincere believers in Christ, and his earnest and devoted followers ; men having at heart to practice the divine precepts for the love of their Divine Author, and the sake of the excellence such practice begets, much more even than for the honor such fidelity may win them ; men true to God, to his truth, to themselves and their conscience, in every age of life, in every walk and rank of society, in every calling and trust, under every difficulty and trial and temptation.

It were, at best, ill taste and worse policy, in beginning a book of instruction, addressed to the men of our own time, to hint at present degeneracy, or to allow it to be thought of the model character we would hold up for admiration

> " Such a man
> Might be a copy to these younger times,
> Which, followed well, would demonstrate them now
> But goers backward." *

It shall be seen, before we have got through many chapters together, that, however we may deplore the spread of unbelief and scientific materialism in the nineteenth century, it is, nevertheless, most fruitful in the purest, the noblest, the best forms of heroic manhood, and even of Christian saintliness.

Comparisons of our own age, its institutions, tendencies, morals, and manners, with the past, could, just at present, only distract the mind from our real purpose. We have

---

* " All's Well that Ends Well," act i., scene ii.

need only of all the inherited wealth of light and gracious helps which His fatherly providence has garnered for us, who is the Creator, the Governor, and ever-present Guide of humanity. Let us only look around us, count the magnificent advantages of our position on this point of time and space, and heartily endeavor to be true to ourselves, as He who is the Way, the Truth, and the Life, wills us to be, and we shall not fail to be the True Men, whose deeds and achievements shall surely glorify our Father in heaven as well as our earthly country.

> " This above all,—To thine own self be true ;
> And it must follow, as the night the day,
> Thou canst not then be false to any man." *

Excellences found in the Men of Our Day.

Our true self, then, is what we are in God's mind what he wishes us to be in our day and generation, so as most to benefit the world amid which his design hath placed us. Let each man of us learn to be, and set himself manfully to be an

> " Active doer, noble liver,
> Strong to labor, sure to conquer," †

and we shall not only fill our place well in Church and State, but help to our utmost to make the present age hold a glorious place in the annals of the world.

No—the age of chivalry has not so utterly passed away, but that the spirit which animated the knightly institutions of old, still remains to inspire lofty aims, sentiments of the most exalted and self-denying generosity, and deeds of chivalrous daring and heroic self-sacrifice, as worthy of eternal remembrance as those that ever graced the lives of a Godfrey, a Tancred, or a St. Louis.

All this shall be made evident as we proceed. Mean while, however, lest our young readers should be led to think that we are going to propose for their imitation an

---

* Shakspeare.   † Robert Browning.

excellence of impossible attainment, or virtues too far above the paths in which they must needs walk through life, we hasten to fix their attention on the twofold excellence of character and conduct, which is accessible to every man, from the peasant to the prince, from the boy just entering his teens to the octogenarian, from the general at the head of his army to the lowliest of those in the ranks ;—accessible alike to the day-laborer, the tradesman, the lawyer, the magistrate, the physician of souls, as well as the physician of the body,—to the man most eminent in letters and science as well as to the man who is ignorant of the first elements of book knowledge.

Our True Man should be a Man of Great Character.

As we are merely foreshadowing in this first chapter the most important features of our work, it may suffice to point out here the importance of character in itself and apart from conduct, and the vital necessity for parents of cultivating, developing, and molding strongly the character of their children from the very dawn of reason.

By character here we mean the firm habitual disposition to truthfulness, honor, integrity, generosity, and resolute energy of purpose, without which no man ever was or ever can be a true man. These qualities are formed in the child by the teaching and still more by the example of his parents.

Examples may best illustrate and impress our meaning on the willing mind.

Of a man who died in 1817, at the age of thirty-eight, and whose memory must ever be dear to Irish Catholics—Francis Horner—it was said by a contemporary that the Ten Commandments were stamped upon his countenance. "The valuable and peculiar light"—adds another of his countrymen—"in which his history is calculated to inspire every right-minded youth, is this. He died . . . possessed of greater public influence than any other man ; and admired, beloved, trusted, and deplored by all, except the heartless or the base.   No greater homage was ever paid in Parliament to any deceased member.   Now let every young man ask, how was this attained.   By rank?   He was the son of an Edinburgh merchant.   By wealth?   Neither he, nor any of his relations, ever had a superfluous sixpence. . . . By talents?   His were not splendid, and he had no genius.   Cautious and slow, his only ambition was to be right.

By what then was it?   Merely by sense, industry, good principles, and a good heart, qualities which no well-constituted mind need ever despair of attaining.   It was the force of his character that raised him ; and this character not impressed upon him by nature, but formed out of no peculiarly fine elements by himself." *

The same author (Smiles) goes on to say :   "Truthfulness, integrity, and goodness—qualities that hang not on any man's breath—form the essence of manly character, or, as one of our old writers has it, *that inbred loyalty unto Virtue which can serve her without a livery.*   He is strong to do good, strong to resist evil, and strong to bear up under difficulty and misfortune."

"It was a first command and counsel of my earliest youth,"—says Lord Erskine,—"always to do what my conscience told me to be a duty, and to leave the consequence to God.   I shall carry with me the memory, and I trust the practice, of this parental lesson to the grave.   I have hitherto followed it, and I have no reason to complain that my obedience to it has been a temporal sacrifice.   I have found it, on the contrary, the road to prosperity and wealth ; and I shall point out the same road to my children for their pursuit."

These examples from a Protestant source we have purposely placed first in order, that our Catholic readers may learn how carefully Providence preserves even in the lands which reject the authority of His Church, the precious home-virtues without which there can be neither true private worth nor lasting public prosperity.   More than that, we are not to forget that civilized pagan nations, living

---

* Lord Cockburn, as quoted by Samuel Smiles in " Self-Help," pp. 332, 333.

under the Law of Nature, have always shown the same appreciation of noble manly character. All this should only shame Catholics, who boast the possession of the fullness of Revealed Truth, into the formation in their children and in themselves, of such perfect manly characters, as befit those who are, by their birthright, God's adopted children here below.

The High Sentiment of Honor.

"With our ancestors,"—says Digby, "the Catholic religion was still the base, the pervading spirit, the vital principle of every virtue. From it flowed the high sentiment of honor, the fervor of heroism, the contempt for riches, the zeal of loyalty, the constancy of friendship." And, speaking of honor, the bright crown of all manly character, the poet does but express the unanimous sentiment of all preceding Catholic generations, when he puts the following words into the mouth of a Duke of Norfolk:

> " My dear, dear lord,
> The purest treasure mortal times afford
> Is—spotless reputation ;—that away,
> Men are but gilded loam, or painted clay.
> A jewel in a ten-times barred-up chest
> Is a bold spirit in a loyal breast.
> Mine honor is my life ; both grow in one ;
> Take honor from me, and my life is done." *

Nor must what is here called honor be confounded with mere fame ; there were and there are still many of the noblest souls, who are as careless of what men may think of them as they are jealous of the testimony of their own conscience and supremely anxious to stand well in the secret judgment of the All-Seeing.

"There is nothing that cannot be endured, save dishonor," says the great St. Martin in the fourth century; "observe therefore your own actions, and do not be careless about them because they are hidden from the public eye: for it mattereth but little that none behold them, since you

---

* King Richard II., act i., scene i.; as quoted in "Orlandus."

are a witness to them yourself.   It is the precious qual-
ity of a great soul, not to be vacillating, but ever consis-
tent with one's self, and fearlessly hopeful of the end of
life." *

The Catholic Idea of Honor.

The conception of honor with our forefathers was, there-
fore, what it should ever be with their descendants,—spot-
less integrity in the sight of God, much more even than an
unstained reputation in the judgment of the world. The
former is the sure foundation of the latter ;—and it is chiefly
about it that every true man should be concerned. If we
are without reproach before our own conscience and in
presence of God, there can be but little fear for our good
name among men. Would that the men of our day could
lay this truth to heart and impress it deeply on the souls of
the succeeding generation! Then indeed might we hope,
in this land of unbounded liberty for all good, the return
of that age mentioned by the great Roman orator, "when
men had for moral safeguard, not the boasting voice of the
people, but elevation of character and spotlessness of con-
duct." †

Supreme and loving reverence for the Divine Majesty,
and the filial fear of rendering one's self displeasing to Him
who is most faithful and true, such is the habitual sense in
the Christian soul that helps to keep it free from every secret
stain. It is "the fear of the Lord" under another name.
And where it possesses thoroughly the heart of man, it is
impossible that it should not preserve his outward life from
voluntary stain. The purity and hardness of the diamond
belong to the very first particles which unite at its heart's
core ; the others which the mysterious laws of the Creator
attract around these to increase and perfect the beauteous
crystalline mass, must needs share the qualities of the

* Serm. I.

† Pro A. Cluentio, 35. *Cum homines se non jactatione populari, sed dignitate
atque innocentia tuebantur ;* words that should be written in letters of gold in
every place where laws are either made or administered.

former. The light which fills it, the perfect purity which gives even that light its highest value, belonged to the very heart of the gem. The most beautiful, the most manly, the most heroic characters in the esteem of a rightly judging world, are men whose hearts have never lost their primal purity, souls in whose very center the fire of God's love lives unquenchably, and whose lives shine with undimmed and surpassing splendor, only because from childhood to the grave they "walked by His light in darkness." *

Pagan Conception of Honorable Youth.

"Young people," says Aristotle, "are not of corrupt manners, but are innocent from not having beheld much wickedness ; and they are credulous from having been seldom deceived . And they are easily put to shame, for they have no resources to set aside the precepts which they have learned; and they have lofty souls, for they have never been disgraced or brought low. . . They prefer honor to advantage, virtue to expediency, for they live by affection rather than by reason ; and reason is concerned with expediency, but affection with honor. . . . They are full of mercy, because they regard all men as good, and as more virtuous than they are themselves,—for they measure others by their own innocence ; so that they suppose every man suffers wrongfully."

Conception of it?from the Old Testament.

See how that most beautiful adamantine quality, formed in infancy and childhood by the joint action of the Divine Spirit and of motherly training, shines with unremitting luster in Samuel, perhaps the most perfect character in the Old Testament. True, his saintly mother, under divine guidance, had led the life of a Nazarite ; nothing that could intoxicate passed her lips, and these lips were skilled in prayer. This was her chief delight. And this twofold

---

* Job, xxix. 3.

spirit of prayer and heroic abstinence did she communicate to her God-given boy.

He was a life-long Nazarite, vowed to abstinence and consecrated to the divine service before his birth. A twofold passion swayed his entire existence,—absolute fidelity to the God of his fathers, and ardent devotion to the freedom and moral greatness of Israel. With his mother's milk he drank in that absorbing love of the Divine Majesty which was the very soul of his life; the awful presence became from infancy to him a familiar reality, illuminating his whole career, like a sun that never sets. Toward the scarcely veiled face of the Lord the eye of Samuel,—child and youth, in obscure manhood and glorious old age,—was ever turned night and day; he, too, walked before God and was perfect.

These were the features of the child's character, when his pious mother brought him to the Sanctuary at Shiloh, clothed in the long white linen robe her own hands had woven for him. And when, yearly, she wove and brought him another, the beautiful spiritual and manly character that unfolded itself, seemed as much the result of her pious nurture, as the robe which fitted his increasing stature was the loving work of her motherly hands.

Samuel,—child, prophet, liberator, judge of Israel, guide and intercessor of his people and their rulers,—offers, from first to last, a model of simple unwavering fidelity to God, to his own people, to conscience, and to honor.

Hearken to the touching dialogue that took place, when this model magistrate gave over, in presence of the assembled nation, his political authority into the hand of their chosen king.

"Samuel said to all Israel   I am old and gray-headed; . . . having then conversed with you from my youth until this day, behold, here I am. Speak of me before the Lord and before his anointed, whether I have taken any man's ox or ass, if I have wronged any man, if I have oppressed any man, if I have taken a bribe at any man's hand: and I will despise it this day, and will restore it to you."

"And they said : Thou hast not wronged us, nor oppressed
us, nor taken aught at any man's hand." *

Modern Examples : St. Louis, King of France.

From the spectacle of such a perfect character thus ad-
mired and praised by a whole nation, and held up in the
Divine Book to the admiration of all succeeding ages, one
reluctantly passes to mix with the rushing crowd along the
paths of our daily life, as the half-rested traveler leaves the
cool shade and the refreshing waters of an oasis to face once
more the sand, the glare, the heat, and the oppressive soli-
tude of the desert.

There is, however, an example nearer our own times of
perfect virtue in a man of the world, which may well com-
pare with the blameless and beneficent career of the great
Hebrew prophet, without creating in the reader any fear of
contemporary allusions.

How his Character was formed.

Who does not know with what incomparable tenderness
and solicitude the canonized Louis IX., King of France, was
reared and educated by his mother, Blanche of Castile,
deemed herself, by those who knew her best, to be worthy
of a place among the saints ? She had come of too heroic a
blood not to value in her son the chivalrous virtues and
qualities which should grace a Christian king. She saw to
it during her regency, that he received an intellectual train-
ing quite extraordinary in an age when persons of high rank
set but little store on literary attainments. Louis was an
accomplished scholar and statesman, as well as a peerless
knight and commander. What, however, distinguished him
above all others, was his perfect Christian character. To
form this in her boy, the God-fearing queen would intrust
to no one but herself his instruction in the truths of reli-
gion, and his training to the practice of every virtue neces-

---

* 1 *Kings* (1 *Samuel*), xii. 1, 2, 3, 4.

sary to a Christian sovereign. "God knows, my son," she would often say to him, as he nestled near her heart, while a mere child, or sat near her in boyhood, "God knows I love thee as well as ever mother loved her dearest. Yet would I rather see thee at any moment stretched a corpse at my feet, than know thee guilty of deadly sin."

How the docile child retained through all his eventful and heroic life, the molding then given to his character, we shall have more than one occasion to judge ere the end of this book. And remembering in after-years all the pains taken for this purpose by his admirable parent, Louis was fain to bestow on his children the same loving labor. "Before he lay down in his bed," relates his intimate friend and biographer, "he was wont to have his children brought to him, and related to them the actions of good kings and emperors, and told them to take example by such men. And he likewise set before them the deeds of bad princes, who had lost their kingdoms in consequence of their licentiousness, rapacity, and avarice. 'I remind you of these things,' he would say, 'that you may keep your souls free from them, and draw not on yourselves the divine wrath.' He also made them learn their prayers to Our Lady, and made them recite their Hours twice a day, to accustom them thereby to assist at the Hours (in the church), when they should have come to govern their own lands." *

Nor, in thus dwelling on the formation of character, and recalling again and again the qualities which enter into chivalry, do we for a moment wish it to be understood that our every word is not addressed to the popular masses much more than to those whom wealth, or birth, or position place at the head of the community. It is most especially the laboring classes in town and country that we are anxious to see "generous and devoted, faithful, and indifferent to their

---

* De Joinville, "Life of St. Louis, King of France," ch. xv. The "Hours" spoken of here, are the Canonical Hours for the recitation of the divine office in cathedral or collegiate churches. It was then customary for all who could to assist at these, or to recite them in private from their "Book of Hours."

own selfish interest, full of high honor, and not aiming to follow the erring multitude." The chivalry which is the very spirit of true Christian manhood, is not the character of a social class, or the distinctive quality of the highly born, or the result of the special training given to a privileged few. The generosity, the self-sacrificing heroism, which áre its primary virtues, have ever been found in the poorest and lowliest, as well as in the foremost in rank and honor. " I can give you privileges and fiefs," said a Christian emperor to a favorite who begged to be ennobled, "but I cannot make you noble."

The nobility of soul, which we here hold up to your admiration, is the joint product of God's grace and your own generous coöperation. Parents can and do contribute greatly toward the creation of this nobility of soul and conduct; it is, however, under God, the result of one's own fidelity to the divine Voice ever speaking in conscience, to the divine Light ever showing steadily the path of duty and honor, and to the impulse of the Divine Spirit urging the babe of the beggar as well as the son of the prince to aim high, and do nobly, and be in all things true to the light and the truth within them.

How Character should shine forth in Conduct.

"I have neither riches, nor power, nor birth, to recommend me; yet, if I live, I trust I shall not be of less service to mankind and my friends, than if I had been born with these advantages." * Thus spoke at the age of twenty a poor lad, who had been brought up in the shop of his father, a carver in wood, and who was, when he wrote these words in his private diary, a druggist's apprentice. The world knows to what a height of pure fame he attained by dint of heroic labor; while the laborious life found its fittest and sweetest reward in the peace and blessing of the church of his fathers, which took the weary traveler to her embrace.

---

* Sir Humphry Davy.

It is conduct, that manifests "the active doer, noble
liver." All man's faculties, with God's light in his mind
and the mighty impulses of the Spirit ever moving his
heart, are given him that he should *do*, that he should
work, that the light of his life-work should go abroad to
his fellow men, showing them how to live, to labor, to con-
quer! It is to enable him to work earnestly, to live nobly,
to conquer surely in the strife with difficulty and hardship
and temptation, that the mother's loving nurture and wise
training, the father's example and sustaining friendship,
are given to the child and the youth; and that, in man-
hood, the sympathy and encouragement of other noble
workers are vouchsafed to him, as Jonathan was sent to
David, to be his stay and his joy in dreadful trials.

Every Human Soul capable of High Culture.

Let the young men whom these words may reach, bear
in mind the old French proverb about farming, *Tant vaut
l'homme, tant vaut sa terre* ("It is the man who makes the
land"). Just as the richest soil is worthless in the hands
of an ignorant or idle possessor, even so will the intelligent
and industrious husbandman create a mine of gold out of
the poorest soil. On our planet, to be sure, there are
very many tracts that we may regard as incurably sterile,
incapable alike of rewarding the labor of the plough or
the toil of the miner. This cannot be said of human souls
and the pregnant years of human life.

The mind and the heart of man, though born in a sheep-cot
or the hut of a savage, are a soil capable of bearing a rich
and an immortal harvest of Godlike virtues and merits.
The years that fill even a brief life, are a mine of merit,
richer and more unfailing than the gem-bearing fields of
Brazil or Golconda, or the gold and silver laden chains of
the Rocky Mountains.

Let every boy, let every youth lay to heart, — as he
remembers the life-work appointed to him, — these
dread words of the Holy Book: "Woe to them that

are faint-hearted ! . . . Woe to them that have lost patience ! "   *

Do the work you have to do bravely and well. The disposition to seek to be perfect in everything one sets one's hand to, to make the most of the task allotted for the present day and hour, is a divine instinct, which, if followed faithfully, will lead to certain eminence, to eminence in learning, in wealth, or in statesmanship ; to eminence in art, in poetry, in eloquence, or in sanctity, according to one's chosen sphere of labor.

Look forth upon the various walks of life, in Church or in State : you will find that the men most eminent and most honored in every profession and employment, are the men who have put their heart in their work ; who have begun with the determination to do as did the great king of Juda, who " wrought that which was good and right, and truth before the Lord his God, . . . desiring to seek his God with all his heart; AND HE DID IT AND PROSPERED." †

Create your Opportunities.

Do not wait for opportunities. You would only resemble the stolid traveler in the fable, who, having come to a river which lay in his path, sat down on the bank till the waters had all flowed by. *You* would seek for a ferry, or make a raft on which to cross : God gives man invention to enable him to find resources against the difficulties toward his progress. The difficulty itself is oftentimes the most golden of opportunities. At any rate, men of resolute temper seek and find, or make their opportunities, just as the industrious husbandman often makes the very soil on which he grows his crops. Have you not seen one man prosper and grow rich on land on which its former possessor grew hopelessly and helplessly poorer year after year ? Have you not seen many a stout-hearted farmer and his sons, with no capital but their courage, their perseverance, and the strong arms

---

* Ecclesiasticus, ii. 15, 16.   † Paralipomenon (Chronicles), xxxi. 20, 21.

that served a resolute will, cover many a stony field with an
abundant harvest, and convert an unsightly and unwhole-
some swamp into a rich meadow or a well-stocked pasture?

Nay, even as these lines are written under the inspiration
of the lovely spring weather, yonder lie within view the
once barren and rocky northern slopes of Central Park,
covered with a wealth of tree and shrub and flower, all
hastening to put forth their vesture of tenderest green.
We old citizens of New York remember the time, not a
quarter of a century ago, when a few scrubby firs scattered
along these crags, and a few patches of grass and weeds
alone formed a contrast with the naked and unpicturesque
rocks. Now, on the contrary, all the vegetable wealth of
other lands has been added to the varied riches of our
native flora, to create a paradise, and the very granite it-
self has been covered with a gorgeous mantle of flowering
shrubs and graceful creepers.

Thus can intelligence, industry, and perseverance convert,
what appeared a hopelessly dead and barren nature, into
life and beauty and perpetual joy.

Opportunities! Life is one grand continuous opportu-
nity from infancy to our latest day. The conscientious,
the resolute, and the thrifty turn each hour into golden
treasures; the listless, the stolid, the sensual, like our
Western Indians, allow the teeming mines to lie idle at
their feet, with countless treasures unknown, unappreci-
ated, undeveloped.

Have a Purpose in Life.

Give us, therefore, in the conduct of life, men who have
a purpose, who know what they have to do, and are deter-
mined to succeed; whose firm trust in God above them only
increases their faith in themselves: MEN WHO NEGLECT
NOTHING; who constantly discipline their own minds,
their own hearts, and exercise over their own powers and
passions a sovereign control: men whose watchword in all
their undertakings and difficulties, in all their alternations

of bearing and forbearing, is DUTY; and who, in their labors, their successes, their failures, find themselves superior to fatigue, to good or ill luck, to praise or to blame,—because they begin and persevere and hope against hope itself, through a sense of duty,—of a sacred debt due to God and their own conscience.

How Education should prepare for the Work of Life.

Education, training, discipline, cultivation of heart and mind, at home or at school, can only aim at one thing: to prepare young men for the business of life, for conduct, self - improvement, self - control, and success in the work, which the Divine Will sets apart for every individual, as the sole purpose of his existence.

In the material world we know what is the result of a constantly accelerating force, acting upon a body moving in a given direction, and in what an amazing ratio its velocity increases minute by minute, and hour by hour. It so happens that the Creator, both of the moral and the material universe, has stamped them both with such marvelous and striking analogies, that the spectacle of power exhibited in any field of the inanimate and unintelligent creation, may serve as a help toward studying its counterpart in the spiritual order.

For there are spiritual forces created by Him who is the sole source of life and of power; and they are ordained to act on the souls of men from the moment these are set forth by the Almighty Hand on the path of duty, and in the direction of their eternal destinies. Call these forces acting upon man's rational nature, graces; they are given as light to his mind, enabling him clearly to know his duty toward God, toward himself, and toward his neighbor; given as instinct, impulse, inspiration to his will, enabling him to live up to the light that is in him. These mighty impulses, if obeyed faithfully by the soul—which can freely reject the proffered aid and vital force, as it can freely accept and follow the divine direction, urging it ever

2

upward and heavenward—have an accelerating character; they augment, in a constantly increasing ratio, the soul's power of getting nearer to God,—nearer to him in perfection and spiritual beauty. They lift her with an augmented velocity to new heights of goodness, of charity, of courage, of generosity, self-denial, and self-sacrifice. They enable her to become more and more Godlike at each moment of her earthly career.

Just as in the mysterious depths of space in the starry heavens, the various bodies which eye or telescope can discern, are impelled onward in their various courses with a rapidity which appals even the scientific imagination, even so in the world of souls are there depths beyond depths, reaching away to limitless horizons, and heights above heights of acquired holiness, merit, and glory, making great and good human souls differ from each other and transcend each other in excellence, as bright star surpasses brightest star in splendor.

Superior Excellence demanded of the Men of our Day.

Hence, whatever in the past may have been the various glories of great men—men distinguished above their fellows for Godlike virtue much more than intellectual superiority —yet must we rest well assured that it is the Divine Will, that we in our day and generation, should aim with His help, to rise higher still in goodness, in generosity, in nobility of conduct.

For—and we must not mislearn this vitally important lesson to every one of us—the formation of a great character and the attainment of this same nobility of conduct, depend on our helping ourselves. The experience and practical wisdom of all past ages have expressed a golden truth in the saying: "God helps only who helps himself.'

It behooves every parent, every serious-minded person in the community to weigh well the following words, written by a well-known writer on the education given in Great

Britain. How far they apply, if at all, to our own country, our readers must judge for themselves.

"There is an ambition," says Smiles, "to bring up boys as gentlemen, or rather *genteel* men ; though the result frequently is, only to make them gents. They acquire a taste for dress, style, luxuries, and amusements, which can never form any solid foundation for manly or gentlemanly character ; and the result is that we have a vast number of gingerbread young gentry thrown upon the world, who remind one of the abandoned hulls sometimes picked up at sea, with only a monkey on board." *

Very different must be the result, if the great principles advocated in this book, and the memorable examples which illustrate their practice, are made the basis of the moral training given in families, schools, and colleges, or adopted as a guide by men of the world capable of influencing the young and inexperienced who look up to them.

Let our Young Men be God-fearing and Dutiful.

Whatever else our young men may be, when formed at home by such parents as we are about to describe, and trained in Christian schools by God-fearing and accomplished masters, they will be at least conscientious and God-fearing themselves.

This is the first and greatest need of our age.

They will be also dutiful and high-minded. For the young man whose soul from childhood has been filled with that lofty sense of duty, as of a sacred, indispensable, and ennobling obligation due to the Most High God, will be disposed to discharge every office intrusted to him, as if he were immediately accountable to the Divine Majesty. Hence everything shall be done perfectly, because done for the sake of Him who is the most loving of Fathers, and the most generous of benefactors.

High-minded must ever be the men who are penetrated

---

* "Self-Help."

with this sense of duty, and act upon such lofty motives.
He who beholds the Infinitely Great and Holy in every per-
son to whom he is bound to yield lawful obedience, will not
feel himself degraded in being subordinate to those who
may be his own inferiors in birth, in education, and refine-
ment. He will not fulfill his duty conscientiously, or go
even beyond his duty in his endeavor to do well, because
he is ambitions to obtain praise, or fearful of incurring
blame. He is only supremely desirous of pleasing One who
values the loving wish much more even than the perfect
performance.

And this high-mindedness will be thus a safeguard against
that baneful and tyrannical human respect, which is so apt
to make old people as well as young omit the good they
ought to do, and do the evil their conscience condemns, lest
they should draw on themselves the displeasure, the ridi-
cule, or the vain judgments of bad men.

The dutiful and the high-minded will ever be the faithful,
the trustworthy, true to the death, because true to God and
to themselves.

Need, in our Day, of the High-minded and Dutiful

Surely there is great need of such in our day.

And because they are thus dutiful and true,—they will
be diligent, laborious, persevering, self-denying, and self-
reliant, because placing their main dependence on the All-
Mighty and putting forth to please Him, in their every
work and endeavor, their whole strength and industry.
Such men are,—everything taken into account,—the best
calculated to succeed.

And such men,—be they born never so lowly,—are God's
true gentlemen,—the men whom all are forced to respect,
—because they are incapable of meanness, fraud, or un-
truthfulness.

These are a few only of the features of the True Man so
needed in all countries and at all periods of the world's his-
tory, but especially needed at a time when noble living will

avail infinitely more to save religion and society than elo-
quent discoursing or the most learned and beautiful writing.

Yes! the road of true manliness and unblemished honor
which we are to travel over together, leads up by steep and
toilsome paths to the only reward worthy of gentle souls.
Like the maiden-knight of the ideal Christian chivalry, if
we would keep our souls pure, and win the ecstatic joy of
coming to close communion with the veiled Majesty of our
Father, we must be ready to do and bear what the crowd
recoil from.

> "I leave the plain, I climb the height;
>   No branchy thicket shelter yields;
> But blessed forms in whistling storms
>   Fly o'er waste fens and windy fields.
> A maiden-knight—to me is given
>   Such hope, I know not fear;
> I yearn to breathe the airs of heaven
>   That often meet me here.
> I muse on joy that will not cease,
>   Pure spaces clothed in living beams,
> Pure lilies of eternal peace,
>   Whose odors haunt my dreams;
> And, stricken by an angel's hand,
>   This mortal armor that I wear,
> This weight and size, this heart and eyes,
>   Are touched, are turned to finest air." *

---

* Tennyson, "Sir Galahad

CHAPTER II.

IDEAL OF THE TRUE MAN'S HOME.

Nor do I find that the Heaven of heavens, which is the Lord's, can be better called than Thine House, which contemplateth Thy delight without any need of going forth to another. . . . That chaste City of Thine, our Mother, which is above, and is free . . . clinging unto Thee with sublime love, shineth and gloweth from Thee like a perpetual noon. O House full of light and splendor! I have loved thy beauty, and the place where dwelleth the glory of my Lord, thy builder and owner.—ST. AUGUSTINE

THERE is a most beautiful and affecting passage at the close of the very last historical book left us by one of the greatest of patriots and legislators, reciting the magnificent prospect afforded him, just before his death, of the beautiful country divinely promised to his race. From the top of a mountain, at its southernmost extremity, he beheld the lovely home of his people stretching out before him in its length and breadth, smiling like the Garden of God in the world's prime. The sight was the last earthly reward bestowed on upward of a century's labors, hopes, and sufferings, before the eternal rest came to the great pilgrim and prophet.

Can we not, at the outset of our quest after true manhood, its ideal types, and glorious realizations, cast a glance at God's beautiful earth before us, in which He bids us to create ourselves a paradise with his own assistance, bethinking us of the Eternal Home which is to be our rest, and animating ourselves to make of the earthly home its image and counterpart?

Is it not significant of a deep purpose that we should read in the very first pages of Holy Writ, how "the Lord God

22

took man and put him into the paradise of pleasure, to dress it, and to keep it " ? * There is no doubt but this Garden of Delights, selected by the All-Father from out the wide and lovely land of Eden, was the blissful home which he destined to our innocent First Parents and their innocent offspring. Fairer far than all the earth beside, the manifold beauties which this abode displayed, its peace, its security, the visible manifestations vouchsafed to its inhabitants of the Divine Presence and of the angelic spirits,—were all intended to lift up man's thoughts and hopes toward the Eternal Paradise, prepared for him and his, as their resting place after labor and the crown of all the merits acquired by trial here below.

Fair, indeed, as was the portion of earth thus set apart by the Creator for the dwelling of his privileged creatures, and filled, as we may fancy it, with all the delights that made it a vision and foretaste of Heaven,—yet did God leave much to man to do, in order to make of that Garden a home which should be truly his own,—the creation of his own love and industry.

Adam had been created outside of this Garden of Delights, in some less favored portion of the vast domain reserved for his descendants. He thus was enabled, when transferred by his Divine Benefactor to the earthly paradise, to judge by comparison of the immense superiority of his new abode to all that his eyes had beheld hitherto. This brief experience prepared him to improve by his own husbandry even the teeming soil of paradise, and to guard with unwearied watchfulness the untold wealth,—intrusted to him not only in all the produce of this fairy spot, but in his own soul and its destinies, in the companion soon given to him in Eve, in their united innocence and bliss, and in the welfare of their offspring.

Thus, in the Home bestowed on him who first on earth bore the name of father and discharged its duties, we find that there was imposed a double law, regarding solely home-happiness and well-being,—the law of labor and of vigilance.

* Genesis, ii. 15.

This law is still the blessed necessity which ennobles the life of man, and creates within his earthly home all that it can possess of bliss and nobleness : *Every true man has to work to create his home*, when he has it not ; to preserve and increase its stores, where he receives it by inheritance ; and he has to watch over its honor, its happiness, its security, with a most loving care.

We recall this primordial law, as well as the existence of the home to which it immediately applied, not that we may insist on its scope and fulfillment in this chapter—that must be reserved to another part of our work—but that we may set forth the design of the Almighty Wisdom, as displayed in His own labors in preparing us a Home eternal in the heavens, and in aiding us to be ourselves worthy of it in our own home-life here below.

The Work of the Almighty Father is to prepare our Eternal Home.

In setting before your minds, O Christian men, who take up this book and peruse its pages, the great central fact in all religion and in all history, that the mighty "Work of God in the midst of years," * the divine work of Redemption in its complete economy, is but the preparation in time of the Home of eternity, there is a twofold fear that oppresses the writer. Were he to express in befitting words the glorious reality so magnificently and still so imperfectly described in Scripture, he would feel as if the reader might justly suspect him of exaggeration. And when he would attempt to convey in the simplest terms the overwhelming truth about God's love for the human race, as manifested in the almost deified condition reserved in the life to come to His faithful servants, and in the Godlike rank and virtues, which are to be the condition of the true Christian in the present life, he cannot but dread lest the

* " O Lord, I have heard thy hearing, and was afraid. O Lord, thy work, in the midst of years bring it to life ; in the midst of years thou shalt make it known."—*Prophecy of Habacuc*, iii. 2.

infirmities of language should fail to convey the great transcendent truth.

And yet the entire scheme of God's work in creating the world and man, in appointing to him a supernatural rank and destiny, in raising him up through Christ, when fallen from his high estate, in creating through Christ a Spiritual House and Kingdom for the whole race, which is only a type of the Eternal Home and Kingdom, and in making of that Home above the masterpiece and crowning work of His power, His wisdom, and His love,—may be best stated to the mind alike of untutored childhood, and of cultivated manhood, by saying that the joint labors of God the Father, of Christ His incarnate Son, and of the Divine Spirit abiding with man evermore,—consist in preparing for mankind a HOME in the heavens worthy of God's utmost magnificence, and of enabling mankind in this life to deserve the unspeakable glories of that Eternal Home.

Do not weary yet of the golden thought held out to you, like a potent spell-word, which, if you grasp and retain it lovingly, will open to your soul many ravishing prospects and sunny horizons stretching away among the eternal hills. Hear, rather, one or two mighty voices whose accents thrill upon the reverent soul, startling it like lightning flashing from opposite sides of the heavens.

"From the beginning of the world they have not heard, nor perceived with the ears; the eye hath not seen, O God, besides thee, what things thou hast prepared for them that wait for thee." *—"Eye hath not seen, nor ear heard, neither hath it entered into the heart of man, what things God hath prepared for them that love him." †

Hear how he whose pen was said to drop honey, the great St. Bernard, comments on this passage:

"Tell us, O Thou who preparest these things, what it is that thou preparest:—'WE shall be filled with the good things of thy house.' ‡—But what are these good things? Wine, oil, and bread?—With all these we are familiar; we see them with our eyes, they pall upon our taste. What we

---

* Isaias, lxiv. 4.   † 1 Corinthians, ii. 9.   ‡ Psalm lxiv. 5.

seek is what eye hath not seen, O God, besides thee.
Here it is : God shall be all things in all of us. In the pres-
ent life our reason is liable to frequent error in its conclu-
sions, our will is swayed by a fourfold disturbing influence,
and our memory is confused by obliviousness of every kind.
To these three infirmities is thy glorious creature sub-
jected, O God, sadly to his discomfort, but not hopelessly.
For He who satisfieth in good things the desire of the soul,
will Himself be to our reason the fullness of light, to our
will the deep and overflowing tide of peace, and 'to our
memory the unbroken course of eternity.

"O Truth! O Love! O Eternity! O blessed and bliss-be-
stowing Trinity! for thee doth this threefold wretched-
ness of mine ever miserably yearn, exiled as I am from
Thee!" *

The Chief Work of every True Father among men, is to create a Home.

It is clear, from all this, that, after the salvation of one's
own soul, which must underlie the aims, thoughts, and
actions of every Christian man, what is chiefly to be the
end of every true father's efforts, is the building up and
sanctifying of a home, if he has none ; or the maintain-
ing and perfecting it in all honor, peace, prosperity, and
happiness, where it exists.

This is, in God's design and under His expressly declared
will, the first and chief object of a true man's solicitude.

Thus, while the divine Architect of the universe, con-
jointly with the angels who are the ministers of his fatherly
providence over us, and with all true men who are laboring
in conformity to the divine will,—is preparing in heaven a
dwelling-place for all his faithful children, more magnifi-
cent than human intelligence can conceive of,—even so
must you, beneath His eye, blessed and aided by him and
his Angels, set about rearing your home or making of it the
image here below of that House of God on high, where, in

---

* Sermo ii. in Cant.

the words of St. Bernard, all shall be "Truth, and Love and Eternity,"—truth in your faith and your life, charity in your dealings with your household and all outside of it, and eternity so far as you can secure it, in the independence gained for your dear ones, in the spirit of faith and honor which you bequeath to them, in the very homestead itself which is to be a lasting center for their children's children.

Nor, in the place of Him who, true Father as he is, knows no acceptation of persons,—is this primary and all-important duty of providing, maintaining, and brightening the family home, the exclusive duty of the great and the rich. There is not a poor laboring-man, who makes it his care to procure shelter, food, and raiment for his dear ones,—that is not obliged to aim at having his own home for them, and of making that home an image of heaven. There is not a youth who takes on himself the responsibilities of husband, who binds to his own lot the young wife of his choice,— who does not thereby bind himself to separate her from the whole world, to give her a home of her own, where she shall be sole mistress and queen.

Whether you be of high or of low degree, a man of wealth or a poor man depending on the earning of each day, whether advanced in years and with much experience of life's difficulties, or just setting your foot on the path,— be earnest in your resolution to work in building up your home, and with it the honor and happiness of a family, and sing in your heart as you begin the effort of each new day and hour!

This is the Golden Rule of life for all of us, men of the world, or ministers of God's sacraments, to set our hands earnestly and joyously to the joint work God appoints us to do—

To build up True Christian Homes !

The teaching and guidance of the priest are ordained only as a help to fathers of families,—from those who rule States, to those who are the lowliest and poorest. The help of the governing classes, in their turn, as well as of the wealthy, is, by the law of Christian charity, due to their dependent and fortuneless brethren. So that the whole effort of religion and of the most favored members of the social body, should aim at assisting the poor man to create for himself a home, and to adorn it with all the best virtues of fatherhood.

This is the need of the age. We must have true Christian fathers and true Christian homes. Socialism and Communism present a frightful caricature of the helpful brotherly love which is the soul and the bond of unity in all States obeying the law of the Gospel. The earnest and successful labors of the directing classes to inculcate parental duty, to practice and enforce the sweet home-virtues, and especially to aid the laboring-man in securing for himself the privacy and the sanctities of home-life, constitute the only efficacious corrective to the pestilential errors of communistic declaimers and conspirators.

The charity which we thus urge upon the men of our day is not the exercise of a new virtue, nor the application of a new remedy to social evils unheard of till now.

The very birds of the air, the very insects in the field would teach mankind how to make of the creation of the home a joint labor, and a labor of love as well. To be sure, we know that it is the special part of a man to provide a home for his companion and their children, as well as to labor for its support and to watch over its security. We are here talking not only of the house which shelters the family, but of the love which brightens and warms it, and of all the admirable virtues that should make its chief ornament. Even in the building up of the material walls, the poor man's wife will have to be most frequently his loving assistant, while in all the affections and virtues that make it a paradise, both have to contribute a generous share.

Just now, however, as the apostles of evil are endeavoring to inculcate on the mind of the laborer, that home and its sanctities and duties are the creation of the laborer's worst enemies, it will be well, after seeing the example which God sets to man in His own most glorious work, to take a lesson from the bird and the bee.

Man Taught to Labor by the Birds.

See how they labor together, impelled by that instinct or half-intelligence given them by their wise Creator, to construct a nest in which they can shelter and rear their young. And how admirable are both their labor and their intelligence! Just when the first sure signs of returning spring and settled weather tell the husbandman that he can trust his seed to the ground, we see in our northern climates the birds in pairs selecting proper sites for their nests. The amount of labor, industry, and perseverance, which even the very smallest of these feathered tribes display in this, surely ought to be a lesson to the observant among us. Both birds are equally diligent in collecting materials and in rearing the walls of the structure, though it would appear that the task of giving the interior its shape, and of lining it with the soft materials that are to keep the eggs warm and to shield the callow young during their first period of helplessness, is left to the female,—not a little suggestive of the mother's office in regulating and adorning the interior of her home.

They often work from the first peep of dawn till after the last glow of twilight to complete their undertaking. And what intelligence is displayed in the selection of the site, the choice of the materials, and the wonderful and varied industry with which these materials are employed for their destined purpose! For among birds there are miners, and carpenters, and masons, as well as weavers, tailors, and felt-makers, manifesting in their craft a skill so marvelous, and such a science of adaptation to climate, locality, and danger, that one is struck with admiration in studying the masterpieces which these feathered artisans produce. These weaver and tailor birds know also how to associate into guilds for mutual protection against their many foes, and their numbers render them secure against the most powerful birds of prey.

Taught by the Bee and the Ant.

Need we descend to the well-known examples of the bee and the ant ? Indeed, the admirable constructions of these little insects (we omit to mention so many other species well known to the reader), are more like the homes of civilized folk, than the most elaborate nests of birds, whether solitary or gregarious. The nests of these are, for the most part, temporary, made of perishable materials, and destined to rear the brood of the season. Not so the hive of the honey-bee, or the prodigious structure reared by the white ant ; these are permanent homes, where generation after generation of laborers is born and reared, and whence, the old home becoming too narrow, and not admitting of enlargement, colony after colony will issue forth to create new homes, adorned by the same intelligence, laborious habits, thrift, order, sobriety, and indomitable perseverance displayed in the ways of their ancestors.

Yes, all nature teaches man these golden lessons of industry, loving co-operation, mutual aid, and dependence order, purpose, system, devotion to the welfare and happiness of others, union of minds and hearts and hands under God to create and preserve anything lasting and glorious.

What is man without a home ? More helpless and wretched than the beast, the fowl, or the insect. He is both the enemy and the prey of every creature on the face of the earth. But with a home, which he has labored to create, or to preserve and perfect, which he lights up with the lofty examples of his life, where,—like God Himself in the world,—he only lives to do good and make others good and happy, where the love he gives is returned to him a hundred-fold by the dear ones who owe him everything,—is not man a most Godlike being ?

With this rapid glance at that sweet and sublime ideal which Religion holds up to the true man, let us now turn to the beautiful and soul-stirring realities of actual life, to the mighty divine-human forces at work beneath our eyes in creating and embellishing true Christian Homes.

CHAPTER III.

We make the world we live in ; and we weave
About us webs of good or ill, which leave
Their impress on our souls.

THE world which is to be to you a fairy-land where all is
perpetual spring and unclouded sunshine to the soul, is
your own home, *as you make it ;* it will be the ever-present
image and foretaste of that other land where joy is none,
nor peace, nor love, nor hope, if you fail to fulfill these sacred
home-duties which are to you the law of life. Where there is
self-caused misery within the home, there can be, for any man
who has the fear of God, but little happiness or enjoyment
in the wide world outside. To a husband and a father, with
a home still left to him, the roses with which pleasure would
crown him outside of it, would be a crown of piercing thorns,
the laurels bound round his brow would seem a diadem of
flame, and the most delicious fruits of the world's banquet
would turn to ashes and bitterness in his mouth. God,
who ordained the home-virtues as the foundation of the
moral world, owes it to himself and to us, that no father of
a family shall find solid happiness or lasting honor any-
where else than by the side of his wife, in the midst of his
children, and beneath the roof which the divine blessing
has hallowed as his home. If he has won her love, their
reverence, and the admiration of the outside world, the
wreath that she will weave for him will seem dearer and
more enviable than the diadem of kings, the caresses of his
children sweeter than the enthusiastic applause of multi-

31

tudes, and the meal spread forth by love on his own table, more delicious than the viands of the gods.

How many homes have we not seen among the laboring poor where the simple, and often the scanty, fare, seasoned by contentment and true love and a good conscience, was, in very truth, a foretaste of the banquet of heaven! How truly were the mutual affection and the delight in each other that welled up in these pure, simple, brave hearts, the magnificent reward of Him whose ecstatic presence even in this life overflows hearts unoccupied by worldly affections, as the rising tide fills with its rushing waters the bare bays and creeks of the seaboard!

Learn we then to "make the world we live in," "to dress and to keep" the paradise, "the garden of delights" we call our home. In that twofold labor the Divine Author of man's being would not have him to be alone: He gives the man of the world a companion, a helpmate, a friend, dear, devoted, and to be cherished beyond all that is not God. The true man's first duty, after God, is to his wife.

Conjugal Love the great creative and conservative Force in the Home.

Since the days of Adam and Eve there has been a great outcry against the latter, as if she were the sole or most guilty cause of that primal offense which lost our race the earthly paradise. It is certain that our first father, who had been weak enough to listen to the tempting voice of his companion, was also unmanly enough to throw the whole blame of his own guilt upon her. Ever since, the descendants of this unhappy pair have been divided as to the proper share of husband and wife in the ruin and misery of homes from which God's blessing had been banished. When a home is blessed with peace, and order, and love, and prosperity, there never is any dispute about the relative merit of the parents. It may be taken for certain that both have lovingly labored "to dress and keep" their sweet garden from the approach of evil.

To secure this harmony of action, and the union of hearts from which it flows, all the religious helps instituted by the Creator from the beginning, and afterward perfected by Christ, are intended. There can be in the home neither happiness, nor peace, nor prosperity, nor the blessing of children growing up in the fear of God, nor the respect of friends or neighbors, without this deep, true, holy, and lasting love of husband for wife and of wife for husband. We are not treating here of the qualities which young people, while yet they are free, should consider in the life-companions they are about to unite to themselves in matrimony. We suppose the marriage to be an accomplished fact, and are solely concerned, at the present moment, with the necessity and the means of preserving, fostering, increasing, and perfecting that union of two souls devoted eternally to each other, without which the married state is likely to be little else than a life-long bondage, and with which it is certain to be a life-long joy, even when the path to be trodden lies through hardship and struggle.

The Husband's distinctive Part in the joint work.

Manly hearts would not believe us or forgive us, were we not to declare at the outset, that the task of the husband, as the head of the family and the stronger by nature, consists in doing all that devoted love can do to cherish the God-given treasure of a true wifely heart.

To cherish the Love of a Perfect Woman.

Let us discuss the only two suppositions to be admitted here :—of a virgin heart kept by God's angels for the des-. tined husband, like a gem of incomparable beauty and price hidden away and locked up by a king for the bridal day of his son and heir ;—or of a heart either unloving, or occupied with the love of another.

In the first case, and presuming the husband to be the Christian man that he ought to be, governed by conscience,

3

and seeking in his choice of a companion the fulfillment of
the divine pleasure,—then is the treasure of love bestowed
on him by the great sacrament of matrimony, exactly de-
scribed in the beautiful sentiments attributed by a modern
poet to old Catholic Portugal ·

> "How do I love thee? Let me count the ways.
> I love thee to the depth and breadth and height
> My soul can reach, when feeling out of sight
> For the ends of Being and Ideal Grace.
> I love thee to the level of every day's
> Most quiet need, by sun and candle light.
> I love thee freely, as men strive for Right;
> I love thee purely, as they turn from Praise;
> I love thee with the Passion put to use
> In my old griefs, and with my childhood's faith;
> I love thee with a love I seemed to lose
> With my lost saints,—I love thee with the breath
> Smiles, tears, of all my life!—and if God choose,
> I shall but love thee better after death." *

Catholic moralists teach,—and it is the sentiment of the
Church,—that just as men are divinely destined and called
to the priesthood, and the life of higher perfection under re-
ligious rule, even so are they destined and called to the mar-
ried state. In each of these conditions true holiness of life
may be attained,—nay, it is the will of Him for whose glory
all conditions of life are bound to labor, that the man of the
world should be spotless and perfect in his state, as much
as the priest in his sacred station, or the monk in his clois-
ter. And to enable each one to fulfill the end of his proper
vocation, our Father and God has set apart for every one
of us an ever-present and ever-ready storehouse of graces,
out of which the divine hand daily and hourly, all through
life, bestows on each a measure limited only by the reci-
pient's own previous generosity in the use of the heavenly
gift.

Of the graces thus prepared for the use of every man
assuming the responsible duties of wedded life, the greatest
is the undivided love of a true woman. To the gift which

---

* Mrs. Browning's "Translations from the Portuguese."

such a one bestows on you, in putting her hand in yours at the altar, what is there on earth to be compared in value? You, too, can say with the supposed lover of the land of St. Elizabeth:

> "What can I give thee back, O liberal
> And princely giver . . . who hast brought the gold
> And purple of thine heart, unstained, untold,
> And laid them on the outside of the wall
> For such as I to take or leave withal,
> In unexpected largesse?" *

Guilt and Folly of not Prizing such a Gift.

Yes, this is more than a royal gift. For at royal bridals, though the East and the West may have been ransacked for the jewels which the bridegroom bestows on his bride, what are they to the love which does not go with them, or which, when bestowed, is above all the gems that earth and ocean can yield?

Do men, even when most assured of possessing this treasure, act as if they prized it at its worth? Do they, from their bridal day and ever after, make it their duty, a most sacred duty to God and to their dear companion, to study to cherish and increase this love in the tender and sensitive heart of the woman they have chosen from out all womankind? There are so many men, and they calling themselves Christian men, who, once married, seem to think that they may feel secure of their companion's love, and that no neglect of theirs, no lack of manly virtue, can lose them the love of that heart so trustfully given to them.

Experience is there, however,—a sad and often tragic experience, to prove all too eloquently how a husband's neglect chills and blights the healthiest growth of wifely affection, how the betrayal of unmanly weaknesses soon shatters the ideal young love had been worshiping, and how ill-usage but too often converts the deepest and purest conjugal devotion into a hatred still deeper and undying.

---

* The same.

Hallowed mutual Love all-powerful for good.

Love is the mightiest force of the moral world, all-mighty for good when directed toward the august purposes ordained by Him who is the Creator both of the world of spirits and of the world of matter, and who delights in aiding the workings of the human heart much more than in controlling the winds and the waves, the play of the lightning or the pathways of the light, much more even than in regulating the vast and mysterious movements of the starry universe. There never yet existed two young hearts kept pure for each other by the Great Author of our nature, and united for life-long companionship through the most ancient and sacred of His ordinances, whom He did not destine to be to each other a source of purest bliss, a mutual power toward all excellence, and the parents of a race of Godlike men and women, *if they would themselves only be faithful to the light that is in them!*

Here lies the secret of so much sin and misery, of so many scandals among every class of society, of the ruin of so many homes and the breaking of so many hearts. The mighty force of lawful love, is placed, like every other most precious gift of God to man, in the keeping and under the control of man's free will. He is left free by his Maker, to use the gift or neglect it, to apply it to the divinest purposes or to pervert it to the worst.

Man has but a limited control of the mighty elementary forces of nature. The storms which sport with his best-built ships on the ocean, the inundations which yearly devastate his fields and wreck his habitation, the earthquake-power that levels the proudest cities in the twinkling of an eye, and ingulfs whole continents in the deep, the very fire given him for so many useful and salutary ends, all show him continually that he is not their master. Nay, more than that, the very steam which he generates and utilizes as the agent of his most triumphant progress, annihilates him at every turn, as if to convince him that his most glorious conquests can never be achieved over elements that he was not born to subdue.

The strength of man and his chiefest glory lie in his mastery over his own soul, and in his power of binding to himself the souls of others. His worst sin consists in the neglect of subduing his own evil passions, of cultivating and developing the good that is in himself; in the neglect of his duties toward the souls knit to his own, given him to guard from evil, to advance in all good, to love as God has loved us, by continual devotion and self-sacrifice in favor of the beloved.

Man responsible for the Fall in Eden.

The story of the two first human beings ought to be a lesson full of warning and most wholesome instruction for every human pair, who start in life together under the sanction of God's blessing. No,—Eve was not the author of the transgression that ruined human happiness and sullied human life at their very origin. Eve was not the head of the race; she was derived from Adam and created for him; we stood not or fell not in her and through her. Man was the head; in him it was decreed that the entire race should stand or fall. When the woman whom he was bound to guard and watch over far more jealously and diligently than over his beauteous domain of Paradise, fell, in great part, it may be, because he was neither diligent nor watchful in his charge over her unsuspecting innocence and comparative helplessness,—*we* had not yet fallen. Her sin was her own, and was not to be imputed to us. Had Adam continned innocent, then had we not forfeited the sublime rank to which in him all human nature had been elevated. He fell, tempted, to be sure, by his now guilty companion; but he fell freely, with his eyes open, with a full knowledge of the consequences of his disobedience, with a lively sense of the immense debt he owed to his Creator and Benefactor, and he fell to gratify his own sensuality. No other motive is assigned in Scripture.

His fall, utterly unjustifiable, and utterly disgraceful as

it was, dragged us all down; and the ruin caused thereby required the coming down to our level in our assumed flesh and blood of that Eternal Son, through whom all things had been made, and by whom alone the ruin of all things could be repaired.

Even so now, let us not close our eyes to the luminous fact,—the ruin of the Home comes through man: woman's baneful agency is but indirect, accidental, at the very most, secondary or subsidiary. *The head of the Home is man,* the head of society is man; the destroyer of the moral world is man; its restoration and salvation must be through woman.

At any rate, certain it is that at the head of the moral order here below is man; when he fails, then there follows disorder everywhere.

Is this preaching? We know not; we would fain think it is not. Yet so earnest are we under the pressure of our great conviction, that we must set the truth forth as it forces itself upon us.

Man's Responsibility for Home-Love and Happiness.

In the home of the lowliest laboring-man, to which he has just brought the woman of his choice, there is present in the force of her pure, maiden love, and in the added force of God's grace, given to these two souls, to love each other withal and to do their life-work, a power infinite in its virtue and eternal in its duration, provided the husband understand the trust which he accepts therein, and freely use it *with the divine assistance.*

For, as surely as God is the Creator and Life-giver, so surely does He place his power and Himself at the disposal of that young husband for the fulfillment of his task, for the cherishing of the twin-soul wedded to him, and destined to be his helpmate in dressing and keeping their paradise. This lesson is addressed to Catholic men especially, who are not unacquainted with the doctrine of their Church on the nature of the various sacraments, and on the virtue of that mighty aid from on high toward all our good actions that we call *grace.*

At every instant, when that aid is vouchsafed to our mind by the light given it to see the good to be done, and to our will by the interior energy to follow where that light leads,—God himself is with the light he pours on our path and in the powerful impulse which urges the heart to go forward.

Perpetual Devotion enjoined on Young Husbands.

It is His will, then, that the young husband should cherish with infinite care and tenderness that most precious flower of love, which is to be, under God, the very soul of his happiness and his power for good till his dying day. His plain duty, therefore, from that day forth, is to make "to-morrow" even more delightful to his companion than "to-day;" to make his love for her, his respect for her, his delicate and even watchful care of her, his chivalrous devotion to her (for all that is true love), like the stream, which is but a tiny ripple of water at its birth, but deepens and widens ever as it flows onward to the sea.

Listen to the soul of pure conjugal love as a Protestant supposed Catholic women to conceive it ; and learn to measure your own upon its exquisite tenderness and delicacy.

> " I feel that I shall stand
> Henceforward in thy shadow. Nevermore
> Alone upon the threshold of my door
> Of individual life, I shall command
> The uses of my life, nor lift my hand
> Serenely in the sunshine as before,
> Without the sense of that which I forbore, .
> Thy touch upon the palm. The widest land
> Doom takes to part us, leaves thy heart in mine
> With pulses that beat double. What I do
> And what I dream include thee, as the wine
> Must taste of its own grapes. And when I sue
> God for myself, He hears that name of thine,
> And sees within my eyes the tears of two."

We must return later to this subject, full as it is of most precious teachings,—and say at present one word about the other alternative of the young bridegroom's lot,—that he has found, namely, in his bride anything save the ideal his love had dreamed of.

How Mental Inferiority in the Wife is Remedied.

What is to be done when a husband is rudely startled from his dream of life-long companionship with a woman endowed with all the virtues and perfections his fancy had painted, to find that he is wedded to the very opposite defects or vices?

It is a terrible question to answer. And yet is it not an unfrequent one. There are but few guides of souls that have not to help a disappointed and despairing husband toward finding a practical solution to this formidable and seemingly insuperable difficulty. For non-Catholics the ready solution would be in divorce and the consequent formation of new ties. With Catholics there can be no thought of divorce. The remedy is only to be found in the sacramental grace itself, and in the heroic virtues which its unfailing efficacy enables the young husband to practice both in reforming what is deformed in his wife's character and temper, and in raising higher in his own heart and life the level of all goodness and forbearance.

Example.

In a charming series of sketches from actual life, published by a gifted American lady some thirty years ago,* is related an instance apposite to our present purpose, of what may be considered a most painful deficiency in a wife.

A young French nobleman, temporarily residing in New York, fell in love with and married a lovely Irish girl, who was simply a seamstress. He was unutterably shocked,

---

* "Portraits of My Married Friends," by Uncle Ben.

soon after their union, to discover that his young wife, who had won and filled his heart much more even by the beauty of her soul than by the uncommon charms of her person, was absolutely destitute of all literary education. She did not know the first letters of the alphabet! That he did not find this out before marriage, was due to his very slight acquaintance with the English language, as well as to the correctness with which she spoke it and the grace and refinement of her manners, all of which she had acquired in the family of " Uncle Ben."

This discovery, though it cast a shadow on their wedded bliss, did not estrange the husband from his innocent, beautiful, and devoted wife. He neither upbraided her with her ignorance, nor accused her of willfully deceiving him. With admirable sense he set about remedying the deficiency of his companion, and was heartily seconded by herself, she being at bottom a woman of excellent judgment and character.

To avoid the possibility of exposing her ignorance to the eyes of his friends or of the social world, he gave up all society, associated with his business connections only outside of his own home, and so far as was strictly needful. He surrounded her in their lodgings with all the elegances and luxuries that could elevate her taste, and he taught her their value. With his aid and that of her former kind mistress's daughters, she soon learned to read and write. These imperfect beginnings filled her with unspeakable delight and a keen desire of further improvement. The gentle husband encouraged every effort, trusting to the natural talent and innate refinement of his dear one for a complete realization in time of all that he anticipated for her.

Meanwhile a daughter was born to him, who promised to be as beautiful as her mother. The latter, however, now that she had a child to rear, felt so deeply the deficiencies of her own education, that she must have been completely disheartened but for the sweet words of comfort and encouragement of her noble husband.

Alas! theirs was but a brief union. He had received

a distinguished scientific training, was a graduate of the Polytechnic School of Paris, and had an active share in the construction of the Croton Aqueduct and Reservoir. A fever contracted by exposure carried him off, consoled, at his last hours, by the angelic devotion of his young wife, and the ministrations of their common faith.

It became needful that she should go to France, whither her father-in-law pressingly invited her, offering her his home as her own. But how was she to conceal from him and his aristocratic connections her humiliating ignorance of all things which a lady is supposed to know? In this extremity "Uncle Ben" and her daughters became her efficient aids. She devoted, under their care, the short interval before her departure to the study of what was most needful, her progress being proportioned to her fervor for self-improvement.

In France, she made a most favorable impression on the aged and widowed nobleman, who loved her dearly for the sake of his only son, as well as for her own. A French master was called in to teach her the language of her new home, of which she scarcely understood a word. She was filled with inexpressible terror lest he should find out her ignorance, and speak of it to the family, to the housekeeper, especially, who had hailed her arrival with any feelings but those of welcome, and who was all too anxious to humble the admired and lovely stranger. So the French master was admitted by the latter to her secret, and won over to her interests. The neighboring Convent of the Ladies of the Sacred Heart afforded her not only a much needed refuge in her bereavement, but gave her enlightened friends in the fresh troubles that beset her path.

To her kind instructresses in New York, however, she had chiefly recourse for help. They literally educated her by letter. We have her letters to them now before us, from the first to the last, and our readers would be astonished, in perusing them, to see how much was to be learned not only in the most elementary branches of education, by one who had learned nothing in childhood or girlhood, but also in the requirements of social life in the highest ranks of a great civilized country.

In less than a year she learned to speak and write French with ease. To those around her she now had the air and the manners of a lady of culture; and, in truth, her natural talents aided by her own most conscientious efforts, had produced most striking results.

At this juncture some English friends of her father-in-law were invited to spend a season with his family, and Kate was the only person there who could entertain them. Fancy the poor thing's agony lest she should again be found out and betrayed by her visitors. Then began a new series of appeals to her New York friends for instruction on every imaginable subject, from degrees of longitude and latitude to the nature and uses of the thermometer and barometer. Nothing could daunt the intrepid learner, till she had succeeded in amassing an amount of varied information that set her at ease in every society she went into.

She was still in the summer of her beauty and grace, when her hand was solicited by a man of birth and fortune; and here we leave her, with the question: What would have become of herself and her first husband, had she not found. in him that high-born sense of self-respect, which did not permit him to allow the outside world to know the secrets of his home and his heart? or, if his true love for his companion and his gentle forbearance had not encouraged and aided her to lift herself up to his level?

Difficulty of dealing with Weak Women.

Bitter as must be a man's disappointment, when he finds himself wedded for life to a woman in every way inferior to himself and to the sphere in which he moves, the deficiency, as we have just seen, can be remedied where he is kind and patient, and she is willing and eager to learn. It is a rich nature totally uncultivated or overrun by the weeds of neglect: the weeds can be plucked up, and the rich soil made to bear a glorious crop by patient and careful husbandry.

But what if the wife resemble the *landes* of Brittany, where there is only a few inches of arable earth, cold and wet, on the underlying granite, and where nothing but furze and barren heaths can grow? What if the soil be the cold, naked rock, or the barren sand of the wilderness?

All comparisons here, if taken in their literal sense to convey the exact truth, must mislead the reader. There is no human soul (we are not here treating of idiots) incapable of culture ; and we shall see presently how the patient, industrious, and gentle skill of a true man, aided by the unfailing grace of the Creator, can work miracles in the natures that appear stricken with hopeless sterility. Nevertheless, as we must present the difficulty to the reader in its real magnitude, let us see what are these weak womanly natures out of which one might think nothing could be made, or these perverse natures, which can no more be made to bear wholesome fruit than the bramble can be made to bear figs, or the furze or heath be made sweet food for cattle.

The ancestor of an English statesman at present very prominent in European politics, warned his son, three centuries ago, in these words: "Thou shalt find there is nothing so irksome in life as a female fool."

"Female Fools"—what they are.

There are women, certainly, who can be fitly described in no other words ; pretty in face, it may be, but silly, empty-headed, lazy, idle, and as incapable of serious thought and sustained exertion, as mercury is of the temper of steel. These are weak women, or the "female fools" of old Lord Burleigh.

Such women are the product of a defective education,— whether given at home by an incapable mother, or at one of these schools where girls, like nails in a nail-factory, are all made exactly after the same fashion, without regard to natural disposition or future avocations. But how happens it, that sensible men, with their eyes open, choose such companions as these?

The mistake made in the selection is but too often to be laid to the husband's account. The headlong passion which is so apt to be caught by a handsome face, and does not stop to ask if the intellectual and moral qualities correspond to face and figure, if the practical training in all that pertains to the management of a household has not been neglected, or sacrificed to the few flimsy accomplishments acquired in a boarding school,—all this he must blame himself for. The Church is so supernaturally wise in the rules which she lays down for the guidance of young people about to contract the weighty obligations of matrimony! She will have them prepare themselves by prayer, by the reception of the Sacraments, by purity of soul, by the most sacred self-respect and modesty, to obtain the divine light on the course they are going to pursue. The fundamental and far-reaching maxim impressed upon all who are deliberating on the choice of a calling in life, or, having chosen it, are selecting the best means of filling its duties, is, that God's will must be sought before and above everything, and that to it our will and inclinations must be subordinated.

Men who choose them, Greater Fools.

It is impossible,—where God-fearing young people have been taught, in preparing for marriage, or in the choice of their companions for life, to implore light to know the divine will, and where they have prayed fervently for such light, kept their souls pure to receive it, and their hearts free to follow it,—that God should not direct them aright and guard them against the fatal mistake of such a choice as we are now censuring.

Those who are true to their conscience, true to the light within them, and careful to seek the divine will in the momentous matter of marriage, are but the very few even among our Catholic youth; the immense majority rush into matrimony blindly, without a thought of God, and intent only on following the impulse of passion or the voice of worldly interest.

We care not to insist at length upon this delicate matter. Only, we ask young men, who have neglected the divine guidance, when such mighty motives should have induced them to seek it, whether they have not themselves to blame for making a fool's choice? Let not the, sentiment of self-condemnation, however, become either discouragement or supineness. You have discovered your error,—all too common a one, in our day; now set yourself manfully to retrieve it.

How such Wives can be Educated.

But how? How is it possible to transform a "female fool" into a sensible woman? Can these empty heads be ever filled with useful knowledge? Can silliness be made serious? or inveterate indolence be stimulated into habits of wholesome activity and profitable labor? Can the whole character of a soul, hitherto neglected, be changed?

Most assuredly,—with His assistance who is ever first to prompt us to every generous resolution, and ever by our side to sustain us while carrying it out,—and with the help of our own quiet and persevering energy in coöperating with that ever-present goodness.

Man's Strength made to support Woman's Weakness.

In the first place, see to it that you keep your disappointment to yourself. Let neither word nor look of yours betray even to your companion, that you are conscious of any deficiency in her. If she loves you truly, then you have in the fullness of her affection and in the trust she reposes in you, one of the most powerful means of effecting your purpose. Do not inquire whence her "weakness,"—her softness, indolence, incapacity,—have arisen. Weakness needs to be sustained by strength. You are strong, and must prop up the weak one, that is henceforward to lean on you alone. The graceful creepers of our Southern forests receive from the lordly trees to which they cling, not only support but sustenance. Many of them derive their nourishment entirely from the trunk on which they live.

It is God's ordinance that the husband should impart to his wedded wife not only the strength which supplements her weakness, but the living energy that enables her to bear abundant fruits of every womanly virtue and graceful accomplishment.

We have known instances where husbands have succeeded, by the silent but eloquent lessons of their own example, in teaching their wives to be orderly, industrious, energetic, model housewives, mistresses, and mothers, —where by gently stimulating womanly pride, they have made them so repair all the evil habits of early training, as to become most companionable in society, as well as most efficient helpmates at home. In some of these we have known a husband to be most ably assisted by his mother or sister,—though it is not often that a weak wife will accept the influence of an accomplished mother-in-law, or of a clever sister-in-law.

The truly Christian forbearance and patient industry on the part of a husband, which we here inculcate, was most ably seconded by his mother in a case that deserves especial mention.

A Noble Example of such Transformation.

A young lawyer of good family and great promise had been smitten, during a vacation spent at a fashionable watering-place, with the girlish beauty and artlessness of a lady to whom he was introduced, and she, on her side, was not less taken by the manly grace and evident goodness of the gentleman. His parents were living in a distant State, and he did not think it necessary to consult them, having a handsome income of his own with the fairest prospects of success in his profession. His wish had ever been to find a wife uniting true goodness and purity to personal beauty; and she had been taught by her mother to prefer to all others a young man of her own faith whose past life

afforded every assurance of unblemished virtue. The young
people thought they had found their ideal in each other,
sought each other's company, became speedily engaged
and were married after less than a month's acquaint-
ance, the parents of the bride alone assisting at the nup
tials.

During his brief wedding-tour, the bridegroom discov-
ered, to his utter dismay, that he had married a beautiful
woman, indeed, but that what he had mistaken for artless-
ness was silliness, and that his wife, though unacquainted
with evil, was totally deficient in practical sense, as well as
in solid accomplishments of any kind. The blushing timid-
ity of the beautiful girl which had first attracted his atten-
tion and won his sympathy, he found, on a nearer view, to
be the self-conscious effort of a girl allowed to grow up in
uncontrolled ignorance and laziness, and who now shrank
from public observation. She was sensitive and not with-
out a certain pride. This was to prove her salvation.

He had contracted, under the discipline of his excellent
mother, the habit of monthly confession and communion.
The haste with which their nuptials had been celebrated not
having permitted them to do more than make a very unsatis-
factory confession, he profited by their stay in Philadelphia
over Sunday to prepare himself for holy communion, and
had no difficulty in persuading his wife to do the same.
Fortunately for him,—as he afterward said,—they both
applied to the venerable Bishop Kenrick ; and to him the dis-
appointed bridegrom opened his whole heart, accusing him-
self bitterly of the haste with which he had acted in choos-
ing his companion, of having allowed his judgment to be
misled by the charms of a fair young face, of having neg-
lected to consult either of his parents before pledging his
troth to an utter stranger, and, worse than all, of not hav-
ing prayed to God for light and guidance. Indeed, he con-
fessed, he had been afraid to pray, lest some secret inspira-
tion from on high should thwart his hope of possessing
without delay a prize so fascinating to the outward sense.
He disclosed his disappointment and his fears for the future

to a fatherly heart most able and most ready to give him timely advice.

The young man was bidden never to make known to any person but his mother the weakness and utter incapacity of his bride. He was to love and cherish her, to show her, both in their own greatest privacy and before others, every mark of honor and respect, laboring meanwhile to associate her in all his own private studies, pursuits, and recreations; he was to get her, as soon as possible, a house of her own, and to take to all appearance unbounded delight in superintending with her its upholstering, decoration, and management. In a word, he was to teach her what and how to do, while seeming to be only interested in seeing her at work.

That he was, at first, and even for a long time, but very partially successful, we are bound to say; that he succeeded in making her at length a wife after his own heart, we cannot affirm; still God did crown his patience and fortitude with results he could not dare to hope for during the first years of his married life.

Her silliness, inefficiency, and sad lack of mental cultivation were to him the cause of daily and hourly mortification. He never knew when she would say or do something unseemly. Indeed, she was almost certain to say and do the wrong thing, when she was most anxious to say and do the right. Yet her husband heroically kept his resolution of never snubbing her or of betraying before others his humiliation and annoyance.

Share of the Mother-in-Law.

It so happened that when the young husband arrived at his parents' home, his mother was prostrated by a long and tedious illness. She saw at a glance what a mistake her son had made, and neither she nor his father ever ventured to utter one word of reproach. They read in his looks how keen was his disappointment, and understood from his admirable behavior toward his wife, that he had determined

4

to repair his fault by unremitting devotion to her comfort
and improvement.

The mother thanked God fervently for this, and with the
instinct of a true woman and a true mother, she resolved to
win the heart of her daughter-in-law. She would show a
preference for her company above that of her own daugh-
ters ; she professed to feel better each time the timid, blun-
dering stranger conversed with her or ministered to her
comfort. Every flower she brought to the sick-room was
placed on the table within reach of the invalid. Every little
article coming from the bride's hand was made much of
and displayed conspicuously. Thus was the latter power-
fully attracted to the sufferer.

A True Mother's Wisdom.

Meanwhile the young couple had been preparing their
own residence, the mother-in-law being consulted with a
childish delight on every detail pertaining to the furniture
and arrangement. When her health was so far improved
as to permit her doing so, she was prevailed upon by her
children to pay them a visit ; and, once in the house, she
was kept perforce by its mistress, who devoted herself to
her in earnest. This circumstance was a most providential
one for the new home. The little silly wife,—thanks to the
joint but skillfully concealed efforts of the sick mother and
her daughters,—was initiated into all the mysteries of
house-keeping, and trained to preside at her own table, to
receive the most brilliant and numerous company, and thus
to do the honors of her husband's house with as few mis-
takes as possible.

When afterward left alone to her own resources, her pride
was stimulated to keep everything in the beautiful order es-
tablished by her mother-in-law,—her husband all the while
secretly aiding his companion in her laborious effort at
system and regularity.

To be sure, there were cloudy days in these first years of
their union. But there was also sunshine. The outside world,

never slow at guessing, and guessing correctly, where lie the difficulties of young married life,—had too many amusing anecdotes to tell about the queer blunders of the brilliant lawyer's not very brilliant companion. Few there were, however, who did not respect him sincerely for his chivalrous devotion to her, his constant deference to her every wish, and wonder, as well, at the marked improvement in her manners and her conversation. Everybody believed them most happy in each other ; and he certainly never allowed even her to suspect that he was not the most blessed of husbands.

The Noble Husband's Reward.

He rose steadily in his noble profession,—and as he rose, he lifted with him to his own level the weak, dependent creature, who now looked up to him with a love that almost amounted to adoration. The children born to her were reared with infinite care. Both parents drew all their strength, as well as their chief happiness in life, from their habits of sincere piety. Though they were wealthy, their life was one of generous self-denial, their home, their heart, and their hand being ever open to distress and the need of all less favored than themselves. How could God refuse to bless their efforts in rearing children worthy of Him ?

The self-sacrificing sense of duty which had sustained the husband through so many years of trial was crowned with a heroic death during the first years of our great civil war. His conduct from the hour that he awoke disappointed from his dream of early love, till he parted voluntarily with his wife and children at the call of his country, was that of the true man and the true Christian. He, his mother, sisters, and wife, followed simply in what they did and bore and forbore, the time-honored rules of Catholic morality. You will say, perchance,—this was genuine good sense, as well as enlightened piety. We shall not gainsay it. The supernatural wisdom of the Gospel only perfects our nature in its views of duty and its generosity in living up to it. The Catholic man need only be faithful to the teachings of his Great Mother to be the model husband, the loving and devoted father, and the heroic patriot, as well. Of every true son of that Mother, in life as well as in death, it must always be said :

> " His life was gentle ;. and the elements
> So mixed in him that Nature might stand up,
> And say to all the world, THIS WAS A MAN ! " *

What may be done with the Vicious.

It is when a husband is wedded to perverseness of temper or disposition, or, still more, when he is appalled by discovering vicious habits where he had expected to find every womanly virtue,—that there is need of all the strength and fortitude of true Christian manhood.

Nor is it easy to say who has the heaviest cross to bear, —the husband tied to a woman blameless, indeed, so far as moral purity is concerned, but otherwise unsociable and ungovernable,—or the man who has brought vice to rule his home.

With the misfortune of the latter,—worthy of the helpful sympathy of angels and men, we can venture only to deal briefly. We have known good men, at least in the judgment of the world and of their own family, afflicted with this irreparable calamity. Of course, where such a union is contracted without any pretense of ignoring the antecedents of the wife, the unworthly husband deserves no commiseration. Should he apply, when the consequences of the choice he has wittingly made press hard upon him, to the guide of consciences for comfort and advice, no true priest will refuse either the one or the other. It is a poor soul,—perhaps two souls,—to be saved from perdition,—or a great scandal which must be prevented from becoming greater,—and so the minister of mercy will deal with these souls in extreme need in the spirit of his divine Master and Model.

---

* Shakspeare, " Julius Cæsar," act v., scene v

Infinite Prudence and Generosity needed.

When, on the other hand, the husband's sad mishap is known to him alone, or so secret that there is but little danger of its being blown abroad, and when the sick soul with whom his life is linked is willing to be healed, then the path to be pursued is a plain one. The unhappy husband is bound to save his own honor, and bound, as a Christian, to aid in healing and saving a soul. To no one living,— save only in so far as he may have to consult his spiritual guide,—ought he to lay bare the wound in his own heart or the sin of his companion. A confessor eminent as well for his learning and experience as for his piety, will be for such a man the friend of friends, the most precious aid ever sent to mortal man in his direst need by Him who, being our Father, is ever anxious most lovingly to provide for our pressing wants.

Let a husband, circumstanced in this way, cast about for such a man of God, and his honor as well as his happiness (so far as happiness is here possible) will be safe in his keeping. From such a friend he will learn what course to follow in dealing with the guilty wife, how he is to temper gentleness with austerity, and how far any show of affection may serve to mitigate or to sweeten the bitterness worse than death of a guilty heart striving to recover itself.

When He, who is the Infinite Majesty and the unapproachable Holiness, descended to our level, becoming one of a fallen, crime-covered race, that in his merciful human arms He might lift us up with Him to His own divine rank, how did He teach every man of us to deal with the souls that had fallen lowest and wandered farthest from innocence and right?

See Him at the table of the Pharisee, surrounded by the proud censorious sectarian friends of his host, and observe how yonder woman, noted throughout the city for her sinful life, approaches the Master stealthily,—but oh! so trustfully and so reverently! It is sin, self-conscious, wretched, humbled to the dust, seeking to lay its intolerable burden at the feet of God, and drawn toward His present, visible Mercy with the united forces of its own misery and His unbounded helpfulness. How she weeps at these blessed feet! How sweet aré the tears which well up from the bitter depths in her soul! Then the long tresses are cast loose to wipe away from His feet the traces of her grief, as if it had left a stain behind! And the irresistible impulse of the new-born gratitude is to touch with her lips these same feet that had traveled so far to seek her soul!

If it be true,—and the most august and venerable authorities induce the pious mind to believe it,—that it was this same "sinner" who followed her Benefactor to the Cross, who stood with His Mother beneath its dreadful shadow, amid the terrors of the earthquake and the darkness, the threats, the violence, the blasphemies, and mockeries of the brutal crowd; who watched by His remains, and waited near his sepulcher, when only one man among the chosen Twelve, and one only from among the hundreds of his disciples, dared to render the last sad honors to the glorious Dead;—then we know what repentant love can do, and what divine generosity can fill a heart renovated by God-given sorrow, and overflow in a life redeemed from shame by forgiveness and a love proportioned to the mercy shown.

This must be the eternal model held out to manly pity while dealing with the erring,—with those especially who have the nearest claims on one's affections.

See how mercifully that most loving Kindness shields the poor penitent at His feet from the prurient curiosity and pitiless judgment of the host and his uncharitable circle of guests. He exalts the heroic faith of that heart-stricken one, immeasurably above the scant courtesy of the Pharisee and his household. "I entered into thy house; thou gavest me no water for my feet: but she with tears hath washed my feet, and with her hairs hath wiped them. Thou gavest me no kiss; but she, since she came in hath not ceased to kiss my feet."

If the soul which reads this page is one which God has

stamped with the nobleness of true manhood, then may we be dispensed from further dwelling on a subject so full of subtle danger to the inexperienced. We who need forgiveness and are not sure of deserving it, pitiless that we are toward the erring, would do well to ponder these sentiments of a womanly heart well tried by suffering:

> "Two sayings of the Holy Scriptures beat
> Like pulses in the Church's brow and breast;
> And by them we find rest in our unrest,
> And heart-deep in salt tears, do yet entreat
> God's fellowship, as if on heavenly seat.
> The first is JESUS WEPT, wherein is pressed
> Full many a sobbing face that drops its best
> And sweetest waters on the record sweet;
> And one is, where the Christ denied and scorned
> LOOKED UPON PETER. Oh! to render plain,
> By help of having loved a little and mourned,
> That look of sovereign love and sovereign pain
> Which he who could not sin yet suffered, turned
> On him who could reject but not sustain!"

Oh! manly hearts, capable of every divine sentiment and Godlike·deed, do not "reject" Him in the persons of his most needy ones; but learn to lift up, and strengthen and "sustain," those dearest to his mercy, because most in need of it,—and what may you not hope from Him?

How to Deal with Perverse Wives.

With mere perversity of disposition and temper, it is even harder to deal than with the fallen and guilty. The soul gently, mercifully, and tenderly dealt with by forgiveness, and the generous aid bestowed toward newness of life,—feels prompted by all the noblest instincts of its nature to be humble and reverent and docile in its demeanor toward its helpmate and physician.

Not so with that perversity which has its roots in pride and utter selfishness. Pride, its parent, has never taught it to respect others or to yield to them in aught; and selfishness, which is its nurse, has accustomed its bantling to consider nothing but its own wants and caprices.

One man's noble but utterly wretched life is now before us, a life open to many not only in its public merits, but in its domestic griefs.

His was a nature as innocent, as guileless as a babe's, giving out the light and warmth of his great soul as freely, as unreservedly as the sun distributes its beams. From his destitute boyhood and struggling youth upward to the close of his most useful and honored life, that rich nature of his continued to glow, to enlighten, to cheer others forward in every noble pursuit. And all that,—in spite of the young, beautiful, but perverse companion, who made his home dark and cheerless by her ungovernable temper, and starved a heart which yearned for love and home-comfort.

Why these Types of Women are mentioned.

How many such wives are to be found in all classes? How often is the home of the rich man, whose wealth and position are the reward of a whole life of unceasing application to business, rendered unendurable by such perverseness as the above! And how many sober, hard-working, and noble-minded mechanics and laboring-men, are driven to the tavern, to intemperance, and to ruin temporal and eternal, by these domestic furies, who have never learned to govern either their temper or their tongue!

Are we saying this to excuse or cloak over the sins of the men in the household,—husbands, sons, or brothers? or, are we holding up the infirmities of the weaker sex to censure, in order to shield from blame the vices of the sex which should ever be the support, the guide, the model, of wife, of daughter, and sister?

No, certainly. We are, like guides over the snow-fields and passes of the Alps, only pointing out from an eminence, the treacherous fissures in the ice where so many unwary travelers have already perished, or the precipitous mountain-slopes rendered famous by many a fatal mishap. We know of countless, countless homes made unhappy and unendurable to husbands, sons, and daughters, by the untamed temper of those who should have been the angels of these homes, making them the bright, peaceful, restful places to which their dear ones might come after toil to find the sweet image of God's Home on high. We state the fact simply in order to address ourselves to the manly hearts in whom we trust, and to urge them by every most powerful motive to exercise a double share of heroism in counteracting the unavoidable evil

Fortitude required to overcome Perverseness.

Marvelous and incredible as are the effects of a noble woman's patient, uncomplaining fortitude and unwearied industry in maintaining a home and hallowing it in spite of a husband's unthriftiness and vice,—there is something still more deserving of admiration in the patient endurance of a husband tied to a shiftless woman whose wicked tongue never tires.

We have known of a family of eight children, born of such a graceless mother, and reared through the saintly examples of their father to be, all of them, model men and women. The father himself, a poor shoemaker, taught every one of his children reading and writing, as well as the elements of Christian doctrine, made them, from childhood, love to share with him his daily practices of piety, to kneel with him monthly at the Table of the Lamb, and to aid him, as they grew up, to make of his home a place so sweet and so restful, that the priest of the parish was wont to bring his friends there to show them a model Christian household. Two of the sons learned their father's trade, and in course of time his business increased and brought him far more than plenty. The other boy became a distinguished civil engineer, and three of the girls, when we last heard of the family, had married well-to-do tradesmen, and made admirable wives.

But what of their mother? it will naturally be asked. She died, stricken with paralysis, after twenty-one years of married life,—a portly dame, who had brought to her husband for dowry a handsome face, the scourge of a tongue that nothing could quiet but the icy hand of death, and a temper which neither the examples of her husband and children, nor the exact performance of her outward religious duties, could ever sweeten. One would think that she had been sent to that household to afford its inmates a perpetual occasion of practicing the sweetest domestic virtues. Few among their neighbors and acquaintances were allowed to suspect the existence of such shocking infirmities in the wife and mother.

The secret of this true manhood in this lowly-born and scarcely educated craftsman, was his high sense of duty; and it was the idea of duty which governed the conduct of his noble children toward their mother. The husband, docile to the voice of his conscience, when on the very threshold of his married life he discovered his wife's infirmities of judgment, temper, and conduct,—resolved forthwith to devote his life to the one purpose of reforming her if he could, or of bearing with her, if he could not. But, whether he could or not, he owed it to God, he thought, that he should be master in the house of his own soul, and overcome his wife's violence by invincible patience, and repair the consequences of her shiftlessness and utter incapacity by his own application. He loved her tenderly when he sought and wooed her; that love survived to the end in spite of her manifold defects. And she, in spite of that other wrathful spirit which seemed to rule her own, never ceased to love him truly. She boasted to all who knew her that he was the best of men, and confesssed herself unworthy of him. One resolution he formed during the very first month of their union,—that he should never taste intoxicating drinks so long as he lived; and he kept it sacredly. His sons found no difficulty in walking in the footsteps of a father, whose life in every one of its most secret details, could bear the scrutiny of God's recording angel.

How could such children help honoring their mother, and, like their father, never even among themselves, alluding to her weaknesses?

Will you say that such examples are almost above the
ordinary strength of human nature? We can only reply
that they are in exact conformity with the examples shown
forth in the Gospel, and intended for imitation in the ordi-
nary every-day life of Christian households. To convince
you of this, weigh well the pregnant teaching of the follow-
ing chapter.

The life of a man who is happily married to a woman
after his own heart and after the heart of God as well, is, de-
spite the trials and sufferings incidental to the lot of the best
and truest men,—like a safe and smooth voyage down our
great South American streams, amid all the magnificences
of nature. On the contrary, such a life as that at which
we have been glancing, is a journey through sandy wastes
and treeless mountain-solitudes, where only pools of brack-
ish, bitter water offer to the wayfarers any chance of re-
freshment. Did not the God who made the whole earth
command the great Hebrew leader of old, as his famishing
people lay down near such poisonous pools as these, to cast
into them a wood which He designated, and were not the
waters thereby made sweet and wholesome?*

Have we Christians, after eighteen centuries of Christian
life, yet to learn what is the virtue of the Cross to sweeten
what appears hopelessly bitter in home-life, and the power
of the Crucified to lighten life's most intolerable burthen
for every man who will take up his cross and follow Him?

We bid the reader to the study of the following chapter,
as we would to listen to the divinest harmonies ever created
by human genius.

---

* Exodus, xv. 22, 24 ; Numbers, xxxiii. 8.

CHAPTER IV.

PARADISE AS REALIZED IN THE HOME OF THE TRUE MAN.

'Ω χαῖρε, μέλαθρον προπυλά θ' ἑστίας ἐμῆς,
Ὡς ἄσμενος σ' ἐσεῖδον !

Oh ! hail, my roof-tree and threshold of my home,
How glad I saw thee !

The Catholic Church attracts those who love the simplicity of natural manners, by the harmonies of a restored creation. . . . The Catholic Religion is not presented to us as separated from nature, but in conjunction with it forming a grand whole, fostering all the domestic affections with manhood, gentleness, liberality, and all the virtues which conduce to the happiness of HOME, banishing not more the luxuries which militate directly against the social state in general, than the false notions of spirituality which would interfere with the free action of the natural relations. For, as a recent author says, *the beauty, peace, unity, and truth of life repose on that religious equilibrium which protects the flesh against the pride of the spirit, and the spirit against the invasions of the flesh.* . . . In truth, nothing is so natural as Catholicity—nothing so full of heart—nothing so favorable, therefore, to all the sweets of Home. Virgins and boys, mid-age and wrinkled elders, soft infancy that nothing can but cry, all are in the secret of its charm.—KENELM HENRY DIGBY.

LET it not be thought that we dwell at too great a length upon this notion of Home, and all the duties and charities inseparably connected with home-life. When one looks abroad upon the nations which once constituted Christendom, and examines seriously the causes of social and political prosperity or decay, this great fact stands forth as evidently as a bright beacon-light in the darkness over a dangerous reef: *The strength or weakness, the vitality or decadence of nations, is to be measured by the purity of their home-life, by their sacred regard for Home, its authority, and its sanctities.*

60

Take any one people among whom Home,—from that of the sovereign or chief magistrate to the lowliest and poorest citizen,—is protected by law, manners, and a wholesome public opinion, against everything calculated to loosen or to weaken the sacredness of the marriage tie, the rights of parental authority as sanctioned by the Christian law and immemorial custom, or the duties of filial love and reverence,— and you will find the nation distinguished for private worth, political honesty, and an enlightened love of freedom.

Abuses there may and will be in the administration of the best human institutions; but where the homes of a nation are sincerely and thoroughly Christian, public corruption must find a certain and most effective remedy in a public opinion fed by the purity and honesty of private life.

The labor bestowed on describing the Home as it ought to be, and as it still is in many Christian lands, is surely a labor well bestowed, and the pains taken to make the description of home-life so enchanting, that all may feel its charm, must assuredly be blessed of God, the Author of our nature and the unwearied promoter of its highest welfare.

Guard inviolable the Sanctity and Privacy of the Home.

In the magnificent new countries in America, Asia, and— it may be—Africa, which Providence throws open to the thrifty and over-crowded populations of Europe, it is free to every man worthy of the name, to build up a home of his own. It was, and is still, the boast of the freeman living under the common law of England and these United States, that his home was his castle, all his own in its length and breadth, and as high as the heavens. It must be the fault of a degenerate race, neglectful of never-to-be-abdicated rights, if the inviolability of their homes and the hallowed privacy of family life, are surrendered into the hands of the policeman or given up to the lawless curiosity of the public press.

At any rate, no one may deny that it is free to every

willing and true-hearted man to create for himself a home as happy, as honored, as lasting as those visited in the present or past ages by God's richest blessings.

Every such home should be one founded on God-given love. "No man or woman," says a Catholic writer, "has ever felt true love without feeling a desire to become better, and to thank God for His having given therein a foretaste of the joys of heaven." *

"Where faith (says Digby) has stamped its character on the maiden's heart, where man is reminded of the graces of her whom he delights to serve, woman's divine air and her countenance, her words and her sweet smile, can so separate him from all evil influences, that no obstacles upon the road to truth will be able to detain his feet from pressing forward to embrace it ; and then hand in hand he is led to his second home, where love and truth made one with it, will remain with him thenceforth forever."

This is the only sure foundation of the Home,—a true mutual love hallowed by the blessing of Him who made the human heart, and tempered by the fear of His dread majesty. Of the divinely appointed means of sanctioning this mutual love, of preserving and increasing it through life and beyond the grave, we have to speak elsewhere.

The True Home, is the True Love which brightens it.

As, however, we do not here understand by the word "home," merely the walls which inclose parents and children, with the roof which covers them, but all the charities and all the sanctities, which can make of the poorest laborer's fireside a heaven on earth, and without which the luxurious mansion of the wealthy man or the splendid palace of the prince, is only a gorgeous sepulcher filled with the skeletons and ghosts of dead hopes,—it is both fitting and necessary that we should dwell somewhat more in detail on these home affections and associations.

To the lowliest-born, as he looks back across the wide

---

* *Études sur les idées et sur leur union au sein du Catholicisme.*

gulf of years to his native spot and the roof under which he passed his infancy and boyhood, there may arise memories of a wealth of love so surpassing, of virtues and qualities so ennobling,—that his soul swells with unspeakable gratitude and a holy pride at the very thought, while it evermore spurs him to emulate the work of his parents, and to sanctify his own home by the same deeds of piety and goodness. And how often does it happen, that the man born in the lap of luxury or reared amid the splendors and pleasures of a court,—finds his soul stirred by no sweet memories of early love, by no recollections of Godlike goodness and virtue in parents, relatives, or early acquaintance! How many hearts have starved and pined for want of the love lavished on the child of the cottager or the mechanic! How many souls, nobly born and nobly gifted, have been degraded, poisoned, ruined in childhood and youth by the profligacy of parents, or the systematic corruption of the tutors or companions assigned to them!

We know it by experience and observation,—there may be an imperial wealth of love, of tenderness, of purity, piety, and self-sacrificing heroism, beneath the humble roof of the poor journeyman mason or of the hod-carrier who waits upon him, while the children of a Louis XIV., or a Frederick the Great, may never know what fatherly affection or motherly tenderness means.

The Poor Man's Home may be Rich in Love; the King's, Poor.

Happy the man, in no matter what station born, who, in calling to mind the home of his childhood and the sweet and venerable images of father and of mother,—only recalls in both a united stream of love and devotion, which bore him along through infancy, boyhood, and youth, as if he were lifted on the bosom of an unchanging flood of joy and peace and harmony! He cannot think of his mother without feeling his heart melt within him at the remembrance of one, who was in his eyes more than an angel,—a visible embodiment of God's own exhaustless goodness and un-wearied patience; a vision of gentleness, devotion, unvarying sweetness, a love that never slumbered or changed save only to increase. And beside her cherished image stands in his soul that other one, of his father,—the second sun of his life, feeding with its warmth and brightness the steady glow of maternal love. He can only recollect the strong man, sustaining, inspiring, cheering the wife of his bosom; aiding her, cooperating with her in the performance of every duty that made their home bright or their name dear to the neighbors; carrying herself and her children in his strong arms and on his loving heart, when the road of life was too rough or too dangerous; and singing in his heart all the while a song more divine than ever sounded at springtide through forest or grove!

This, however, is only a very feeble and unsatisfactory description of the manifold blessings and most blissful influences arising from the perfect mutual love and united life-work of father and mother in the Home. Where such a close union reigns, what is not the happiness of the children! what harmony among servants and dependants! what edification to the neighbors! These expressions do not at all convey the full truth as it is in our mind, and as we have beheld it in reality.

God designed that the creative power of this love in the Home should resemble that of His own unspeakable charity in the everlasting kingdom, that of the sunlight here below.

This Love makes Home a Heaven.

It does indeed make the Home the image of Heaven. For there the infinite love which binds together in one most blissful being, life, and society, the Three Divine Persons, is the same which forms the bond of eternal affection, joy, and happiness of the glorious society of angels and men, united in fellowship with their Creator and Father. Even while in the flesh, Ignatius of Loyola was vouchsafed what would seem a glimpse of the beatific reality which is to be in the life to come the reward of faith practiced in this. He was given to see or to understand so clearly the ineffable way in which the Three Persons are one, the Son, proceeding eternally from the Father, and the Holy Spirit from the Father and the Son,—that in his case the veil had been withdrawn. This extraordinary favor would appear to have been granted in return for the absolute generosity with which the high-minded soldier had torn his heart away from the pursuit of all earthly honor and glory, from the deepest and purest natural affections, to become in the hand of God a passive and docile instrument for the mighty work reserved to him. It was but a glimpse vouchsafed him into these eternal depths, in which he beheld the three infinite Persons like a threefold flow of being and light and love springing evermore from the one original fountain, and returning thither in its irresistible tide of charity, only to seem to overflow itself, and flood all the blessed society of men and angels with its splendors and its ardors.

How a Glimpse of the Eternal Love created Apostles.

Thenceforth the soul of Ignatius, like a piece of cold metal once plunged in a vast kindred mass in fusion, remained for ever penetrated, inflamed, illumined, and transformed by the glorious vision. He could not rest till he had collected around him a chosen band of men like himself, communicated to them the light and burning love which overflowed in his own soul, and sent them forth, like Francis Xavier and Peter Favre, to kindle the flame of God's love to the uttermost ends of the earth. Thenceforth, also, his soul could scarcely bear its separation from the blessed company above, and from the undisturbed contemplation of that Divine Reality, one little glimpse of which had set his heart on fire. Prayer and meditation became almost his only food, and so sweet was the love which filled his whole being, that he wept unceasingly. Threatened with the loss of sight, and weakened otherwise in body by the

5

vision, which departed not from his soul by day or night,. he was bidden by his physicians and his spiritual direc tor, to abstain from protracted contemplation or frequent thought of divine things ; but as he walked about his little garden in Rome, the sight of a single flower would recall the hand that made it, and that uncreated Beauty whose sight from afar and through the mist had ravished his soul, and filled him with yearnings that nothing here below could appease.

And so this great parent of so wide-spread a religious family of priests and apostles, would draw each one of his children to his own glowing heart and send him forth all aflame with the unappeasable desire of daring, doing, and accomplishing what was most heroic for the glory and ser- vice of that Adorable Majesty.

Hallowed Creative Love of a True Husband.

So it is in a family where the husband's soul has been touched, purified, and kindled into holy love by the fire from above ; he will communicate his fervor to the wife of his bosom ; the two hearts, aglow with the same divine flame of charity, will daily become more and more one in thought, in feeling, in purpose, in life. How can they help making their children and their servants like to themselves ? How can neighbors, friends, relatives deal with them in frequent intercourse without experiencing the effects of the super- natural ardor that surrounds them like an atmosphere ?

Beautiful Examples of Conjugal Love and Home-Bliss.

We cannot pass away from this consideration without affording the reader, in illustration of the practical truth set forth here, a glimpse into the private correspondence of a man of the world, who united in his own life the rare blessedness of possessing a model wife and an ideal home, —and the twofold honor of belonging to a family most deservedly dear to Catholic Ireland, while becoming himself in America a model patriot and statesman. The letter from which the following extract is taken was written in August, 1842, eight years after his union with the wife of his choice, and after a literary enterprise, which he had undertaken from the loftiest motives of patriotism and religion, had brought on himself, his companion, and his six little children, utter pecuniary ruin. His young wife, from motives of economy had, with his consent, retired for a few months to the home of her noble father several hundred miles away, and daily received from the busy lawyer such letters as this, replete with the fervent piety and unfailing fortitude of the Christian :

"How much quiet and heartfelt happiness we shall yet enjoy together with the divine blessing! We shall trust everything in His hands. I was never so struck as I was to-day with the beautiful passage in the Gospel for this Sunday. *O ye of little faith! Be not solicitous, . saying, What shall we eat? or, What shall we drink? or, Wherewith shall we be clothed? For after all these things do the heathens seek. For your Father knoweth that you have need of all these things. Seek ye therefore first the Kingdom of God and his justice, and all these things shall be added unto you.* How much of strength and consolation is found in these words! and who that has faith could make these earthly wants a subject of anxiety or solicitude? How full of affection and tenderness is this reproach of our Saviour, complaining that we should doubt the kindness and care of our Father who is in heaven! . . . *Our Father knows our need!* Let us do our duty,—seek the reign of his justice over us,—and leave the rest with Him.

"I have been filled with this disposition to-day, more than I have ever been before, thanks to the divine goodness. . . . I was reading yesterday in the Life of St. Francis Xavier, when he beautifully refers to this truth, writing amid sufferings and dangers which no mere mortal strength could endure among the half-barbarous populations of India. 'Believe me, my beloved brethren,' he says, addressing his brethren in Rome, 'it is in general easy to understand the evangelical maxim, that he who will lose his life shall find it. But when the moment of action has come, and when the sacrifice of life for God is to be really made, oh! then, clear as at other times the meaning is, it becomes deeply obscure; . . . so deep, indeed, that he alone can comprehend it, to whom God, in his mercy, interprets it. Then it is we know how weak and frail we are.' May God grant that we shall always comprehend this maxim.

"It is enough, almost, to fill such a cowardly, self-indulgent sinner as I am, with despair to contemplate the zeal and intense devotion of this great apostle. Indeed, I should despair, if God did not pity and sustain me with hope that I may yet strive more earnestly and effectually than I have done hitherto in his service. To speak to any one but you of what passes thus in my mind, would appear, perhaps, an unseemly exposure of what had better be kept within one's own breast. But, partner of my heart and soul, partner, I hope and believe, of my life for ever, I communicate with you as unreservedly as I would with my own spirit. And I know that I derive advantage from so doing.

"I have thought much to-day of the great anxiety with which I regard all worldly matters, and I have resolved, with the blessing of God, never to let the issue of any worldly affair, or the opinion of the world, disturb me. I will labor with the same zeal, perhaps with a better zeal, for success in all things; but without solicitude for the result, or any regard for the troubles and difficulties attendant upon the prosecution of my labors.

"What a blessing it would be, if I could obtain this spirit from God! The Gospel of this day and some account of St. Francis Xavier that I read last evening have filled me with these thoughts; and I beseech you, pray, my beloved angel, that they may not be lost on me.

"The account of St. Francis Xavier which I read, was contained in a powerful article for the last Edinburgh Review on the Jesuits. I shall send you a couple of *Tribunes* (Mr. Greeley's paper) containing extracts from the article.

When you read them, you will feel as I did how conspicu-
ous is the presence of Christ with His Church in the lives
of men of such extraordinary sanctity. My sloth and cow-
ardice appear more criminal than ever when I think of
what sufferings and labors St. Francis Xavier had to con-
tend with ; and how utterly idle I have been, how often I
have procrastinated, how often I have turned aside from
the performance of my ordinary worldly duties through a
dread of the labor which they would require. May God
grant I may keep the resolution I have now formed *to think
nothing of labor that is a duty, or that charity requires!*

"For you also, my own love, and for our dear children,
I implore the same divine grace."

In very truth the trials which beset the life of this true-
hearted man, gave, until his dying day, perpetual opportu-
nity of practicing the heroic devotion to duty, the perfect
and most loving conformity to the Divine Will, that char-
acterized the great Apostle of India. To the latter, indeed,
had been given in the midst of his overwhelming labors, so
sweet a sense of the divine presence, so inflamed a love of
the Master he served,—that by day, as he passed through
the streets on his apostolic errand, the people would behold
his face all aglow with the interior fire, while from his lips
would burst forth the rapturous ejaculation : "O Most Holy
Trinity ! O Most Holy Trinity !"—as if he were already a
glorified spirit gazing on the Unveiled Essence on high ! At
night, when the crushing and varied labors of the day were
over, Francis was wont to withdraw to the silence of some
neighboring chapel to give vent to the torrent of praise
which he could not restrain, or, frequently, to seek the
solitude and cool air of the cemetery, and there kneeling,
and throwing open the folds of his poor cassock, he would
bare his breast to the night air, as if to cool somewhat
the fire which consumed his heart, exclaiming the while,
"Oh! not so much sweetness, not so much sweetness, dear
Lord ! "

With the good and upright magistrate whom we have
been mentioning, God's wise providence dealt otherwise.

He, too, was a man of prayer; and, when tried to the utmost, —as his faithful companion often related,—he would kneel for hours in his bedchamber before an oratory, his arms extended upwards as if on a cross, the tears streaming down his cheeks, and his silent heart-cries ascending to heaven in praise and supplication.

A few days before the date of the letter quoted above, and when his heart was bitterly assailed by undeserved calamity, he wrote to his wife as follows:

"I have just risen from my knees, where I have prayed with tears, my loved wife, to the Almighty God, and to his Blessed Virgin Mother, for us both and for our dear children, imploring His grace and guidance in doubts and difficulties, and that he would bring us speedily together in peace, and union, and health, and happiness, and *His love.* I besought the Blessed Virgin to take us as her children and present our hearts before Him, and beg of Him to purify them and strengthen them in all good purposes, to obtain His aid in our troubles, and that we may receive willingly, with filial affection and submissiveness, whatever trials He may call upon us to undergo."

The Flame which Feeds a True Husband's Love.

This, then, was the flame in which his heart and that of his companion ever sought to be more and more chastened. Nine months after their union he could write to her, on receiving a letter from her:

"Never since you left me was I so delighted, so happy as at that moment. The contents of the letter, the fond, affectionate heart and soul that breathed in every line were in no wise calculated to lesson my rapture. They stimulated it, rather, they added to and strengthened it. And oh! how I longed for the moment when I could tell you of all the love that burns in my soul for you! and how worthy you are of more, more, far more than any human heart can offer for your acceptance. Yes, my little angel, your purity, your goodness, your unstained love are worth more than all the realms of earth, than all which Time—the past, the present, and the future of this life,—can offer to the enjoyment of man. I feel humbly grateful to the Almighty Hand that has conferred on me a treasure so pure and priceless!"

And farther on in the same letter:

"My beloved, good mother, how I wish I were near her now, if my presence could be a comfort to her! There is a bond of attachment between me and my good dear mother so tender, affectionate and reverential, that while there is life in me nothing can weaken or disturb it. You can understand, my own gentle, affectionate girl, how I must have felt and how I still feel at having left a mother to whom I am so firmly attached, and at a time when she claimed my help and protection. . . . We had all come away from our friends and native land, and had toiled together amid many privations. . . . They believed my presence to be essential to them, and to leave them so circumstanced was a trial indeed. But may God give me the means of showing them that I was not insensible to their claims.

"How much more intimate, easy, and natural do I find the communion between *our* minds to be, than even between myself and my nearest relative, parent, or sister. I cannot write as fast as the ideas come to me when I am writing to you. I let flow my whole mind at once, and without reserve, when you are the beloved object I address. I need not stop to select words or phrases. I want only to place my whole heart before you, and let you read it. How blessed and sacred indeed is the union between us! Never did I at any moment conceive of such a holy, limitless confidence, such a perfect blending into one of our hearts and our very being, as I have felt to exist between us since our marriage. May God continue this blessing to us! and I feel that He will   "

These fervent protestations of conjugal love and of the deep admiration on which that love was founded, are heard through his correspondence, year after year, till his death, like the ascending tones of a litany. Every year and week and day seemed to reveal to the pure soul of the husband some undiscovered perfection in the wife, which heightened his veneration for her as well as his gratitude to Heaven for the bestowal of such worth on himself.

"Dearly as I loved you," he wrote toward the close of the first decade of his married life,—"much as I esteemed you, good and excellent as I believed you to be before we were united for ever, yet I did not then know half your purity and excellence. I often think how little I knew, before I could call you mine, of the gentleness, the pure confiding affection, the devotedness, the fortitude, the energy, the childlike innocence, the clear intuitive perception of truth and right, of what is the highest virtue and the highest wisdom, of the firmness in pursuing the course of duty, all of which constitute the character of a true and genuine woman.

" I had always formed the highest estimate of the female character, and had always had—I thank God for it—some of the best examples before me ; but in no other relation of life, save that of husband, can a man see and understand, intimately and without disguise or reserve, all the various attributes and virtues of a woman's heart and soul. And, even in that dear and holy relation, how often does man's sterner and more material nature render him slow to discern, appreciate, or sympathize with the above precious gifts and dispositions, that only require the breath of love, with words and deeds and a heart of answering tenderness, in order to be revealed to him in all their exquisite delicacy and loveliness.

"You are, thank God, my own love, the model of all this excellence ; and it is from the contemplation and intimate knowledge of your character, that I have formed the conception of what woman was designed by her beneficent Creator to be."

Ay,—there is the indispensable condition toward calling forth the full and magnificent luxuriance of a true womanly nature,—" *a heart of answering tenderness.*" This tenderness is to the development of her womanly and wifely qualities, what rain and dew and sunlight and a congenial soil are to the growth of the tree or the flowering plant.

Nevertheless, while surrounding her and her children with all the comforts and refinements within reach of their modest income, he believed it to be conducive to her spiritual growth to encourage her oftentimes to sacrifice her most innocent pleasures and gratifications in favor of the poor, of some great religious purpose, or even for the great gain of being in this more Christlike.

" I would dearly like "—he wrote—" that I could make this world a fairy-land to you, in which no thought or wish of yours should remain ungratified. It pains me much, at times, to be forced to disappoint your expectations and to deny you pleasures that wealth enables so many others in your position to enjoy. And yet I cannot help thinking that I should do you a grievous wrong, were I to suppose that you would not be more happy in performing the duties of a sensible, discreet, affectionate, and domestic wife and mother, than when engaged in all the gayeties and exciting pleasures and amusements which mere money can purchase. The temper of your soul would lead you to prefer your home-duties, even though at the cost of sacrifices and deprivations that were very painful. I *know* this, my darling ; I have had, time and again, the evidence of it in your daily life, and my heart has duly appreciated it."

The True Foundations of the Home.

And thus, in these passages taken from the inmost life of a true man, and destined never to meet any other eye than that of his worshiped companion,—we have laid before us the deep, sacred, and safe foundations of the Christian Home,—of the Home as we need it, as God designed it and still wills it, and as it ever existed, hallowed and respected through so many past ages,—the Home of our fathers.

One or two more gems from the conjugal crowns of this truly Christian pair,—and we shall hasten to close this chapter. On the twenty-eighth anniversary of their union, during the autumn of the first year of our great civil war, the husband thus wrote to his absent wife :

"Up here in my quiet little third-story room, and all over the house wherever I have been ; and in the field, on the road, on the lake,—looking abroad and around me, and above me and below ;—looking far away over the woods and the hills, and the misty mountains, or down at the little rivulet or the grass-plot beneath me ;—wherever I turned or whatever I saw, whether speaking or silent, or alone or surrounded by others, I thought only of you and saw only you,

on this the twenty-seventh anniversary of the day when God blessed our union and made us one forever.

"I sighed with regret that I could not be with you ; and at every step and turn, at every light and shadow of the landscape, the longing of my heart was on my lips : 'How I wish my darling wife was here ! How happy it would be if she were with me !' And I sometimes said to E——, 'How often your dear mother has looked at these scenes with me ! and how we used to enjoy them ! How I wish she were here to enjoy them now !'

"The day was cool and lovely, and the breeze on the lake invigorating ; so we rowed and walked about a good deal ; and I talked to the children of our anniversary, thinking of all the past and the present, and of all our darling ones who are with you, and of dear F——,* and of the sweet beloved ones who are gone before us. I told E—— it was St. Michael's Day ;—that the great Archangel was the patron Saint of our marriage. 'Yes,'—said she,—'he is the patron Saint of the soldier, the Archangel of battles, the patron of those who have to fight and battle in the world !'—'Well then,'—said I,—'he has had fitting clients, and our Saint was well chosen. For we had to battle with the world from the start, and he has been, I know, our good Archangel, our loving, watchful, and efficient patron, fighting for us against the Powers of Darkness, against the world and all evil, and gaining for us many a victory when we knew not how it was done !' And so I believe it to be,

---

* The eldest son, then an officer of the Federal Army in Missouri.

my own dear little wife, who have trodden with me so
many perilous paths with such a light cheerful look and
all the childlike trust and hope of inexperienced inno-
cence.

 "I can see you still,—a little girl, almost a child in your
unsuspecting 'ignorance of an evil world,—with a bright
glow on your cheek, walking or tripping lightly beside the
tall and strong man whom you trusted, over a wooded path
through brushwood and thorns, your face so young and
bright and cheerful,—almost like an angel's,—a slight ex-
pression of sudden pain sometimes clouding it as a thorn
sharper than the rest unexpectedly tore your flesh.

"And, after a long experience—after much travel, much
joy and brightness, much weariness and not unfrequent
experience of sorrow,—the little girl is seen to have become
the wise and holy woman, patient, courageous, and cheer
ful still; and, while counseling and encouraging her com
panion,—the strong man,—now almost fainting on the road
—she seems in his eyes more than ever an angel.

"With thoughts like these I have been filled all day, and
I have taken up this note-paper to give expression to some
of them.   How deep and how great is my debt of gratitude
to our Heavenly Father!"

Surely our readers will be grateful to have one short
glimpse of this noble husband's twin soul, and so to hear
from out its depths the echoes of these God-given harmo-
nies of wedded love :

"A few thoughts on my wedding anniversary, September
29, 1866.

 "AT GLEN-ELLEN.

"Here, in this lovely spot, this beautiful valley, the
twin-vale of my cherished native place,—let me call you
around me, my loved ones, to look back with me through
the long vista that leads to my wedding-day.

"Oh! how can I describe to you that home in which I
learned all that is good in my heart!   I must close its
door,—lest my strength should fail me : those who then
loved and cherished me with such a watchful and tender

care, have now gone from my sight. Do they this day know my gratitude ?

"Our wedding-day! the day we celebrate! It had a fickle, changeful sky; the dark clouds and rays of fair promise intermingled in its skies like the light and shade of coming years that lay before us in the unknown future.

"The morning of that day was cold and chilly as the world's charity. At its noonday the snow and sleet became rain, and fell in showers, like the tears we have both since dropped in the cup of chastening sorrows. With its evening came bright sunshine,—omen of the glowing love-light that floods every nook and corner within our blessed home.

"Such was our wedding-day. And such has been our life.

"Since then, the day has oft returned. It has come in weal, and it has come in woe—in woe, oh! how deep! And now this blessed day comes in light;—not in light unclouded, but in the noonday sky of other years when the driving snow and sleet softened into rainbow showers.

"My darling husband! Chosen companion of my life! Beloved of my heart above all others, and, next to God, the source of the ever-flowing fountain of joy in my soul,—let me on this day renew to you my vows of love made in the presence of that dear home-circle, when my parents gave me to your care. Let me here promise to be to you a faithful wife and heart-companion 'till death do us part.'

'How well you have kept your promise of that day, my beloved husband!

"Cold and bitter blasts have swept over us since then; and how lovingly you have shielded me from their fury!

The icy chill of a heart in agony, has been melted into tears by your consoling tenderness and devotion. And when has not sunshine been made more bright by your presence, my darling ?

"My children! Oh! what visions of happiness rise before me at this call! My children far and near! Angels of my earthly paradise! Precious offerings of my life's labor for Heaven's acceptance! Jewels, *set by God,* in my marriage crown! You are our honor, our glory, our pride, and the warmth of our hearts!

 "Come, this day, nearer, closer to my arms. Let me take you, each and all, and lay you at the feet of our Lord, and ask Him to bless you for your devoted love of us, your parents. Thank Him, my children, that you still have this sweet sanctuary, your parents' hearts, in which to rest you with a never-failing security.

"I would gladly celebrate this day by showering gifts upon you all, my husband and my children. Out of the deep fountains of a wife and mother's heart take for yourselves oceans of love."

The Close and Crown.

Little did parents and children imagine, while enjoying the deep bliss of this anniversary, that, when another came around, the husband and father would be no longer there, —the model-man to all of them, in the mirror of whose life they had ever seen reflected the noblest virtues of the Christian and the citizen. To him might be applied in the fullest sense what a great and holy writer of the fifth century applied to an illustrious layman of his time:

"I have leisurely inspected the daily actions of this distinguished man, and found them worthy of being described. What is the chief praise?—He maintains a house in uncorrupted purity ; his servants are useful, . . . tractable, polite, obedient, and contented. His table feeds the strange guest no less than the client. Great is his humanity ; but greater still his sobriety. His mind is serious ; he maintains public faith. With all this, the reading of the sacred scriptures is frequent, so that he feeds his mind even at his bodily repasts. In a new form of life he unites the gentleman and the monk. . . . Toward his household he is neither harsh in his manner of speech, nor disdainful of counsel, nor perservering and exact in detecting offenses. He rules those subject to him not with a domineering authority, but with such gentle equity, that one might think, that instead

of governing his own family, he was only administering the
estate of another.   Truly, all men of our order (clergymen)
might derive a most useful lesson from his example ; for,
without offense to them, I must say it—I am a warmer ad-
mirer of a priestlike layman than of an unpriestly cleric." *

How a True Man should Choose his Companion, and Cultivate her Heart.

Need it be said here, that it does not fall to the lot of
every man, even of very good men, to possess such a wife?
The obvious answer must occur ,to every serious-minded
reader : The Church of God,—that is, God Himself through
the Church, prescribes to parents the utmost care and pru-
dence in selecting companions for their children about to be
married ; while to the children she recommends recourse to
prayer, the reception of the Sacraments, the avoidance of
sin, a desire to fulfill the will of God by making a right
choice,—and, in choosing, a preference for the gifts of mind
and heart and true piety over the mere attractions of face
and form.   Where the desire to please God and to obtain
such life-companionship as is best fitted to one's spiritual
welfare and solid happiness, as well as the advancement of
His service, is the leading thought of young man or maiden
preparing for matrimony,—there is little danger but that
God will direct them aright.

We must not, however, anticipate on what has to be
treated fully in its proper place.   Suffice it to say at pres-
ent, that even when parents have solely consulted the Di-
vine Will and the best interests of their son in choosing for
him or in directing his choice,—or even when he has been
given a woman endowed with all the natural and super-
natural graces that make her a treasure beyond price,—
much, very much still remains for the young husband to do
if he would call forth all the wealth of his treasure, and ap-
ply it to the best uses.

---

* *Plus ego admiror sacerdotalem virum quam sacerdotem.*—Sidonius Appolina-
ris, Epistolarum, l. iv. 9.

A rich womanly nature demands to be known, to be appreciated, to be developed by the deep love, the ingenious tenderness, the unfailing devotion, the delicate and respectful attentions,—ever growing in assiduity with each successive year,—of her young husband.

You have chosen, from out the varied wealth of the garden and the forest, the loveliest and rarest flower that attracted your eye ; will you have it brighten and perfume your home to the utmost ? Then study its nature, its habits, what soil it likes best, what companions suit it (for plants and flowers also have their preferences), what degree of moisture, of heat, of shade, or of sunshine. Gardeners will tell you that wild flowers from the meadow, the woods, or the mountains, will seem to change their nature under the care of an intelligent and loving hand, and in a few seasons become so beautiful that they seem to have been transformed by culture. Not that only ; but the flowers most beautiful by nature are so much improved by the art of the gardener, that their charms are not only increased tenfold, but varied continually so as to create ever new surprise and delight. And who does not know that the horticulturist's skill can enhance to a wonderful extent the qualities of the most delicious fruits of our fields or our gardens ?

This is "to Dress and to Keep" the Home-Garden.

To you, O man of the world, your home-garden, your paradise,—the source of your purest and dearest felicity on this side of the grave, is the mind and heart and soul of your wife, your companion, the mother of your children. Her soul, her life, is given you "to dress and to keep;" and on your appreciating her nature and her worth, on your knowing how to call forth by your love, your care, your devotion to her service, by the sunlight of your examples much more even than by your mere love and tenderness,— must depend whether or not you shall have a home-garden, a paradise,—or a hell upon earth.

There is no delicacy, no purity of thought and word and

act,—no feeling of respect or reverence so, exalted,—no chivalrous devotion to the honor, the unblemished name, the generous and holy purposes of a true woman,—to be compared with the all-embracing sentiment of God-given love in the sinless soul of a man, united, through God's blessing, with the maiden chosen in accordance with God's will. Catholics, who are thoroughly acquainted with the sacred character of the matrimonial union, who know what untold graces are set apart for their whole after-life by the sacramental blessing, enter upon married life with mingled joy and fear,—because they are made aware both of their responsibilities and of the mighty aids divinely given them, to make of their whole career one long day of rejoicing, because it must be one long day of generous devotion to duty.

The husband's first duty, under God's service, is to his wife. He must give himself to her as she has left all to follow him. His must be,—from his bridal hour to his dying day,—one long, uninterrupted, most loving and unstinted service to her. He must, every day that he rises, set her image higher in his heart; reverence her more, seek to have others know her worth better, and show her greater honor.

It is the death of conjugal love, where respect diminishes in the heart instead of daily increasing, and where that delicacy and courtesy in word and manner which we call outward respect, is dispensed with on pretext of nearness and intimacy and unreserve.

Make it, therefore, the law of your life, that as the years of your wedded life pass by, they shall find, beside the ever-blooming flower of love in the center of your home-garden the flower of undying reverence. One cannot live without the other. And to the wife we must say : If you would have your husband's love and respect to know no fading,—make it a sacred duty to God, every day of your life, to invent new methods of showing your companion that your love is ever young and fresh as the flowers that bloom on high in the City of God.

Let men of culture and position, who owe to those beneath them,—much more than to those of their own level,

—the light of good example, read and ponder carefully every word in the following exquisite lines from a woman :

> " If I leave all for thee, wilt thou exchange
> And *be* all to me ? Shall I never miss
> Home-talk and blessing, and the common kiss
> That comes to each in turn, nor count it strange,
> When I look up, to drop on a new range
> Of walls and floors, . . . another home than this?
> Nay, wilt thou fill that place by me which is
> Filled by dead eyes too tender to know change ?
> That's hardest ! If to conquer love, has tried,
> To conquer grief tries more, . . . as all things prove :
> For grief indeed is love and grief beside.
> Alas ! I have grieved so, I am hard to love—
> Yet love me—wilt thou ? Open thine heart wide,
> And fold within, the wet wings of thy dove."

A priestly voice is daily and hourly wont to guide the young amid the first trials and bitternesses of wedded life, as well as amid the storms which attend on its noon and its setting. The reader knows also how precious and safe a refuge fathers and mothers alike find in that guidance, when worldly wisdom and worldly friendship are of no avail. It was, nevertheless, best that these lessons should be given from the experience of persons of worldly station. We have listened to the most intimate secrets of a true manly heart, still in death for many a year : the accents seem to come from the depths of the sanctuary. And this last wayside flower of poetry we have culled, as we seemed to pass from the altar and the awe of the cemetery, will also have its pregnant reminder.

Yes,—loved,—nay, infinitely dear,—as are the ties of the home of childhood, when a woman turns her back upon it and puts her hand in her husband's hand to walk the earth alone with him, it is as if a deluge had swept over her past, and her spirit, in going back in thought to the fireside of father and mother, found nothing but a ruin, with her loved ones all dead to her. In her grief for the separation, she turns to the Ark of her husband's home and heart like the dove sent forth by the great patriarch ; has she not a right

6

that her husband shall open his "heart wide and fold within, the wet wings" and drooping spirit of her to whom he is now all in all ?

There are so many who fail, on the very threshold of their new existence, to understand the yearning of their companions for the home-life they have lost, and to make up by unselfish and unbounded tenderness for this great loss !

We crave pardon for dwelling thus at length on the necessity,—so all-important, so indispensable,—of this union of hearts between husband and wife. Without it there is no home, no home-life, no true family. We have insisted upon it, because without it there can be no life-work done to any good or meritorious purpose by the wedded pair, become thus most miserable yoke-fellows. God only grant them to say, each to the other:

> "The world (our home-world) waits
> For help. Beloved, let us love so well,
> Our work shall still be better for our love,
> And still our love be sweeter for our work,
> And both commended, for the sake of each,
> By all true workers and true lovers born."

Most blessed are those who can thus look back to the parental home, and dwell with rapture on the memory of such a union between the father and mother who reared them ! Still are they not to forget, that this great gift of hallowed conjugal love was only bestowed for the dear and sweet work of making home a paradise not only for their children, but for their own parents, if privileged to possess them and shelter them there, for their servants, and for their friends.

Work together with United Hearts.

Home should be a paradise for the children. Would that all who are above the cravings and anxieties of poverty, would understand this ! Whatever excuse the poor, the over-worked parents of a large and growing family may plead for the neglect of their little ones, or the discomforts and disorder of their squalid fire-side, none such can be claimed by the man who has not to fear for the morrow, or to tremble for the next week's rent.

It is where wealth, independence, comfort, have been dispensed to parents by a kind Providence, that the obligation is increased a thousand-fold for father and mother "to dress and to keep" their garden.

The duty falls on the father first. He is the head of the family; he is the provider, and the protector. The wife and mother governs within, and dispenses love, kindness, care,—the bread of the soul and the bread of the body, to every member of the household. She watches over the fire on the hearth, and sees to it that there is warmth, sunlight, and cheerfulness for all; she also it is who keeps alive the fire of religious faith and neighborly charity on her domestic altar and in every soul intrusted to her. The husband only stands by her side twice a day, morning and evening, when they are both the united ministers of the family sacrifice of prayer and praise. Throughout the remaining hours of day and night the wife and mother feeds the sacred fire and the lamp of piety.

Happy the wife who is ever sustained, encouraged, and cheered by her husband in every labor that has for its object the formation of true children of God in all her dear ones, as well as the promotion of every scheme and industry for making home-life delightful!

It is wonderful how the poorest natural ability in a wife can be called forth and developed by a husband who is careful to study her and to encourage her every effort for the improvement of others as well as for her own. How much more marvelous are the results when the wife's great natural gifts are further increased by the stimulus of a husband's praise and generous appreciation! What will she not accomplish to make her dear companion happy! And what a sweet reward she finds in that happiness for her own labors in favor of children, servants, and the poor of Christ! Thus it is that her work,—their joint work, rather,—is still the better for their love, and that their love is ever the sweeter for their work,—and that all outside their blessed home "commend both for the sake of each," and are themselves by such examples stimulated to become in their turn "true workers and true lovers."

Appeal to all to aid in creating Blissful Homes.

Shall we proceed ? O you to whom God has given in this world's wealth and independence, the ready means of creating and adorning such homes as these, will you not show your gratitude toward the Giver of all good and your solicitude for the dearest interests of your own children, by a willing and zealous coöperation in this divine work of making your household a shining example to all ? Is the social body in our young and magnificently endowed America, by allowing premature corruption and decay to fasten upon its leading classes, to resemble the most lordly tree of our forest, which begins to die at the top and propagates sterility and death downward to its lowest branches and its very roots ?

Shall you not rather,—you who are the crown and ornament of the whole body,—open your minds to the conviction, that it is through you that life and healthful energy and well-being and moral beauty, are to flow and to spread from, above downward and around to every class and home ? Let the laboring poor, the ill-requited, weary toilers of city and country-side,—who are, like the hidden roots of a mighty tree, the obscure feeders of the entire social body,—let them be cared for, loved, cherished, encouraged and aided in their hard toil by all above them,—and the love they will feel in return for the love shown them, will be like the plentiful vital sap pumped up from the genial earth by every root and fiber, and sent coursing in warm healthful currents through trunk and branch, to the topmost spray of the goodly tree.

Be it our care,—clergymen, legislators, magistrates, men and women who wield the mighty pen, merchants, manufacturers,—all to whom others beneath and around them look up for light, guidance, and support, to see to it that every industrious toiler dependent on us and within reach of our influence and our aid,—*shall* HAVE A HOME *of his own!* And teach him by your own example how to make his home bright, religious, refined, happy!

Oh! let us be up and doing betimes! For the social world, in our day, so far resembles the troublous and changeful era of St. Gregory the Great, that to the established and time-honored distinctions of rank, to the prosperous, wealthy, and influential classes of society,—and to every individual man among them,—this prophetic warning of the great Pope may apply

"We are uppermost to-day, and laugh at the struggles of those who seek to rise to our level : let us tremble lest they should soon rise on our ruin! For no one is less secure of his own position, than the man who only knows how to laugh at the misery of his less fortunate rival." *

---

* *Timendum est ne, etiam nobis cadentibus, surgat qui a nobis stantibus irride-tur ; quamvis stare jam non noverit qui non stantem noverit irridere.*—Lib. xxv., Moralium.

CHAPTER V

DARK SHADOWS FROM THE RUIN ; AND LIGHT FROM THE HEARTH.

> " The hearth in hall was black and dead,
>   No board was light in bower within,
>   Nor merry bowl nor welcome bed ;
>   ' Here's sorry cheer,' quoth the heir of Linne."
> OLD BALLAD.

> " At school I knew him—a sharp-witted youth,
>   Grave, thoughtful, and reserved among his mates,
>   Turning the hours of sport and food to labor,
>   Starving his body to inform his mind."
> OLD PLAY.

WHILE the bright vision of a home,—marked, indeed, with the cross like all true Christian homes,—is still floating before our mind's eye, and before the sound of love's divinest harmonies, from around the domestic altar, has died away amid the noise of the street, let us withdraw a moment, as to some shady spot far enough from the dust and the roadside, and listen to one or two brief tales,—the one glancing at a life wasted and a home ruined, the other at a life of early helplessness, poverty, and heroic struggle directed toward building up a home.

The crowd of ill-clad and half-starved laborers, of pale, emaciated, and overworked boys and girls, are hurrying past us to their daily toil. Who knows but more than one of these discouraged husbands and parents, on listening to what we here say, may take heart to make their home brighter and their poverty richer by patience and content? Who knows, too, if the noble example of a child more help-

less than any of the young folk we see from here, may not
spur many a one among them to heroic labor, self-respect,
self-reliance, trust in God, and success beyond their fondest
dreams?

So be it! And so, this repose between two long stages of
our journey, may cheer you, dear reader, to pursue the
mighty theme which grows on us.

The Homeless Wanderer.

We can never forget the sad extremity of one aged suf-
ferer found by the police at the steamboat landing on a bit-
ter morning in early February. He had been given a free
passage on a steamer from the interior, had found shelter
during the night in the engine-room, where the stokers, some
of whom were Irishmen, recognized beneath the soiled gar-
ments a countryman and a gentleman, and in the terrible
cough which racked the poor invalid's chest, the sure sign
of a speedy end to his sufferings. So, the kind-hearted
fellows shared with him their own scanty fare and the
warmth of the coal-room;—and when they had arrived at
the term of their journey, their guest left them with many
thanks and blessings, to knock at the door of an old ac-
quaintance, on whom, in better days, he had conferred more
than one obligation. His, however, had been a downward
course for many a long year; he had dissipated his large
patrimony, thrown away splendid natural gifts improved
by the most careful cultivation, and had again and again
wrecked the home which he had won back by his fitful
industry,—wearying the generosity and patience of his
friends, till he became an outcast, utterly broken in health,
in heart, and in temper.

He was almost a dying man, however, when on that bit-
ter Sunday morning in February, he stood shivering at the
door where he had so often been welcome, and gasping
forth to the heartless menial who opened it his name and
his pitiful prayer for help and shelter. The door was closed
brutally in his face, till the master's will was ascertained;

and the master's answer was a peremptory order to give the poor wretch nothing,—no, not even a kind word !

Stung with indignation and rage, the latter turned away, and blundered blindly through the storm back the way he had come, till on the wharf he fell exhausted and fainting. At the police station the letters found on him disclosed his profession, as well as the names of several prominent citizens, and to the house of one of the latter the wretched wanderer was taken.

Not in vain did they knock for admission at the door of that hospitable home. Its master was under no obligation to the sufferer ; but that he suffered and was apparently near his end, moved himself and his family to the most brotherly compassion. A physician was sent for in all haste, and meanwhile the sick man was given a most comfortable room and bed, together with such restoratives as were deemed most needful.

These, with the remedies prescribed by the doctor, seemed to revive the sinking flame of life in a body wasted by long excesses and recent privation. At evening and through the night, the sudden change from the deck of a steamer, the inclemency of the open streets in winter, and the horrors of a police station-house,—to the elegant room in which he lay and the gentle attentions of his hosts, so roused the spirit of the patient, that he was able to sit up and converse.

With this momentary return of vitality, all his old recklessness came back ; and he told several of his late adventures and mishaps with zest, mixing his account of himself with bitter and merciless scorn of his own family and of the friends who had cast him off. A better and more hopeful spirit had, however, seemed to rule his utterances when the kind host and his wife were lavishing their first charitable care on him. As he gazed round the room, he would exclaim, as if waking out of a dreadful dream, "Oh, the bliss of having a home ! the bliss of having a home !" To this first soft mood, however, soon succeeded one of fierce antagonism to all mankind, and violent denunciation of those who had wronged him. His anger seemed to consume the

last remnants of his physical strength, flaming forth more
fiercely and luridly in the intervals of his broken rest.
When the physician returned early the next morning, he
found his patient very much worse, but most anxious to
live,—"that he might,"—so he expressed it,—"triumph
over all his enemies, and recover his lost property and
home."

The physician felt himself bound to tell him that he must
entertain no hopes of recovery. "Not recover, doctor!"
broke forth the miserable man · "not recover! Why, I
am not fifty years old, and I am still hale and hearty. I
only want three years of life to redeem the past and put my
slanderers to shame." The physician bade him put away
these false hopes, and open his soul to sentiments more be-
fitting one who must very soon appear before the great God
in whose hand were life and death. " Very soon!" gasped
the other; "why, you don't mean to say I am dying?"
"You most assuredly are," was the firm, though gentle
answer. "Dying!" screamed the poor wretch, as he al-
most started from the bed. "Oh, no! do not tell me so.
I cannot afford to die at present. Let me only live a year,
and you shall see what I can do. I have broken my wife's
heart, beggared and disgraced my children. Help me to
live one year, and I shall merit their forgiveness."

And thus pitifully, frantically he went on pleading with
the physician, "for a month, for a single hour!" "Can
you not give me a single hour, curse you!" he cried.
"What is your skill worth, if you cannot give me one hour
of life?"   And so the fearful passion and despair of
that death-bed went on increasing in gloom and horror, while
this guilty life was fast ebbing away. "Oh, I cannot die,—
I will not, will not!" the hapless creature would continue to
repeat, as spirit and body writhed under the united terrors
of the wasted, misspent past and the dark, eternal future.
"God is bound to give me life," he went on, as the foam
gathered on his lips. "Yes! you cannot refuse," he would
say, lifting himself from his pillow, and wildly extending
his arms upward, half in supplication, half in blasphemous

menace. "I mean to reform *now*,—I mean *now* to do better;" . . . and his strength would utterly give way beneath the icy hand of the dread Avenger.

It was in vain to speak words of comfort, to recall the infinite mercy of God's fatherly heart, who would take the will for the deed. "No! no!" he would repeat; "I *must* repair, I *must* live!" To look upon that despair was more harrowing, more appalling than tongue or pen can describe.

Scarcely had that guilty soul departed, when a most fearful change took place in the dead man's features. Their expression became so ghastly, so unspeakably terrible, that the ladies present fled wildly from the room, making vain efforts to banish from their imagination that terrible face in which was depicted all the agony of everlasting despair.

While the undertakers were sent for, a veil was thrown over the head of the corpse ; it was forthwith placed in a strong double coffin, firmly screwed and nailed down, and never afterward opened, even to satisfy the dead man's relatives.

> " *King Henry.* . . . If thou think'st on Heaven's bliss,
> Hold up thy hand, make signal of thy hope.
> He dies, and makes no sign ; O God forgive him !
> *Warwick.* So bad a death argues a monstrous life.
> *King Henry.* Forbear to judge, for we are sinners all.—
> Close up his eyes, and draw the curtain close ;
> And let us all to meditation." *

Let this one example suffice as a warning to men who, deriving from their parents independence, wealth, and position,—feel no incentive to labor or honorable exertion, squander in idleness and vicious enjoyment the fruits of their parents' industry, have no sense of their accountability for all these inherited advantages, or for the ill use of talents and education, and the waste of fruitful years,—and make of their existence upon earth a curse to others as well as to themselves. Alas,—there are many such ; and would that the lesson of this wasted life, like a light placed on high near a much-frequented coast, famed for appalling ship-

---

* Shakspeare, Second Part of King Henry IV., act iii., scene iii.

wrecks,—could teach our young men to avoid the reefs on which so many lives have been lost, and to steer far away from the fatal currents that have borne so many thousands to ruin!

On the other hand, we have such noble instances of heroic endurance and perseverance in laboring to create a home,—and that, too, among men born in every class of society, and contending with the most adverse and, seemingly, discouraging circumstances.

How a Son repaired his Father's Ruinous Extravagance.

One man's bright life now comes up before our mind's eye, like the summit of some mighty mountain towering aloft above the whole earth for hundreds of miles around, which, left behind by the traveler at early morn, is seen, at the close of day, when the landscape is shrouded in gloom, glistening far up in the heavens with the last glories of sunlight. His father had, by a life of reckless extravagance, lost every acre of the broad lands possessed for generations by his family, and left his only son nothing but debts, which the latter vowed he should pay to the last farthing by his own industry. He was an officer in the army; and as a military career promised no opportunities of fulfilling what he considered a sacred obligation, he threw up his commission, and betook himself to farming in a new and richly endowed country. Being unmarried, he felt himself at liberty to choose the pursuit which seemed most adapted to his own abilities, and best calculated to bring him speedy and lawful wealth. He, therefore, betook him to sheep-farming,—attached to him by his kindness of heart and his gentleness, much more than by the ascendency of his superior intelligence and culture, several rude men, who had been rather a terror to the settlers till then, made them sober and steady workers like himself, taught them the value of truthfulness and honesty, shared most generously with them the profits of their joint labors; —and, increasing rapidly both his flocks and his profits, became at the end of six years the wealthiest proprietor in his district. Having settled his companions on farms of their own, which he helped them to stock and taught them to manage, he sold out his own interest for a large sum, sufficient to pay off his father's debts and to secure himself a modest independence for life, and returned to his birthplace.

The parental debts were paid some months before he set out on his homeward journey, and the balance of the money was intrusted to enterprising bankers with whom he had entertained frequent business relations. Indeed, he had more than once been urged to become a partner in the concern. During all these years of unceasing struggle with his own inclinations and habits, much more than with the strange and deep humiliations of the life he had adopted,— he had cherished one purpose above all others, that of creating an honored and happy home for one to whom he had been affianced in early youth, who had never consented to separate her destiny from his, and whose almost daily letters had cheered him amid gloom and depression, and strengthened his soul to undertake and undergo what otherwise he must have deemed impossible.

She became his wife a few weeks after his return, and while the thought was uppermost in his heart of purchasing back from the present owner a portion of his patrimonial estate, building himself a home on it, and devoting the remaining years of his life to the task of recovering the remainder.

He did succeed in persuading the proprietor, sadly in need of money, to part with a portion of the land, and paid him an exorbitant price for it. But, when he came to order plans for a modest dwelling-house to be erected thereon, he was thunderstruck at learning that his bankers were insolvent.

Religion, however, much more than pride of race, had ever been the mainspring of his resolution, and it now saved him from discouragement. He was passing rich in the love of a wife who prized him for his work, not his wealth. Together they sought consolation and counsel where it is ever sure to be found,—at the Mercy Seat ; and together they resolved to face the privations and the struggles which had already brought him the means of achieving the independ- ence and comfort so suddenly and sadly compromised. The generous husband would have spared his beloved com- panion the trials which a brave-hearted man, in spite of his gentle nurture, can always face successfully, but which few delicate women can endure. What man, however, is braver of heart than a true woman ? And so, the faithful wife would not hear of further separation from him she had loved with such true single-heartedness.

The country in which he had retrieved his fallen fortunes had undergone many changes: tracts favorable to sheep- farming or other like occupations were no longer to be had for the seeking. To find them, one had to go far into the interior, to incur greater fatigues, greater risk, far greater expense, and with far less prospect of efficient aid from needy emigrants. The gold-fields, on the other hand, opened a new and more tempting prospect of sudden gain ; and to the gold-fields our hero and heroine directed their steps.

With an energy that the devotion of his worshiped wife and the sacred purpose on which he had set his heart could alone sustain, he bent himself to the fearful ordeal before him. He had brought with him from home money enough to secure her the privacy and some of the comforts of a home superior to the wretched temporary abodes that sheltered the immense majority of miners. But while he applied himself to his self-imposed task, she became the angel of this wild and lawless community ; induced those of her own faith to rear a rude but commodious chapel, where she called them together on Sundays, recited the mass-prayers and rosary with them, read beautiful instructions from her little stock of pious books, catechised the children, gave good advice and needed comfort to all who sought her, and learned where she could find sickness and distress to alleviate. In good time, she also secured occasional visits

from the nearest missionary. In all this she seemed only
to be her husband's helper. For his goodness made his
fellow-miners find him out long before the fame of his
former success and generosity had reached them. Not
many months had elapsed in this hard life before he fell
sick of a dangerous fever, and while he lay at death's door,
his first child was born to him ; the entire motley popula-
tion forgetting their greed, their religious differences and
national animosities, to minister to the comfort of the pair
with a delicacy, an assiduity, and a constancy begotten
of heartfelt veneration and gratitude. The husband and
father recovered slowly at first ; but when the delirium
allowed him to recognize his wife and to look upon the face
of his babe, a mighty wave of healthful energy seemed to
pass over his soul, and to lift him above his illness. He
was grateful, too, that the dear companion of his trials had
been spared from a heavy visitation of sickness ; and his
heart melted within him at all the marks of respectful and
affectionate interest lavished on himself and his dear ones
by the men and women around them,

Indeed, while he lay on his bed of sickness, the miners
had volunteered to work by twos and in succession at the
mine which belonged to the invalid, just as their wives
watched successively in the sick-rooms to tend both the
sufferers. Nor was this charity without its present reward.
For rumors went abroad that everything succeeded with
the men and women who were thus foremost in their charity
and devotion. At any rate, during the illness, the work-
men happened upon a vein of gold of extraordinary rich-
ness, the produce of which was treasured up most con-
scientiously for the sick man. He recovered to find himself
rich far beyond his most sanguine expectations.

Of this wealth,—as could be surmised,—the owner made
a most noble use. The men who had stood by him were
assisted, every one of them, to secure themselves independ-
ence and a fortune. A noble church took the place of the
former rude wooden chapel, and schools and other institu-
tions soon grew up round the church. The estate at home

returned to the brave-hearted heir; but he had pledged himself, together with his wife, that, while no debt should encumber the inheritance of his children when it descended to them, he should rear them to labor and industry, and teach them by the example of their parents to bestow on charity and on the self-helping.poor the surplus revenues his fathers wasted on self-indulgence.

Happy, most happy, and most blessed was their household, husband and wife vying with each other in practicing piety toward God and charity toward the neighbor. Nor, despite the long and bitter trials of the past, did they murmur or repine, when sickness and death visited their little flock of lovely children. The Christian mother knew that the angel who marked their door-post with the sign of the cross, as he came to bear away their first-born from them, was the messenger of infinite Mercy and Wisdom. Many a blessing, from every lowly home far and wide, was daily uttered on the noble man whose heart and hand were ever open to the needy or the erring, winning the deep love of the poor much more by the eloquence of his unwearied devotion to their interests and his spotless life, than by his enlightened liberality in stimulating the industrious and helping every manly effort made toward honest independence. But who can tell the worshipful feeling of reverence with which his angel wife was regarded? She had seen the laboring poor at their worst, and had discovered how much their virtues excel their vices, how rich a soil their hearts afford in which to sow the seeds of gratitude and of every Godlike quality. And so, does she to this day move among her devoted poor neighbors,—paupers there are none,—the living image of that Goodness which only came down on earth to renew in man the divine likeness.

Noble Devotion of a Swiss Orphan Boy.

Most unlike the two men whose story we have just been telling, in its beginnings and progress, was the life which we are about to sketch in its main features. The advan--

tages of high birth, gentle nurture, and careful education, taken together with the power for good which inherited wealth and position bestow,—are a mighty trust in the hands of mortal man, and involve a fearful responsibility toward the Almighty Giver. Where an early fear of Him who is the Judge of the whole earth, is instilled into the mind, and the Christian sense of generosity and accountability is carefully fostered in the children of the well-born and wealthy, the good done by the proper use of riches and position, by the influence which superior culture and superior station command, is incalculable.

Where, however, a man born without any of these social advantages, and left from childhood to struggle against every evil example and tendency, without education and without proper direction or encouragement, the castaway child develops into the self-reliant boy and the man of indomitable energy, industry, and stainless integrity, till he becomes a prince among the benefactors of his race,—there we have a miracle of true manhood. Such is the man whose story we now recall.

We shall call him Johann. He was born near Burglen, the birthplace of Tell, two months after the sudden death of his father. His mother married again a native of the Lower Engadine, whose profession of peddler led him to frequent alternately the Forest Cantons and the beautiful cities and hamlets of Northern Italy. The child was in his fifth year when his step-father, who had been guilty of the double crime of murder and highway robbery, found his way with his wife and family to Genoa. There, the better to conceal his identity, he found employment around the Cathedral of San Lorenzo, till such time as he could secure passage for himself and his wife and their youngest child in a merchant ship bound for Sumatra. The wretched wife and her babe died on the passage, poisoned, it was believed, by the unnatural husband and parent, who was imprisoned on his arrival, but escaped, and, after many adventures, found his way to New Zealand, where he perished miserably.

Johann and his half-sister, some two years younger than

himself, had been made over by contract to one of these in-
famous *padroni*, or dealers in Italian children shipped to
England and America, and held as veritable slaves by their
inhuman masters.   Taught music or some other art, these
innocents were hopelessly condemned to labor for the sole
profit of their owners, and made to endure a life of de-
gradation so awful, that unspeakable filth, poverty, and
starvation were often the lightest part of the burthen of
misery.   Johann, on being stolen from his poor heart-broken
mother, was allowed to retain nothing of his raiment even,
but a rude silver locket, so black and battered that it was
deemed worthless; it contained, however, his certificate of
baptism.   He was called by another name, and forbidden
under the most awful threats of punishment ever to men-
tion his mother's name or his own, or to acknowledge any
one as his parent but the wretch who took himself and sev-
eral other children to London.   Fortunately, or unfortunate-
ly, for the little creature, he caught the small-pox, almost
immediately after his arrival in that city, the disease assum-
ing a most virulent form, accompanied by fever and deli-
rium, which, on his recovery, completely obliterated all
memory of the past.   His padrone meanwhile sailed for
New York, deeming Johann lost, and transferring all claim
to his services to another of the tribe remaining in London.

The child, who was not lost sight of by the latter, recov-
ered; but left the hospital very feeble, half blind, and
seemingly imbecile.   Picked up one morning in January,
as he lay famished, half-unconscious, and half-frozen in one
of the by-lanes of Southwark, he was taken to the room of
a poor shoemaker's wife, who, childless herself, received the
little waif as some great gift of God.   And, surely, he was a
blessing in disguise, sent by the Father of the orphan, to a
soul overflowing with divinest charity,—one of those lowly
ones so dear to Christ, so rich in the gifts of the Spirit, so
far advanced above the learned and the great ones of this
world in the sublime paths of sanctity.   Nevertheless, she
was the wife of a drunken husband, whom she had mostly
to support by her own thrift, and whose insane fits of vio-

7

lence made her life as insecure as it was miserable. Amid
all this poverty, sin, and wretchedness, this beautiful soul
grew daily in holiness and merit.   The atmosphere of good
ness and purity that surrounded her filled her vicious com
panion with reverence while he was sober, and when in
toxication transformed him into a wild beast, the very
majesty of his wife's virtue awed him into respect and sub-
mission.

On the day when this good, admirable woman, as she re-
turned from early mass at a neighboring church, found
Johann and took him to her heart and her home,—the hus-
band happened to be half-crazed by a long course of de-
bauchery. He drove both his wife and her charge back
into the street with fearful oaths and threats of violence.
A neighboring woman sheltered the two till the drunken
man's fit was over, leaving him plunged in a lethargic sleep.
It was the wife's opportunity. She watched tenderly over
the slumberer, caring meanwhile for Johann's pressing
needs ; got him clean linen and such warm raiment as she
could, made him partake of a hearty meal, and forced him
to take rest in a quiet corner of her lodgings,—the very
place where she was wont to pray and meditate herself
when she most needed the sweet refreshment ever found in
communion with God.

The husband, on awaking to the consciousness of his
guilt and the sense of racking pain consequent upon his
shameful excesses, was all submission to his gentle wife's
will, and welcomed heartily the little stranger. Thencefor-
ward, Eunice,—for such was her name,—had two sick per-
sons to care for and to support. But she was not forgotten
in her dire need. One of these noble English ladies, whose
high birth is their least merit before men and their least
recommendation to the love of God and his angels,—stum-
bled into the poor apartment, and promised to return. Eu-
nice had never yet asked or accepted relief under any form,
and her soul could not brook the idea of obtaining assist-
ance from any one so long as she could work herself. Work
she could not now, however ;—and the assistance was prof-

fered in so delicate and generous a form, that her self-respect was spared, and the boon gratefully accepted.

The husband soon died ; and the slow fever which consumed poor Johann yielded to the tender nursing of his second mother, and the comfort and peace which surrounded him. His convalescence, without bringing back the memory of his childhood, restored him to the full use of his other faculties, and within six months he was a strong, healthy, and beautiful boy of eight. Eunice, during his illness, had opened the locket round his neck, and ascertained his parentage and religion. She now devoted herself to his education. Fearful, nevertheless, lest some one should steal or take away perforce her treasure from her, she accepted a position of trust in a country residence obtained for her by her benefactress. There she had not been more than a few weeks when she sickened and lay at death's door for months. The boy, whose manly character began to display itself in this extremity, watched over her whom he called his mother with an intelligence that won the admiration of their masters, and tended her and worked for her with such unwearied love, that their sympathies were deeply excited.

It was while thus lavishing on his adopted parent all the tenderness of his nature, that the boy formed the resolution of supporting her by his industry, and of working till he could get her a home of his own. The kind mistress whom they served purchased the little fellow a basket or pack filled with needles, thread, and some more costly articles in favor with ladies and serving-maids, and encouraged him to try his luck first of all in her own mansion and among her dependants, and then among her lady acquaintances in the near neighborhood. No one could refuse to buy from the bright, beautiful boy, whose high soul shone through every feature,—so that, before two months were over, he had increased tenfold not only his stock in trade, but his custom.

The invalid,—for such she now was,—could, with the aid of her generous friends, venture to rent a small but very neat house in the neighboring town, and set up a little stationery and soft-ware shop, which she attended herself, while her boy extended his excursions to several populous villages of the district, and managed to make himself useful over night in a pottery, whose master took a great liking to the child.

His boyish frame was unequal to this excessive fatigue, and the great strain on the nervous system of one who was growing very rapidly, brought on symptoms of brain fever. He could afford to rest, however, for his heroic devotion had been blessed, and the little shop was patronized by rich and poor alike, who felt drawn to the saintlike widow and her orphan charge.

Up to that moment, Johann had scarcely learned to read. During the fits of delirium that accompanied this last illness, he raved continually about books and learning a trade and going to America to make a fortune for his dear mother, as he ever called Eunice. The physician who attended him was so touched by all that he heard about the pair, that he mentioned the matter to a friend of his, a wealthy ship-owner of the town, who was, besides, largely interested in the lumber trade both of Canada and of the Pacific coast. This gentleman called on Eunice, found Johann much better, and was charmed by the boy's manly beauty, intelligence, and spirit, as well as by the indescribable magic of Eunice's conversation and manner.

He became henceforth their declared protector. Johann was placed as an errand-boy in the ship-office, and sent three days in the week to an excellent school. His progress in learning was prodigious. He seemed to know by intuition what his master would teach him, obtained a thorough knowledge of arithmetic and algebra, was filled, at the sight of the designs and plans which covered the walls of his benefactor's office, with a thirst for acquiring the science of ship-building. The boy, while filling the functions of confidential secretary to the head of the firm, was allowed to qualify as apprentice in the trade of shipwright. His salary, which his employer insisted on paying him, went to make Eunice entirely independent, and much more than the salary went to the same purpose. So that the gentle sufferer could give her noble boy a home supplied with all the restful comforts required by his feverish activity of brain and body, and bestow, besides, large alms on the poor.

Johann was thirteen when he made his first communion. This event produced a wonderful change in one who was already precocious in mind and character. In preparing himself for the reception of the Divine Sacrament, his tenderness of conscience compelled him to open his heart to his employer about several peccadilloes which his boyish temper had led him to commit since he had entered the office. His friend, who was a stanch opponent of the Catholic faith, listened in amazement to this accusation of acts in which not a trace of voluntary guilt could be discovered. At the same time he was deeply touched by the purity, innocence, truthfulness, and high honor revealed by that one glance into a soul so privileged.

Johann was intrusted with the most confidential part of his protector's correspondence, and sent more than once to London on errands of great secrecy and importance. Everything he undertook succeeded in his hands, because to rare practical judgment and natural tact he joined absolute singleness of purpose. He devoted himself entirely, without a thought of personal vanity, to whatever he was given to do, applying his whole mind to it because it was his duty. Nor did he seem, when the thing was done, and his employer was loud in his praise, that he had done anything uncommon or what anybody else would not have done as well as himself. With all that, the boy was ever ready to oblige every person around him, from the oldest clerk to his master's little footboy. Thus it happened that his wonderful simplicity and the absence of all pride in his conduct made him a universal favorite.

His rapid advancement, therefore, made him no enemies, and lost him no friends. In the ship-yard to which he was drawn by an irresistible attraction, he seemed to understand everything at a glance. The principles of the science of naval construction, the nature and value of materials, all were grasped by his marvelous intellect with a quickness and sureness that made learning to him an amusement.

At twenty he had become so useful to his kind protector, so indispensable indeed in the transaction of business requiring secrecy and dispatch, that he was made a junior partner in the concern. This extraordinary good fortune made no change either in Johann's outward bearing or in his interior sentiments. His soul seemed filled with reverence and gratitude toward his benefactor, and devoted love for his mother; his tender piety to God being the source of his affection for the two beings on earth who had been to him the images and instruments of the divine goodness.

Thenceforward his history was one of continuous and wonderful success. How his fertile invention discovered new methods for improving the strength and velocity of sailing vessels,—for steam was not then known; how he traveled over both hemispheres to discover the richest forests and to establish centers for the vast lumber traffic in which his house was engaged; and how, wherever he went, his winning manners, his generosity toward his subordinates and workmen, the lively interest he seemed to take in every individual, and the mixture of gentleness and firmness with which he dealt with the refractory among them, caused his presence to be hailed with delight, and his departure to be regretted as a personal loss by every man in his employment.

One fixed purpose ruled his conduct toward these,—to encourage every married man to have his own little home, giving them such wages as enabled them to live comfortably and free of debt. With that, he would provide the children with schools in which they were taught the elements of a good common education, while every boy able to be apprenticed was articled to some good master tradesman in the shops attached to his manufactories and ship-yards. Ample provision was also made for religious instruction.

His chief delight, however, was to see the home-life and home-virtues cherished by all those who came beneath his control or influence, or were the recipients of his bounty.

In a thousand ways, as his young, bright face passed like a sunbeam through the industrial villages which thrived under the protection of his house, he would show his love for children,—for the parentless and the outcasts particularly. They were somehow drawn to him by a powerful magnetism : he kept a list of all such, and of the families to whom he intrusted them, and from whom he took especial care that they received most kindly treatment.

In these good works every shilling he could spare was spent. His own home, the home of his adopted mother rather, he made most comfortable, without ever adding to it anything that savored of luxury. In this he was guided by the wishes of Eunice as well as by his own inclination. There was in their dwelling a simplicity that was not without its elegance, but nothing more. Or, if there was any other distinctive feature about his and her home, it was in the many visitors of every rank who came to honor in the saintly invalid the woman who had reared such a noble son, and in the constant coming and going of the poor and the distressed whose need was relieved quietly, and each one of whom was bidden to depart noiselessly, with the injunction of the Divine Master, "See thou tell no one."

Johann was supremely happy in seeing his mother beloved and reverenced. He had obtained the legal authority to bear her maiden name,—not that his upright nature or manly disposition could allow him to blush for his own,— but because he gloried in owing her everything, and in devoting to her the life she had preserved and helped to make so honorable and so useful. He could not bear that any steps should be taken either to punish the padrone from whom he had endured such horrible cruelty, or that the course followed by his step-father should be ascertained for he feared that the discovery of his guilt might rest like a stain on the memory of his dead parent.

Into the house which he had created for Eunice, nothing could induce Johann to bring a bride. His love for his benefactress, and his ardent and enlightened charity for his laborers, seemed to fill his heart and to leave no place for any other love. He was in his thirtieth year when she was taken from him, and at thirty, hundreds upon hundreds of homes in the Old World and the New blessed him for their comfort and happiness. Her death only served to give a mightier impulse to his indefatigable activity for the good of others, and to the great industries of which he was the soul.

We shall now let the veil drop on that life, which, fruitful as it was in noble labors crowned with success, and in countless deeds of the purest beneficence, would never court praise or publicity. The rain which is a blessing to the earth and crowns the most fervent prayers of the husbandman, is not that which the heavens send down like a cataract amid the flash and terror of the lightning and the loud roar of the thunder-storm. It is that which falls as silently and gently as the dew at midnight, dropping on the parched bosom of the earth, causing the seed to germinate, to grow up, and to ripen,—giving new life to the drooping flower, a more vivid green to forest and field, and filling the land with gladness.

We would wish the voice of these examples to reach thousands of boys, who know that they are born to toil, and many thousands more of young men whose hands are hardened by toil,—so that its eloquence might stir their hearts to industry, endurance, and perseverance in building up a home that God's angels may delight to visit, good men to honor, and the poor to bless in their prayers.

Should there be among our readers any who have wasted the golden years of their life, created nothing, but destroyed rather,—then let them once more take courage and begin again!

> "Up, mortal, and act, while the angel of light
>   Melts the shadows before and behind thee !
> Shake off the soft dreams that encumber thy might,
>   And burst the fool's fetters that bind thee !
> Soars the skylark—soar thou ; leaps the stream—do thou leap ;
>   Learn from nature the splendor of action.
> Plough, harrow, and sow, or thou never shalt reap :
>   Faithful deed brings divine benefaction.

' The red sun has rolled himself into the blue,
    And lifted the mists from the mountain :
The young hares are feasting on nectar of dew,
    The stag cools his lips in the fountain,
The blackbird is piping within the dim elm,
    The river is sparkling and leaping,
The wild bee is fencing the sweets of his realm
    And the mighty-limbed reapers are reaping.

" To spring comes the budding ; to summer, the blush ;
    To autumn, the happy fruition :
To winter, repose, meditation, and hush ;
    But to man, every season's condition ;
He buds, blooms, and ripens in action and rest,
    As thinker, and actor, and sleeper ;
Then withers and wavers, chin drooping on breast,
    And is reaped by the hand of a Reaper." *

    * Robert Buchanan, " Wayside Poesies."

CHAPTER VI.

˙UNHAPPINESS.

Cato the Censor held that there was more merit in being a good husband than a great senator.—PLUTARCH.

To the farmer nothing is more important, than to have near his house an unfailing spring of water, ready to his hand during the longest heats of summer and the severest winter frosts. Hence, the first thing the settlers throughout our vast continent attend to, after they have found a tract of rich, arable soil, is to seek for a stream or a spring of wholesome water, near to which they may erect their homestead. To turn away the stream or to poison the spring would be to render the homestead uninhabitable · it would be the act of the worst of enemies.

What an enemy's hand might do to render the family home intolerable, the head of the family himself but too often does to poison every spring of domestic happiness, and thereby to destroy or imperil the very existence of the family itself.

If the prosperous farmer, or the settler struggling with the first difficulties of the forest or the plains, must feel grateful when warned against criminal designs threatening the health and life of his family, have we not a right to expect attention, if not gratitude, when we warn heads of families against foes of their household no less to be dreaded?

Home is no home, and home-life at best but a long "purgatory," if he who is its head and chief ruler, instead of being, by his devotion to its every interest, by his self-control and self-denying virtues, the main cause of comfort,

106

peace, security, and happiness, becomes by his imperfections or his vices, the source of all unhappiness to his dear ones.

We wish, with all the delicacy and charity of a priestly heart and hand, to describe briefly the principal defects that lead to discomfort, discord, misery, and wretchedness in homes where God intended that all should be serenity, sunshine, joy, and bliss unalloyed.

The first of these,—one which it should be the struggle of a lifetime to overcome and eradicate, is infirmity of temper.

Infirmity of Temper—Irascibility.

Its most troublesome forms are irritability and fault-finding. Of that headlong passionateness, which is properly anger, we do not wish to say much. Proneness to anger, when not checked in childhood, and allowed to grow up with a man's growth, is almost as ruinous in its evil example and in its consequences to the professional or business man, as the worst forms of intemperance. For headlong anger is intoxication, depriving its unhappy subject of the use of his reason, rendering him incapable of using aright, for the time being, any of his mental faculties or bodily senses. Hence, it is classed by theologians and moralists among the Seven Capital Sins,—among those, namely, which are the fruitful parents of crime and disorder.

The irascibility or irritability we point out here, as a thing so much to be dreaded, avoided, and courageously put down, is only a milder form of the same dreadful distemper, but one scarcely less hurtful in its effects. As this is not a moral treatise, we can only point out the remedy,— early habits of self-control, and life-long watchfulness over this domestic foe and inseparable companion,—a watchfulness that can only be aptly compared to that kept over the movements of a chained mad dog. Loosen the chain but for a moment, and you feel the fangs of the rabid animal fixed in your flesh, and its poison coursing through the blood and maddening the brain itself.

There are men most generous in every other way, endowed with the noblest qualities of heart and mind,—whom this unrepressed infirmity render a burthen to themselves and an intolerable torture to all around them.

We have known a young husband who had conquered a most honorable social position and no less honorable wealth by hard labor and sterling integrity, who had won the admiration and warm esteem of a large circle of distinguished men, by his uncommon ability and a largeness of mind and heart still more uncommon. He also won the admiration and maiden love of a woman not less gifted than himself in mental and moral excellence. He had provided for her a home in which a princess might be proud to live, so elegant was it in its noble simplicity, so exquisitely adorned with all that could suit the most cultivated taste or charm the most poetical fancy. And with his home, his wealth, his position, and his name, he gave her a heart that no other love had ever filled.

Nevertheless, six months of wedded life had not elapsed, when the young wife's love began to wane, and with her love her health declined. She had discovered that the man, whom she had chosen from among a crowd of admirers and suitors, and to whom in her inexperience she looked up as to one far above herself and above others, was one subject to that baneful and humiliating infirmity of an irascible and uncontrollable temper.

In her own father's home, she had never once beheld either her parents or her brothers giving way to the sudden and unaccountable outbursts which seemed to upset, when she least expected it, the soul and the very nature of her husband. She cowered and shrank before these fierce exhibitions as she would before some wild beast that might have leaped suddenly into her room through the open window or doorway.

Too proud to resent by words, expressions or acts which degraded her and lowered her husband infinitely in her estimation, she could only weep in secret, and pray to God to give her strength. For she soon felt her great love slipping away from her, like the dying reverence for an idol de-throned and shattered utterly.

Her husband would come home wearied from a day of professional exhausting toil, his whole soul frequently over-strung to its utmost tension by mental activity ; and she, in the long hours of absence, would devise a thousand loving artifices to cheat him of his weariness, and to unbend by sweet distractions the mind that had been so long on the stretch.

He, who had disciplined himself to severe self-control in public and in the transaction of professional business, had never taught himself in the privacy of his hitherto solitary home, to keep a strong rein over his temper. He had not learned that the true gentleman is he who is every inch and in every word and gesture a gentleman, in his private chamber especially, and before his valet. How much more is this true of the Christian ! And, in our case, how much more true of the husband !

A wife is not made happy or heart-satisfied by being made in public her husband's honored companion, on whom he bestows, with evident affection and assiduity, all the marks of sincere esteem and respect. It is the atmosphere of their privacy, when no eye is on them but that of God and His angels, that must be unclouded, bright, warm, blissful, and undisturbed by one unseemly word or act ;— this alone constitutes a wife's perfect happiness. She must see nothing in the man she loves utterly, and who is all in all to her, that she cannot love, admire, respect. If the self-control assumed in public and kept on like a mask while beneath the public gaze, is cast aside when alone with his wife, and the countenance wears the distorted form of passion, and the soul, hitherto serene and unruffled, be-comes all at once, like a storm-tossed sea, hideous with monstrous forms rising from the depths below,—then is love in imminent danger.

Six months of such disappointment, torture, and humili-ation the young wife endured, without ever permitting one word of complaint or remonstrance to escape her, or without relaxing in aught her daily devices for her husband's comfort and amusement, when an unusually violent outburst of irritability brought matters to a crisis.

They had been invited to a family anniversary in the evening, and were to be the very center of the happy circle. She had prepared everything for her husband with more than ordinary forethought, wishing him to rest sweetly on his return home and to wear his best looks afterward before the assembled family. His room had been made even brighter and pleasanter than usual, and a bunch of the flowers he loved best had been daintily gathered and arranged by his little wife, whose hand had placed a thought of love in every flower more fragrant than its own perfume.

He came in very much exhausted. It was an intensely hot day, and the heat told heavily on a nervous system that had endured great strain throughout the day. He was, however, not conscious of any predisposition to irritability; he met his wife with his wonted joyous smile and affectionate greeting; partook heartily of the refreshment which she had prepared, kissed the sweet and fragrant flowers on his dressing-case, and made all the currents in the young wife's veins run on delightfully. They were truly, in their sweet rooms, as they presently began to dress for the evening, the very ideal of blissful connubial love. But, all at once, some shirt-buttons would not fit, and there were hurried words of impatience, a necktie did not suit, and there was a muttered oath which made the young wife start in the adjoining room, and then the shoes were too tight and hurt his feet; in tying the strings, one of them broke, and the shoe itself was torn off the foot by the now thoroughly enraged man, who flung it from him, striking with it his wife as she was coming unperceived to quiet and pacify him. There was a scream, and as he looked round he saw her put her hand to her face and sink fainting against the doorpost. The shoe-heel had struck her violently on the temple, cut her, and the blood was flowing copiously on the white dress of the insensible girl.

To seize her in his arms, with the tenderest words of grief

and love, to bear her to her bed, summon the servants, and do all he could to restore her to consciousness, addressing her the while in the most affecting terms of self-accusation and reproach ;—all that was the work of a few moments. The maid had witnessed the accident, and told the other members of the household exactly what had occurred. So that all blamed their irascible master as much as they sympathized with their fainting mistress.

She had opened her eyes for a few moments to see her husband kneeling in agony by her bedside, and had drawn his head toward her to kiss him tenderly but mutely ; and then she sank into a second swoon longer, deadlier than the first. Why distress the reader? The young wife and mother had received a terrible shock, from the effects of which it required the utmost skill of her physicians to save herself and her babe.

But the danger to both caused a complete revolution in the husband and father. During the months that his wife lay helpless on her bed of sickness, he had vowed to God and promised his own soul to repress at once and forever that irascibility which had well-nigh proved fatal to her, whose worth he never knew so well as when she had well-nigh fallen a victim to his own ungoverned passion.

Not one unpleasant incident ever afterward dimmed the serenity or clouded the brightness of their most happy life. He was too firm a believer in the wonderful ways of Providence, not to feel that the dreadful consequences of his sin had been only averted by supreme human skill and God's merciful kindness. Thenceforward he showed himself the meekest and most patient of men,—worshiped by his servants for his gentleness and many other virtues ; while his grateful wife blessed the Heavenly Father for having made her suffering the occasion of such a blissful and lasting change in her loved husband.

A Great Life marred by Irritability.

Another instance of the effects of this deplorable irritability, we are moved to mention here, because the man who was subject to it, marred thereby a life of magnificent promise. Splendidly gifted, carefully educated, placed from earliest manhood in a position of all the most favorable to the exercise of his great natural and acquired abilities, this man, whom we knew and loved well, disappointed the expectations of his family and the prophecies of his friends, —neutralizing all his marvelous gifts of head and heart by this single ungovernable passion, and ruining all the good he otherwise did by this excessive irritability, which made him pull down with one hand the fair structure he had reared with the other.

Painfully conscious of his own infirmity, his whole life was an unavailing, because a too feeble, struggle against his fell enemy. His shining qualities, and the continual occasion of using them imposed on him by his profession, only rendered his failing the more conspicuous to others,— like a great flaw in a vase of the most superior design and workmanship, or a fatal crack in a bell of extraordinary dimensions, and placed aloft in a cathedral tower to call a whole people to prayer and praise, and to sound abroad over a city on solemn festivals as the consecrated voice of Religion.

It is but a vain, we had almost said, a criminal, excuse for such wayward passionateness and unrepressed irritability, in any man, especially in educated and professional men, to say that it is a disease, inherited with one's blood, and increasing in intensity with age. We are speaking of men,—held by their families, their neighbors, and the public, as responsible persons in all the ordinary transactions of life. Responsible to God they most assuredly are, for neglecting to repress in youth and early manhood, the enemy within the house of their soul,—whose subjection and annihilation every man of us knows he can achieve with His help who is always near us to bestow all the strength rendered needful by our own most extreme infirmity.

Fault-finding.

Akin to this fiery disposition of the irascible, is that other of fault-finding, which would seem to attach itself, as rust does to iron, rather to cold than to ardent natures. It is even a more hateful infirmity than wrathfulness. For, without pretending to excuse or extenuate the guilt of the passionate and the irascible, we may remark, that it is the fault of souls generous, loving, devoted, and self-sacrificing in a great measure : it may even be said to be the excess or the defect of some of the most admirable qualities in human nature. Not so with the odious disposition toward fault-finding. It belongs to selfish, narrow, ungenerous natures, as cold as the cuttle-fish which seizes with its long arms upon all that comes within its reach, and mangles them without pity or discrimination. Fishermen on the coast of France, often haul in with the wholesome fish in their nets some of the young of this destructive species. If they happen to leave them together in the boat or on shore for a single night, it is ten to one but they will find on the morrow all their choicest fish utterly ruined and emptied of their substance by the merciless and voracious cuttle-fish.

The fault-finding husband, in like manner, wears out the life and destroys little by little the happiness of his wife and entire household. A wife may exert herself to the utmost to govern, regulate, and brighten the home, to make its interior the very picture of comfort, peace, and restfulness ; she may call forth, as much through the promptings of true love, as from a deep and pure sense of duty, all her skill to please, to amuse, to cheer and charm her husband. She may be in heart and disposition, as well as in person and appearance, an angel welcoming her wearied companion to the joy and repose of her paradise: of what avail will her every grace and charm be against the icy manner, the cold sneer, and the cruel words of dispraise, which are the only answer to her warm welcome, the only return for the loving forethought and care and labor bestowed on making the home bright and sunny for his coming ?

There are men who are indefatigable workers, clear-headed and successful business-men,—who take real pride and pleasure in providing for wife and children a home lacking no element of outward respectability and creature comfort ;— men, too, who do not seek distraction, amusement, or distinction outside of their home. And yet these men have the talent of making their homes hateful to the children for whom they labor, hateful to wife and servants and friends,— because they pass over a thousand praiseworthy things in their wife's management, in their children's proficiency, in the conscientious labor of their servants, to seize upon the one little defect that appears to them blameworthy. Their wife's warm greeting is sneered at as affectation and demonstrativeness, and her reserve as a want of proper affection. The soup on the table is always either too hot or too cold, the roast-beef overdone or too rare, the tea and coffee either too strong or too weak ;—and these criticisms are all the more liberally indulged in that there are the more present at table. Indeed, friends or strangers dining there for the first time, would be induced to believe from their host's liberal dispraise of everything, that the poor wife was the most careless or the most incapable of managers the cook the most ignorant or stupid of kitchen-knaves, and the servants chosen from among the most unservice able of the tribe.

In the drawing-room the music is treated in the same illiberal manner as the cooking. What is sung or played grates on the ear of *paterfamilias ;* and the daughter is asked to play something she has never practiced, or the son to sing a melody he has never studied. So that all desire of improvement,—so far as the head of the house can do so,—is effectually quenched in the bosom of wife, and children, and servants.

Of what avail is the most devoted attention to business, the most encouraging and remunerative success in one's profession, or the bestowal on one's family of all the means of physical comfort and liberal education,—if the home is made, by constant and indiscriminate fault-finding, like a darksome ice-cave in which not one little bud of heartfelt joyousness will dare to unfold itself?

Nor is this the worst. Indeed, it is only a very softened picture of the home of the fault-finder. We know of one man, married in his first youth to one of the loveliest girls, and belonging to one of the very best families in a great State,—who made life so intolerable to his devoted and accomplished young wife, that it broke her heart, ruined her health, and sent her an incurable maniac to the insane asylum, while he still primes it at political meetings, or shines as a star of the first magnitude in the most fashionable circles.

Moodiness.

A third form of ill temper is moodiness. For there are men who have succeeded in quelling the fierce outbreaks of anger and impatience, who have even gone so far as to set a strong guard upon their tongue, restraining the wrathful, censorious, or sarcastic utterances which caused so much pain to others, and so often wounded both justice and charity. But the very effort required to keep down the rebellious spirit within, or the desire of avoiding the occasion of giving way in word or deed to their effervescent feelings, would induce these mistaken souls to seek complete isolation, or to preserve a moody and obstinate silence, not a whit the less irksome to others than the open violence, or the bitter invective to which they were wont to yield.

Moody people thus only take refuge from one weakness in another, like the victims of Asiatic cholera, who only escape the fatal grip of the dire pestilence to succumb to typhus fever.

Moodiness takes several forms in different men, and not unfrequently in the same man. The moody husband will be all smiles and cheerfulness one day, like a sunbeam to the hearts of wife and children; but the very next day he will be all gloom, and silence, and storm. In the morning

he will leave his home the pleasantest of men, but will return in the evening the most disagreeable and troublesome.
. His moods come and go as unaccountably and as suddenly as the changes in an April sky. Just as the traveler never knows if he can trust the fair promise of a sunny morning at that uncertain season, and will, if he be wise, not go forth without waterproof or umbrella; even so those who live with a moody man can never trust to his present temper, though all smiles and serenity, but have to be always armed with patience and forbearance, so as not to be surprised and overwhelmed by the suddenness and violence of his change from sweet to sour, from mildness to the downpouring of wrath.

Nor is it easy to say when such a man is more unbearable, —when he suddenly gives way to successive or continuous spasms of ill humor, censoriousness, and impatience, keeping his whole household in a ferment for days, and communicating to wife and children and servants his own ague-fits of interior wretchedness,—or when he subsides into a gloomy silence lasting day after day, and making the atmosphere of his home as unendurable as the darkness and cold and oppressive stillness of a long night near the Pole.

Surely such moral and mental infirmity in a man often proud of his gifts, his position, and reputation,—is as baneful to the comfort and happiness of all around him as would be the frequent and persistent visitations of some odious disease, which would torture every outward and inward sense without destroying or endangering life.

A Notable Example of Moodiness

One memorable example may suffice to show such persons how fearful and utter is the ruin caused in the wealthiest and most refined home, as well as in the lowliest and poorest, by this unchecked moodiness.

Two of the most distinguished families in one of our Middle States had cemented, as they fondly thought, a deep and ancient friendship by marrying an only son to an only daughter, both the idols of their respective parents, and both to all appearance most worthy of their utmost affection. The young gentleman was a graduate of West Point, clever, accomplished, well mannered, of a handsome person, winning and courtly address,—such a man, indeed, as would most powerfully attract a young, innocent, and artless girl, who had never learned to fear the angry and fitful depths that may lie behind the bright sky of an open, handsome face.

Innocent, artless, in very truth, most beautiful and most graceful, was the bride which the handsome and wealthy West-Pointer had won;—and all who knew him not intimately, prophesied that the union would be most blissful. There were some, however, who knew well how uncertain was the calm self-possession the young bridegroom could assume, how changeful was the serenity of that brow, and how treacherous the bright smile which he had ever worn before his bride. His parents were but too painfully conscious of the fitful passionateness that lurked beneath that fascinating exterior. But their religion had not taught them the duty of acquainting the intended bride or her parents with the capital defects or vices that might imbitter the life and ruin the happiness of a wife. Alas! there are but too many parents who believe this to be their duty, and nevertheless neglect it, thereby making shipwreck of the lives and not seldom of the souls of the innocent and unsuspecting.

Not a week of the honeymoon had elapsed when the beautiful bride, so proud of her brilliant husband, and so wrapped up in his happiness, made the discovery of the moodiness that was to be her bane. In the very midst of the joyous festivities gotten up in their honor by devoted relatives and admiring friends,—the most trifling accident would call forth a fit of sullenness, gloom, and silence,— like a thunder-clap from a summer sky, or the instantaneous gathering of dark storm-clouds over the face of the brightest noonday.

The young wife had brought from her home and inherited from her mother that deep tenderness and patient love, which can perform miracles of devotion and self-sacrifice. She loved her husband with her whole heart, for she had clothed him with all the perfections of her cherished ideal. And she was very slow to admit that her husband's long and distressing fits of alternate irritability and sullen moodiness, were not the consequences of some hidden distemper, —of a mind overtaxed by too close application, or of nerves disordered by the long and severe dicipline of a military school,—instead of being the outgrowth of peevishness, waywardness, and ill temper, allowed to spring up unchecked in an only son by a mother's fatal indulgence.

With the complete forgetfulness of self, and the unlimited devotion to the comfort and pleasure of the loved object, that are the very soul of wifely affection, she devised and exhausted, week after week, and month after month, all the sweet industries by which a woman can soothe the pangs of both body and spirit ; but all were to no purpose. The hopes she fondly clung to, that the overstrained mind should soon recover its balance, that the endearments of her beautiful affection and the peace and quiet of her beautiful home, would calm the disordered nerves and soften every asperity of temper,—disappeared one by one ; and the dreadful reality stared her in the face, that she was united to a man, whose moods were as sudden, as uncertain, as destructive of all happiness and home-life,—as those of a lunatic.

So with her hopes her love waned, constantly increasing dread and despair filling up their place in the young heart. She bore up against all her ills for years, however, without complaining to parent or friend. She had looked forward to the birth of her first babe, as to an event which might stimulate her wayward husband to serious efforts at self-amendment, or at least awaken in his soul new affections, a new sense of responsibility, and deep reflections on the pains he had caused the mother of his child, and on the clouds his temper had cast over the first stage of their wedded life.

Whatever regrets for the past may have visited him, or whatever transient resolves he may have formed, they did not outlive the rejoicings which welcomed the arrival of the son and heir. Three other children were sent to cheer the young mother; and with the birth of each the dying root of love and wifely trust would put forth a few timid leaves, —so fondly will a woman's heart persist in hoping against hope itself!

At length she sank beneath the intolerable load of ills which she had borne so silently and uncomplainingly. Her father had watched her drooping form and spirit, and his intercourse with his son-in-law, as well as the indignation caused among their neighbors and acquaintances by the ill conduct of the latter, forced the parent to interfere and save the life of his child.

It was too late. All the tenderness of her mother, all the devoted care of brothers and sisters, all the caresses of her little daughters who would not be separated from her, were alike powerless to arrest the progress of a disease, the seat of which was in the heart. She pined away, and died broken-hearted.

Her husband retained his son with him in the now desolate and widowed home. But not even that desolation in all its utterness could change that proud spirit, or rouse it to repent of its selfishness, or to exorcise from his hearth the fiend that had changed all its joy into mourning and blighted all the fair blossoms of early connubial love.

The widowed husband wrapped closer around himself the dark and forbidding garment of his moodiness and sullen perverseness of temper. His daughters had chosen to cast their lot with their dead mother; thenceforward they were dead to him. His son had clung to the paternal roof with the hope of inheriting the paternal estate. He, too, grew up to be a young man of fair abilities, handsome presence, and engaging manners.

The father, growing wearied of the intolerable solitude and desolation which surrounded him, thought, in one of his softening moods, that, if his son married happily, the

home might again be brightened by young faces and glad-
dened by pleasant sounds. Till then, although he had
given his boy a good education, he had nevertheless afforded
him no opportunity of turning it to any useful purpose.
The allowance made to the young man barely sufficed to
clothe him decently, without permitting him to indulge in
any of the most innocent recreations of persons of his own
age.

What then was his astonishment, when, one morning, at
the breakfast table, his father asked him if he had never
thought of marrying? "I should be happy to see you
settled in life, my son," he continued. "For the house is
rather dull for one of your age, and has been a long time
without pleasant company." "But, father," returned the
other, "I have at present no means of my own, and am,
therefore, entirely unable to support a wife. That I have
not sought to enter on the active duties of any profession,
is due to your own desire." . . . "Let that be no obstacle
to your marriage," the father replied; "I shall gladly
furnish you immediately with the money necessary for
your equipment, and shall advance you, on your marriage,
ten thousand dollars or more, to enable you to practice
your profession independently. Have you found no young
lady who could make you a good wife?" Yes, the son
had been thrown into the company of a charming young
person, belonging to a most honorable family, and there
had sprung up a warm affection between them. Acting,
therefore, on his father's urgent advice, the young man
asked his lady-love to become his wife, was accepted by
her and her parents, and everything,—as his father had
desired,—was arranged for their speedy marriage.

Returning home without a moment's delay, his soul full
of joy and triumph, he informed his parent of his success,
and of the arrangement made for the nuptials. The latter
received these tidings without any sign of pleasure or inter-
est, acquiescing apparently in what his boy had done, but
saying not one word about advancing any money for the
necessary expenses of the wedding. He had relapsed into

one of his blackest moods, and his son did not dare to press him by untoward questions or demands for money, while the cloud was on him.

So, with the aid of some generous relative he was able to meet the needful outlay, and was married, his father excusing himself, under some pretext or other, from being present at the nuptials. He could not bring his bride home at once, both because he was absolutely penniless, and because he was not sure of her getting a warm welcome from his capricious parent. When he appeared before the latter, however, he told his tale simply, and begged his father to execute the promise kindly made of advancing the money necessary to set him up in his profession.

"I have had nothing to do with your marriage," was the startling reply; "and I mean to have nothing to do with providing for yourself or your wife. I owe you nothing, and shall give you nothing." "But, dear father," the other forced himself to say; "it was at your own solicitation that I sought a wife, and acting on your promise of a liberal settlement, I have taken the woman I loved, and with your express approval. What am I to do?" "Do what you like," was the brutal rejoinder; "it is no concern of mine. No man has any business to marry who cannot support his wife."

These words at first almost threw the wretched bridegroom into a fit of despair. He knew it to be useless to make any further representation to the heartless parent, who seemed only to have deceived his own child for the express purpose of torturing him. He left his father's home that day, never again to return to it, and set himself manfully to work to support his young wife and create a home for themselves and their children. It was a hard and a long struggle; but he succeeded.

Meanwhile his moody and self-tormenting father was more wretched than ever in his cheerless abode. The same perverseness which steeled him against the most touching demonstrations of his young wife's love, now prevented him from making,—much as he desired it,—any advances to his alienated children. He would have given his entire fortune and many years of his life to have them once more back in his loveless, comfortless home. As if, in very truth, an evil spirit possessed him, urging him to repel all show of affection from his friends and obliging him to withstand the yearnings of his own fatherly affection, he lived on unloved and unhonored, and died as he had lived,—the destroyer of his home.

CHAPTER VII.

HOME DESTROYERS (CONTINUED).

Look in my face ; my name is MIGHT-HAVE-BEEN ;
I am also called *No More,—Too-late,—Farewell ;*
Unto thine ear I hold the dead sea shell,
Cast up thy Life's foam-fretted feet between ;
Unto thine eyes the glass where that is seen
Which had Life's form and Love's, but by my spell
Is now a shaken shadow intolerable,
Of ultimate things unuttered the frail screen.

DANTE GABRIEL ROSSETTI.

WE have seen a few of the dark foes whom the Enemy of God and man leagues with himself and his fallen angels to mar all the most merciful designs of the Creator on human society,—on the Home, especially, which is or ought to be the nursery of Godlike manhood.

Within the Earthly Paradise, as its Divine Author planned it in the beginning, we know how many perennial fountains of live-giving waters gushed forth and made everlasting springtide in the place.

"Through veins
Of porous earth with kindly thirst up drawn,
Rose a fresh fountain, and with many a rill
Watered the garden ; thence united fell
Down the steep glade, and met the nether flood,
And now divided into four main streams
Runs divers." . . .

There, too, was the Tree of Life, yielding man, by a loving provision of his Maker, the healthful nourishment that fed every vital source in the body, while keeping every faculty

123

of the soul fresh and disposed for all the labor of intel-
lectual life.

Why will man, instead of enjoying beneath the shadow
of God's wings, all these manifold sources of health, and
sweetness, and strength, and joy, turn his back on God and
them, and follow the beckoning of his soul's enemies, to
seek outside his little paradise, false pleasure, food that
poisons both soul and body, misery, degradation, and death?

Let not the reader, however, misinterpret the lesson of
the Divine Book, or misunderstand what is sought to be
here conveyed. We are but too apt to attribute to the hid-
den working of the Evil One or his allied spirits, the moral
degradation and temporal ruin wrought around us in the
lives and homes of men by *their own sin*, originating in
their own mind and heart, and consummated by their own
free will, in spite of the lights and warning voice of con-
science.

Of course, we do not and cannot deny it,—for it is the
plain sense of God's revealed word both in the Old and in
the New Testament,—man is assailed by his inveterate and
sleepless Foe in many ways, and has, as well, much to fear
from the seductive words and examples of his fellow-men.
Nevertheless, his true danger lies within his own heart : he
is, himself, his own greatest enemy.

Hence, for once that our temptation and the occasion of
our fall come *from without*, ten times, a hundred times,
the sole cause of our sin and its consequences may be traced
to ourselves. The guilty thought and imagination are the
spontaneous growth of our own soul, as well as the subse-
quent resistance to conscience, and the final full and free
consent given to evil.

There is nothing more pitiful in the brief story of the
downfall and arraignment of our First Parents, as plainly
told in Genesis,—than Adam's shifting the guilt off his own
shoulders to his companion's, and her imitation of her hus-
band's pusillanimity and cowardice, in throwing the blame
on the Serpent.

In this prevaricating weakness, we all show our ourselves

but too truly the offspring of these great criminals,—by transferring to the Tempter the primal blame for our misdeeds. Alas,—if we look well into our own soul and the truthful record of our own conscience, we shall most surely find that we are, ourselves, our own worst tempters, and, most frequently, our sole tempters.

Let us have the courage, then, to call our soul to a candid account for our transgressions. In looking into our own consciousness, and scrutinizing impartially the causes that have led to make of our lives a something so different from what God had designed and we had once hoped ourselves,—we shall find that our own hands have marred the plan of God and of the nature He so richly endowed. There is not one of us,—when some sudden illness or catastrophe places the soul on the verge of eternity,—to whom conscience does not hold up the twofold truthful image of what "I am" and what I "Might-have-been." Beneath the all-revealing splendor of that light which issues from the near Judgment Seat, I cannot help seeing, with overwhelming evidence, what God designed me to be, with all the possibilities placed by Him at my disposal,—and side by side with that most loving and glorious plan, stands staring me in the face, that other image of what I have made myself. All my past life, with its misused graces and lost opportunities, like a horrible reflection of myself, cries out to me

" Look in my face : my name is MIGHT-HAVE-BEEN."

I seem, as the last waves of time, receding for ever, leave me stranded on the beach, to stand upon the shore of the Dead Sea of all my hopes, in which lie buried opportunities, graces, untold treasures of strength vouchsafed to lift me up to God's own level,—and just as the foam of the last wave frets my feet, my own heart is like a shell picked up from that desolate strand ; and holding it to my ear, I hear within it the echo of that abyss of time over which I have passed in vain. And the sound it brings to me, says : For thee time is "No More !" Thou wouldst fain profit of graces and opportunities, when it is all "Too Late." Thou wouldst live as becometh a child of God, a fellow-citizen of the Angels, a dweller in the Heavenly Jerusalem,—when it is all in vain : thou must perforce bid "Farewell" to the society of the Angels, to the bliss of the Supernal City, and to that God who is their light and their love,—to all an eternal "Farewell!" The horrible image of what I made myself throws on the dying soul a dark "shadow" and a chill intolerable as of the everlasting death, while behind the thin "screen" which separates the ending present from the endless future, appear dim visions of that last doom, still "unuttered," but "intolerable."

If the true-hearted husband and father would, therefore not be haunted and maddened in the last dreadful extremity by the apparition of his lost "Life and Love" rising up before him, to show him what both life and love in the home might have been, let him begin now in earnest to make that home his true and sole paradise.

Seeking Pleasure outside the Home.

There is another class of husbands who are the enemies of their own domestic happiness,—such as seem to think that home can afford them neither congenial society, nor rational amusement.

Of course, we are perfectly aware, that many men of every rank in the community are driven to the tavern, the low theater, or the club-house, by deplorable selfishness or apathy of a wife or a mother, who will not or cannot make home attractive to the husband or the son. Elsewhere we have shown how the husband has to exert himself, as in the performance of a most sacred duty, to contribute his share, and if need be, the principal share, in all that makes the domestic hearth warm, bright, joyous, and delightful. Let the heart of a true man only be set on making of his own home the most attractive and soul-satisfying spot on earth, and he cannot fail of success. This is one of the fundamental and indispensable duties of a father and husband's office, and God is bound to assist him in his earnest endeavor, nay, God and his angels are interested in promoting his purpose.

We suppose, however, in what we have to say here, that the fault is not on the side of the wife, the mother, or the daughters : that they are most anxious to keep the gentlemen of the family at home, most desirous to devote themselves to their comfort and amusement, and every way capable of rendering the evening hours and the Sabbath repose most pleasant and profitable.

It not unfrequently happens, in a country such as the United States, where steady and persevering industry is pretty sure to enable the laborer to rise to wealth and position, that a real difficulty is thus created for the husband. He has risen, and has given his family a luxurious home. But his wife and, sometimes, his daughters as well, have not risen with him. He is ambitious to mix with the cultivated society among which his fortune enables him to move. But he cannot invite to his home men who are his equals in wealth, and his superiors in birth and in long-acquired social standing ; nor,—were his daughters sufficiently educated to make up for their mother's deficiency, would such gentlemen,—save only for some passing political purpose, —be willing to accept his invitation, or to admit him and his to their home circles. Meanwhile there is in the bosom of men of this class a yearning for " better society," which impels them to turn their back on their own fireside and seek so much of this society as they can find on the neutral ground of certain clubs and associations. Hence the danger of utterly neglecting what is due to one's own home, and of seeking and never finding the happiness inseparably attached, for the husband and father, to the company of his wife and children. Hence, too, the many temptations thrown in the way of men, who have plenty of money, without the sweet attractions of home-enjoyment to hold them from pursuing a downward course of distraction and dissipation.

We have seen this evil,—so frequently to be met with in

a society like our own,—remedied only by such wisdom and piety as we mentioned in a preceding chapter.*

Similar, and more touching instances of devotion to the dear ones who, having shared the early battle with poverty, have a right to share in all the home-bliss that affluence can bring,—are to be found all around us. For if there are many (shall we say too many?) who are all too anxious to assert themselves and make the most of their newly ac-quired wealth,—there are also very many, whom their natural good sense induces to be satisfied with the solid and substantial comforts of a modest home, of a sound education for their children, of devotion to the friends who have stood by them in the dark hours, and of the blissful satisfaction of being for the poor and the suffering within their reach God's watchful eye and helpful hand. There is not a priest on our wide missionary field all over the North American continent, who does not know many such homes as we are here describing in a few faint outlines. One, in particular, we shall sketch briefly, throwing over the picture such a veil as may cover the sensitive, shrinking modesty of the model husband and wife.

The Man who Drank of the Waters of his own Well.

He had been forced to seek a refuge in America, by political troubles in his native land, in which his family had been seriously implicated,—though he had himself taken no active part. Still the indiscriminating passion, which usurped the place of public justice, having marked him also out for punishment, left him no alternative but flight and exile. Landing at New Orleans, he met with alternate success and ill fortune, and at length his failing health as well as the desire of joining his wife and children lately arrived in New York, led him to go North. He arrived in the great city almost as penniless as when he first landed in New Orleans. But his steady temperate habits, his trust

---

* See pages 47–52, and Chapter IV. throughout.

in God, his quiet, persevering industry, and the indomitable will to succeed, raised him, step by step, to the front rank of business men. All this while, he with his wife and three children lived most modestly, giving without stint the money he earned to every need, and remaining almost unknown to the very clergymen who were the recipients or the distributers of his most liberal charities.

The village near which he had located the factory to which he owed his great fortune, did not contain a single person professing his faith or belonging to his own nationality ; yet he was not the less respected by the very highest in the place, and none the less popular among the laborers whom he employed. His word was his bond in commercial circles, his gentle firmness gave him authority over his workmen, and his intelligent liberality in encouraging the best talent, together with his generous care of the sick and suffering, won him the hearts of all. So, the silent, mild-mannered, simply dressed man moved about in his own little world of labor, the personification of true authority, creating happiness and love by continual beneficence.

To the priest of the distant city to whom he periodically went to confession, he never made his name known during the first period of his prosperity, although he invariably left with him large alms for his poor, or liberal donations for his parochial institutions.

He had labored seriously and successfully to educate himself during all these years, teaching himself all the branches necessary and useful to him in his calling ; but his quick intelligence, his wide experience of men, and his sound practical judgment enabled him to go far beyond the mere letter of what he learned. While giving his children (two girls and a boy) a solid common-school and business education, he was careful to make his wife,—his own twin-soul in disposition and ability,—study with him during his after-business hours. Not even his own children were allowed to suspect the occupation of their dear parents during the long night-hours devoted year after year to self-improvement. Nor, when grown up to manhood and woman-

9

hood, they found both father and mother able to converse
with the most intelligent and accomplished, giving as well
as receiving information on the topics introduced, did they
for a moment imagine that there had been in the early
training of both a defect which nothing but the most per-
sistent labor in after-life enabled them to remedy. The
husband's first effort in that direction had been to speak
and write the English language in its purity, without much
caring to correct his native accent. And this he also made
the first object of his wife's private studies. We have read
letters from both, not only free from grammatical errors of
any kind, but perfect models of simplicity, sound sense,
and good taste. And, for hours together, we have conversed
with them without being able to remark a single flaw in
their conversation. And all this was the result of private
study, after the first period of youth had been passed, and
when both were engrossed with the management of a large
and growing business, and the cares of a family !

What was most admirable, however, was their quiet and
comfortable home, in which furniture and servants seemed
to reflect the quiet, gentle, modest character of the master
and mistress, and in which the children were evidently the
natural growth of the parental tree,—the daughters bright,
intelligent, handsome, healthy, and radiant like their mo-
ther,—and the son what one would think his father must
have been at the same age,—self-possessed, courteous with-
out affectation, cordial in word and manner, low-voiced in
conversation, and warming gradually into real eloquence on
subjects that interested his convictions.

It was evident, even to the casual visitor, that the mem-
bers of this family were all in all to each other. The father
never would accept invitations from the most distinguished
men in the community, who entertained a deep respect for
the man's upright character and uncommon sagacity, and
were anxious to cultivate a more intimate acquaintance
with a household, a glimpse of whose interior resembled a
view from the dusty and sun-broiled thoroughfare of a
green, shady resting-place beneath the high trees, where

wild flowers scent the cool air and the song of birds make the stillness vocal.

No one who had ever enjoyed the hospitality of that abode of unaffected simplicity and true self-respect, but wished to return again. None of that family ever spent a single day or night away from that true home in which their whole heart dwelt, but longed to be back again in its atmosphere of love and peace and sunshine.

We hold up a mirror to many a true-hearted man, to husbands and fathers dazzled by the glare of a false and dangerous respectability, misled by a wrong estimate of the real nature of home-life and domestic happiness. We pray that theirs may be the unspeakable enjoyment which crowned the life of a husband, who felt that he had in himself and the virtues of his loved companion too rich a store of goodness, greatness, and self-content, to seek outside of his own home-life for any one satisfaction necessary to himself and his dear ones.

Men who seek the Bitter Waters of the Desert.

From this home,—like the skylark's lowly nest hidden far away from the roadside, amid the hay and fragrant clover, or like that of the nightingale buried in the soft mosses and undergrowth of the deep forest,—we turn to the desolate home of the man of fashion or dissipation, resembling the heaps of sand on some river-bank, in which the Australian bird * deposits her eggs, leaving them to be hatched by the burning tropical sun, while the young brood are deprived of a mother's tender and watchful care or of a father's protection.

When,—as we have shown in the last example,—it is within a husband's power to create himself a paradise, in which body and soul may find repose, refreshment, and all true contentment after labor and at the end of life, what folly and what guilt are not the man's who throws his

---

* The TALLEGALLA, or Australian BRUSH-TURKEY.

money, his time, his health, and his heart away on outside
pursuits,—like waters poured out on the barren desert
where tree or shrub or flower will never grow!

For,—after all,—wealth inherited or acquired, a social
position obtained from one's family or conquered by one's
own merit, talents, time, health, and opportunity,—every-
thing which enables a man to be conspicuous, influential,
to be a living power for the common weal or the good of his
own dear ones,—is heaven-given, and may be wasted like
water poured out on the barren sands. You have wealth, a
home that may be honored, a family that may be happy,
health and strength and fruitful years before you;—will
you be the steady light of that home? the very heart of that
family's happiness? Will you make what remains of life,
like the crown of the palm tree when loaded down with
its ripe, delicious fruit? Then seek within your home, in
the company of your wife and children, the sole satisfaction
which can secure your own felicity and contribute to theirs.

Look around you, and see, in this great city, in every
city throughout the land, in the great centers of population,
wealth, and industry that you are acquainted with from
personal observation or the reliable report of others,—how
many families are made wretched or utterly ruined, how
many lives are degraded, how many hearts broken, how
many reputations are blasted, and how many honorable
careers are brought to the most shameful ending,—by the
fascinations of the club-room or the gambling-house!

We have known, through their results,—just as one learns
to judge the pitiless might of the angry ocean from the
wrecks and the corpses cast up on the beach,—the terrible
consequences of club-life in Paris and London, as well as in
New York. We know that the tide of custom which carries
men away from the quiet and duties of home-life to the
club-room and the gambling-table, is daily gaining volume
and velocity. Can no warning voice be raised? Modern
science has invented a most admirable system of storm-
signals, warning vessels setting out to sea of the danger
which threatens them on the waves, and these signals are

only the result of a still more admirable system of weather observations.

Can the sacred science of the theologian and moralist, or the zeal of a priestly heart, not invent and apply some such warnings to the souls that are still on the firm ground of domestic duty faithfully discharged, but who are sadly tempted to try the ventures and enjoy the excitement of these currents of social life so full of shipwreck and sorrow?

The wrecks themselves and the sight of their victims may serve to warn the unwary, the venturesome, or the tempted.

A Young Mechanic's Fearful Example.

Here is a young artisan who has been all his life a model of filial devotion to his parents, absolutely irreproachable in his morals, most esteemed as a tradesman, and handsomely remunerated for his labor, at the moment his parents induce him to marry a girl of his own class, in every way suited to him by her education, practical tastes, unsullied innocence, and true piety. The marriage and the very comfortable establishment made for the young people, are the joint work of their two excellent families, as much as their union is the result of real mutual affection.

All the relations and friends who have seen them in their new home have pronounced them most happy, and their handsome little dwelling a picture of comfort. A few months of unalloyed bliss have passed over them, disclosing to each the solid and lovable qualities of the other, and thus drawing closer the sacred bond between them. Till that hour the young husband, though possessing many warm friends and admiring acquaintances, has never belonged to any club or association,—never, indeed, been inside a club-house. Not so his companions in the workshop. The foremost among them and one of the junior partners of the firm, belong to a very influential club of tradesmen, unmarried men for the most part,—on whose roll of membership are the names of very many distinguished mechanics

in the city. Our young husband is made to believe, now
that his independent position as a married man opens
to him new prospects of fortune and advancement,—that,
in their business, a man cannot hope to reach any high de-
gree of eminence, unless he belongs to a club like theirs.
This is the chief reason which prevails on the inexperienced
youth to join them.

He does so reluctantly and with many strong misgivings.
But he does so because the support he is promised from his
fellow-members, will, he thinks, enable him to reach that
point of success and prosperity, which will contribute so
materially to his wife's happiness. From her, however, he
keeps his membership a secret. The single evening spent
at the club, has been that on which he was elected and re-
ceived the warm congratulations of his associates. So, he
hopes,—indeed, he is sure,—that his duties toward them
will not take him away from the company of his young
wife, or interfere with his domestic duties.

The First Cup.

To be sure,—once the election was over, and the new
member had made his neat little speech, and shaken hands
with all present,—refreshments were partaken of in the ad-
joining restaurant, and he had to drink a health or two.
This was an innovation in his hitherto orderly and strictly
abstemious life. For he was the son of a man who had
gained in youth a great and rare victory over habitual in-
temperance, and who had been most careful to preserve his
children from the curse which had blighted his own most
precious years. It so happened, too, that his reception into
the club took place a few days only before the Fourth of
July, and he was invited to make one of the addresses cus-
tomary on the occasion. Then he was charged with pro-
posing a toast at a puplic banquet to take place in the
evening under the auspices of the club.

All this filled his young wife with secret forebodings of
evil. His life-long habits of sobriety had been one of her

husband's chief recommendations to her parents, one of the solid reasons on which her own esteem for him was founded. She noticed his excited and strange manner on his return home the night of his election, but forebore from either question, remark, or reproach. On the Fourth of July he came in very late after the banquet, and came in intoxicated, noisy, and violent! She had spent the day in agony; she feared she knew not what, as the birds and brute beasts feel instinctively the approach of an earthquake, as sea-birds divine the coming of a tidal wave and fly promptly to the shore and the highlands.

So did the gentle and pious girl take refuge from her own unexplained fears in prayer, lifting up her heart to God in the highest. Indeed, she was still on her knees, when the hurried ringing of the door-bell startled her, making her heart beat violently. She could not stir from the spot on which she had been kneeling, endeavoring to overcome the faintness and the sudden heartache she felt, as they bore in her husband, swearing, struggling with his companions, and uttering threats of vengeance against some real or imaginary foe. His rage increased on seeing his young wife pale, silent, riveted to the spot on which she stood, and staring at the scene before her with frightened and fixed eyes. She soon recovered herself, thanking in a few words the two worthies who were only a little less intoxicated than her husband. After much exertion she succeeded in pacifying him, and inducing him to undress and take the rest he needed.

The next morning found him sick in heart and head. Not one word of reproach was uttered by the little wife; nor did she so much as allude to the scene of the preceding night. This ought to have touched the husband more than anything else. But in truth his brain had not yet recovered from the effects of the last day's excitement and of the deep debauch with which it had closed. So, although he vowed interiorly that he should never again be seen in such a state, he did not express to his wife by word or look the sorrow he really felt. On the contrary, he put a bold face on it, saying that "men were men; that he had to do a man's part in public and on great occasions; that his speeches had been well received, that many had highly complimented him, and that he had to comply with the custom of gentlemen on such public occasions, to drink toasts to his friends and admirers ;   . and much more to the same purpose.

To all this the wife made no reply, save by the tears which fell silently down her cheeks. The husband observed them with a keen pang of anguish ; but, with that perversity of judgment and feeling which many men, "honorable" and educated and high-born men,—mistake or feign to mistake for manliness and independence,—the culprit only blustered and bungled the more as he went on justifying his own moral cowardice. He was yet speaking when one of his associate workmen came in according to appointment, and both sallied out together, leaving the young wife to her grief and her sad forebodings.

They sallied out, breakfasted together at a neighboring restaurant, seasoning their breakfast with some needed stimulant, and then went to the factory.

Fast in the Folds of the Serpent.

Shall we continue the details of this sad story? Here was a young man about to contract one of these dreadful habits which bind the soul with chains as firm as those which hold down the inhabitants of the City of the Eternal Death. A friendly hand might have led him away from the fatal downward path, which to him was a path almost untrodden, and certainly unloved. His wife, young as she was, could and should, with that deep, clear-sighted wisdom that is one of the gifts of woman, have been this friend, had he turned to her. But the Tempter was at hand in the fellow-workman who had called for him, and who had remarked the young wife's tears that morning, and hastened, when they were alone in the street, to twit his companion on his being "hen-pecked," and tied to his wife's apron-strings.

A well-seasoned tippler himself, and a man who had already broken one wife's heart, he related to more than one in the workshop that his young friend had been severely lectured by his bride for returning home jolly on the Fourth of July. So, after laboring hours, the young husband,—who had now sobered down and had been making very serious resolutions of amendment, was surrounded by a group of inveterate drinkers, who bantered him mercilessly about his meek subjection to his wife.

From that hour he fell, like a forsaken ship, into the hands and under the direction of these unprincipled men. Vainly did he stuggle to escape from the thraldom they exercised. Week after week he followed them to the club and the tavern, at first only "to assert his manhood and his independence," as was the slang of his fellows; and soon, to gratify the craving for alcoholic excitement, which had now become his ruling passion.

Dragged down to Perdition.

To his poor young wife he manifested, alternately the most touching sentiments of tenderness and repentance, or those of downright brutality,—of brutality when crazed by drink,—of repentance and love, when thoroughly awakened from the temporary insanity produced by alcohol. She never permitted herself one word of reproach. When her husband returned to her weekly, body and soul deformed by the evil spirit that entered into him with alcohol, she only sought to soothe him and hide him away from every eye. God alone saw the tears she shed unceasingly, as she besought Him to accept her life as a sacrifice of atonement for her husband's guilt, and to grant in return the grace of final repentance to her lost one.

The heart-rending agony of grief and shame which the poor wretch underwent in the intervals between his relapses, was something most pitiful to behold. The good priest who had married them also added his fatherly advice to the promptings of remorse; and there followed a few spasmodic efforts of amendment. But the examples, the jests and sneers of his bottle-companions, were too powerful for a will naturally infirm, and growing weaker by every new resolution violated, and every additional sin of intoxication.

And thus the young inebriate continued his downward course with accelerated speed,—till he lost his position of foreman in the workshop, lost at length all opportunity for work, which his health and habits rendered him unfit to perform, and lost to his creditors of the tavern the very roof above him, the handsome and comfortable home bestowed on him by his good father.

Ruin, Death, Insanity.

The latter took the young and heart-broken wife to his own home, lavishing on her the warmest and most tender care. She survived only by a few hours the birth of her first babe, and the babe itself had no sooner been regenerated by baptism, than its spirit rejoined its mother on high. They laid them both to rest together, the little blossom on the parent stem; while the husband and father sought a refuge against his grief and despair in furious and continual intoxication,—till at length reason gave way forever, and his parents had to place the madman in an insane asylum.

The Scandal Spreads from Above Downward.

This young mechanic was only one of the tens of thousands who in any one of our States, daily travel down the road to ruin, following in the footsteps of their betters. The Mechanics' Club and the connected tavern are only a copy of so many aristocratic resorts of the same nature, with their restaurants, their unlimited facilities for gambling and dissipation, and their hordes of wealthy and fashionable husbands and fathers, who learn there to forget and violate all their most sacred home-duties,—wasting the often hard-won wealth and the golden opportunities of mature life, in ruining soul and body, and bringing as well, ruin and desolation to the home they were made to gladden and glorify.

How many well-born men, who were on their way to honors higher than birth or gold can ever purchase in a free country, and who are at this moment the inmates of the public prison or of the insane asylum, because they preferred to the charities, the duties, the repose and delight of home-life, the glitter, the excitement, the manifold fascinations of club-life, and betrayed their conscience, their honor, and their trust to gratify the habits of criminal extravagance and dissipation contracted there!

How many men once most happy and most honored,—favored public officers, successful merchants or manufacturers, lawyers and physicians trusted with the honor and health of families,—men blessed with accomplished and devoted wives, with doating and most virtuous children, who have allowed themselves to be fascinated by the sounds and sights and amusements of the club-house, and of what the club-house leads to,—and are now gone before their time to a dishonored grave, after bequeathing to wife and children a name which all the waters of the Hudson could not wash clean! And how many others are left, after making a wreck of fortune, reputation and home, to drag on a wretched existence, unhonored, and unloved, despised alike by their fellow-citizens and themselves!

To be sure, it is in the power of the rich man to neglect his wife and family, and to make his home of the tavern, without bringing poverty on those who call him husband and father, or without having his offenses laid bare to the public eye or visited by the reproof of the magistrate or so much as a notice from the officers of the law. We happen to hear of many of these so-called "Cottages," or pet taverns, patronized exclusively by the wealthy, where the recreant head of a family, because he happens to be blessed or cursed with a superabundance of money,—can hide himself away for weeks and months, every one of his vicious appetites pandered to, and the consequences of his debauch most carefully screened from all but his boon companions.

And when wealth and station, when culture and the most responsible professions are thus made to teach the laboring classes the very worst lessons of example,—is God going to perform a miracle by saving society from the destroying hands and corrupting examples of the governing and leading classes?

How the Leading Classes must Lead.

The leading classes,—if they would lead at all to any purpose under a republican form of government —must lead by the ascendency of virtuous example. It is agreed on all hands by the men most competent to forecast our future weal or woe from a scientific survey of the present, that on the purity of home-life in every class of the community, depends the longevity of the nation as well as its prosperity. Leading classes there are, of course, among us, as elsewhere,—and the home of the mechanic and the laborer will be evermore modeled on that of the man above him in wealth, office, station, or profession. The life of the clergyman, the lawyer, the physician, the magistrate, the merchant, or the manufacturer, will be instinctively studied by all who look up to them for teaching and guidance, for direction, support, and employment. Your servants, your daily laborers, all who depend on you or come in any way within the reach of your influence and example,—will copy you so far as they can in their way of living, their amusements and recreations.

Hence it behooves every home among the governing and leading classes,—that the example it sets, like the radiance of a light-house near a dangerous coast,—should be steady and guide surely amid darkness and storm.

We have seen the baneful influences of the club-house and the aristocratic tavern copied by the naturally ambitious classes of mechanics and skilled laborers. We see, —to our grief and dismay,—that the young people of both sexes belonging to the poorest of the working classes, are

zealously copying the worst forms of fashionable amuse-
ment, in their cheap theaters, cheap dances, Saturday night
free balls,—and such like.

They swarm to them from the crowded down-town dis-
tricts like flies in midsummer to a putrid carcass or a heap
of fermenting vegetable matter ; and, on Sunday mornings
more especially, as we can testify, they are to be seen issu-
ing in noisy swarms from these hotbeds of corruption,
intoxicated with alcohol, sensual excitement, and passion,
crowding the street-cars,—young girls and young boys ut-
terly forgetful and regardless of modesty, decency, and
self-respect,—returning to their homes as a blight and a
curse, or prowling through the streets ready for every law-
less deed of violence and murder !

No preaching can avail to stop the festering of this mighty
mass of corruption,—no doctoring can avail to stop this
gangrene which has fixed itself on the young of both sexes,
the twin-roots of the society of the future,—unless the men
of the leading classes, by the shining morality of their own
lives, and the beautiful teachings of homes made attractive
and blissful, shall encourage and enable the poor man,—the
laborers from whose hearths these swarms of pleasure-seek-
ers issue,—to make their homes so bright and delightful
that young maidens and young boys shall never leave them,
—but to join pure hands and virgin hearts at the matri-
monial altar before building up blessed homes of their own.

Oh ! let no one, who knows how lightly we have, in
these last pages, passed over an evil that chaste minds
would not care to fathom, blame the writer for saying thus
much and no more. Let all, on the contrary, who have at
heart the preservation and perfection of home-life in our
midst, bethink them only of contributing each his best en-
deavor toward thus making our homes, in every class, the
nurseries of true men and true women,—innocent before
marriage, chaste and stainless after marriage, God-fearing,
self-respecting, and self-denying.

With this not unnecessary digression, we close this first
part of the present subject-matter, reserving what remains
for another chapter.

CHAPTER VIII.

BAD HUSBANDS (CONTINUED).

When you will have passed this gate (of Fortune), another inclosed space extends beyond it : do you perceive at its outskirts these magnificently attired women ?—Yes, who are they ?—Their names are Intemperance, Pleasure, Avarice, and Flattery.—But why are they stationed there ?—They are watching for all those who have received any gifts from Fortune —And what do they do next ?—When these favorites of fortune approach, these women dance with joy, embrace these men, praise and flatter them, and urge them to stay where they now are,—holding out to them the promise of a life of ease, without suffering or sorrow. As soon as any one of these men, fascinated by the witcheries of these women, surrenders himself to Pleasure, the life he leads seems to him at first to be most delightful ; but very soon these delights appear to him to be empty delusions. Indeed, as soon as he awakes from his intoxicating dream, he sees that while he was enjoying his visionary bliss, both his goods and his person have been utterly wasted. Hence, having now dissipated all that he had received from Fortune, he becomes the slave of these female tyrants, who force him to obey them in all things, to perpetrate all manner of enormities ;—such as to become a forger, a profaner of holy things, a perjurer, traitor, highwayman,—an embodiment, in one word, of all the vices. And when he has consummated all iniquity, they hand him over to Justice.—CEBES, *Prospect of Human Life.*

CEBES, one of the most illustrious of the disciples of Socrates, has left us but a few fragments of composition. Even these, however, suffice to show, as do the writings of Xenophon and Demosthenes, the influence of the great Athenian's teaching on the mind and heart of the disciple.

In the "Prospect of Human Life" * he uses the Oriental form of allegory to point out, as in a vast picture, the per-

---

* Generally appended to the editions of Epictetus.

nicious influences that turn the multitude of men aside
from the path of virtue and true wisdom, render them the
slaves of Error, Passion, and Vice, and lead them to endless
pain. Imposture sits with Wise Experience at the very gate
of Life (the author describes the false Philosophy of his age
and country together with the errors and vices which tyran-
nized over the then heathen world). Turning aside from
the latter, which warns every human being what path to
take in order to find the great teacher, Truth, and to arrive
with his aid at lasting felicity, the blind and blundering
multitude crowd around the lofty seat of Imposture, drink
of her poisoned cup, are given over to error and ignorance,
to vain opinion, and vicious enjoyment.

We are now concerned with such of the crowd as blind
Fortune has loaded with her favors ;—for the reality which
was before the mental and bodily vision of the Athenian,
Cebes, differs in no essential point from that which meets
the eye of the religious philosopher in the nineteenth cen-
tury of Christian civilization.

We have been studying a few types of the bad husband ;
a few more, belonging to classes neither less numerous, nor
less interesting, remain to be considered in this chapter.
Cebes makes men loaded with the gifts of Fortune come
beneath the influence of " Intemperance, Pleasure, Avarice,
and Flattery ;" we shall reverse this order, leaving the in-
temperate husband to crown the sad list of home-destroyers,
and begin with such as may be classed under the head of
"Flattery," or, rather, of Vanity.

Weak Ambition.

In the companion book to the present work * we spoke of
the love of display as one of the most dangerous enemies
of the wife and mistress of the home,—of vanity, which
nourishes this foolish ambition, as the path to dishonor.

This sort of weak ambition,—of vanity, rather,—is by no
means uncommon among our men, not alone among such as

* " The Mirror of True Womanhood," pp 123, 124, 125, 126.

rise to affluence and position without possessing anything
like mental cultivation, but more especially among the edu-
cated who have risen into wealth and fame by dint of per-
sonal effort, and thanks to their superior culture.

It will not be considered as an invidious distinction, if we
here say that, in the community in which the author lives
and over which his observation has ranged with special care,
a large proportion if not a very large majority of such hus-
bands, were natives of the New England States.   There, the
pride taken by the people in making common-school edu-
cation embrace so many branches elsewhere reserved for
the college, the university, or the art school, has begotten
in a multitude of young people an ambition and an apti-
tude to rise to eminence as professors of pure science, or as
civil engineers and inventors.   Every day one sees some
New-England boy thus forcing himself by talent and genius
into the front rank of industry and fortune.   It is to their
cases, and to others like them, that our animadversions
more particularly apply.

How the Weakly Ambitious are Ensnared.

A young man so reared and highly gifted marries while
he is obscurely struggling to rise.   His wife is one of these
pretty, bright, well-educated, and attractive New-England
girls to be met with all over the land, in town and country.
She is, at the time of their union, quite her husband's equal
in every respect, very often his superior in birth and for-
tune.   As theirs has been truly a love-match, their home-
life is a most blissful one so long as the husband's battle
for distinction and success lasts.   She is, during these years
of struggle, and often of poverty, not only the loving wife,
the tender mother, and thrifty manager of the home, but
also and especially her husband's companion, counselor,
friend, and consoler, sustaining him when discouraged by
failure and opposition, and cheering him on to face and
vanquish every obstacle, till at length he triumphs.

He triumphs; fame and fortune now smile upon him,

capitalists place unlimited means at the disposition of the successful inventor, or court association with one whose practical genius has outstripped in a given direction the science and skill of the most popular manufacturers or speculators.

With success comes a new ambition, new wants, new habits, new aims and tendencies. He finds himself transferred from his obscure native town and his modest abode to the great metropolis, where alone that rare plant, Genius, can find a congenial soil and atmosphere. He must have either splendid apartments at the most fashionable hotel in which to receive becomingly the men of wealth and position who seek his alliance or his acquaintance ; and, next, he must, as his fortune rises still higher, have a brilliant mansion of his own. Besides, the fruit of his genius, he is told, must not be confined to his own country ; it will also thrive in foreign lands and obtain the patronage of foreign governments and peoples.

And thus, he finds himself, step by step, carried upward by the wave of success to a world quite different from that in which he has hitherto moved. And with himself, his wife and children have been suddenly lifted into the dazzling world of wealth, fashion, pleasure, and unbounded vanity.

The wife, brought up in the simplicity and severity of a New-England country home, does not take kindly to very many of the ways of this fashionable and dazzling world, with whose incense her husband is intoxicated. She is "too puritanical" in the estimation of her husband's associates, and too "countrified" in the judgment of their elegant wives. Still, these condescend to patronize her and court her acquaintance as a part of the homage due to her companion,—the rising man.

Thus, by degrees and insensibly, the husband is led to look down upon his wife, to consider her as inferior to his new position, if not to himself. So love dies out in the intellect before it is killed in the heart. Should it so happen that, in his business trips abroad, his wife should accom-

7

pany him, the result most probably will be to make him
contrast unfavorably her quiet, simple, homely tastes with
the wit, the brilliancy, the grace to be met with in women
of the upper middle class in European capitals. Nor is it
unlikely that he will become acquainted, while there, with
the deplorable laxity of opinion, entertained on the matri-
monial relations by the Voltairian husbands of these women.
And so, while his mind is poisoned by anti-christian princi-
ples current among the very men he most admires, the pure
love of his early youth and later manhood is daily losing
all hold on his heart.

  How open is an ambitious or a vain man so disposed, to
the poisonous suggestions of an unprincipled acquaintance
to whom he looks up with deference! or to the wiles of a
still more unprincipled woman, lying in wait for a husband
like him, shaken in his fidelity to his lawful wife, and un-
consciously yearning for a companion more suited to his
improved fortunes, his brilliant associations, and his newly
born taste for high life and its pleasures!

  For, — and many a true-hearted wife knows it to her
cost,—there is, unfortunately, in our great cities no lack
of women whose sole aim in life is to insnare some such
wealthy victim, whose fortune shall minister to their un-
unslaked thirst for pleasure and display, utterly reckless
the while of the faithful hearts they may break, of the
misery and desolation they may bring to homes hitherto
blessed with all domestic virtue and happiness!

  Men fired by ambition, blinded by passion, are but ill
suited to cope with the wiles and witchery of some

<blockquote>
"Lady elf,
Some demon's mistress, or the demon's self."
</blockquote>

To men fallen into bondage to such clever and wicked
women, the cup of misery to be drained thenceforward is
all the more deep and bitter, that they retain some con-
science, and remember how innocent and worthy of all love
is the wife they have forsaken. Such men dare not sue for
a separation in the courts, and they scorn to use the abomi-

nable facilities for divorce furnished by men who are the disgrace of the legal profession, and sanctioned by local legislation that perverts all the holiest purposes of law. They profit by the forsaken and outraged wife's horror of publicity, to screen their own shame beneath the insecure veil of half-secrecy, and give her name to the seducer. Thus they drag from one foreign city to another their secret with them, and with the guilty secret they drag about the sure pledge of the retribution that must overtake them.

Retribution.

The public have not forgotten the sudden and tragic ending of more than one of these scandalous careers,—scandalous at least in the unblushing effrontery with which a brilliant fortune was lavished in unholy gratifications, even when that fortune itself had not been acquired by means which honest men abhor. We remember how the shadow of the divine hand long hung above the home of the profligate, who flattered himself with impunity because Vanity Fair did not discard himself and his accomplice, and who saddened religious hearts by the spectacle of crime successful, unpunished, and apparently secure in its happiness; but the bolt from heaven fell at length, and the home of the criminal, the place of his burial, and his very name were,—like those spots where, in Pagan Rome, the lightning had fallen on a guilty head,—inclosed and held forever ground that no human foot should tread upon.

Let us believe it most firmly,—though the Almighty Father and Judge of mankind does allow individuals as well as communities to flourish while they most shamefully abuse their free will, and seemingly defy and deride His most patient justice,—that Justice shall have its day for the nation and for the man, as surely as to the longest, longest Arctic night succeeds the dawn of God's sun in the heavens.

Two instances stare us in the face as we write; one of a man who abandoned the young and admirable wife of his youth, having fallen beneath the charms of some Lamia.

>"Not a drop of her blood was human,
>But she was made like a soft sweet woman."

He loathed the serpent in whose coils he was fast bound, as much as he had once loved and respected the spotless bride he had first taken to his parents' home. The fear of discovery and the terrors of his own cowardly conscience followed him in his dark ways while on his native soil, and pursue him now abroad like the fabled Furies of the ancients, attached night and day to the footsteps of the man who had profaned the altar of his own home-sanctuary and quenched with his own hand the sacred fire on his hearth. Men who do not divine the secret of that once happy home left desecrated and darkened forever, or who cannot read the agony of the wretched husband's breast, will applaud his genius and minister to his vanity : the world which only worships success, fame, and fortune, may crowd nightly the saloon in which the false wife queens it with the children of her guilt around her, while the true wife far away gives up her whole existence to good works, and her heart to the one hope of God's mercy. But not one day of intoxicating success ends for that faithless husband, but he says with agony in his heart of hearts as he lays his head on his sleepless pillow,

>"O to-day and the day to come after !"

Ambition, Infidelity, and Nemesis.

The other instance, one of swift and terrible retribution, was but little if at all spoken of in the public press, or in the gossip and scandal-loving world for which our daily press caters. A beautiful wife, in every way but one the superior of her unworthy husband, had been discarded by him for one far her inferior in graces of mind and charms of person,—simply because the wife was extremely young and modest, while her rival was passionate, and well experienced in all the ways of Vanity Fair.

The former was induced by her wily husband to travel abroad and to remain for years in European capitals under the tuition of the best masters, in order to complete,—as her husband said,—her early education, and thus to enable her to shine on her return at the head of the establishment he was meanwhile creating for her. The persons who accompanied the artless girl were in the pay of her unprincipled husband, and instructed to expose her inexperience to the most terrible dangers. Her unsuspecting innocence as well as the pure love which filled her heart for her husband, served as a twofold shield against even the thought of temptation. And she returned to her husband doubly accomplished,—we need not say, and a thousand times more worthy of the love of one so utterly worthless.

She found her husband waiting for her, not in the splendid home of which he had so often written to her,—and which she was never to set foot in,—but at a quiet hotel, where apartments were ready for her. There was in his manner a something that fell chillingly on her young heart, and a mystery in the atmosphere with which he skillfully surrounded her, that she was afraid to penetrate. He was, —he said,—obliged to go suddenly to Europe on very urgent business, and her coming home unexpectedly and without timely warning, had only anticipated by a few weeks their meeting in Paris.

She did not believe all this ; for she had discovered of late many little things in her husband's conduct and letters which made her suspect both his good faith and his veracity. And now, being told that she was to remain behind while he went abroad, and that she was to remain in her present lodgings without so much as attempting to visit the lordly mansion of which he had written so much, she was thoroughly roused, and accused her husband of deceiving her for some purpose she feared to understand.

He became enraged, and in his rage threw off the mask he had worn with so ill a grace. He plainly told her he loved her no longer, and that he loved another. He threatened her with instant separation, if she made any resistance to his will. If she made up her mind to bear with the inevitable he would settle the new mansion on her with a liberal annuity. If not, and if she chose to defy him, he had those in his pay who would swear to such conduct of hers while abroad, as should secure him a decree of divorce from her, and leave her penniless with a dishonored name.

She heard no more. A death-like swoon followed the revelation of her husband's unspeakable baseness. For several days the wretched and forsaken wife lay between life and death, and then came a brain-fever. Meanwhile the husband had left for Europe, having sent his paramour and her child in another vessel a few days before he set sail himself.

Several months elapsed ere the poor young creature's slow convalescence allowed her to think seriously or speak of her forlorn condition. A sealed letter from her husband had been placed in the hands of his lawyer, renewing the offers made on that memorable day when she found that her idol was vile clay. She spurned both the offer and the advice of the lawyer, and, as her parents had come to her in her extremity, she told to them her tale briefly and simply, affirming at the same time, that if her father could only accompany her, she would follow her husband and unmask his villany wherever she happened to find him.

The letter left with the lawyer she retained for this purpose. Her father, whose brave spirit she inherited, consented readily. His modest fortune was sufficient to enable him to meet their expenses, and he would willingly expend it all to vindicate the honor of his child, and to punish her unworthy husband. So, they both set out firmly bent on prosecuting their purpose to the bitterest ending.

They learned on their arrival in London that he was negotiating with one of the continental governments the sale of a valuable patent of his own. In that capital the young wife had spent a most agreeable autumn and winter, had been presented at court by the minister representing her own country, and had made many friends among the highest aristocracy. For, in truth, her beauty, sprightliness, and many accomplishments had gained her all the more admiration that they were accompanied and heightened by childlike simplicity and genuine modesty.

Her husband, emboldened by the reports of her deathly
sickness and tedious convalescence, had everywhere intro-
duced her rival as his lawful wife ; and, by some providen-
tial permission they were both to be presented at court on
the day after the arrival of our travelers in the capital.
There had been a change in the legation, and to the new
minister her husband and herself were total strangers. The
injured wife instantly adopted her plan of action. She
drove without a moment's delay with her father to the hotel
of a nobleman, into whose family circle she had formerly
been more than once admitted, and laid before him her
wrongs, and what was to happen on the morrow.

He was much struck by the sad change wrought by grief
and sickness in the lovely girl who had endeared herself to
his family, and at once took a fatherly interest in her case.
Yes! he would present her and her father at court on the
morrow, and take care that they should have precedence of
the false husband and his companion in guilt. They must,
however, preserve a strict incognito and the most inviolable
secrecy. The nobleman meanwhile sought the prime min-
ister, and laid the matter before him in confidence. He
warmly espoused the side of the injured wife and her father,
and took other measures for punishing and exposing her
dastardly husband. The beautiful stranger was remem-
bered by many courtiers and noble ladies in the royal
antechambers, and greeted with genuine cordialty as she
leaned on the arm, of her noble friend. The presentation
was made, and then came the turn of her unsuspecting
husband, who was waiting in another room. Suddenly,
as his name was called out for the first time, and he and
his paramour were advancing in answer to the call, a high
officer of court appeared, and openly accused the culprit of
presenting another woman as his wife, whereas at that mo-
ment his lawful wife and her father were standing in the
Presence Chamber conversing with royalty.

We need not pursue in detail the story of the guilty pair.
He was allowed to escape,—most probably at the solicita-
tion of his kind-hearted father-in-law. He disappeared for-

ever from public notice, either having capped all his crimes
with suicide, to avoid the reprobation of the world'on whose
breath he lived, or to escape the avenging pangs of his own
conscience.   The woman to whom he had sacrificed honor,
home, and happiness, was indebted to her generous rival
for her liberation from prison.   She never returned to her
native land.   As to the young wife herself, we shall leave her
to the tender care of her parents and the obscurity in which
she chose to bury a life devoted solely to the good of others.

The Mirror of True Companionship and Felicity.

From this class of husbands we must not part without
holding up, for one moment at least, the mirror of another
life and another home,—as an incentive to the inviolable
fidelity and constant devotion which are characteristic of
all true men, and which should be the special attribute of
the man to whom God has given genius, and with it the ob-
ligation of shining example.   Men such as those whose
aberrations we have been describing, have it in their power
to do so much for the loved and loving companion of their
early years,—just as the faithful wives of such men have a
wealth of wisdom and of tenderness to bestow on their hus-
bands amid the noonday glare and the golden evening of
their later life !

Let us glance at a home, happily still bright and warm
after more than half a century of wedded bliss and united
literary labor.   Surely, the man who rises to universal fame
by his pen and his pencil, may well stand as a peer to the
great inventor, and in his home-life serve as a model to the
intellectual toilers of both hemispheres.

AFTER FIFTY YEARS.
September 20, 1874.

Yes ! fifty years of troubles—come and gone—
  I count since first I gave thee hand and heart !
But none have come from thee, dear Wife—not one !
  In griefs that saddened me thou hadst no part—
  Save when accepting more than woman's share
  Of pain and toil, despondency and care,

My comforter thou wert, my hope and trust
 Ever suggesting holy thoughts and deeds :
Guiding my steps on earth, through blinding dust,
 Into the Heaven-lit path, that Heavenward leads.
So has it been, from manhood unto age,
In every shifting scene of Life's sad stage,
Since—fifty years ago—a humble name '
I gave to thee—which thou hast given to fame—
Rejoicing in the wife and friend to find
The woman's lesser duties—all—combined
With holiest efforts of creative mind. .
And if the world has found some good in me,
The prompting and the teaching came from thee !
God so guide both that so it ever be !
 So may the full fount of affection flow ;
 Each loving each as—fifty years ago !
We are going down the rugged hill of life,
Into the tranquil valley at its base ;
But, hand in hand, and heart in heart, dear wife :
 With less of outer care and inner strife,
 I look into thy mind and in thy face,
 And only see the Angel coming nearer,
 To make thee still more beautiful and dearer,
 When from the thrall and soil of earth made free,
 Thy prayer is heard for me, and mine for thee ! *

The beautiful friendship, the close companionship in
labor and trial, in honor and obscurity, and the abiding
trust reposed by each of the wedded souls in the other,—
all so touchingly and gracefully alluded to in this affect-
ing tribute of a husband to a wife after fifty years of the
closest union,—must serve as a fitting close to the instruc-
tion we have been giving, and a no less apt preface to what
we are about to say.

---

* Samuel Carter Hall. This estimable gentleman and his wife (Anna Maria
Fielding, a native of Dublin) are too well known to our readers, by their many
popular works, to need any introduction from us. Mrs Hall's "Sketches of
Irish Character," "Lights and Shadows of Irish Life," and "Ireland, its Scene-
ry and Character," are found in every private library, while Mr. Hall's "Art
Journal" is still a favorite with all lovers of art. But far transcending all
literary merit, is the beautiful home-life of this venerable pair.

7*

The Secret Husband.

There are husbands who fail grievously in a point of duty as well as of deep interest to themselves,—and make it a rule to conceal from their wives their business transactions and troubles, thereby depriving themselves of counsel which would have saved them from ruin.

We are not speaking here, of course, of professional men, lawyers, physicians, and others, who are intrusted with secrets that concern the honor and vital interests of families or individuals,—or of statesmen bound to inviolable secrecy in matters relating to the public service. The violation of secrecy in any such matter is always a grievous sin. Nor is a husband intrusted with such weighty matters in any way justified in betraying them even to his wife, under the pretext that "husband and wife should never have secrets for each other." This only holds in the matters which concern their own affairs, and in which each has an undoubted right to know both the favorable and unfavorable sides.

Women are gifted with extraordinary wisdom and sagacity. They see at a glance the hidden reason of things; seize with unerring certainty principles and consequences that escape the eye of man, distracted as he is by preoccupations from which the female mind is happily free.

We have, among other memorable examples of the blessed influence of female counsels both in domestic and in public affairs, that of St. Margaret of Scotland. Not only did her advice induce her husband Malcolm Canmore to make of his court and household a model for every Scottish home, but she made of Scotland a center for European commerce in a warlike and barbarous age, fostered at home all the arts of peace, founded colleges, churches, missionary establishments, and promoted agriculture, manufactures, nd the fine arts. Her husband did nothing without her onsent,—and when he followed his own judgment and that of his headlong nobles in opposition to her,—as in the war which cost him his life,—he had always reason to rue it.

Even so was it with St. Louis, King of France. The wonderful wisdom which his mother displayed both in the administration of the kingdom during his minority and in his own education, caused him to consult her ever afterward on all matters of moment. And he trained his queen, Marguerite of Provence, to be, like his mother, his constant and principal adviser. Thus, when taken prisoner with his sick knights in Egypt, he would accept no terms of ransom from the Saracens that had not been sanctioned by the queen, who was in Palestine. And when the infidels expressed their astonishment at his deference for a woman, his proud answer was, that the woman "was his lady and his companion."

Were a more recent instance required in persons of royal station, we should remind our readers of the determination of Queen Isabella, the Catholic, to pawn her crown jewels in order to pay the expenses of the momentous expedition which discovered America. King Ferdinand and the entire royal council had set their faces against the scheme. But the Spirit of God moved the heart of the Queen as He had the soul of Christopher Columbus, and of her might be said what the poet has sung of her illustrious servant:

> " Him by the Paynim bard descried of yore,
> And ere his coming sung on either shore,
> Him could not I exalt—by Heaven designed
> To lift the veil that covered half mankind !" *

To business men, as well as to others, there are difficulties which a woman's ready wit and deft fingers will unravel, when men's self-sufficient and slow wisdom would only perplex matters and render them inextricable. If the husbands to whom we address ourselves be the true men we believe them, they will follow the example of the great statesman and heroic soldier-king, St. Louis, and make of his wife, the mother of his children, "his lady and companion," to be consulted before and above all persons on earth, because more interested than the whole world in

---

* Rogers, " Voyage of Columbus."

giving him good advice, and often far more able to do so than any one living person.

How many admirable women have we known, dear reader, wedded to men whom a stupid prejudice about women's radical unfitness for business kept from ever opening their mind to their companions, till the tidings of their common ruin burst upon them, like a sudden deluge sweeping fortune, home, and everything before it! If the wife had been made acquainted, step by step, with her husband's embarrassments, it is ten to one, but she had found a sure way out of them; or, had not that been possible, she would have taken wise precautions against the evil day. But what a cruel wrong is done to her judgment, her heart, her home, and her dear ones, when she is kept studiously in the dark till fortune, home, and happiness are swept away from her as by a flood coming down on them in the night!

We say this much on a very practical subject, and pass to one of still greater practical importance;—the shiftlessness of some husbands, the greed and avarice of others, and the prodigality of still another class. We can only devote a few short paragraphs to each.

The Shiftless Husband.

The world knows of very many such; and by the world, which worships success and honors the thrift that leads to it, the idle and shiftless head of a family is treated with universal and merited contempt.

That in European lands, where some men are born to wealth and high rank, there should be found many who, in anticipation of their inherited honors and riches, indulge in a life of ease, and never learn the value of work done for its own sake, or the blissful reward which attends application to healthful study and to self-improvement, as well as the self-approbation of a conscious devotion to the welfare of others,—is a matter of course.

In England, with its hereditary nobility, its landed gentry, and its entailed estates, if there be found among the privileged classes one man who spends his youth in utter idleness and ignorance of all ennobling pursuits, there are at least ten who devote their whole time to labor for the good of others much more than for the cultivation of their own intellectual powers or the development of their material resources. The heirs to a great title or to splendid ancestral wealth, are for the most part to be seen among the most laborious of the public servants, or the most industrious promoters of local enterprise and industry. It is the strength of England that her aristocracy, whether of rank or of wealth, thoroughly understand the meaning of *Noblesse oblige*, and will not allow themselves or their sons to lose the leadership of the country by listlessness, indolence, or incapacity to manage their own estates and the interests of their county, as well as the affairs of the nation.

The young man who dawdles and dreams till a coronet drops on his empty head, or unlimited wealth relieves him of debt and permits him to indulge his sloth or his sensuality, is the exception among his peers, as he is their scorn.

But that in a country like America, where every son of the soil is free to be the architect of his own fortune and fame, and the creator of his own greatness,—there should be found men to say to themselves and others, that "a gentleman is not born to work,"—sounds like a practical absurdity. Yet have we seen such un-American Americans, and heard them proclaim this new code of gentility to their own children as well as to others.

Of course these are no true men; on the contrary, they disgrace the very name of manhood, and are either totally ignorant of what constitutes manliness, or affect to ignore it in their utter abjection. For a man, to vindicate his claim to the essential attributes and the simplest virtues of manhood, must do the work of a man, and display in the performance of his life-work the qualities which make up what all denominate manliness.

Unmanly Men.

In the face of these plain truths, that a creature calling himself a man should take on himself the duties of a husband, undertake to provide a home for the wife he has chosen, and to feed and educate the beings who call him father, —while consuming his days in sloth, trusting to the provision made for him by his parents to supply all their wants and to furnish him the means of gratifying his own low inclinations and appetites,—without ever seriously endeavoring to add to this provision by his own personal labor and looking forward to the death of some rich relative for some legacy that may stand between himself, his wife, his children, and starvation,—is simply monstrous !

These unmanly men neither dig, nor plow, nor sow, nor reap ; the rising and the setting of God's sun does not mean for them the beginning of labor, and of rest after labor ; the seasons come and go for them without teaching any practical lesson or furthering any useful purpose.   They are like the foul and cowardly birds of the Dismal Swamp, that have neither the strength nor the energy to hunt down a living prey, but look out for the animals that perish in the treacherous and pestilential waste, and then perch themselves on the surrounding trees, watching patiently the progress of decomposition, and whetting their hungry beaks for the auspicious moment.

These ignoble birds of prey that are evermore speculating upon what death may bring them, seem gifted only with an unlimited faculty of consuming what they never toiled for of wasting what they have not husbanded or garnered up.

To appeal to the reason, the conscience, the sentiments of these men, were as bootless as to preach to a flock of vultures.   Either the guilty neglect of the parents who edu cated them,—or, rather, who left them to grow up without training or discipline of any kind,—is to be considered as the prime cause of their own degradation and of the misery they bring on others ; or the habit, indulged from boyhood,

of expecting to inherit the wealth of others, killed in them-
selves all desire of self-improvement, and prevented the for-
mation of the blessed virtues of self-reliance, self-respect,
and independent exertion.

Where these men are shiftless and helpless without being
intemperate and dissolute,—the evil, comparatively, is tol-
erable to the poor wife left to depend on her labor for
the bread of her children, as well as for that which feeds
the worthless husband. We have seen these miserable
husbands pass from stalwart manhood to robust old age,
perfectly satisfied with themselves, as vain of their quality
of gentlemen and of their privileged exemption from labor,
as the peacock that airs his plumage on the housetop and
displays his brilliant colors to the admiring sun, while his
female is indefatigable in some remote walk of the garden
or the forest in purveying for her tender brood,—anxious
only that her lordly mate shall not cross her path or perse-
cute their common progeny.

Leave we the despicable tribe of shiftless husbands ·
they resemble the wretched multitude whom Dante met
with outside the walls of Hell, unworthy of the society of
either the Blessed or the Damned :

> " From his bounds Heaven drove them forth,
> Not to impair his luster, nor the depth
> Of Hell receives them, lest the accursed tribe
> Should glory thence with exultation vain.
> . . . Their blind life
> So meanly passes, that all other lots
> They envy. Fame of them the world hath none,
> Nor suffers ; mercy and justice scorn them both.
> Speak not of them, but look, and pass them by." *

Grasping and Avaricious Husbands.

It is a sacred duty for the head of a family to make suita-
ble provision for his household, for the husband to place at
his wife's disposal the fruits of his thrift, as it is her duty
to dispense it prudently within the home : it is the bounden

---

* INFERNO, iii. ; Cary's translation.

obligation of both to lay up for their dear ones and for
their own old age. Thus providence and economy are
among the first virtues enjoined on parents. We omit all
mention here of the duties of hospitality and charity.

Equally opposed to the wise forethought which urges a
parent to labor and lay up for his dear ones, and to pru-
dent generosity which should guide himself and his com-
panion in the use of their store,—are greed in acquiring,
avarice in retaining, and prodigality in wasting what God
gives for such definite and holy purposes.

It is a virtue,—a blessed one too,—to be industrious and
indefatigable in providing against the present and the future
need ; it is no less a virtue to be moderate in using for one's
personal comforts or wants, generous in meeting the neces-
sary demands of family life according to one's condition,
and generous as well in giving hospitality, and in meet-
ing the requirements of religion, charity, and patriotism.
There are men who, while they bestow liberally for all these
various purposes, what they have labored hard to acquire,
are still careful not to leave the home they have either built
up themselves or inherited, without abundant means for
maintaining its splendor after their own day.

But what shall we say of fathers of families who make of
the labor of amassing riches, not a means for the happiness
of their families,—but an end ? who earn and hold money,
not for the purpose of using it for the comfort of their dear
ones or their own, but simply for its own sake,—to have it,
to own it, to make it grow, and grow, and grow forever,—
like a tree bearing golden fruit that no one,—nor them-
selves, nor others,—may either gather, touch, or taste, in
this life or the life to come ?

It cannot, in the gold-seeking and worshiping age in
which we live, be too strongly insisted on, that money is a
means to an end, not the end itself,—a means of making
life happy and honorable, of helping others toward useful-
ness, honor, and happiness ; but not in itself an end, so
that the possession and the hoarding of money should be
for itself alone, without aiming at anything beyond that.

Hence the absurdity and the guilt of so giving one's self
up to making money, that in doing so, one forgets con-
science, health, the claims of one's family, the needs of the
poor, and every other generous and useful purpose which
money is calculated to promote.

It is not so unfrequent a thing to hear, in this great city
of New York, of some wretched creature who died of sheer
want in a garret or some filthy corner, deprived of all
human aid, of all the comforts of society and religion, of
all the consolations of earth and heaven, reputed in life ab-
jectly poor, and most industrious in having others believe
so, and yet dying worth thousands!—thousands that will
profit nobody, nor the wretched soul gone to its account,
and which was not created to make money for money's
sake, nor even the poor of the neighborhood whom not a
penny of it shall ever reach, nor the unknown family and
relatives whom the miserable hoarder forsook or forgot, in
order to indulge this solitary and absorbing passion of add-
ing little to little without cessation.

> " O wealth, with thee is won
> A worm to gnaw for ever on his soul
> Whose abject life is laid in thy control !
> If also ye take not what piteous death
> They ofttimes make, whose hoards were manifold,
> Who cities had and gold,
> And multitudes of men beneath their hand ;
> Then he among you that most angereth
> Shall bless me (Fortune), saying, ' I worship thee
> That I was not as he
> Whose death is thus accursed throughout the land.'
> But now your living souls are held in band
> Of avarice, shutting you from the true light,
> Which shows how sad and slight
> Are this world's treasured riches and array
> That still change hands a hundred times a day.

> " For me,—could envy enter in my sphere,
> Which of all human taint is clean and quit,—
> I well might harbor it
> When I behold the peasant at his toil,

Guiding his team, untroubled, free from fear,
He leaves his perfect furrow as he goes,
   And gives his field repose
From thorns and tares and weeds that vex the soil :
Thereto he labors, and without turmoil
Entrusts his work to God, content if so
   Such guerdon from it grow
That in the year his family shall live ;
Nor care nor thought to other things will give." *

Meanness, Greed, Cruelty, and Misery.

One home we cannot but think of with unalloyed grief, for it touched us nearly. The wife, of gentle blood, uncommon beauty, and goodness greater than her beauty, was wooed and won by a man her equal in birth and almost her equal in age,—a young and brilliant officer high in favor with the government. She brought him a fortune which more than sufficed to support them handsomely, but which was allowed to accumulate till her dying day, while his own yearly income went far beyond the expenses of their household. Seven children were born to them, not one of whom ever inherited any share of the fortune of either parent.

His absorbing passion, almost from the first year of their wedded life, was to accumulate money, fearful,—as he often expressed it to his familiars (friends he had none),—lest his children should some day be left penniless. Unfortunately the marriage settlement gave him the sole management of their joint property ; nor did he rest satisfied till his wife had been bullied and persecuted into making over her property to him in his own absolute right.

She was not an extravagant, nor even a worldly woman. She was conscientious, solidly pious, fond of her home and devoted to her children,—a woman whose qualities should have made any husband happy, and could have adorned any station.

He never allowed her to dispose of a single dollar of the

---

* Guido Cavalcanti, " Song of Fortune," in Rossetti's " Early Italian Poets."

revenue of her own property, nor even to regulate the expenses of her household ; no, not so much as to purchase what was necessary for the table. He was his own caterer ; went daily to market with the first light of morning ; and disdained not to haggle with fishwoman and butcher, till he had shamed them to his own terms, buying rarely any but the cheapest fish or the poorest meat.

He half-starved his children, making up in liberal sleep what he refused them in substantial and necessary diet, and he starved their souls as well. For he would not allow them to be educated up to their condition ; nor would he permit them to associate with those of their own class, being unwilling that their raiment should be superior to their spare diet or their scanty schooling.

He would have his wife,—whom he shockingly ill-treated, —dismiss her servants, and attend to the household work as well as the education of her children. But she at length rebelled against a tyranny and a brutality become the more intolerable, that the unmanly husband had taken to solitary tippling after the daily official duties were over, and never went to bed sober.

At length his violence forced her to take refuge with her nearest relative far away. She never recovered from his latest ill-usage. The children, one after another, were driven from their most unhappy home ; the father married his cook, and died leaving to her and her children the little he possessed at the time. For by a just retribution of fortune, his accumulated wealth had been vested in ruinous ventures, and was swept beyond his reach, leaving him the most wretched and one of the vilest of men.

The Spendthrift Husband.

Of this very numerous class we need only discuss one or two varieties ;—the others are so much akin to the intemperate and the debauchee,—that we shall not consider them separately.

There are spendthrifts who are not addicted to the odious

vices begotten of sensuality. Their wasteful extravagance
has its source in other, higher, and more refined tastes.
The reckless indulgence of these tastes, however, works a
no less fatal ruin to the family substance and home.

There are husbands, whose sole purpose in life is to make
their wealth the means of outshining their neighbors : men
troubled with an inordinate amount of vanity, and with
very little brains; who are utterly unable to calculate their
own resources, and spend without ever stopping to consider
how much they are unable to spend.

Many of our readers will recall William Dorritt, Esquire,
" the Father of the Marshalsea," gifted with but two facul
ties,—the heartless vanity that accepted the services and lib
erality of strangers as well as the boundless devotion of his
own child as the homage due to his own transcendent supe-
riority, and the blind prodigality with which his inherited
wealth was squandered for the mere purpose of eclipsing
others and asserting his own gentility. Of course, vanity
being always mean, this arrogant self-assertion, in the hour
of ill fortune will condescend to beg and to borrow, and in
the hour of prosperity will basely ignore the friends whose
purse and hand were ever the most open ; and equally, of
course, this purse-proud meanness will make itself most
prominent at the very height of good fortune, by tyranniz-
ing over dependants, browbeating all persons of equal or
inferior rank, and by cringing like an Oriental slave to supe
rior rank or ability.

These men, even when not afflicted with this morbid van
ity, cannot keep out of debt; for they cannot refuse them
selves any of the beautiful and costly things which strike
their fancy. This is the least odious form of extravagance,
—the passion for books, for objects of art, or for other costly
hobbies. It tends, none the less, to ruin the happiness and
independence of the home, and to imperil its very exist-
ence. For, this extravagant and uncontrollable fondness
for things which are above one's means, keeps the husband
band continually in debt, deprives the wife and children,
not only of the comforts and enjoyments belonging to

their condition, but frequently of the bare necessaries of life.

Such men are in reality overgrown children, who ought to be kept in perpetual tutelage ; who are incapable of managing their own affairs. Their extravagant tastes are but a higher and more refined sensuality, just as ruinous as the drunkard's proclivities.

The extravagant, however can be made amenable to reason ; for their brain is not habitually crazed with drink and their intellectual powers weakened or obliterated by beastly indulgence. They can understand that indebtedness is slavery ; that to take from the most urgent needs of one's family what is expended on mere intellectual or artistic pleasure is a grievous wrong.

CHAPTER IX.

THE INTEMPERATE HUSBAND.

In the third circle I arrive, of showers
Ceaseless, accursed, heavy and cold, unchanged
Forever, both in kind and in degree.
Large hail, discolored water, sleety flaw
Through the dun midnight air streamed down amain.
Stank all the land whereon the tempest fell.
Cerberus, cruel monster, fierce and strange,
Through his wide threefold throat, barks as a dog
Over the multitude immersed beneath.
. . . So passed we through that mixture foul
Of spirits and rain, with tardy steps.

INFERNO, vi.

. . . Weakness is thy excuse,
And I believe it ; weakness to resist.
If weakness may excuse,
What murderer, what traitor, parricide,
Incestuous, sacrilegious, but may plead it ?
All wickedness is weakness : that plea therefore
With God or man will gain thee no remission
In vain thou striv'st to cover shame with shame,
Or by evasions thy crime uncover'st more.

MILTON, Samson Agonistes.

THE sense of the most enlightened Christian ages, basing its judgment on Holy Writ as well as on the fitness of things, deemed it equitable that the punishments of eternity should be a real expiation of the guilt, and by the sense that had sinned. Hence, intemperance in all its loathsome forms, is represented by the great poet,—as punished in a land of eternal darkness, where the abject multitude were immersed in "a mixture foul" of discolored water and sleety slush, large hail and rain pelting the sufferers unceasingly, and filling the land and the atmosphere with intolerable stench. Over this vile and filthy fold of the drunkard,—as over

166

some miry farm-yard with its swine,—the monstrous form of three-headed Cerberus,—the gluttonous and insatiable, kept sleepless watch, rending the prostrate forms with his cruel fangs, and filling the hideous darkness with his continuous barking.

Surely, when one considers calmly what that form of intemperance is which we designate as habitual drunkenness in a husband and parent,—it must be evident that the eternal death as here described, is but the natural consequence and just retribution of the drunkard's present life. For the intrinsic guilt of intoxication consists not so much in the gratification of the animal appetite for strong drink, or of the craving for the pleasurable excitement which is the first stage of inebriety,—as in depriving one's self knowingly of the mastery over one's bodily faculties and, above all, over one's reason.

It is this temporary loss and suspension of the highest powers of the soul,—of those which are Godlike in man, that constitutes the specific guilt of drunkenness. The sin of the suicide, the self-destroyer, the man who takes away his own life,—is a something most awful to contemplate. It is the throwing away, by one act of despair or defiance, of all the gifts of the most bountiful Creator, the unmaking of all the gracious plans of His most wise providence in favor of a human soul; it is the setting aside, against all the laws of nature and nature's God, of one's responsibilities to Him and to our kind in the present and throughout the boundless future.

This, and much more than this, is all comprised in self-destruction. But intoxication, whether by alcohol or by opium, is the beginning of self-destruction. It ends,—as every enlightened reader knows,—by destroying the body, by debasing and destroying the soul, by destroying the home, breaking the wife's heart, disgracing and ruining the children. It brings man, destined for the close companionship of God and his angels in the life to come, down to the level of the beast in this world. . But, no! this is most unjust to the beast.

It is but too familiar an expression with us when we see a man surrendering himself to the excesses of inebriety, to say that "he is making a beast of himself." The brute is never false to its nature, never sinks below the level of the instincts, the intelligence that nature has given it. Nothing is more temperate and abstemious than the irrational animal which we are wont injuriously to compare with degraded man, when he acts against the laws alike of his spiritual and his animal nature. The dog, even in its extreme thirst, will lap up daintily just enough of water to satisfy its need. It is most dainty, when it has no choice between pure and impure water, in barely lapping once or twice of the latter; and under no pressure of appetite will it so much as taste of what it knows to be poisonous or hurtful. A very ferocious bear in the *Jardin des Plantes*, at Paris, was condemned to be killed by the authorities. The keepers resolved to destroy it by poison. So they impregnated the bread and injected the meat they threw to it with the most deadly substances known to the chemist. The animal, although kept without food for several days to render it the more ravenous, was too wary to follow the promptings of its hunger. It smelled the treacherous food over and over again, turned it on every side, and then went away. Presently, however, — as if it had been devising some plan to meet the difficulty,—it returned to where the poisoned food lay, and pushed it steadily toward its water-trough. Then, after washing it copiously again and again, smelling after each ablution, it came to the conclusion that it might safely taste it. It did not eat it up all at once, but by small pieces, washing each of these over again as a further precaution. This being reported by the keepers to the magistrates, they revoked the order for the animal's destruction. It deserved to live.

It is also well known how much labor and fatigue the camel can undergo amid the burning sands of Africa. This most useful beast is the very impersonation of temperance, performing the longest journeys under the most trying circumstances, living on the scantiest fare and depending on the supply of water laid up in its complex stomach.. It is a supply on which its master often depends in the direst extremity of thirst,—the frugal animal thus saving the life of man at the expense of its own.

We do the beast a foul wrong when we say, that man by drunkenness sinks down to its level,—whereas it is only by sheer violence that brutal man can bring the beast down to his own level by making it drink perforce. Yet, though you may reduce the poor brute to helpless intoxication, do you not bring it down to your level. It has no moral law to guide it ; and, if it had, you can only make it drunk by sheer violence done its nature and in spite of its own desperate struggles.

This outrage was perpetrated on the brute once,—and during a war which we shall not designate here. A besieging army had been for months beleaguering a mighty fortress ; and, as the siege dragged its slow length along, the officers were wont to spend the uncertain intervals of battle in such amusements as they could find or devise. Neighboring regiments had their festive meetings, and their leaders but too often forgot past dangers and the perils of the morrow in most unseemly dissipation. One of the most notable frequenters of these clubs was a young officer who was always accompanied by a magnificent Newfoundland dog. One evening,—the eve, indeed, of a day since become famous,—the gallant friends had indulged in longer libations and louder mirth than ever ; they had "made a night of it," not knowing, they said, who would survive the struggle on the morrow.

Just as they were about to separate, some one remarked that the Newfoundland dog was the only sober individual present, and thereupon it was moved and resolved that the dog be made drunk. So, there are these gentlemen, these brave defenders of their country's honor, engaged in holding the poor struggling animal down, while they poured wine and brandy down its throat. The innocent and temperate animal resisted frantically the outrage done to it by the united strength of these " lords of creation ;" at length,

8.

half strangled, half poisoned, sick and helpless, the poor
dog writhed on the ground, rejecting, with the native vigor
of its unimpaired stomach, the poison it had been forced to
swallow.

So, the dog as well as its master had to be "carried
home" that night. The struggle of the morrow passed by
without completely ending the siege. Of those who had
been actors in the inhuman scene just described, we know
not how many perished. But, not very long thereafter, the
survivors met, as before, to make merry, and with them
came the master of the dog,—and the dog also,—though not
quite all the way.

He had followed his master, forgiving, faithful animal
as he was, the cruel injury done himself, on that memora-
ble night;—had followed his master through the camp
from tent to tent, and line to line, till they drew near the
house or tent used as a club-room. As they approached it,
the dog fell behind his master, and when the latter at the
very door turned round to call the animal to him, the other
turned and fled with the speed of the wind. No coaxing
and no threats ever afterward could make the ill-used dog
come near the spot where high-born, educated, and brave
gentlemen had once reduced him to their own level of
physical helplessness,—but not to their own depth of moral
degradation.

We know that it is becoming fashionable in our midst,
to set aside the salutary severity with which the Church in
former times visited both the man who died by his own hand
and the man who drank himself to death. With the wan-
ing of true religion, charity, dissevered from truth, becomes
cruelty, and our caricature of mercy in her maudlin minis-
trations, becomes the worst of unkindness. True charity
loves as God loves, the soul before the body, and in its work
of saving the former it also saves and sanctifies the latter.

Our modern doctors and moralists will have it that the
despair of the suicide,—the supreme wrong done to the
Infinite Mercy and exhaustless patience of the Creator, by
renouncing it and putting one's self beyond its pale,—is

insanity, rendering the doer of the most dreadful of deeds irresponsible for his' act. They will have it, too,—these modern blind leaders of the blind,—that drunkenness is disease, that habitual drunkenness is chronic disease, by which the brain becomes so weakened, that the will loses all control over its own inclinations.

Oh, we do not deny that just as successive acts of virtuous self-denial impart to the will a continual increase of strength and generosity, even so a long series of guilty indulgences weaken it in the like proportion. We know that habitual generosity and self-sacrifice, aided as they are by the ever-present grace of God, will end by making the Christian man a Godlike being in his strength to overcome every obstacle to virtue, and in the supernatural facility with which he performs the most heroic deeds of holiness.

Knowing, also, what the wise pagans proclaimed long ages before Christ,—that vicious acts breed vicious habits, and that habitual vice is the worst form of slavery,—we must only recall to parents and to all who have the training of youth, this fundamental truth in practical morality : The man who commits one sinful act knows, that by so doing he only disposes himself the more readily to commit a second, and that the second renders more easy still the committing of a third,—every successive fall from the level road of virtue increasing, almost immeasurably, our downward velocity. The drunkard's guilt, in his very first sin, consists, not only in his offending against God and himself by transgressing the Divine Law and the law of his own nature, but in acquiescing in the immediate and necessary consequences of his sin, such as the inability to discharge obligations and duties incumbent on him, the scandal given to others by his evil example, and this very rendering of a second act of drunkenness both more easy and probable.

The child should be warned against the formation of evil habits, and taught that evil habit is a chain of adamant by which the soul fetters its own freedom,—the most glorious and sacred of all the gifts of the Creator. This weakening, fettering, and destroying of the soul's innate freedom—its

most Godlike attribute and power,—is known, or ought to
be known to every human soul in possession of its reason,
as the inevitable consequence of evil acts become evil habits.
This is the very nature of sin.   Most true, therefore, in the
estimation of all ages, is the affirmation of the great poet:

<blockquote>" All wickedness is weakness."</blockquote>

The first act of wickedness weakens the will, takes away
a part of its power for good ; every succeeding act adds to
the weakness in an increasing ratio.   This weakness, this
wickedness is "shameful,"—shameful in the eyes of God
and men.   The man who consents to the first sin, the first
weakness, does a "wicked" thing, precisely because it is
destructive of his own strength, his own dignity, his own
happiness and that of others, as well as injurious to the
most high God.   Just as it is no excuse of a man's folly,
that, without any justifiable reason, he has again and again
and again gone into a leprosy or a yellow-fever hospital till
he has caught the plague in its worst form, although warned
by physicians and others of the consequences of his fool-
hardiness ; even so it is with the drunkard.   He has been
warned against the first act of intoxication, and the second,
and the third, till the habit grew on him and possessed his
soul as with the virulence of the most deadly disease.

<blockquote>" That plea therefore
With God or man will gain thee no remission."</blockquote>

And, where a man is at the head of a family, with a lov-
ing wife to care for and to cherish, with children to train,
like the young of the eagle, to the loftiest flights of excel-
lence, and the pursuit of virtues that lift the soul far above
earth and its groveling satisfactions,—the contracting of
habits of intemperance, or the exposing himself to contract
them, is fearful guilt, and most awful responsibility at His
judgment-seat who will hold the husband and father ac-
countable for the life, the honor, the happiness, the souls
of wife and children.

And the higher a man is born, the more richly he is

endowed with talents, worldly wealth, and great opportu-
nities, the more favored he is by education and position—
and the more terrible is that responsibility ; because all
these are powers given him to make his home-life blissful,
and his home the center from which his own power for all
good may radiate far and wide.

The American public has been obliged to recall, in the
recent death of a most estimable lady in New England, not
only that she was destined to become the bride of the most
gifted poetical genius that ever shed luster on American
letters, when, at the age of thirty-nine, he was found dead
intoxicated with a broken bottle by his side ; but that his
career of profligacy had already been a long one,—dating
from his very boyhood.   Only two years before his death,
he buried his lovely wife, the *Annabel Lee* of his well-
known song,—buried her after having broken her heart,
and dragged her through the mire of his own degradation
and the extreme poverty brought on by incessant debauch.

Most touching and most instructive it is to recall a few
passages of that gifted and guilty man's writings, in which
he records both his love for this innocent young thing and
his remorse for the misery caused her.

> " And this maiden she lived with no other thought
>   Than to love and be loved by me.
> *I* was a child and *she* was a child,
>   In this kingdom by the sea ;
> But we loved with a love that was more than love,
>   I and my Annabel Lee ;
> With a love that the winged seraphs of heaven
>   Coveted her and me."

At the very time when poverty and its saddest privations
were preying upon the homeless wife, and nothing seemed
able to reclaim the wretched husband from the degrading
passion that preyed on his life and his honor, he wrote the
poem of "The Raven,"—one of the masterpieces of Ameri-
can poetry.   The "Raven" was that same dreadful passion
whose fatal hold upon his will left him neither power of
resistance nor hope of eternal salvation.

Listen to the awful utterances of that immortal verse, every word and line of which seems to have been written under the inspiration of that demon-haunted fever which ever attends upon alcoholic excess.

"This I sat engaged in guessing, but no syllable expressing
   To the fowl whose fiery eyes now burned into my bosom's core;
This and more I sat divining, with my head at ease reclining
On the cushion's velvet lining that the lamp-light gloated o'er,
But whose velvet violet lining with the lamp-light gloating o'er,
     She shall press, ah, nevermore!

"Then methought the air grew denser, perfumed from an unseen censer
Swung by seraphim whose footfalls tinkled on the tufted floor.
'Wretch,' I cried, 'thy God hath lent thee—by these angels he hath sent thee
Respite,—respite and nepenthe, from thy memories of Lenore!
Quaff, oh quaff this kind nepenthe, and forget this lost Lenore!'
     Quoth the Raven, 'Nevermore!'

"'Prophet,' said I, 'thing of evil!—prophet still, if bird or devil!—
Whether tempter sent, or whether tempest tossed thee here ashore,—
Desolate, yet all undaunted, on this desert land enchanted—
On this home by Horror haunted,—tell me truly, I implore—
Is there—*is* there balm in Gilead?—tell me, tell me, I implore!'
     Quoth the Raven, 'Nevermore.'

"'Be that word our sign of parting, bird or fiend!' I shrieked, upstarting—
'Get thee back into the tempest and the Night's Plutonian shore!
Leave no black plume as a token of that lie thy soul hath spoken!
Leave my loneliness unbroken! quit the bust above my door!
Take thy beak from out my heart,* and take thy form from off my door!'
     Quoth the Raven, 'Nevermore.'

"And the Raven never flitting, still is sitting, still is sitting
On the pallid bust of Pallas, just above my chamber door;
And his eyes have all the seeming of a demon's that is dreaming,
And the lamp-light o'er him streaming throws his shadow on the floor;
And my soul from out that shadow that lies floating on the floor
     Shall be lifted—nevermore!"

To the inveterate drunkard bound, like Prometheus, to his habits with chains which no effort of his can break, the remorse preying on his heart is worse than the beak of the vulture tearing the entrails of living man. And in that ter-

---

* The italics are our own.

rible remorse the most intolerable pang does not come from the constant remembrance of what the drunkard "might have been" and of what "he has brought himself to,"— so much as from the torturing knowledge of the shame, ruin, misery, he has brought upon his dear ones.

The young wife who chose him to fill her heart and her life with happiness, because she believed him to be what she was herself,—spotless, manly, true, strong to support her through life, devoted to duty, to home, to God, and to all the sacred and manifold obligations of husband, father, and Christian,—knew him not. And she awakened from her dream of innocent love and hope, to find the husband of her choice to be, like one of those horrid monsters of Scandina-vian fiction,—a man having to all appearance the stature, the strength, and the beauty of the gods, but who was only half of an empty shell, a mask of humanity without heart, or flesh, or blood, or feeling.

We have seen many of these young wives entrapped into marriage with such half-men by some strange error of their own heart and judgment, by the ignorance and neglect of their own parents, or by some unworthy artifice of the half-man and his parents;—and they struggled on for years and years to conceal from every eye, even that of their nearest relatives, the dreadful secret of their own misery, rising beneath the load of their heavy cross to sublime heights of heroic self-sacrifice ; arming themselves with invincible patience, meekness, and forbearance, in order to reform their companion, and to enlist in the work of reformation the good God and his angels. Their union reminded one of the cruel method devised by the abominable tyrant Mezen-tius,* who bound the living to the putrid dead, that they might thus slowly perish of horror and loathing.

It is not, however, the torture of soul arising from the

---

* *Mortua quin etiam jungebat corpora vivis,*
Componens manibusque manus, atque oribus ora,
(Tormenti genus) et sanie taboque fluentes
Complexu in misero longa sic morte necabat.

ENEID, viii. 485–488.

deception practiced on herself and the agony of having thus
to live bound forever to one loathsome to every interior and
exterior sense, that is the greatest suffering of the wife and
mother ; it is to see her home made desolate, her children
worse than orphaned, every means of sustenance sacrificed
piecemeal to the unhallowed appetite of him who should
be the sustainer and provider of the home. This is the
death-like shadow which falls on the home of the drunk-
ard, frequently from the very first days of his married life ;
this is the gloom, worse than that of the Valley of Death,
amid which his bride finds herself condemned to dwell, —
the darkness and the despair increasing day by day, as the
husband pursues his downward course. This is the raven
that

"Still is sitting, still is sitting,"

above the door of the home which wifely devotion and
motherly love are vainly laboring to brighten ; this is the
dark form of evil boding which haunts her waking and her
sleeping hours like a living horror. Its " eyes have all the
seeming of a demon's," its cruel beak is ever tearing her
heart, and its prophetic voice,—as month of misery suc-
ceeds to month, and as the years come and go without
alleviation to her intolerable burthen, ever seems to utter
in her ears the fatal " Nevermore ! " No,—there is never
to be for her sunshine around the hearth, joy in her chil-
dren's endearments, assurance that the father's name will
not blight the prospects of her daughters, or that his vice
will not cling like inherited leprosy to her sons.

We men are but too apt to commiserate the lot of the
drunkard even in the last stages of his reckless and selfish
course, when irreparable ruin has fallen on his home, and
irremediable disease on himself. We say that " it is a
pity ; the man is so generous, so warm-hearted, gifted with
such rare qualities of soul ; so lovable, when he is himself,
so sociable," etc., etc., etc. Priests and others who have
only seen him outside of his family circle, and when his
fits of maudlin repentance were on him,—solely, or princi-
pally considered the wreck before them, beholding only in

the man the qualities or gifts which he had neglected or perverted. We do not deny either that this infirmity attaches itself most frequently to the man of lively fancy, facile talent, warm heart, and open hand, or that,—when degraded and ruined by the misuse of his gifts,—the poor prodigal is still deserving of helpful sympathy and charitable compassion. It is not to be forgotten, however, that the Prodigal Son in the Gospel narrative, was unmarried, and that his debaucheries had not ruined a home, broken a wife's heart, and brought children to disgrace and beggary.

As we are holding up the mirror of truth to men, we must remind them of what the wife is suffering in her cold, cheerlesss, darkened home, while the self-ruined husband is parading his native generosity of disposition, and soliciting the sympathy of his old acquaintance, as if he were the victim of other people's injustice, instead of being the destroyer of his home, his family, and himself.

You, dear reader, who know with what a priestly charity and tenderness we are anxious to touch on all these details, will agree with us that these "unselfish" and warm-hearted drunkards, are in their own wretched homes and toward their families, the most cruelly selfish, cold-hearted, and unfeeling of husbands and parents. Is it not true, that in looking upon that sad wreck of humanity we call an habitual and irreclaimable dunkard, we give all our pity to the fallen man before us, and forget the wife and the children at home, whom his merciless and heartless self-indulgence reduced to want and starvation?

Have you not heard of, have you not seen, these men living for years upon the earnings of wives, who had not been brought up to such labor? Have we not known these men to steal and drink the money so hardly, so heroically earned by their delicate and drooping companions for the support of their suffering children, to keep a roof above them, and scant fire on the hearth, and scant bread on the board?—Yes, we have known these "warm-hearted," unprincipled brutes to steal from the wife a whole week's earnings, and spend the whole of it in the neighboring tavern, treating their vile companions all round to cup after cup of the drugged alcohol,—till not one penny was left to get bread for the hungry children on the Sunday morning? And, viler than this vile husband and his peers of the bottle, viler even than words can express, the tavern-keeper dealt out cup after cup of the murderous beverage so long as the money lasted, fully aware the while of the sore, sore need of the hapless wife and hungry children at home!

Unselfishness, indeed! Have we priests not known more than one of these same men, praised by their casual acquaintances for their amiability and open-handed liberality to be drunk daily while a mother or wife lay on her death bed, drunk while she lay in her coffin, and to have come staggering drunk to her grave? Have we not known wretches so utterly reckless of all sense of honor and shame that they would have stolen the marriage ring off the finger of mother or wife in the grave to buy one last glass of alcohol?

Talk of unselfishness! Have we not seen these utterly selfish and utterly unmanly men forget all the most sacred feelings and imperious duties of the husband and the parent, and indulge in their wildest freaks of intoxication, when their sick wives most needed tenderest nursing and lay at death's door for many days in succession? Yet these abominable brutes would return from their long nightly or daily debauch to enter perforce the sick-room and imperil the helpless sufferer's life by noisy demonstrations of affection or bursts of passionate abuse.

The fiend, that seems to possess the souls of men who indulge in the dreadful poisons invented by modern distillers, seems to transform his slaves into fiends after his own image and likeness,—impelling them to show a devilish ingenuity in torturing the poor, patient, overtaxed woman who has to bear the double curse of their name and their companionship. . . . Shall we continue on this subject?

O men, O true men, who read this page, forgive the writer for penning truths so disgraceful to human nature,

:so painful to the reader, and so unspeakably painful to the writer himself. If, in holding up the mirror to you, such diabolical forms appear, where the divine features of the true Christian man,—the child of God in life and manners, —should alone appear,—let the fearful apparition only stimulate us all to a salutary hatred of the besetting vice of our age.

Where is the radical remedy? it may be asked. We know but one. The rearing of our boys in such ignorance and such horror of intemperance, that they may be like holy Samuel, or Elias, or John the Baptist, or the thrice-blessed descendants of Jonadab the Son of Rechab, Nazarites from their birth, never tasting wine or strong drink of any kind. Oh! if this book could bring forth such fruit in every family in which it is read, how gladly would the writer sing his *Nunc dimittis !* *

There is, however, one class of men to whom, in particular, we address this concluding paragraph,—those, namely, who are engaged in the traffic of intoxicating drinks. We remind distillers, that, while we should under no circumstances interfere with the necessities and the liberty of lawful trade, there are certain modern expedients in their special business, which are alike beyond the necessities of lawful trade, and a criminal violation of the freedom it should enjoy. It is not only the distilling of alcoholic liquors from substances which render the liquor distilled essentially deleterious, but the drugging of pure alcohol so as to make it injurious or poisonous, or the selling for wine or for any other like well-known drink, what is a dangerous or deadly counterfeit, skillfully disguised.

But it is to tavern-keepers, and all who are engaged in retailing alcoholic stimulants, that our words would fain appeal with all the earnestness and charity of a priestly heart.

---

* " Now dost thou dismiss Thy servant, O Lord,
According to Thy Word, in peace,
Because my eyes have seen Thy salvation."
ST. LUKE, ii. 29, 30.

We have seen fortunes,—great fortunes, even,—made in this dangerous business, and made, too, by men who did not care what they sold or to whom they sold,—provided they found and kept their customers till these had given the last penny they had, and taken much more than they could bear of intoxicating drink. We have seen these men flourishing suddenly, their children springing up around them like these trees of rapid growth, that take root in an unwholesome Southern swamp, live a short and brilliant season, and pine away as suddenly as they had grown up without leaving healthy fruit or a lasting progeny behind.

The blessing of God does not come with money made in violation of His most binding laws ; money so made is also burthened with the curse of widowed mothers, of heartbroken wives, of children rendered homeless, penniless, and parentless. And these terrible curses will melt the money in the hands of those who inherit it, and often consume the possessors themselves.

Only think of it. Here is a man calling himself a Christian, a Catholic, having a family to rear, and wishing to educate them according to the dictates of the faith of their baptism. He knows that it is a deadly sin to allow any person to become intoxicated in his house ; and yet, because his customers may get as much to drink as they please at the next tavern, he thinks they may as well get drunk in his house. " If I do not give them as much liquor as they want,"—he reasons,—"they will get it elsewhere ; and my customers will leave me." So, he refuses no one, and gives, to any extent.

This is not the worst. There is among these customers one man, the father of a family, who is an habitual drunkard, who is,—to the tavern-keeper's certain knowledge,— drinking his wife and children out of house and home ; and who, besides, is leading a life of intolerable disgrace and misery. He has been warned by the neighbors of the ruin this man is bringing on his dear ones ;—he has been warned again and again by the drunkard's unfortunate wife. And yet he allows that recreant husband and father to remain and your children after you?

CHAPTER X.

THE FATHER.

Love from its awful throne of patient power
Folds over the world its healing wings.

No more truthful and beautiful conception of the paternal office in a Christian household, can be conveyed than by saying that Fatherhood is Love, all-powerful Love, that it should occupy an "awful throne"—one surrounded with affection and veneration, in the home; that its authority should be at once a sacred and a "patient" power; and that its right exercise must result in healing, at their very roots, the inveterate sores of which society complains.

Yes,—fatherly love and authority, acting in the name and place of God, would be to that sick, perverse, and overgrown child,—the youth of the nineteenth century,—a "patient power" which

"Folds over the world its healing wings."

We need in the Home, as it is now assailed by rampant errors, subversive of God, of authority, of order, reverence, and love,—the conviction firmly seated both in the soul of the parent and in that of his offspring,—that a father is in God's place; and that, just as he must make it almost the one chief aim of his life to have his children so consider and reverence him, even so must he do himself his utmost to be to his dear ones the living image of God's love and patient power.

As the great secret of establishing over the minds and

182

hearts of all within the household the lovingly accepted in-
fluence of his august power, lies in being most like to God
in word and deed, so 'fathers will bear with us while we re-
quest them to read and ponder well one or two passages
from men, who have been most truly what we wish to make
our readers,—kings over the minds and hearts of those who
called them "Father." We shall thereby show all the more
easily and convincingly what is the nature, and what the
extent of a father's authority.

In what Fathers are to Imitate God.

St. Thomas Aquinas, called by the veneration of Catholic
ages "the Angelic Teacher," says that Christian men are
bound to imitate God, to copy in their conduct what is re-
vealed to us of His outward manners,—His truthfulness,
wisdom, meekness, patience, justice, liberality, mercy,—
and so emulate all the other divine attributes in so far as a
created being can follow and imitate the Creator.

Another, and an older saint, Bernard of Clairvaux, teach-
ing a Pope his duties,—in an age when the Pope was re-
vered as the Common Father of Christendom,—thus ad-
dresses him :

What is God ? The all-powerful will, the most loving
power, the everlasting light, the unchanging reason, the
supreme felicity ;—who createth souls to make them par-
takers of His own nature; . . . who inflameth them with
zeal for His service, and maketh their zeal fruitful by His
grace ; . . . who imparteth the strength to practice God-
like virtue ; . . . who filleth them with His Godhead to
make their bliss perfect ; . . . and who rendereth their
supreme felicity unchangeable by making it eternal like
Himself." *

What more magnificent than this faculty of becoming
within your homes the living image of this Goodness which
ever yearns to pour out on its intelligent creatures an ever
fuller and fuller measure of its exhaustless wealth of love,

---

* Lib. v. de Consideratione, c. ii.

till, with the dawn of eternity, it can overflow all bound-
aries, like the victorious ocean-tide, and encompass the
loved object within its rapturous depths? Cannot a true
father become more loving, more generous, more devoted
every day?

Let us show how this divine ideal should be one of prac-
tical daily and hourly life, to every man who holds toward
others the sacred relation of father,—how it is imitable by
him in every one of his actions,—in the discharge of every
possible duty inside and outside his home.

When men of the world,—high or low,—are told to take
God as their ideal or pattern, they are apt to think and say
that the perfection demanded is too high above them, and
impossible of attainment. "You might as well," they are
tempted to say, "tell us to understand what is the nature
of the fire which burns eternally in the bosom of the Sun
or of the light which it sheds through the universe. We
have near our hand means of procuring heat and light for
our dwellings without being at the trouble of studying the
nature of the solar atmosphere or of the mighty globe it
surrounds."

The Divine Exemplar walking in the ways of Men.

True. But our "Sun of righteousness" has come down
to us, veiling his light and tempering the heat of his near
presence, that our weak senses might bear this very near-
ness. We have seen Him,—not as the glorious Being who
dwells above in light unapproachable and manifests His un-
clouded essence and perfections to the gaze of the Blessed,
—but as a child growing from helpless infancy through
boyhood and youth,—a true man in all his ways and affec-
tions and virtues, as well as very God in the powers which
he wielded to confirm his mission and his teaching.

It is these sweet human virtues, of every-day life, especi-
ally as practiced within the lowly home of his mother,—that
we would have parents study and acquire by practice. Then
only could they teach and enjoin them on their dear ones.

To fathers in the household (and, in their own measure, to all persons having authority over others) is the divine exhortation addressed, "Be you . . . perfect as also your Heavenly Father is perfect." *

I. *Fatherly Love should be all-embracing, like God's.*

Let yours be perfect love! And how few there are among the wisest, the most learned, the most experienced of good fathers even, who understand what that supernatural charity, that perfect, all-embracing, all-enduring love is, of which He who is Father over us all affords us the sweet and wonderful model!

It embraces His Enemies among the Heathen.

To those among His human creatures who are most forgetful of Himself, most bitterly, hostile toward the very notion of a Godhead,—who blaspheme Him by their words and their writings, who make of their whole lives one long act of rebellion and defiance of His authority, who are upon earth the embodiment of irreligion, impiety, vice, and wickedness,—see how good, how patient, that Fatherly Love is! Not one of His laws is suspended with respect to the evil-doer, not one of the manifold provisions of nature ordained by that Almighty Love is withdrawn. The sun still rises over him, despite the countless days so horribly misspent, and the sweet repose of night will come again after a day of sin, and God's angels will guard from danger the life of the enemy of God, as unvarying and patient in their watchfulness, as are the stars which look down from the firmament on the sleep of the wicked and the repose of the just.

The great sun in the heavens continues, day after day and year after year, to dispense its light and vital warmth to the man whose whole existence is an outrage to the Creator; the air he breathes loses nothing of its wholesomeness,.

---

* St. Matthew, v. 48.

the heavens above his head and the earth and ocean around him, are unchanged for him in their magnificence and their beauty.

It embraces Bad Christians.

There is, however, another order of things in which the unspeakable patience and tenderness of that same Fatherly Love is displayed to all its children without exception. Take the "Household of the Faith,"—that most wonderful creation and world of all in which man knows himself to bear toward his Maker the real relation of son,—not in that vague and remote sense in which every being that owes its existence to the Almighty may be said to be his child,— but in that lofty and sublime sense in which all who are born by baptism of the blood of the Only-Begotten Son, are most truly partakers of his sonship. There are in the house of the Father very many who disgrace their sonship, who live a life unworthy of the unbaptised and the heathen, who are most keenly conscious of their own unworthiness, and deplore, while they persist in it, the monstrous inconsistency of leading a beastly life in a heavenly station.

Its Infinite Mercifulness.

And yet all this while, the Fatherly Love in its unwearied patience, in its unutterable tenderness, in its awful reverence for those who are the Sons of the household,— throws over the secret sins of the fallen an impenetrable veil, deals with their most open sins with infinite mercifulness, —urging the guilty soul by incessant touches of shame and regret and longing to return to that Goodness who cannot refuse to forgive,—and throwing over every step made by the returning sinner, the darkness of a secrecy so full of respect, and pity, and gentleness for the humiliated and repentant soul! Think, O fathers, of that most divine story left us by the Incarnate Mercy, and which is the history of His dealings with the soul of every one of us,—the Parable of the Prodigal Son.*

If we would, therefore, apprehend that Infinite Love in all its fatherly tenderness and generosity, we must conceive it not only as all-embracing, having no manifest preference for some of its children over the others, and excluding openly none of the underserving from the light and warmth it dispenses ; but we must conceive of it as drawn in a special manner toward the erring and the fallen. This is the supernatural aspect of paternal charity. And this point, on which we dare not insist too much, every right-minded and true-hearted parent will instinctively understand and appreciate.

Fatherly Love of St. John the Evangelist.

A most beautiful instance of this irresistible impulse of true fatherly love, as understood among Christians, occurred in the very infancy of the Church, and is related by one of her earliest and most eloquent historians.*

St. John the Evangelist, while visiting one of the churches of Asia Minor, had remarked among the crowd a young man whose mien and bearing bespoke uncommon gifts. The preternatural insight of the apostle of charity read in that soul a mighty capacity for all great deeds, if properly cultivated,—and which, if neglected, might become a power for evil. The youth was then in the first fervor of his conversion, and, amid the fearful temptations to evil which beset youth in that most beautiful but most licentious land, he needed special watchfulness and care from his religious guides.

St. John, whose angelic life and winning gentleness had so powerfully attracted the young convert, intrusted him, on his departure for Ephesus, to the local bishop. "In the presence of Christ, and in the hearing of thy people," the apostle said, "I give this youth to thy keeping." The trust could not be refused ; it was even accepted with readiness. As it often happens, however, the very fervor of the youth

---

* Eusebius, "Ecclesiastical History," book iii., c. 23 ; where he quotes as his authority Clement of Alexandria.

lulled the bishop into a fatal security. He fancied that one
so good and so generous had nothing to fear from the seduc-
tions which assailed every sense on that enchanted shore,
and, more particularly, from the company of his young pagan
friends and associates. The strict discipline in which the
young man lived in the bishop's house, was relaxed after
he had been baptized and confirmed. It was thought that
the sacramental grace would prove a sufficient protection
against the manifold evils of pagan life and conversation.

Human respect—the fear of being true to conscience in
presence of the dissolute or the impious—together with the
powerful incentive to sensuality where the whole world
around him ministered to the senses, soon caused the un-
guarded youth to fall, and to fall to the lowest depths of
guilt and crime. He was outlawed, and betook himself to
the mountain passes, where he became the chief of a band
of highway robbers, the boldest, bloodiest, and most reck-
less of them all.

When the aged apostle returned to that city, he missed
his protégé among the clergy and select youth of the
Church. "Where is the youth that I and Christ with me
intrusted to thee in presence of thy flock?" were the first
words the fatherly heart could find in its alarm. "He is
dead!" was the answer. "Dead! how, and when?" the
apostle demanded. "Dead to God and to all virtue," was
the mournful reply.

John would not be satisfied until he had learned all, and as-
certained where he was likely to find his prodigal. So, though
in extreme old age, broken by labor and suffering, he would
not rest till he had brought the lost sheep to the fold. It
was in vain to represent to him that the wild mountain tracts
in which the robbers dwelt were almost inaccessible to man
and beast, or that the men of blood who found shelter and
impunity there, spared neither age nor sex; the apostle set
out without a moment's delay, repeating to the recreant
bishop, who tried in vain to oppose his mad project: "Oh.
what a guardian have I set over the souls of my brethren!"

"When he reached the retreat of the robber band," the

historian continues,—"he was surrounded by their scouts. He had no thought of avoiding them and no fear of the violence they might offer. He only shouted to them : 'I have come to seek your chief ; bring him to me !' The other came fully armed for a hostile encounter ; but, on perceiving the man of God, he turned and fled. John, who was on horseback, followed him, crying out as he went: 'Why fly from thy father, my son ? I am but an old man, feeble and unarmed. O my poor child, stop and listen: lay aside all apprehension. There is yet hope for thee. I shall be answerable to Christ for thee. I am willing to die for thee, as He did, and ready to give my soul for thine. Only stop, and trust to me ; for Christ it is who sent me after thee ?' "

The Wolf becomes a Lamb.

The fugitive, overcome by the appeals of that love he knew so well, turns on a sudden and falls prostrate at the feet of his pursuer. He has cast away his weapons, and with his face buried in the dust, he pours forth a flood of tears, concealing the while that guilty right hand which has shed so much innocent blood. John is kneeling by his side, mingling his tears with those of the guilty one, and protesting to him solemnly that he will not rest till he has obtained his pardon from Christ. He has no horror of grasping, despite the other's resistance, that murderous right hand which tears of true repentance are already beginning to cleanse from its stains. He brings him back in triumph to the church in which he had been baptized, remains with him in prayer, vigils, and fasting, pouring forth his whole soul to the Great Shepherd of the flock, to implore His mercy on this lost one which he had reclaimed.

The apostle would not quit his side, calming the terrors and remorse of that guilty soul, by sweet and gentle words, " charming the evil spirit out of him,"—says the historian, by the accents and artifices of his fatherly love. Nor would he commit the care of that sick soul to any one till he had led him step by step to expiate his enormous guilt, to repair by the most heroic acts of virtue the scandals of his sinful life, and to become foremost in generous goodness as he had been foremost in crime.

It is, we would fain believe, a rare thing to have to recall the sinner from such depths as these. And yet, considering what we daily see, and hear, and read of,—there must be very many homes in every class of society, where deep guilt in some child demands all the arts of a father's love to soften the sinner's heart, and all the resources of his tenderness to raise him up to repentance and newness of life.

We do not, however, hold up the mirror of these Godlike examples, in order to make parents behold therein these extreme cases, in which deep guilt or degradation in a child could only be remedied by heroic charity in a parent.

The love we would inculcate here, is that love which expends itself in the thousand and one little home-charities of every ordinary day and hour, that go to make the household so deeply happy in the sunshine of a father's affection, while it tends to make every child there good, and to keep him good.

How the Divine Ideal is realized in the Family.

Yes, yes; you laughed, dear reader, at our effort, a moment ago, to make you take the Sun in the Heavens as the model of your practical tenderness toward your dear ones. We know it,—it is the sun nevertheless that imparts to the glorious planets of our system their brightness and their vital warmth. But let the planets go ! Have you a garden near your home? or beautiful fields and woods around it? or lovely flowers within it? and are you one who takes a hearty pleasure in beautiful things?

Then feast your eyes on the colors and shades which clothe earth and sky around and above your home at morning, or noon, or sunset; look into the face of every flower that blooms in your garden or at your window,—as if in each you read a delightful page of that endless book of beauty, which is only the pale reflection of His charms, in whom alone resides the essence and perfection of all that is most fair and most bright. Know you not that the magnificences of earth and sky, and the varied beauties and fragrance of grove and garden, of cloud and daintiest flower, —are as much the creation of the Sun in the Heavens, as are the brightness of the evening or the morning stars?　.

And so,—you, who are the suns of your own homes, you can by the light of your examples and the warmth of your fatherly love, make the souls, the hearts, and minds and lives of your dear ones more beautiful and fair to look upon, than the most gorgeous flower that ever bloomed beneath the sun. Will you refuse to give to these souls, to these dear and precious lives their coloring and their beauty in the eyes of God and men and angels?

II. *How to Love Wisely.*

Let your love be a wise love. Wisdom is indispensable to all who have the charge of training and governing others. But, you will ask, what is that wisdom which should temper the father's love in his government of the household and the rearing of his children? Wisdom, in so far as it regards the understanding, is the knowledge of the peculiar nature of things, of the purposes for which they were made, and of the means to make each thing fit itself to its purpose. In practice, it is the directing of others according to this clear knowledge of their destinies and their capacities.

The wise architect, besides the thorough knowledge of the principles, rules, and practice of his art, seizes in every work of his the object for which he builds, and exactly suits the building to the uses for which it is destined. He is the best and wisest builder who so plans and executes every structure intrusted to him, that it is the best of its kind,—the best dwelling-house for rich or poor, the best church edifice in view precisely of the worship to be held therein,—the best for the climate, and for the people ; the best for durability, and the best in proportion to the means of those who rear it.

The wise father studies carefully the dispositions of each of his dear ones,—just as the musician studies the capacity of his instrument and the power of each of its chords,—just as the wise gardener acquaints himself with the habits of all and each of his fruit trees, so that each one may be so trained, so cared for, as to yield its utmost in due season.

The Divine Art of Training Children.

The art of cultivating, developing, governing souls (we say nothing of bodily strength and health, in themselves so exceedingly important), is of all arts the most difficult, requiring the highest wisdom, skill, and prudence. We have known parents,—nay, we see such every day,—who seem gifted with almost a divine insight into child-nature, and endowed with somewhat of the divine skill in managing their various capacities and dispositions. They display a like superhuman prudence in training such as are weak, or perverse, or fractious,—addressing themselves, in their method of education, to the affections of each child, calling forth what is noblest and purest and best in their nature, and making them, even from earliest infancy, to love to do what is repugnant to sense or to inclination.

Unwise Love.

Other parents there are,—excellent in many respects, religious, exemplary, gentle,—under whose care children grow up like fruit trees that are never pruned, or grafted; around whose roots no loving hand has dug to loosen the soil or to manure it; from whose trunk hurtful parasites or insects have never been removed. The trees are of the choicest kind, the soil is of the most favorable, and grafts from the very same stock produce, in the neighboring garden, fruits the most abundant and delicious. But the neighboring gardener makes of fruit-growing a labor of love *and a science.*

We have seen parents,—themselves the sad subjects of

inherited moral disease, love their children with a love so absorbing and so unwise, that, knowing them to be prone to the parental weaknesses, they could nevertheless refuse nothing to their appetites ;—nay, they would glut these poor diseased little ones with every aliment most fitted to develop in them the fatal germs of the ancestral vice !— This was not loving either wisely or well.

Example of Heroic Wisdom in a Father.

The heroic love of one father, and the marvelous success that rewarded his culture, deserve to be held up to the ad miration of our readers.

He was a lawyer,—the son of a man whose transcendent talents might have placed him in the front rank of any profession, but whose incorrigible intemperance had marred all his brilliant prospects, consigning himself to the madhouse and leaving his six orphan children to utter poverty. The son of whom we speak here, was the last of four brothers, and the youngest but one of the whole family. His mother died when the boy was in his third year, a year after his father had become a hopeless lunatic, and six months after giving birth to her sixth child. The two youngest children were adopted by a maiden aunt ; of the four others we need make no further mention than to say, that the oldest son drank himself to death before he was thirty.

Our little hero found in his aunt and adopted mother, that supernatural love and wisdom begotten of true piety, which enabled her to discharge the duties she had assumed toward her little orphans, with rare devotion and success. The infant,—a little girl,—was saved and brought up by a miracle of tender nursing, so fragile was the life she inherited. The little brother was watched over with more than a mother's care. The slender means of his aunt were so husbanded by her that she could send him to college in due time,—and his progress in learning was prodigious. His nature was a most passionate one ; but the piety imbibed at home and sedulously fostered by his admirable masters, as

13

well as the recollection of his father's failing and fate, acted on the boy and the youth as a powerful restraint.

It was his good fortune, on entering college, to meet with a spiritual director who had known his father well, and who was most anxious to save his boy from the terrible enemy of his family and happiness. He encouraged the latter to come to him as to a second parent in all his troubles, taught him to overcome his fierce outbursts of temper, and to refuse his appetite everything that was a delicacy or for which he felt a strong liking. On his leaving college, he addressed him in almost the words of the good Father Clifford to the celebrated naturalist, Charles Waterton ; * obtained from him a solemn promise of life-long abstinence from everything intoxicating.

The promise in his case, as in that of Waterton, was kept to the end of life. He grew to fame and to affluence as well, dying at the early age of forty-two, leaving five boys behind him, every one of whom was trained from his cradle not only in abstinence from wine and strong drinks, but even from tea and coffee. They were noble boys, healthy, robust, bright,—models of manly strength and beauty, as well as of all manly virtue. Their father made them his constant companions from childhood, making them delight in study and in the practice of all goodness. He asked them to do nothing which he did not do himself,—so that abstinence seemed to them no sacrifice. So far as we know, not one has ever turned aside for a moment from the path in which they had learned to walk with their excellent father.

---

* "One day, when I was in the class of poetry, and which was about two years before I left the college (Stonyhurst) for good and all, he called me up to his room. 'Charles,' said he to me in a tone of 'voice perfectly irresistible, 'I have long been studying your disposition, and I clearly foresee that nothing will keep you at home. You will journey into far-distant countries, where you will be exposed to many dangers. Promise me, that from this day forward, you will never put your lips to wine, or to spirituous liquors. The sacrifice is nothing,' added he ; 'but in the end it will prove of incalculable advantage to you.' I agreed to his enlightened proposal ; and from that hour to this, which is now about nine-and-thirty years, I have never swallowed one glass of any kind of wine or of ardent spirits.' "—NORMAN MOORE, *Life of Charles Waterton,* prefixed to the " Essays on Natural History," London, 1871.

Is not this the way,—approved by nature and blessed of God,—to neutralize and eradicate the fatal germs of ancestral weakness and vice? And was not this to love wisely and well?

Another Example of Wise Love in a Father.

Another instance, in which a like fatherly wisdom saved his child from hereditary consumption,—may suggest a no less useful moral, and shall now be related.

A man of wealth and position had seen his wife and four children taken from him successively by that insidious and implacable distemper. One child, a daughter, was left to him. How could he save her? By a sort of inspiration he resolved to harden her frame, as she grew up, to every influence of the atmosphere, while accustoming her to simple and nourishing diet and to regular though not excessive out-door exercise. From childhood she was made to take a daily cold bath, and when vacation time came yearly for her father, he took her with him to the mountains, lived with her in the open air, in a tent, and made her swim for an hour every morning and evening, even through the cold autumn weather. She is now a lovely woman, the robust mother of a large family of children, whom she brings up after the manner she was herself trained. Will this method prove an effectual remedy to the inherited disposition to consumption? We shall not dispute it with the doctors, nor trespass on professional ground. But surely there is a virtue in generous abstinence, as well as in the healthful use of nature's own appliances, besides the blessing which the God of nature bestows on all generosity and self-denial.

Sublime Example of the Rechabites.

There is,—to confirm such fatherly wisdom and generosity as we would fain inculcate here,—a most memorable example left us in Holy Writ.

When the Hebrew tribes were painfully threading their

way from Egypt through the frightful labyrinth of the Sinaitic Peninsula, — a family of Madianites, — who had, probably, known Moses during his long exile in their midst, —cast their lot with him and his people, renouncing the idolatry of their ancestors, and becoming thenceforward invincibly faithful to the one true God. Even when Israel had fallen away into licentiousness and corruption,—these generous converts only seemed the more bent on honoring the God of their choice by purity and austerity of life.

The fearful sensuality which characterized the Phœnicians and Canaanites, had made on these simple-minded Arabs so painful an impression,—that they refused to live in cities, lest they should become contaminated by the luxuries of city-life. A portion of them withdrew to the northern extremity of Palestine, and the remainder settled in the pastoral wildernesses of the south, not far from the cradle of their race. In the times of the early kings of Judah and Israel, when the majority of the people seemed to have given up forever the worship of the true God, and to sully their homes and lives with all the abominations of the heathen, the chief of this tribe of Cenites or Kenites was Jonadab, the son of Rechab. To preserve his descendants from this dreadful apostasy and its punishment, he bound them by solemn oath to drink no wine, to plant or possess no vineyard, to build no houses, and to live always in tents far away from the atmosphere of cities.

To this solemn engagement these Rechabites ever afterward continued faithful, affording so shining an example of constant purity, piety, and austerity amid the increasing degeneracy of the Israelites, that God allowed them to share in the ministrations of his temple,—as if they belonged to the priestly tribe,—and pledged Himself to perpetuate their race forever.*

Even when the blood of the Apostle James was being shed near the Temple,—almost on the eve of its final destruction, the generous voice of a Rechabite "cried out protesting against the crime." †

---

* Jeremias, xxxv. 19. 　　† Eusebius, "Ecclesiastical History," ii. 23.

God not to be surpassed in Generosity.

We are not without proof that the Divine Goodness has magnificently kept his promise to this race of noble men. Benjamin of Tudela in the twelfth century mentions that he found the Rechabites to the number of one hundred thousand, fulfilling to the letter every part of the promise made to their glorious ancestor, tilling the ground, living in tents, pasturing their herds and flocks, and abstaining from everything which could intoxicate. In the present century, a European teacher, Dr. Wolff (1829), found the Beni-Khabr (sons of Rechab) to the number of sixty thousand in one place in Arabia, walking in the law of their fathers.

The conclusion must force itself on the serious-minded reader. Jonadab saw that to preserve himself, his brethren, and their descendants from physical degeneracy and extinction as a race, as well as from the deep guilt of idol-worship, he must adopt and practice absolute and perpetual simplicity, austerity, and purity,—utter and perpetual renouncement of all the luxuries of civilized life, and the pleasures of the table. He did not hesitate. And for nearly three thousand years there are the descendants of that man, beneath the gaze of the whole world, sacredly keeping to the promise made to God·by their fathers! There is nothing like it elsewhere in profane history.

Surely, this generous parent and reformer loved his children wisely and well!

This is what one father did three thousand years ago,—a simple Arab, unused to all the devices ministering to the comfort and enjoyment of life, for which we have coined the lying name of progress;—he, this high-souled man who feared God and loved his children,—swore for them to be true to God and to be self-denying. And no lapse or length of time has made them swerve from their oath!

On what an "awful throne" did these glorious descendants of a true man place their father! And how truly did the "patient power" of that strong, wise, and fatherly love

of long ago, cover his descendants and the world in which
they dwelt with its "healing wings"—as if the might and
love of Jehovah himself shielded them from harm amid the
political revolutions that have never ceased to convulse their
country,—more destructive in their effects than the simoom
and its whirlwinds of burning sand!

Would that Christian fathers in our midst could nerve
themselves to such generosity and self-sacrifice! God alone
knows how deeply, how fearfully our nineteenth century
needs it.

III. *Liberality, Hospitality, Charity to the Poor.*

As to the other virtues which should distinguish the
father in his government of the home,—we may dismiss
them in a few words.

That he may ever be in the eyes of his dear ones the
living representative of the divine perfection, let him be
careful to add to the wisdom, and patient, all-embracing
love, we have spoken of, the liberality and hospitality
which make his home lovely to the friends or the stran-
gers he admits to his table, or to the poor and the needy
in whose behalf he acts the part of God's open-handed
steward.

Let him, no matter how hard has been his battle with the
world in amassing wealth or securing comfort and independ-
ence, never allow his children to believe that his heart is set
on what he possesses. This superiority to riches and pos-
sessions, this independence of all that men value most,—
will be only a higher degree of likeness to' the Heavenly
Father, who is supremely independent of all created things,
even while He ministers to our needs with such magnificent
liberality, and decks heaven and earth with such beauty
and splendor.

It is needful to a child's estimate of his father's great-
ness of soul, that he should find him ready to give up the
whole world for God, and so drawn to the Infinitely Great
and Good and Fair,—that he can only love all things out-
side of God in conformity to the divine will and pleasure.

Fatherly Love must be Firm and Authoritative.

Wise and fruitful of good a father's love cannot be, unless it be at the same time full of that gentle, calm firmness which will be obeyed. The will which enforces obedience willingly and lovingly in the Home, can never be one that is violent, fiery, impulsive, and, therefore, changing and inconstant.

A hot, imperious, wrathful disposition may enforce obedience in an army or on board a ship. There authority is despotic and irresistible,—every act of disobedience and mutiny having to be repressed by immediate and pitiless punishment. For no ship is safe, and no army can exist for an instant, in which the voice of the commander may be questioned or set aside by his subordinates.

In the family the father must govern by a mixture of genuine, enlightened love, and calm, indomitable firmness. All who are subject to him must feel instinctively that what the father wills, he wills lovingly, justly, reasonably ;—*and that his will is law.*

It is scarcely possible, where a man is impulsive, passionate, and imperious toward his children,—that his commands can be regulated either by justice, reason, or wisdom. Hence, the minds of the children will rebel against them, though force may compel them to be silent and obey. Where, on the contrary, they know, from their parent's habitual disposition, that he is himself governed, in every order he gives, by reason, calm judgment, and true love for their own welfare,—and where, especially, experience has taught them that he means what he says, and exacts compliance with his will,—there you may be sure to find neither disobedience, nor disorder.

Gentle Firmness and Persistency exemplified in Nature.

Nothing is so wonderful in the certainty with which it accomplishes its purpose and overcomes obstacles seemingly irresistible, as the gentle and persistent working of the forces and laws of nature.

Take up a cocoanut on its native soil and when it has fallen in full maturity from the tree. Its shell is as hard, one would think, as iron, without a break or an opening on its surface. If you would get at the delicious substance within you must employ your whole strength to break the shell. And yet, if you plant that nut in the ground, under the conditions favorable to germination, the pulp within will put forth a little white leaf as soft as cream, and the growth and constant pressure of this soft and tender substance will pierce or burst the hard shell, opening a way to the imprisoned life, that in its time will become a stately tree.

See these ancient cities of Mexico, Central America, and New Granada, with the magnificent temples and palaces which attest the genius and civilization of races now passed away. One, who could have seen these mighty structures in all their glory, would have said that the great blocks of which they are built, and the skill with which these are put together, must surely defy the action of time. And yet the feeble and graceful creepers of the tropics, by sending their tiny roots into every joint and crevice, have separated huge block from block, rupturing and disintegrating the hard stone with its marvelous sculptures,—till the whole now offers to the eye of the traveler but a confused heap of fragmentary ruins.

There is, nearer home, another and, perhaps, a more startling instance of the resistless might of the silent and slowly-working forces of nature. We remember in the early spring of 1847, how a portion of the huge and majestic cliff crowned by the Citadel of Quebec, gave way suddenly, falling over and burying the houses and inhabitants that nestled at its foot.

The water had penetrated into what was at first a little narrow cleft in the rock. But water, in freezing, enlarges its volume with a force that nothing can withstand. So each winter the cleft grew in width, admitting a larger

quantity of snow and ram and gravel. The alternate pro-
cess of freezing and thawing went on silently, impercep-
tibly to the military men who watched in the citadel and the
civilians who slept in conscious security beneath,—till one
spring night the mass of half-melted snow and water was
such that a single night's frost completed the work of ages,
detached a vast mass from the hillside, and sent it toppling
over into the river beneath.

Even now there is, a little above the former rift, a new one
that is yearly increasing, and which no power known to
man can prevent, in its own time, from working a similar
catastrophe.

The force of fatherly government should be thus gentle,
constant, and irresistible. Children, servants, dependants
of every kind, are perfectly conscious of this calm, unruffled,
resistless temper of a parent. Even animals feel and obey
it. The most spirited and fiery horses know when the hand
that holds the reins is strong, firm, and gentle withal,—and
they obey its direction and guidance implicitly. Not so
when the man who guides them is fiery, impatient, and un-
steady. They become feverish, nervous, fidgety, and un-
governable.

How Violence paralyzes the best Qualities.

Need we say more? Let an example or two serve to
impress this vital truth.

Napoleon the First was a man of surprising genius. He
was not only the greatest of generals, but one of the great-
est of legislators. Yet, it has been said of him by one who
knew him well and intimately, that what his sword had
won on the battle-field, his ungovernable temper lost him in
the council chamber. He aspired to be the master of the
world, and had at one time become the arbiter of Europe;
but he had never learned to control either his anger or his
tongue. He thereby made mortal enemies not only of the
allied princes he could have bound to himself by gentleness
and generosity,—but of his prime-minister Talleyrand, who

knew how to dissimulate and be silent, and who became Napoleon's evil genius and perfidious counselor.

His own brothers hated and opposed him. Before his death, at St. Helena, he said: "I have been spoiled by success. Circumstances and my own energy of character have been such, that from the instant I gained military superiority, I acknowledged neither master, nor laws."

In other and far inferior stations we every day see men, who are remarkably successful as business or professional men, and whose home-life is one of disorder, discomfort, misery, and utter failure.

We know of one man whose great talent for organization and energy of character enabled him to colonize one of our loveliest valleys in the interior, and to found one of our most beautiful cities. Yet could he not wield over his own household. that wise, gentle, firm sway without which American boys grow up spendthrifts and vagrants.

If the true father and the true man, for whom these pages are written, is sincerely desirous to see his home-life as blessed as his public life has been laborious, arduous, and successful,—let him learn well the lesson conveyed here. Let him practice self-restraint, and teach it to his children. Those who have never learned to govern themselves, are but ill fitted to govern others,—to govern children especially, who are so wise, so logical, so clear-sighted to perceive the monstrous contradictions between an authority which would impose laws and punish their infraction, while remaining itself lawless, unruly, and most unreasonable.

CHAPTER XI.

THE FATHER'S SUPREME DUTY: TO MAKE HIS HOME THE
SCHOOL OF REVERENCE.

They gave me a master who was rich in high virtue, the Margrave Henry of
Austria, who served women with full loyalty, and spake ever nobly of them as
a knight should. He was mild, bold, and of a high heart, wise with the wise,
and foolish with the foolish; he endured labor for the sake of honor, and his
mouth never spake a bad word; to all his friends he was generous and faith-
ful; and he loved God from his heart. This worthy master said to me:
Whoever would live well, must give himself up to serve a woman. He taught me
much of his gentle virtue, how to speak of women; how to ride on horseback,
and to compose sweet verses; he said, *Thereby will a young man endear him-
self to people, when he can praise women with gentleness, and when he loves them
more dearly than himself: for* (said he) *that which arises from a flattering and lying
mind can never succeed with the good.* Had I fulfilled all that he said to me, I
should have been worthier than I am.—ULRICH VON LICHTENSTEIN.*

Reverence,—the Grand Feature of Christian Homes.

THE happiness of the world and the salvation of society
itself, must depend on the manner in which women, within
the home-sanctuary, mold men to loftiness of soul and gen-
tleness of life, while the father and husband, by word and
example, teaches his sons a sovereign respect for every one
that bears the name of woman.

Do not pass lightly over this thought, as if the practical
chivalry it inculcates belonged to the society of the past, or
as if this supreme reverence for woman could never again
become the worship of all Christian homes and the distinc-
tive virtue of all young men who are proud of their Chris-

---

* "Duties owed to Women."

tian mothers, and proud, too, of doing homage to her who is the ever-blessed Mother of Christ.

More priceless than all the treasures ever buried in the bosom of the deep and recovered by the appliances of human skill, are such fundamental truths as this, which await the serious inquirer in the very first pages of the Gospel.

We all know how the first words of prophecy ever uttered by man,* were inspired by the Deity † and applied to the divine institution of Matrimony. He who came to restore this fundamental ordinance of the divine economy to its primitive unity and firmness, and who perfected all preceding legislation in His law of charity, generosity, and self-sacrifice, also gave, in the lives of his Mother, of St. Joseph, his foster-father, and in his own private life at Nazareth, the examples of the very home-virtues needed throughout all time.

She who was to be the Mother of the Redeemer, had been united to her kinsman Joseph by a true marriage,—a marriage founded on exalted and mutual affection. Both had left father and mother and the whole world to cast their lot together, under God's wonderful guidance, in poverty, toil, obscurity, and perfect union of hearts. It was a union sanctified by so special a grace, that from the virginal love and life of both was to spring and blossom forth that Tree of Life in whose blessed fruits and leaves was to be the healing and salvation of the world. ‡   Just as John the Baptist, His forerunner, was endowed before his birth and through Mary's instrumentality, with a grace that made him shine like the morning star, the precursor of the sun,—even so were both Mary and Joseph privileged with the purity and holiness that fitted them to be the parents and first companions of the Holy One of Israel.

Threefold Reverence practiced at Nazareth.

We find in the lowly home at Nazareth of Joseph and

---

* Genesis, ii. 21, 22, 23, 24.   † Matthew, xix. 4, 5, 6.   ‡ Apocalypse, xxii. 1, 2.

Mary, honored during thirty years by the presence of the incarnate Son of God, the practice of that threefold reverence, which has been characteristic down to the present century, of every Christian family and state,—the reverence for God, for parental authority, and for woman. More than ever, at a time when false science and revolutionary socialism league themselves together to destroy the foundations both of domestic and of civil society, does it become necessary to insist upon this threefold reverence, without which all the glory of our civilization must disappear forever.

The Christian family, wherever it was free, during the past eighteen hundred years, resembled the settler in some one of our lovely valleys in the interior,—along the course of the Susquehanna, the Wyoming, or the Connecticut. He had placed his home high above the stream, so that the sweep of no inundation could reach it ; and for generations had beheld from his secure position the fields and farmsteads far and near laid waste in spring by the devastating waters. But lo! he wakes up from his fancied security one morning to see a portion of the bluff on which he has built, ingulfed in the swollen river, and to discover that the swift-flowing waters are slowly but steadily undermining the very soil beneath his foundations.

This Reverence now more than ever Necessary.

The waters of unbelief are daily rising higher and higher. undermining the hitherto secure foundations of the family and the community ; the captious errors of the socialist and the communist are sinking deeply into the minds and hearts of the vicious and idle who will not work, and of the hard-toiling poor whose work is but ill requited,—like a conflagration which acquires fiercer destructive force from everything it preys upon.

We must build the home far away from the mighty flood and high above the reach of the flame,—on that Rock of Ages which alone can withstand the utmost violence of the deluge, the fiery tempest, and the earthquake. It behooves

us, therefore, to convince ourselves thoroughly of the deep
practical truths to be learned by children and parents, by
rulers and subjects, by families and by nations, of the Hid-
den God, who toils, obeys, and grows in all spiritual loveli-
ness beneath the roof of the Carpenter Joseph.

I. *Reverence for God.*

The prodigious self-abasement of the Word made Flesh
—taken in the whole compass of his mortal life, was one
perpetual act of reverential submission and loving expia-
tion offered for the entire race of man by Him who had
become the Second Adam, to repair the ruin caused by the
blind pride and selfish sensuality of the First.*

The infinite reverence with which the Second Eve, the
Mother of our Life, accepts to be associate with the Cruci-
fied in his labors, humiliations, and self-sacrifice,—is set
forth most eloquently in the simple words of her answer to
the angel, "Behold the handmaid of the Lord; be it done
unto me according to thy word!" And then, how that
absolute and heartfelt reverence for the expressed will of
the Deity, is manifested in the pains such a Mother takes
to separate herself from all the scenes in which her Son is
glorified by the people, only taking her place,—woman-
like and mother-like,—by His side when He is lifted up
on high in shame and agony! And was the cry of that
motherly heart, pierced by a sevenfold wound, not heard
along with His, when He "was heard for his reverence,"
as He yielded his spirit to his Father?

But what of him who was the visible head of that lowly
and most blessed household of Nazareth? what of Joseph,
the "just man," true and perfect in the discharge of his

---

* "Wherefore when He cometh into the world, He saith : Sacrifice and
oblation Thou wouldst not ; but a body Thou hast fitted to me. Holocausts
for sin did not please Thee. Then said I, Behold I come : in the head of the
book it is written of me, that I should do Thy will, O God."—*Hebrews*, x. 5, 6,
7. "Who in the days of His flesh, with a strong cry and tears, offering up
prayers and supplications to Him that was able to save him from death, was
heard for his reverence."—*Ibidem*, v. 7.

office as custodian of God's chiefest treasures on earth, as husband to such a wife, and foster-parent to such a Son?

See, when the first perplexity assails him, how promptly and unhesitatingly he yields obedience to the injunction of the heavenly messenger: "Fear not to take unto thee Mary, thy wife!" How reverently he complies with the divine command when bidden to fly without preparation or provision across the wilderness to Egypt, trusting himself and his precious charge, on the way thither and while there, to the guidance and care of the Most High and his angels! The same reverent and trustful submission shines forth in his receiving the order to return to his own country, and to fix his abode at Nazareth. Were not he and Mary the ready pupils in all this of the Divine Babe who grew up beneath their roof and their nurture,—like the Lily of the Valley beneath the shade of twin palm-trees, embalming with its fragrance and delighting with its simple beauty only the obscure corner of earth on which it grew!

II. *Reverence for Parental Authority.*

Respect for man can only come from respect for God; a loving and conscientious obedience to human authority can only be found in the man who sees the majesty of his Divine Author reflected on the brow of parent, prince, or magistrate. There can be no degrading submission to the voice or will of father and mother in the home, when the child is taught and feels assured that they speak and command in the place of the Heavenly Father. There is nothing but ennobling obedience in observing the laws of Church or State, in accepting the authority of Pope, bishop, and priest,—of emperor, king, or president,—when the reverent eye of faith sees the Eternal Lawgiver behind the earthly legislator, and the knees of the heart are bent to the Infinite Majesty, as man bows down before His representatives here below.

When our Emmanuel gave himself a mother upon earth and consented to pass for a time among men as the son of the Carpenter Joseph,—He did so with the design of teaching all after-ages in His own person how they were to reverence father and mother.   He interrupts the obscure life of toil, poverty, humility, and obedience which he was leading at Nazareth, to show Himself in his twelfth year at Jerusalem the true God-Man, already fitted by the plenitude of his wisdom to teach Israel and enlighten the world,—and lo! after proclaiming to his parents and to the audience assembled in the Temple, that he has an indefeasible right to "be about His Father's business,"—he becomes once more the docile and dutiful child, returns with them forthwith to Nazareth, and thenceforth till his thirtieth year "was subject to them," and, as the pregnant years succeeded each other, He "advanced in wisdom, and age, and grace with God and men." *

This is the order of nature, carried out by its very Author when he came to repair and to teach the world : it is and ever must be the law of life and of all intellectual and moral advancement, so long as the world exists and as man continnes to be what he is.

Shall we ever lay this truth to heart—that human society both in the Home and in the State, is paternity, dependence and loving progress in all moral worth, much more than that "liberty, equality, and fraternity," which sets one half of the human race to cut the throats and burn down the homes of the other half?

III. *Reverence for Woman.*

Do we, in this nineteenth century,—this age of boasted progress and freedom from old prejudices,—marvel at that noble ancestor of a long line of emperors, who was so "rich in virtue," and "who served women with full loyalty, and spake ever nobly of them as a knight should"? We forget that she who, being the Mother of our Head, is thereby the Mother of us all, was looked up to by Him with all the reverence which the best of sons ever paid to the best of

---

* Luke, ii. 42-52.

mothers. We forget also that Mary was treated with supreme reverence by the angel, by Joseph, her husband and protector, and by St. Elizabeth, their cousin ; and that this reverence pervaded the entire Christian family down to the age of the Reformers, forming the very spring and soul of Christian chivalry and the guiding principle of domestic education.

Read over the passage of the Evangelist St. Luke, in which is related the Angel's message to Mary, and weigh well the reverent words of salutation :

> " Hail, full of grace,—the Lord is with thee !
> Blessed art thou among women !"

Then listen to the almost adoring words of Elizabeth, who like her unborn babe, was filled with the Holy Ghost, as soon as the Mother of the New Life, the Eve of the new creation, the living Ark of the New Covenant,—had crossed her threshold :

> "Blessed art thou among women !
> And blessed is the fruit of thy womb !
> And whence is this to me
> That the Mother of my Lord should come to me ?"

And then, as the Divine Spirit rushes upon her own soul and opens out before her eyes the book of the future, the trials and triumphs of the Christian church,—her prophetic soul hears every succeeding age bending before herself with reverence and repeating the words of the Angel and of Elizabeth :

"Behold from henceforth all generations shall call me Blessed !"

Joseph's respectful and faithful service to Mary.

From the hour that the Angel discloses to Joseph the august mystery of Mary's Motherhood, he understands, this chaste Joseph of the New Testament, that he is infinitely more honored than Obededom of old. For, it is no longer the figurative Ark of the Mosaic Covenant that he has the

14

honor of sheltering beneath his roof; but the true Ark, and
the abiding presence of the Incarnate Deity bringing with
it untold blessings.*

Thenceforth he understands it to be in conformity with
the divine plan that he should devote himself,—every
thought, and aim, every aspiration and pulse of his heart,
every day and hour of his life, to the service of that most
blessed Mother, and the preservation of that Life of our life,
from its first tender blossoming on the root of Jesse till its
glorious maturity on the Tree of Calvary.

He knows that the Babe intrusted to his keeping is one to
be "born not of blood, nor of the will of the flesh, nor of
the will of man, but of God;" in the light vouchsafed him
from on high, he sees that until the time appointed for his
Emmanuel's manifestation by John, He was to be, in his life
of absolute dependence and laborious obscurity at Nazareth,
as if he were in the eyes of the nation "without father,
without mother, without descent." The blood of David
in the veins of the high-souled Carpenter, and the heroic
spirit of David firing his heart, will thenceforth prompt
him only to deeds of unhesitating devotion and self-sacrifice
to protect both Mother and Babe from the manifold perils
which beset them.

How tenderly, how reverently he watches over her during
the period that Emmanuel remains hidden within the Holy
of holies! How full of sovereign respect, and love and ten-
derness is the solicitude with which he guides her to Beth-
lehem, when "the fullness of time" has come! And who
can appreciate his mingled grief and humiliation, when the
City of David casts forth the Lamb of God in the cold mid-
night hour to be born in a cave by the roadside! And then
follows the touching story of the hurried flight to Egypt,
when Christ, the Hope of the world, and his humble Vir-
gin-Mother, are left, under God, to the care of this other
most true-hearted Joseph,—intrusted with a charge infi-

---

* "And the Ark of the Lord abode in the house of Obededom the Gethite
three months: and the Lord blessed Obededom and all his household."—2 *Kings,*
vi. 11.

nitely above the administration of the broad empire of the Pharaohs.

Can we wonder, that this man, so holy, so true, so hon-ored by God and his angels, who was the guardian of Christ, —the Head and Parent of regenerated humanity,—and of Mary, the type of the Church, should have been so rever-enced in all Christian lands, and that, in our own days, he should at length be solemnly proclaimed as the Guardian and Protector of the whole Christian family ?

We have, therefore, in the very first pages of the Gospel history set before our eyes that Holy Family,—as it has been called by the reverence of Catholic ages,—that most august household in which Emmanuel grew up from infancy to boyhood, from boyhood to modest and gracious manhood, subject all the while to his parents, both Mother and Child respecting in the Carpenter the divine seal of that fatherly authority, whose prototype and fountain-head is in the Eternal God.

Woman ever reverenced in Catholic Households.

There never has been, since Christianity began, a Catho-lic family in which Christ, his Mother, and his foster-father Joseph, have not been a reality most familiar to the mind and dear to the heart. Indeed, every household in Catholic lands has been modeled on this sacred home of Nazareth. The devotion of Joseph to Christ and his interests, his rev-erent service toward the blessed Mother and her Babe, his living faith and unquestioning trust in the all-directing providence of God,—have been the virtues proposed to the imitation of Christian husbands and fathers. Every man within these homes professed to reverence in wife, mother, and sister, the dear and lofty image of Mary's spotless ex-cellence. Nor, all through the countless hosts of chivalrous men, who professed to honor women, was there to be found one true man who had not been trained to imitate St. Joseph, and to reverence in all women Mary Immaculate, the sweet Mother of the children of God.

These men saw with their own eyes, that, in the women
of their families, "Goodness gave greatness, and greatness
worship." * And old Chaucer, toward the close of the
middle ages, gave expression not only to the heart of Cath-
olic England, but to that of all Christendom, when he
wrote:

> " For in reverence of the Heavens queene
> We ought to worship all women that beene,
> For of all creatures that ever wer yet, and borne,
> This wote ye well, a woman was the best . . .
> Wherefore me thinketh, if that we had grace,
> We oughten honor women in every place."

If such was the universal respect paid to women, so many
ages after the death of the Blessed Mother of God, and all
through heartfelt love for her who is also our sweet Mother,
—what, think you, must have been the love and worship
paid to her by the husband into whose hand and heart God
gave her to keep, to honor, to cherish ?

The Rule of Catholic Households.

It is impossible that any true Catholic man should think
deeply of these things, and make of the holy and elevating
sentiments they inspire, a guiding principle in his home-life,
without reverencing and worshiping his wife, the mother of
his children, the angel of his hearth and heart. It is quite
impossible, where true love in the husband is begotten and
hallowed by deep piety toward our Lord and his Blessed
Parents, that it should not be manifested in a chivalrous
devotion toward the wife and mother ; that his home
should not be blessed with noble children,—true " children
of God," ful of loving submission to father and mother,
and prompt to fulfill every duty of home-life and citizen-
ship.

Reverence for Women a Want of our Age.

Besides,—and this observation is not without its oppor-
tuneness at the present moment,—our Divine Solomon is

---

* Ben Johnson, "New Inn."

most anxious that we should find in the hidden and unfail-
ing treasures of instruction laid up for us in .the brief re-
cords of his own private home-life, what is most needful for
our own day and country.   Unfortunately, to very many
Catholic families, these treasuries of revealed truth are
like the magnificent reservoirs of Christ's great ancestor,
Solomon,—constructed so many ages before the Christian
era with such forethought and munificence, they are now
discovered, by English and American explorers, at the cost
of much money and labor.   ·Uncared for, unknown, hidden
away in Jerusalem, half-choked by ruins, or far away in
the neighboring mountains where the gigantic works are
scarce known to rulers or people,—are they not the lively
image of our own splendid birthright of truth, lying around
us and beneath our hand, while we cry out for the living
waters, and the land is desolate in its moral barrenness?

If families and communities in our nineteenth century
will only apply themselves to the study and imitation of
these God-given models of private holiness and public vir-
tue,—if all classes in society will only revive in their hearts
and homes and lives this threefold respect for God and His
Law, for parental authority, and for womanly purity,—we
need not fear the inflow of new ideas or the changes threat-
ened by political revolutions.

The Ideal Excellence of the Life at Nazareth most eminently practical.

The supernatural light vouchsafed in such abundance to
the Blessed Mother and her noble companion aimed at a
life of extraordinary and continual devotion and self-sacri-
fice in the cause of God's highest interests and of man's
salvation.   Their life-work was to be that of Christ.   They
were to be identified with Him, and their actions to be lost
in the splendor of his career,—just as the planets nearest
the sun, though sharing most in its warmth and bright-
ness, are lost in the surpassing effulgence caused by the
very nearness of the mighty luminary.

The obscurity, the apparently purposeless inactivity of
Christ's hidden life at Nazareth, was no mystery to Mary
and Joseph, how much soever it may puzzle the ration-
alists or half-Christian biblicists of our modern literature.
If our divine Model wished to mark out, by the deeds and
virtues of his brief public life, the road which apostolic
men in the church and statesmen in civil society should
be studious to follow,—He assuredly wished no less to
make of the long years spent beneath the roof of Joseph in
toil, poverty, obedience, and growth in all Godlike excel-
lence, a lesson to be taught and imitated by the weary and
heart-sore millions of the laborious poor.

His parents were enlightened from above to seize the di-
vine purpose both in the one and the other ;—and, just as
they set themselves with their whole hearts to study and
copy Christ in his long probationary humility and toil, so
did their inflamed love of the divine glory dispose them to
follow Him.

We can thus conceive, that both husband and wife in
that most blessed household, would encourage each other
to copy to the life all the excellences of the dear Model
they had ever before their eyes,—and even, were that ne-
cessary, exhort Him as he grew up beneath their care, to
run his own giant race of obedience and self-immolating
charity.   Such was the heroic Mother's purpose, when she
"stood" beneath Him in his terrible death-agony, and
with her most assuredly would have been present Joseph,
had he been then among the living, to support and cheer
both herself and her Son in the accomplishment of this
supreme act of comformity to the divine will.

Nearness to Christ in both these august personages,
meant, therefore, the closest fellowship with him in abne-
gation, suffering, and all magnanimity.   It meant, practi-
cally, the closest resemblance to Him whom they studied
more nearly, copied more faithfully, followed more devot-
edly than any of his dearest disciples.

Thus, in the three persons of the Holy Family, we have
the most perfect embodiment of purity ;—and purity, let us

not forget it, is always strength of soul, and the principle of heroism in action. And, as it is impossible to honor and to practice purity without reverencing and honoring woman, so the study of Christ's life at Nazareth and piety toward His Mother, begot throughout early and medieval Christendom, that spirit of chivalry which went hand in hand with the highest heroism in designing and accomplishing great things.

A reasonable curiosity which is not exclusively distinctive of scientific men, but belongs to all of us, leads to seeking out the sources of great rivers and gazing with wonder at the lake or the rivulet which is the head and wellspring of the mighty stream. So let us look for a moment at some of the sources in the household piety of Catholic nations, of the heroism, courtesy, and gentleness of manners which we couple with chivalry and the knightly enterprises it originated.

Hear Christian Spain through her Ildefonso of Toledo: "O my Lady, and my sovereign mistress, Mother of my Lord, handmaid of thy Son, parent of the world's Creator! I pray and beseech thee that I may have the spirit of thy Son, the spirit of my Redeemer, that I may think of thee true and worthy things, speak of thee true and worthy things, and utter whatever is most true and most worthy concerning thee.

"Yes, I desire to become the servant of the Mother of my God; and why I should desire this, they know who love God, they see who are faithful to God. . . . But not so ye, O wise of this world, who by your wisdom are made fools, and who reject this doctrine, who refuse to believe that she alone should have Him for Son, whom every creature hath for its Lord. But I, as the servant of her Son desire to have the testimony of submission to his Mother. Thereby, what serves the handmaid is referred to the Lord, what is shown to the parent redounds to the Child, what is paid to the Queen passes to the honor of the King.

"By this Virgin God has come, and having gathered together the nations and the languages, we have seen his glory as the glory of the only-begotten of the Father. We have flowed to Him from all people, we ascend to this Lord, to the mountain of the Lord, and to the house of the God of Jacob, which is the Church of the living God."*

To Love the Mother means to Love the Son.

And this tender and universal feeling toward the Mother of regenerated humanity only served to deepen the love felt for her Son. What St. Augustine wrote toward the close of the fourth century held true of all those which followed, while the reverence for the new Adam and the new Eve spread with the Church all over the world :

"To them who believe,"—the great Doctor says,—"the beautiful Spouse (Christ) is presented at every turn,—beautiful in heaven, beautiful on earth, beautiful in miracles, beautiful in sufferings, beautiful inviting to life, beautiful not heeding death, beautiful laying down life, beautiful receiving it back again, beautiful on the Tree, beautiful in the Sepulcher, beautiful in the celestial Kingdom. The weakness of the flesh does not turn aside their eyes from the splendor of that beauty."†

How Catholic Ages Meditated on the Heroic Deeds of Christ and His Mother.

In the days of Augustine and Monica, of St. Patrick, St. Bridget, and St. Ildefonso (died 667), it had become the custom for the Christians of both East and West to divide the Psalter into three divisions of fifty Psalms each, which they recited or chanted in public. But for the unlearned poor, and the multitudes who toiled in the city and country, in forest and field, far away from the churches, the sweet custom arose and spread of reciting the Psalter of the Incarnation or of the Blessed Virgin, consisting in repeating the Angelic Salutation fifty times in each division. And this

---

* *De Virginitate Sanctæ Mariæ.*   † *In Psalmum,* xliv.

they did in order to proclaim thereby their living, loving
faith in Him whom all the Psalms and other inspired writ-
ings foretell and proclaim as the Father of the world to
come, while they saluted at the same time with heartfelt
reverence the Mother whom they could not dissociate from
him in life or in death, on earth or in heaven.

Thus, in the age of St. Bede (the venerable), who died in
733, this manner of praying prevailed all throughout France
and England. "The beads used to be suspended with ven-
eration in churches and public places, for the accommoda-
tion of all who wished to use them. We read of St. Eloy
that for a certain devout lady he made a chair adorned with
one hundred and fifty gold and silver nails, that by the
signs of the nails she might repeat the Psalter of Blessed
Mary.*

This led step by step to what is known as the Rosary, a
most beautiful form of mental and vocal prayer, perfected
by St. Dominick in the thirteenth century, and which has
ever been so dear to all Catholic homes and hearts.

Chivalrous Zeal for the Spread of God's Kingdom.

So, all this sweet and devout thought of the mysteries of
Christ's life,—this familiar contemplation of the three great
figures of Jesus, Mary, and Joseph in the studied story of
our redemption, begot in souls, together with the love of
purity, reverence for woman, and a mighty desire to imitate
and glorify the Redeemer, by spreading his faith and his
reign in all lands.

Although the age of chivalry has passed away, and, it is
thought, the spirit which animated it has disappeared for
ever with the institution itself, yet the general favor shown
in our age for the works in prose and poetry which set forth
the glories of ancient knighthood,—would prove that this
spirit is still a living reality. Thank God, we know it to
be such wherever in the English-speaking world the beauti-

---

* Digby, "Compitum," book ii., ch. ix.

ful productions of the Bard of Chivalry * are still read with admiration by old and young.

Also to Purity as the Brightest Ornament of Chivalry.

The piety begotten by this daily meditation of the sublime mysteries of Christ's life and a familiar acquaintance with the heroic achievements of his apostles, martyrs, and principal saints, prompted men not only to become knights for the protection of female innocence and weakness,—for the defense of the Church and the recovery of the Holy Land from Islam, and for the extirpation of infidel and heretical rule,—but it also spurred men on to such enterprises as the recovery of the Holy Grail,† when lost by the sin of its keepers, and to the high and spotless purity which could alone enable one either to see or to recover it.

The virgin-knight, Sir Galahad, who is privileged to recover and possess the sacred treasure, is the youngest of the knights of the Round Table:

> " 'God made thee good as thou art beautiful,'
> Said Arthur, when he dubbed him knight."

Sir Percivale and his Saintly Sister.

A nun, the sister of Sir Percivale, himself a blameless youth, had risen to such a height of purity and holiness, by her fervor in expiating by voluntary austerity, the scandals she heard of in the outside world, that God also granted her to see the Holy Grail as it was borne away from its unworthy guardians at Glastonbury. Says her brother:

> " And so she prayed and fasted, till the sun shone,
> And the wind blew through her, and I thought
> She might have risen and floated when I saw her.

---

* Tennyson: see his " Idyls of the King."

† The Holy Grail (French, *Sangréal*, or *Sang réel*, the very blood of our Lord), was, in the Arthurian poetry, supposed to be the Cup which our Lord used in the Last Supper, and in which Joseph of Arimathea had collected the drops of blood which fell from Christ on the Cross.

> . . . Behold her eyes
> Beyond my knowing of them, beautiful,
> Beyond all knowing of them, wonderful,
> Beautiful in the light of holiness."

So this saintly girl, anxious only to stir up in chosen heroic souls the spirit of purity and self-sacrifice as a remedy to the social poison that was leavening souls in the world, chooses Sir Galahad for her champion,—the one destined to recover the Holy Grail, the palladium of England's Christianity. She binds his sword around him with a belt she has made herself :

> "Saying, 'My Knight, my love, my Knight of heaven,
> O'thou, my love, whose love is one with mine,
> I, maiden, round thee, maiden, bind my belt.
> Go forth ! for thou shalt see what I have seen,
> And break through all, till One will crown thee King
> Far in the spiritual city :' and as she spake
> She sent the deathless passion in her eyes
> Through him, and made him hers, and laid her mind
> On him, and he believed in her belief."

Such was their conception, in these ages of faith, of the purity which adorned the souls of Joseph and Mary, of the ardor which such holy wife could breathe into the soul of such holy husband, of the unearthly love which bound them together in promoting the interests of God and His Christ : such the spirit in which one might imagine Mary addressing holy Joseph and sending him forth to "see what she has seen," and to endure and brave all labor and suffering, in following their common Lord and Love.

This Pure Spirit fruitful in Great Men and Women.

What marvel that such popular belief and piety begat so many great men and women in every Christian land ? Take that great nation, which for eight hundred years was ever in arms against the domineering Mohammedan,—Spain.

"Having great examples of virtue in their Catholic kings and princes,"—says a writer who knew them well,—"the

Spaniards in general live in a most Christian manner. For they observe justice ; they observe the precepts of the Church ; they assist at the divine offices ; they hear sermons ; they venerate priests ; they respect elders ; they love their friends ; they injure no one ; they console the afflicted ; they assist the needy ; they show the right way to those who are wandering from it ; they admonish sinners ; they pardon the penitent ; they keep faith, love the studious, and hate the wicked :—therefore do I prefer Spain to other countries. For I am delighted with the admirable morals of the Spaniards, with their singular urbanity, their noble customs, not alone those of the knights and priests, but also of peasants and husbandmen."*

The Country Population in Spain Uncontaminated.

Nor,—much as the systematic introduction of Voltairian skepticism and the prevalence in the cities of revolutionary doctrines have affected Spanish institutions and manners,— has the mass of the Spanish people been robbed of ancestral faith and piety by the successive social and political revolutions.

Do not think, because the stream, as it flows by the crowded city or skirts the great centers of industry, becomes polluted by the manifold impurities poured into it, that its waters have been contaminated throughout their entire course and even in their well-springs.

We have only to go

" Away from city, smoke, and sin,
Unto the solitude wherein
The happy stream is born,"

and we may be sure that there we shall find the air pure, the crystal fountain stainless, and all around peace and purity.

" Hither the sunshine cometh not,
But leafy branches shade the spot
Where sleeps the baby stream ;

* Marinus Siculus, *De Rebus Hispanicis*, lib. **v.**

And here with folded wings Love lies,—
We feel his breathing, and our eyes
Meet in a happy dream.

"There, looking down upon its face,
We watch the water in the place
From whence it singing flows,
And picture sweetly, while we rest,
A little Naiad in a nest,
Where the wild lily blows." *

Catholic Home-Life Surviving in Protestant Countries.

We may well console ourselves, in view of the dangers with which society and religion are at present threatened, in reflecting that home-education in every Catholic land, is still based on this venerated ideal of our fathers,—the home-life of Nazareth. Even in countries, which regard with undisguised hatred not only the authority of the Church, but the very name of Catholic,—the ancient virtues and traditions of Catholic home-life still continue to be cherished. That is a mercy of Him who is Father over all the families of nations, and who, having "made them for health, . . . there is no poison of destruction in them," † for which he has not prepared an antidote in his own good time. No! the power of evil is not unlimited ; nor is the reign of the Enemy of God and man to endure forever.

A Noble National Character.

Surely we have seen enough of these blessed homes on both sides of the great ocean, not to feel secure of the future, even though the present be full of doubt, and danger, and fear. The greatest man ever born in Ireland, Edmund Burke, wrote at the close of the last century: "The Castilians have still remaining a good deal of their old character, their *gravidad* (dignity of deportment), *leal-*

---

* " Wayside Poesies "

† Wisdom, i. 14. *Creavit enim, ut essent omnia : et sanabiles fecit nationes orbis terrarum : et non est in illis medicamentum exterminii, nec inferorum regnum in terra.*

dad (loyalty), and *il timor de Dios* (the fear of God)." This is more true even of other provinces of Spain than of Castile. It is true of the whole rural population from sea to sea. And these noble characteristic features,—the lofty self-respect and dignified courtesy, the steadfast loyalty to God, country, and honor, that fear of God which is not the abject servility of superstition, but the enlightened sentiment of that Majesty which rules and judges the whole earth,—all that comes from the intimate knowledge and daily practice of these great principles that guided blessed Joseph in Nazareth, and still form the living law for every Spanish father of a family in Europe or America.

What we most need in our day are men conscientiously and invincibly attached to principle,—God-fearing, self-respecting, nobly independent while reverencing the rights of others,—incapable of betraying their conscience, their trust, or their honor ; men uniting to the vigor of body inherited from chaste and temperate ancestors and sustained by personal virtue, to the strength of soul which true piety begets,—that dignified and gentle courtesy which is only the flower and perfume of Christian charity.

Catholic faith, Catholic piety, Catholic home-life begat such a nation of men in glorious Spain during her long struggle with the Moor. If the national character degenerated, and with it declined the national greatness,—it was because other principles and another life, hostile to their ancestral faith, penetrated like the miasms of a plague into Spanish homes, and tainted there the atmosphere which Christian purity and piety ever generate.

How to Preserve and Improve National Virtues.

Would you see, among the Spanish race at home and abroad, the old domestic virtues flourish anew, and with them revive the pristine glories of the proudest nation of Christendom ? Leave Religion free to set up the ideal we have been describing, and men free to make it a living reality in their homes and their public conduct!

We Catholics, by our degenerate lives, are responsible for much of the evil which at present afflicts both Religion and Society. The sole remedy against its increase lies in our honoring the faith of our fathers by living up to its precepts and teachings, to the high ideal which it holds up to our imitation and to the noblest of household examples.

> " Good alone is good without a name,
>   And this breeds honor : that is honor's scorn
>   Which challenges itself as honor's born,
>   And is not like the sire : honors best thrive
>   When rather from our acts we them derive
>   Than our fore-goers. The mere word 's a slave
>   Debauch'd on every tomb ; on every grave
>   A lying trophy."

CHAPTER XII.

PATERNAL AUTHORITY AND HOME EDUCATION

He that honoreth his father shall enjoy a long life;
And he that obeyeth the father shall be a comfort to his mother.
He that feareth tne Lord honoreth his parents,
And as his masters will serve them that brought him into the world.

Ecclesiasticus, iii. 7, 8.

What principally strikes the observer who studies the civilization of China, and what is in reality its distinctive feature, is the preponderance of paternal authority. Indeed, this authority is the chief tie of the family, the fundamental basis of government and laws, and the very soul of religion itself. It preserves domestic harmony, feeds the spirit of obedience toward the public authorities, and hallows both the memory of ancestors and the popular respect for traditions.

Filial piety is in China, what the love of freedom was in Greece, what love of country was in Rome, and what the religious sentiment was in the Middle Ages.—M. L. DONNAT.*

THE mightiest rivers on the surface of the globe have their source in the highest mountain solitudes, most frequently in the vast snow-fields which furnish them perennial waters. The ancient traditions of India will have it that the sacred streams of the Indus and the Ganges rise at the very foot of the mountains that are nearest heaven and the dwelling place of the gods.

So is it with all authority most revered among men, with every institution from which human life and society derive power, happiness, and stability. One has to go back to the cradle of humanity to find their certain origin ;—their sanction must come immediately from Heaven itself

The beginnings of these venerable customs and institutions of the vast Chinese Empire, if traced back conscientiously from century to century, would lead us to the very

* *Ouvriers des Deux Mondes,* vol. iv., p. 116.

age of Noe and his sons: the traditions on which repose the ancestral worship of China, the religion and moral life of the nation and of every home within it, are thus found to be anterior to Moses and his law, anterior even to Abraham and that Chaldæan corruption from which the great patriarch fled.

Thus we can appreciate how ancient and universal was the wisdom enunciated by the Son of Sirach ·

" He that feareth the Lord honoreth his parents,
  And as his masters will serve them that brought him into the world."

That fear, full of reverence, submission, and love, which, before the deluge, formed the religion of Seth and Henoch flowed on through the breasts of Noe and Sem, to be the religion of the renovated human family. It was the law of nature, as immutable as the Eternal God,—that reverence, honor, and love for the Father in Heaven, should be the source of the respect, obedience, and affection which we are bound to show to our parents. Do away with "the fear of the Lord" in the hearts of children, and the home will become a ruin. Let religion and filial piety disappear from the majority of homes of a nation, and you can safely predict its extinction. Just as the vast regions watered by the Indus, the Ganges, the Amazon, and the Mississippi, would soon become a barren and uninhabited wilderness, if their sources in the mountains should fail, because the winds of heaven ceased to bring there either rainfall or snow.

It is then of unspeakable importance that this paternal authority, God-given as it is, fundamental as it must be regarded in human society, should be thoroughly understood and most religiously upheld and reverenced.

Were Christians to forget either its origin or its claims they would be reminded of both by pagans and Mohammedans. Thank God, there is one great society one everpresent and unerring authority, which can never cease to reutter the divine precept, "Honor thy father and thy mother," and to explain its significance and scope to the nations.

15

Divine Origin of Paternal Authority.

It is, then, the sentiment of the Church that the father in the family derives his authority not from the State, but immediately from God himself. The family was before the State, which owes its existence and derives its powers immediately from the people or the association of families and individuals who compose the people, and ultimately only from God.

By no human law or legislator can the authority of the father over his children, and the duties essential to his office, be done away with, confiscated, or superseded. It is the interest of civil society and of its legislators to lend their aid to the divine and natural law in this. Our lawgivers, our magistrates, our voters would only be playing into the hands of the socialists, communists, and levelers, by trenching on the father's legitimate authority within his own household, instead sanctioning by their enactments its rights and protecting its free exercise.

Let us once more repeat it here,—to abridge in the family the father's authority over his children, or to weaken in any way the unity and indissolubility of the marriage tie,—is to move the foundations of the earth !

With this warning we dismiss, for the present at least, this portion of our subject, and proceed to show what is the extent of parental jurisdiction, and what is the corresponding obligation of the father, or, in his stead, of the mother. The reader, of course, will understand us to speak here of education.

Education, the Parent's indefeasible Right.

One of the first injunctions laid on the great Christian Society of Ephesus, was, " Children, obey your parents in the Lord ; for this is just;" * and then the Great Apostle rehearses the Mosaic precept, continuing thus:

---

* Ephesians, vi. 1.

"And you, fathers, provoke not your children to anger; but bring them up in the discipline and correction of the Lord."

With regard to the first part of this injunction, we have said what is abundantly sufficient in the preceding chapter. There is no more certain safeguard against a parent's provoking his children to anger,—to all the rebellious and passionate discontent which an oppressive use of authority creates,—than the wise, gentle, patient, all-embracing love, and firm discipline described there. We have now to insist on the "bringing up in the discipline and correction of the Lord,"—that is, on the duty of education,—Christian education, as is evident from the very words of the apostle.

And now, dear reader, do not be alarmed at this beginning, as if we meant to inflict on your patience a long lecture or sermon on the training of childhood and youth. What we have to say is exceedingly practical, and had better, therefore, be said briefly. It is also exceedingly important, and must be said clearly. At any rate we shall do our best to tell pleasantly a tale so often told, and requiring, nevertheless, perpetual and conscientious repetition.

The object which the great Christian apostle had in view in insisting upon bringing up children "in the discipline and correction of the Lord,"—was, undoubtedly, the formation in them of habits of supernatural virtue,—such virtue having its standard of excellence in the life and teaching of Christ.

This,—as being in reality Christian education,—is to be most carefully distinguished from mere instruction in letters or in worldly knowledge. Our remarks, in this chapter, shall apply to both the one and the other,—keeping very distinct before the mind of the reader, the parent's office in forming the character and molding the soul to Christ-like goodness, from the function of training the mind to the acquisition of knowledge and science.

The author, during many years of his life, has been occupied in the duty of teaching; he is, therefore, deeply impressed with the importance of the teacher's functions at all times, and especially in his own age and country. He has also been all his life a keen student, seeking to complete the early knowledge given him in one of the foremost institutions in America, by serious studies undertaken in advanced manhood—undertaken, too, with the purpose of benefiting American youth. He will not, then, be suspected of undervaluing modern methods or their results, or of holding cheap the science of the age, the ripest fruits of which he has sought so laboriously in the best schools of both hemispheres.

Of scientific and literary studies he will treat after he has said here what a long experience and deep conviction urge him to say on education proper, as distinguished from instruction.

What Education is.

Under the Christian religion, man, regenerated by baptism, is taught that the entire race is called in Christ to a supernatural destiny, through the profession of a supernatural faith, the practice of supernatural virtues, and the use of divine ordinances, that are supernatural in their aims and effects. It is the sacred and indispensable duty of every Christian father to live up to this belief himself, and to see to it that his children are educated up to it.

On this point the Church has spoken clearly, emphatically, definitely: so, there is no room for questioning her mind and purpose thereon. We only insist on it here, because, in our own country, as elsewhere, the right and duty of the parent are made to conflict with what is called the right of the State. Let it suffice that the same St. Paul has said elsewhere: * "If any man have not care of his own, and especially of those of his house, he hath denied the faith, and is worse than an infidel." Is it not a confirmation of the charge given so many ages before that to the fathers in Israel, "Lay up these my words in your hearts and minds, and hang them for a sign on your hands, and place them between your eyes. Teach your children that.

---

* 1 Timothy, v. 8.

they meditate on them "?* And again, at a period much nearer the Christian era, "Hast thou children? Instruct them, and bow down their [neck] from their childhood." †

The Christian generation of the nineteenth century believe and affirm that it is their right and their duty to form their children from infancy to the knowledge of "the truth as it is in Christ Jesus," and to the perfect imitation of his virtues. The injunctions of the apostle, and the Divine Will revealed and declared through him, they believe to be addressed not to the State or the civil magistrate, but to every father in his place and office as head and master in his household. The obligation of seeing to it that parents do comply with this duty, has been imposed on those whom "the Holy Ghost hath placed . . . bishops, to rule the church of God," and in a special manner on him who is, under Christ, Shepherd of the whole flock, and whose office it is to feed both the lambs and the sheep. The maintenance and development of Christian life, as such, is the care of the Christian Society, the Church,—not of the Civil Society, only in so far as the Church requires and accepts its coöperation.

So much for the duty of the parent in Christian education,—as well as its correlative, the right to educate. As to its exercise, we need not say much. It is the province of the mother to train and to form,—it is that of the father to sustain and aid her with the whole weight of his authority and sympathy. Where both parents are true practical Christians, united in mind and heart in this the most essential part of their work,—though they may not have much of worldly learning or worldly means,—they will be sure to bring up their children well.

As, however, we devote a special chapter to "Education in the home of the laboring man and the unlettered,"—we must now give some practical advice on parental duty in directing or superintending the education of children both in the home or in institutions outside the home.

---

* Deuteronomy, xi. 19.　　　　† Ecclesiasticus, vii. 25.

I. *Home Education.*

Where the atmosphere of the home is pure and healthful to soul and body,—though it may be neither the abode of wealth nor that of culture,—its influence on the spiritual growth of the child is most salutary. For both the interior and the exterior man may grow to all goodness and loveliness even in the cottage of the field-laborer, the shepherd, or the peasant, as we read of David growing up beneath the roof of Jesse, of the Blessed Peter Favre developing all his most amiable and most admirable qualities of soul while pasturing the flocks of his father and uncle on the mountains of Savoy,—like the exquisite and sweet-scented flowers of his native Alpine solitudes, unfolding all their loveliness amid barren crags and perpetual snows.*

Nothing can ever wholly take the place of the blessed and manifold influences which the daily words and actions of father and mother, their very bearing and manners, and the mysterious but all-powerful action of the very air that good people breathe, exercise on the children that grow up around them. The earth retains throughout the longest and severest winter, even when all is covered with deep snow, some portion of the vital heat received from the sun in summer; and we know that, even after the sun has set and during all the hours of the darkest night, the air retains the most precious qualities of what is called diffused light; and thus beneath the frost and the snow will the germs of all the earth's beauty and wealth continue to bide the return of spring; thus, too, through the midnight darkness all living things in field and forest will continue to grow till dawn once more brings back the sun.

We have, at the moment we write, one of these obscure, laborious, but most blessed homes quite near us, where the children, amid the silent, gentle, but most powerful influence of their parents' and grand-parents' homely virtues and

---

* See in "The Life of the Blessed Peter Favre" (London, 1873), the early training of one of the greatest men of the sixteenth century.

example, all grow up to that upright, innocent, and honorable type of manhood and womanhood, that so vividly brings before us the dear homes of another land. Yes, yes, —there is a teaching more eloquent than the lessons of the most accomplished masters and mistresses, an education more congenial to man's higher nature, more beneficial to the growth of every faculty of soul and every power of body, than all the book-learning and all the scientific gymnastics of the schools.

It is not that we do not prize the latter at its very highest worth, but that we consider the influence and training of a father and a mother in whom the Spirit of God dwells, and who bring up their dear ones according to the instincts of that Spirit, to be the sole mighty agency of nature, mightily seconded by nature's God, for the unfolding of all that is noblest in the human soul.

The Home-Formation prepares the Substance of the Soul.

This first education of the child in the paternal home, is one that lays the foundation of all future greatness; just as the neglect of such education, or a perverse and vicious one, is the source of all the failures, the misery, the guilt, and ruin of after-life. This first formation (*creation* the old Catholic language termed it) gives to the soul its "grit," as well its shape: it never loses either the mold or the temper then imparted to it. Like the magnificent Japanese vases seen at our Centennial Exposition, the exquisite designs, wrought, after the casting of the vase, into its substance, or the no less marvelously beautiful scenes inlaid on the bronze itself in gold or silver or color, are the work of an artist other than the potter. Thus the first formation of the soul and the character in the home and by the creative influence of the parents and of the whole atmosphere around them,—is like the casting of the vase. It gets its form, its molding in these early years;—the second education of the schools, and the final education in the world amid professional business and the battle of life, may be compared to the designing, the inlaying, the enameling, the chasing, and the coloring bestowed on the molded form to make it in every way perfect and admirable. This extraordinary wealth of ornamentation, however, is only lavished on vessels made of the best materials. Where the metal is base, or where there is a flaw, the artist will not attempt to carry out elaborate and costly designs, for the imperfect or unworthy vessel will not bear them.

At any rate, the action of virtuous and intelligent parents, during this first process of education, may be most aptly likened to the hidden, slow, but wonderful action of nature in forming the most precious marbles or the rarest gems; the marbles of Paros and Carrara, out of which Art has fashioned its masterpieces, are composed of the same substance as the commonest limestone, just as the diamond is identical in composition with pure coal or charcoal. By the action of laws, whose secret is known to the Divine Author of all things,—the beautiful marble is prepared by the hand of nature and made ready for the hand of the sculptor, just as the diamond is crystallized in Nature's own secret laboratory, where no human eye has ever witnessed the process, and laid up for the skill of the jeweler to polish and to set it.

We repeat it, the influence and the action of the best of parents in forming the soul and life of their dear ônes, is in accordance with the laws of nature, with His will who is its creator and lawgiver; it is therefore strictly natural; and even in following the higher impulses of supernatural grace, this formation does not cease to be natural in the full and comprehensive sense in which the Christian philosopher understands it.

This formation makes the marble marble, and not lime; makes the diamond diamond, and not coal-dust. The soul of the child receives therefrom its quality and its form; the education which follows only gives polish, design, ornament, and setting.

Infinite Reverence due to Children.

Hence, parents cannot be too careful and wary in all that relates to the early training of their children. There is not an action, a word, a tone, a look, that is not observed by these wonderfully attentive little eyes; and not a thing observed that is not remembered for a time at least. Every thing in the parents influences these sensitive plants; every thing in the home,—its comfort or discomfort, its cleanliness or uncleanness; the pictures on the walls, the very furniture and its arrangement, all exercise a subtle but most undoubted action on the senses of these tender ones. Like the self-registering instruments of our observatories, they receive and retain impressions made by all the phenomena of earth and air; and because these impressions act upon the secret springs of nature in the soul, life's center, the action produces results that are permanent, sometimes everlasting.

Indeed, it is because the soul of man partakes of the nature of the Infinite and Eternal, that parents should be so solicitous about every teaching and every impression given to their infant children. It is ascertained that there are trees in our American forests that live for upward of a thousand years; the English yew tree lives longer than this, and we know not but others may be endowed with still greater longevity. Thus the impression made on one of these saplings, the twist given to it, the mark set upon it, will remain forever on the tree's substance, and outlive in duration kingdoms and empires.

Your child's soul is destined to outlive the sun in the heavens, to live with God, sharing His life, His glory, His bliss throughout all the unimagined countless cycles of eternity. This is elementary Christian truth. There is not an impression you make on the soul of your babe,—for good or for evil,—that is not of itself destined to be everlasting. There is not a direction or inclination your teaching or your neglect gives to that tender soul, but will persist beyond the grave. There is no lesson of yours, no matter how imparted,—by words, or actions, or the influence of your life and your home,—but is of infinite importance to your child's welfare, of eternal consequence to its greatness here and hereafter. We say "hereafter,"—for it is only in the Eternal City that man attains to the full perfection of manhood. Eternal life is the autumn of humanity, the golden season of maturity and perpetual fruition.

What Seeds should be sown in Young Hearts.

When, therefore, you, O Father, encourage and aid your wife, in every way that your countenance, coöperation, and sympathy can, in sowing in your child's heart the first seeds of generosity, self-denial, devotion to the welfare and happiness of others,—the early love and fear of God, the sense of duty and inflexible honor, the horror of all that is untruthful, hypocritical, and time-serving; you are sowing seeds of immortality.

> "I wonder did you ever count
>   The value of one human fate;
> Or sum the infinite amount
>   Of one heart's treasures, and the weight
> Of Life's one venture, and the whole
> Concentrate purpose of a soul." *

We have seen gardeners in France, where common wine is so plenty, employ it to water certain favorite plants, because the generous liquid imparts to the flowers a richer hue. We have heard of persons in tropical climates injecting the living tree with some deep coloring matter, in order that such precious woods as mahogany might by this process receive a deeper and more beautiful tint. Indeed, modern chemistry has found means of injecting the veins of wood employed in certain important constructions with a liquid that will prevent the wood from decaying and crumbling away.

---

* Adelaide Anne Procter.

All these industries of the gardener, the merchant, and the mechanic, will help a thoughtful parent to understand what undying and varied beauty, what priceless qualities of mind and heart, what immortal vigor and virtue,—can be imparted to the soul of a child by the careful and con scientious culture of father and mother,—by HOME-EDU-CATION.

Special Advice to Fathers.

We must not repeat here the instructions given to mothers on this important subject.* As, however, the father's au thority is paramount in the family, and as he before all and above all is responsible for the vicious education given in the household, we are bound to direct his attention to some few points of no little moment.

Let him see to it that there be in the house neither pic-tures, statues, nor books, unworthy of meeting the eye of innocent childhood and chaste-souled youth. Parents too often need to be reminded that the first and incomparably the most essential purity, is that of the soul—of the mind, memory, and imagination. So many young people of both sexes grow up around us to beautiful manhood and woman-hood without ever having had a thought or a suspicion of evil cross their mind or fancy! One feels, in presence of these spotless souls, as if one beheld an angel descended from Paradise, surrounded with an atmosphere of heavenly light and fragrance.

There is no father, who in his heart of hearts does not most devoutly wish that his little sons and daughters may grow up in this ignorance of all that can stain soul or body, as well as in the knowledge and practice of all the virtues and graces, that can make innocence itself tenfold attractive and powerful for good. Innocence is the virgin gold without alloy or blemish ; the added virtues and graces are the exquisite form given to the gold, the chaste designs and enameling that embellish, and the gems that enrich it. The soul thus kept pure, and then perfected by every

* See " The Mirror of True Womanhood."

manly or womanly virtue, and further adorned by all the
graces and accomplishments of education,—is a vessel into
which God may pour His Spirit, and which He may use for
all His most gracious purposes.   •

No Vile Pictures or Books in the Home.

It behooves, therefore, every enlightened father to ban-
ish from his house the vile pictures and the still more vile
literature of the day.   It is one of the deep schemes of the
atheistical and social revolutionists of our times, to publish
in the cheapest and most attractive forms books of every
description aiming at implanting corruption both in the
mind and in the heart of the popular masses,—of boys and
girls, particularly.

There are works of fiction written in the most enchanting
form, every one of which is based on some theory hostile
to religion, subversive of conjugal fidelity, of filial piety and
parental authority, and illustrated by romantic incidents
that are as sure to deaden or to kill innocence in the soul,
as slow doses of arsenic or strychnine are certain to destroy
within a given time the life of the body.

The revolutionists of Europe showed a diabolical skill in
conveying into the homes of the people whom they wished
to dechristianize and corrupt before they made them ripe
for insurrection, these antichristian and antisocial romances
at a mere nominal price, and these cheap and exquisitely
illustrated works in which all that was most sacred was
caricatured, and all that had hitherto been deemed pure and
chaste was profaned and defiled. .

Deadly Influence of Bad Books in France.

We remember, at Laval and Amiens, in France, to have
watched on Saturday evenings, young working-men and
women forming long files before some cheap book-store,
where these productions were sold or lent for a mere trifle,
to be taken home and fed upon for several days or the en-

tire ensuing week,—filling the whole soul with the intoxi-
cating fumes of the rankest impiety and the most unblush-
ing licentiousness. We knew then what fruits would come
of this devil's husbandry; and has not France reaped them?
and are they not, at this moment, preparing to gather
another harvest of civil strife, social convulsion, and anti-
christian hatred, such as, perhaps, the world has never yet
seen?

French Novels the Soul's Poison.

Is it not notorious that French novels, and indeed, the
whole of the lighter literature of France, breathe a spirit
deadly to the souls of the readers and to all the virtues on
which, in our midst till now, family happiness and purity
were founded? One thing of late has filled us with equal
astonishment and alarm,—that our most distinguished pub-
lishing houses should so far forget their own high position,
the esteem in which they were held by the public, and the
reverence they owed both to the religion they profess and
the morality of Christian families,—as to translate and cir-
culate the infinitely dangerous productions of Georges Sand
and the most seductive French and German novelists.
Surely this is worse than the crime attributed, rightly or
wrongly, to a fanatical partisan during our late civil war,
who purchased abroad in every center of pestilential dis-
ease, the garments of the dead victims, imported and scat-
tered them among our most populous cities, that a multi-
plicity of plagues might effect what armies could not on
the battle-field,—the ruin of our people.

Guilt incurred in Circulating them.

These publishing houses themselves are loud in condemn-
ing our "Dime Novels" and filthy illustrated papers.
But we do not hesitate to affirm, that beneath the enchant-
ing style of the pestilential works of fiction which they
popularize in our midst, a worse poison is prepared for the
unsuspecting mind of youth,—than in the worst of "Dime

Novels." Each is a curse to our people ; the French novel a tenfold curse to our American homes with their traditional beliefs and noble ancestral virtues. And will the propagation of this curse among the Christian families and chaste youth of America, bring a blessing on the publishers, or on those who lend their pens to the vile work of translation ?

It is for fathers of families,—the God-fearing men whom this book will reach,—to exclude these poisonous and pestilential books from their homes. This rigorous exclusion becomes, at present, more than ever necessary. For it has of late become the fashion to issue in the cheapest form the most attractive books in the whole range of English literature. Of these "Libraries," as they are designated, some may be more free from objection than others ; but, for indiscriminate use, in the hands of young people, of children especially, all are most objectionable.

Keep them out of your children's hands,—keep them out of your homes.

Some of our Catholic publishers, anxious to provide an antidote as cheap and as attractive to the taste as the poisonous intellectual food of these "libraries,"—are publishing popular and cheap editions of the masterpieces of Catholic writers. May God prosper their enterprise, and increase a hundred-fold their own means of doing good !

Danger of promiscuous Newspaper reading.

The same precautions and watchfulness should be used by Christian parents, in a very great measure, in the choice of newspapers and periodicals. We are not afraid that any truly enlightened journalist shall take us to task upon this subject. No parent,—we would venture to affirm,—could be more strict in excluding from his home and from the hands of his children, both the vile literature we have been describing, and the indiscriminate use of the daily and periodical productions of the Press,—than several distinguished journalists well known to us. Newspapers are only for men engaged in the active business of the world. *They* take from the columns of the daily journal what is to their own immediate purpose, and let the rest go. Third or fourth-rate politicians alone find in editorial disquisitions the intellectual food they crave for. But children and young people are not politicians. And may their good angels long keep them out of the miry paths of politics!

Besides,—there is no worse school for the mind than our daily papers. The cheap and very imperfect knowledge to be found there on such a multiplicity of subjects, only taxes the memory, without exercising the intellect and the judgment. The superficial learning thus easily acquired, will prevent a man from applying himself seriously to methodical study. What such learners gain in surface they lose in depth. They never attain to real science on any subject. There is a worse injury done to the mind than this,—it is to unfix its firmest beliefs and notions, to leave it without strong convictions or lofty principles. For, it is very hard for a young man to read, day after day, misrepresentations of his baptismal faith and the dearest objects of his veneration; to see the principles he has been taught to consider as immovable as the foundations of the earth, laughed at as superannuated, or absurd, or illusory, without finding all firm ground of respect and belief swept from beneath him.

Let parents believe us, then,—the later in life their sons betake them to reading much of the newspapers, the better for their minds, their hearts, and their fortune, as well!

Be your Sons' Companions.

This is the proper place for recommending to fathers to make themselves the companions of their grown-up sons. Of the watchfulness to be exercised by a good mother in order to keep her boys from dangerous associations, the author has written at length in another work,* and he earnestly requests fathers to ponder seriously the advice there

* See "The Mirror of True Womanhood," chapters xiv. and xv., pages 217-290.

given. It is so desirable that both parents should be guided
in this vital matter, by the same rules! As we have already
said, it must be the father's delight as well as his duty to
make the mother's will the supreme law in this respect.

But we find it impossible to turn our back on this part of
our subject, without again beseeching every father who
takes up this book, to make every effort, every sacrifice of
his own rest, and comfort, in order to make his sons and
daughters find at home all the amusement and recreation
they need, and in order, as well, to share all the out-door
amusements of his grown-up children.

Dearest reader, whoever you are, we suppose you to have
nothing in this world so much at heart, as the making of
your own home the sweet paradise to which you long to
come back, whenever business or duty keeps you away for
a time, and out of which you never go without regretting
the necessity that impels you. Is it not to have one such a
sweet spot on earth that you have labored late and early? Is
not the creation of such a true home—a true heart-rest—the
reward you most covet for all your labors and trials on this
side of the grave? Then do your utmost to make your
home to be for your sons and daughters what it is for you,
the center of all their thoughts, affections, and longings.

Beware of Bad Companions.

One poor young man's terrible fate brings, after many
years, before our mind the blissful interior of such a home,
and the tragic consequences of slighting a parent's admoni-
tions about loose companions.

The victim in this sad domestic tragedy was in his twen-
ty-first year,—the son of a man who had begun by being a
hod-carrier, then a journeyman mason, then a builder on
his own account, and finally a most successful speculator in
real estate, but in every stage of his business a man fearing
God, self-reliant, of equal integrity and business capacity,
honored and trusted by all who knew him, and ever the
modest, unobtrusive man he had been from his early youth.

He had made for himself and his five children just such a little home-paradise as you would expect the true Christian, without pretension or love of display, but with abundant means and natural good taste, to create for himself. No one knew how much of comfort, of goodness, of happiness, and native refinement there was in that "nest of a house," but those who partook of its hospitality, and they were not many.

The two oldest sons had been successively associated with the father in his own thriving business, had been most happily married, and had gone forth from beneath the parental roof to found homes in every way most like their mother's, coming back weekly to her to spend the Sunday's rest in the sunshine of her own delighted smile and her husband's proud affection. The youngest boy,—perhaps over-petted by his parents because he was the youngest, had asked to be sent to college, and had finished with credit his collegiate course. On returning to his parents, he seemed to weary of the quiet of their home-life,—and, if the truth must be told,—of the companionship of his parents and of his brothers and sisters. He had formed a friendship with a college companion, belonging to a family much superior to his own in social position,—and, in spite of the anxious entreaties of his mother and the indignant remonstrances of his father, he spent most of his free time in this friend's company, and accepted even an invitation to pass several weeks with him on a shooting excursion.

This young gentleman, the other, of course, invited to his father's house on their return. The beautiful young daughter of the house, the twin-sister of our collegian, struck the fancy of the fashionable and well-born friend, and the latter at once resolved to make a conquest of her. He was handsome, witty, accustomed to the best society, and played and sang charmingly. The artless girl was smitten by all these accomplishments as well as by the marked attention the young visitor paid her. This happened on the very first night. But both parents, warned by their secret instincts, did not invite their son's friend to return, and lost no time

16

in telling their son with all due precaution and tenderness,
—that the young gentleman's companionship was one they
did not wish for him, and that his intimacy in the family
was most undesirable. Had there been no other reason for
this than the patronizing airs of their late visitor, the hon-
orable self-respect of the parents would not submit to be
looked down upon by anybody. Besides, the young man
was known to be fast, and that was a sufficient motive to
cut off their family from all intercourse with him.

Unfortunately their son was blind to all these reasons,
and deaf to their entreaties, and he had already begun to
turn his sister's head about the conquest she had made of his
wealthy and much-admired friend. The latter, presuming
on this friendship, renewed his visits as well as his attentions
to the now conscious and fascinated girl ; and the visits be-
came so frequent and the attention so marked that the fa-
ther felt himself bound to tell his visitor, that he could
not permit him to continue his intercourse with a family so
much inferior to his own in social position. He therefore re-
quested him to abstain from anything like attention to his
daughter, since an alliance between the families was not to
be thought of.

The other was not to be put off in this way. The father
had spoken plainly to him, and he resented his interference
as an insult to his own family pride, resolving to punish the
parent in the child. He had a zealous ally in the girl's
brother, and through him kept up a clandestine correspon-
dence with her. The girl's infatuation was natural enough,
beset as she was by secret professions of love on the part
of the false friend, and by the guilty persuasions of her
brother. She had a conscience, however ; and deemed her-
self bound to tell all to her mother, laying before her the
letters she had received. Thereupon the honest mason
sought the young gentleman's father and laid the whole
matter before him. He had no desire, he said, that any of
his children should wed outside of their own condition. He
was anxious to secure for his daughter, the virtuous and
industrious son of a man like himself, who had been the

architect of his own fortunes and belonged to his own Church. Any other would only create division, discomfort, and unhappiness in his family.

Meanwhile, the two young men had gone out fishing together, in order to console each other on the untoward opposition their plans met with, and to devise some means of thwarting it. They drank freely all day, and were returning homeward at dusk, when some ill-natured allusion of the half-tipsy lover to the insolence of wealthy shoeblacks and hod-carriers, stirred up his companion's blood. Hot words were bandied, and blows were exchanged, and in the scuffle the boat was upset, but not before the mason's son had received in falling a blow on the temple which rendered him insensible. Neither of the young men could swim ; the senseless man sank to the bottom ; while the other barely saved his own life by clinging to the rudder of the upset boat till fishermen at a short distance came to the rescue. But the unfortunate companion, in the interval, had sunk and come to the surface repeatedly, and now was to be found no more. When, after much exertion, the body was recovered, all life had been long extinct.

And so, into that family which had never known sorrow or sin, late at night, the fishermen carried the dead undutiful son, destroyed in the full flower of his youth, because he would choose his own companions, and be wiser, better than the parents who had so tenderly,—all too tenderly, it may be,—reared him. On the grief of the mother,—the heart-rending remorse of the twin-sister, we mercifully drop the veil.

> " Oh, who that knows where faults may first begin,
> Shall bid not earth be just, before 'tis hard, with sin ?"

On this matter, as well as on many others, which regard domestic education, we must refer our readers to "The Mirrow of True Womanhood," and the Mother's office in the household.*

---

* See, in particular, chapters xii., xiii., xiv., xv.

Training of the Mind.

With respect to intellectual education, it must be further added, that the father cannot be too watchful and firm in preventing his sons from acquiring loose habits of learning, thinking, and studying. It is most essential to the welfare of every boy that he be forced to be orderly and methodical in acquiring knowledge, as well as in using it. Do not give a child too much to do, but make him do well whatever you give him. This thoroughness and accuracy may be a little irksome to him in the beginning; but if you are firm and persistent, the boy will soon see the benefit of working in this way. A mind must be very ill constituted, that does not take a great natural delight in acquiring knowledge, and in making a sensible progress in it. We are so framed by our all-wise Creator, that the soul rejoices as much at mastering a problem of algebra or geometry, at learning to draw a classic head or a beautiful tree in a landscape, as in being the first at base-ball or cricket. We feel a joy and a pride in cultivating and displaying our powers,—a deeper joy and loftier pride at excelling in exercises of the mind than in those of the body.

You must act upon this natural love of progress and excellence, and accustom your boys, in whatever they do, to do it accurately, heartily, and well. For well they can scarcely do it unless they do it with a will. One indispensable condition toward doing everything well is, not only to put their heart in it, but to put their whole mind to it. Attention to one thing at a time, undivided attention to what one is doing here and now,—are golden rules for success. Inattention weakens the mind and prevents it from grasping the subject or taking in the knowledge of what is just before it. It is like the attempt one would make to grasp with the hand, at one and the same time, three different balls, each of which is quite large enough to fill it. "One thing at a time," must be the rule. We have known men, gifted with more than fair abilities, who have succeeded only in becoming "confused" in every subject they would fain study, comprehend, or discuss. Because their mind never had been trained to these habits of accuracy and close attention. Place before their mind's eye the simplest proposition, and, instead of looking at it simply as it is, they will puzzle themselves by seeing, alongside of it, another proposition which is both like and unlike the first,— so that they do not know which is which. These men become the most troublesome of logicians, because they never seize accurately what you say to them, nor see clearly what they mean themselves.

Grammar-School Education.

Happy the children blessed with a home in which they can receive a complete education, moral and intellectual, fitting them for all the duties of after-life! We fear that such homes are very rare among us,—rare, at least, as compared with the immense majority of families less privileged in culture or in means. In Ireland and England during the dark centuries of persecution, home-education was the exclusive mode of training the children alike of rich and poor Catholics. The very necessity of rearing them in the knowledge and practice of their ancestral faith, as well as in all such branches of learning as became their station, made the parents themselves uncommonly careful in acquiring the necessary accomplishments and the methods by which these should be taught to others. Thus were brought up many a generation of devoted men and women,—true to all that we hold as most sacred and praiseworthy. College education was only to be had abroad, or,—in the case of children of the lower classes,—to be got in scraps from itinerant masters, who taught at the risk of their own lives, while the peril of their pupils and of the pupils' parents was little less.

These days have passed in the Sister Islands,—and the dark cloud which there so long oppressed Catholic homes, now rests on more than one continental country;—how long,—is the secret of God's providence. But no man who has read in local history of the trials and heroism of our Catholic ancestors, and who is acquainted with the robust faith, the solid and varied learning, as well as the unshaken attachment to principle of the men and women who have gone forth from these homes,—can feel surprise at the zeal of their descendants for the religious training of the young.

It is far from our purpose,—even could we do so here with advantage or propriety,—to enter into a discussion of principles concerning religious teaching in the schools maintained at the public expense and placed under the control of the State.

We simply affirm the sacred and indefeasible right of the parent to see to it that his child, by whomsoever or wheresoever educated, be not only safe from all teaching and influence calculated to weaken his faith or stain his purity, but also trained in the knowledge and practice of the true religion. It is the parent's imperative and indispensable duty to take care that his children are so brought up at home: the masters to whom he trusts his boys outside of his home, either for elementary instruction or for college or university education, only represent him, and possess over his children that portion of the parental authority that he devolves on them.

If the college or the school cannot or will not give his boys such religious and moral training as is the parent's right and duty to obtain for them, then his conscience will induce him to seek elsewhere such educators as may fulfill the obligation of forming the mind and heart of youth in accordance with the dictates of the divine law.

The Foremost Duty of a Parent.

The religious and moral training of the children, is foremost among parental duties. No matter in whose hands the boy is placed, and how safe soever the guidance of his teachers may be, the father must see to it that the teacher does his duty thoroughly.

It cannot, from this point of view of simple and unavoidable duty, be a matter of surprise that Catholic parents everywhere show themselves so jealous of the purity of the religious doctrines taught their children, and of the irreproachable morality of both masters and companions. Nor, where the atmosphere and teaching of a school is judged pernicious by the parents themselves or their trusted religious guides,—can it be a matter of reproach to such parents, if they use every endeavor and make every sacrifice to secure schools and teachers, safe in point of doctrine and morality, and equal or superior in point of ability to the more privileged or patronized.

This Conscientious Spirit not Aggressive.

Between the imperative sense of conscientious duty impelling both parents and their religious teachers to secure truly Christian schools, and the aggressive spirit that denounces what is wrong and defective without ever building up anything,—there is assuredly a wide difference.

We are for allowing other religious denominations to secure and maintain for their children educational institutions in every way suited to their views of parental duty. But the right we should vindicate for others, we must unhesitatingly and unflinchingly assert and pursue in our own behalf.

Yes,—a thoroughly Christian, thoroughly Catholic system of education for our boys,—is the first and most pressing need of our age and country. The Church has again and again declared it so; and, even in the absence of any such recent and solemn declaration, the voice of authority in the past has spoken loudly and repeatedly, while the clearly expressed voice of God in His revealed word, leaves no doubt as to the duty of parents and the obligation of pastors.

Most blessed of God, therefore, and approved of all true men is the generosity manifested by all rich and poor in this needful work of creating and supporting Christian schools. And, above all, most blessed will be the day when our Hierarchy can spare, from the many pressing wants of their struggling institutions, the means necessary for creating Normal Schools,—the nurseries of accomplished teachers of both sexes!

With these remarks on the greatest need of the century, we pass to the superintendence which the father ought to exercise on his boys daily after their return from school.

This superintendence is but a part of the parent's necessary coöperation in the work which the teacher is doing during school hours. Are we doing parents injustice when we say, that very many, if not most of them, seem not to be aware of the great importance of their helping forward by every means in their own power, the efforts of masters, professors, and all others engaged in educating their children?

Education the joint Work of both Parents and Teachers.

This is a matter not to be passed over lightly. For, after many years spent in Canada and the United States, in the labors of a professorship, and after a serious study of college and university life abroad, the author is bound to say,— that one of the chief reasons,—if not, indeed, the chief reason of the ill success of college education in the case of so many boys, lies at the door of the parents.

The parents at home and the masters and directors in school or college, are bound *to work together* in educating the boy. The work for which they join hands, is always and necessarily the work of the parents. If, at school or in college, those who undertake to educate youth fail in doing their full duty, they sin, in doing so, against God, against the parents, and against the child, especially. But, meanwhile, the parents are not relieved from their obligation of watching with a scrupulous care over the progress of their boys both in learning and in virtue. When the school or the college fails to do its work, or does it wrongly, —then it becomes incumbent on the father to have the wrong repaired, and to use a twofold diligence in making up for lost time.

The great bulk of fathers and mothers,—even of the better educated,—think, or act as if they thought,—that they have done their full duty, when they have sent their children to the Sunday school for religious instruction, and to school or college for secular instruction, or the completion of their entire course of education.

This is a great mistake. You must moreover make sure that your boy reaches the Sunday school in good time, that he is there properly and thoroughly taught;—and it will be both your interest and your duty, if you attend yourself occasionally in the catechism class, and, after catechism hours, question closely the boy about what he has learned. But, will not this be too great a hardship for the child as well as for the parent? So far as the child is concerned, there will be no hardship, provided that you study to make him love to learn his catechism, as you should make him do all else,—by a generous sense of duty.

We remember well, while yet a very young priest in the dear old city of Quebec, that hard-working men would walk for miles to Sunday school with their boys, making the road pleasant for these by lively and entertaining conversation, and, when catechism and prayers were ended, returning to their homes with redoubled joy to share with their children all the sweet and innocent recreation of the Sunday evening. Indeed, the Sunday-school seemed to be the great work of the Lord's day for all the most distinguished men of the place. The then Provincial Secretary, the Right Honorable Sir Dominick Daly, was at the head of the Christian Doctrine Society, and taught his own catechism class, and so did every one of our foremost merchants and young men,—the non-commissioned officers of the garrison also deeming it an honor to take a hand in this divine work.

And thus we were reminded of our own native home, where the gentlest and the best devoted several hours of the blessed Sabbath repose to the religious instruction of the young.

No, no! Do not say it is a hardship either for fathers or for their sons to gather, on the Lord's day, this swee

manna of divine truth ;—doubly and tenfold sweet the God
of the Sabbath knows how to make it to men of good will.

We say nothing of the means employed by zealous and
enlightened priests to render the exercises of the Sunday
school interesting, attractive, and delightful,—such as cho-
ral singing, recitations, and appropriate rewards from time
to time.

In like manner you will see to it that your boys do their
duty at school, and that they study after school hours the
matters given them by their teachers. Omit no effort to
excite and sustain your boys' emulation ; if their masters
are really zealous to push them forward, do you second
this zeal by every means in your power. See their teachers
often ; show them that you are most anxious to coöperate
with them. Without being either obtrusive or unduly in-
quisitive, you can easily ascertain what methods are used
in the school, and what pains taken by the masters in fur-
thering the progress of their pupils.

Respect, Love, and Sustain your Children's Teachers.

But, above all things, beware of the too common and
most hurtful custom of certain parents (and uneducated
parents are not the sole offenders in this respect),—of con-
sidering their children's teachers, and treating them, as if
they were natural enemies to be watched, abused, and
thwarted at every turn. There are parents, who take the
part of their unruly and untruthful children against their
teachers, who look upon every punishment inflicted on the
latter as an injustice which calls for immediate redress.
There are others again who keep their children away from
school on the slightest pretext, or who are utterly careless
of sending them punctually at the appointed hours ; and
having thus broken in upon their boys' studies and seri-
ously hindered their progress,—they will blame and abuse
the masters for the backwardness, the insubordination, and
all the irregular and idle habits of which they,—the parents,
—are themselves the sole cause !

Never,—unless you have carefully and calmly ascertained the fact,—never sustain your boys against the teacher's authority; and, especially, never, when your boys complain of the latter, allow yourself to utter one word of censure or blame. Always lean to the side of authority. You have given the teacher yours in the school; make your boys respect it invariably.

Take a lively and continual interest in your boys' studies. Let them feel that you are more pleased with their daily progress, than if they brought you home gold or some precious object at the end of each day's schooling.

If you are forced to choose another school for your children,—or, when you have not made your first choice,—we should advise you to peruse slowly the following beautiful lines, full of that love of innocence and child-life, which was so dear to the Master.

> " I sauntered where the town and country meet,
> Where Art and Nature battle for the street,
> Where, ere the stones had vanished from my foot,
> The grass laughed up at me a gay salute.
> In leafy contiguity I heard
> The mellow note of some love-brooding bird;
> And nearer still I heard a droning noise,
> Come from a hive of bees or school of boys,
> But which I could not tell, until my eye
> Lighted upon a porch, as butterfly
> Lights on a kingdom of all-mingled bloom,
> Wherein the flowers breathe out their beauteous doom
> And fill the air with souls. To that flower-cell
> I leaned my ear, as to a humming shell,
> And heard the moan as of a fairy sea
> Far in the dim domain of mystery.
> Then growing bolder, I advanced a pace
> Into the trellised porch, and saw the place:
> And, lo! as I do live, a little school,
> Wherein an easy dame kept easy rule,
> And learned, as well as taught, the way to know
> About her sat, but in no formal row,
> Her little students, serious, but unfrightened.
> Surely, I thought, this is a school enlightened,
> Where neither word of wrath, nor lash descends
> To harden knowledge unto hateful ends:

Where rule is quietly taught and quickly learned,—
Things apprehended, if not quite discerned ;
And where bright youth is lifted to a height
From which he sees each glorious height on height,—
Those starry souls by whose effulgent breath
The world is snatched from chaos, man from death.
A pleasant school—a pleasant sight for eye
That loveth spots where nothing seems to die ;
Where winds are soft, flowers sweetly bloom, and man
Fits like a star into dear Nature's plan,
And wins by truth and unreposing duty
The throne of wisdom and the crown of beauty." *

Yes,—that is what parents and teachers, the most advanced in years and in learning, the reverend guides and eminent governors of peoples, can do every day they live, in spite of the longest and widest experience,

"To learn, as well as teach, the way to know."

The oldest of us, the most learned, the wisest,—as they look back over their dealings with the young, would wish to undo much that they did, to unlearn much of what they thought they knew, and to begin again with childhood, and 'learn the way to know,''—the way to know child-nature, in particular, the sweet and love-lit way to children's souls.

Above all, O fathers, be sure,—whether your dear ones are "schooled" inside your home or outside of it,—that their souls are not narrowed down and straightened by the methods followed in teaching them, and that their hearts retain all the freshness, the candor, the simplicity of childhood. Keep them children as long as ever you can !

---

* Robert Buchanan, "Wayside Poesies."

CHAPTER XIII.

PATERNAL AUTHORITY AND PUBLIC EDUCATION.

These Teachers were known to maintain that double commerce which Muratori styles sweet and useful—with the wise living and the wise dead.* The guides of the Catholic School, as the learned men of the Church from primitive times, are still what they once were—clear but mystical—devoted to serve men with an intense affection, but separate from the crowd. Remote from all egotism, it is clear to their disciples that they only obey a high influence, and that their awful task is imposed. This character of retirement and solemnity adds a great interest to their lessons, as to their books. Youth will not turn from them to hear a teacher, who, like the generality of writers now, is one of the public—a man of noise, a man of news, a man of money.—KENELM HENRY DIGBY.

AN unerring instinct in the heart of a Catholic parent will direct him, in seeking for his boy the guides who can lead the latter safely through the walks of classic antiquity, and the bewildering mazes of modern science—like the ill-arranged departments of some Centennial Exhibition—to select the men who have sought eminence in learning through a holy ambition, and who impart it for His love who "is a God of all knowledge." It is a great attraction too for men who have had themselves, very often, to fight a hard battle with fortune, and whose ancestors had to endure all but the loss of life in fostering Catholic education,—to be able to give their sons, their money, and their

---

* *Dulce est eruditionis sectatoribus quotodie com mortuis versari; dulcius profecto futurum, cum vivis, a quibus brevi facilique compendio eruditior in dies discedas.*

"It is sweet to the votaries of knowledge to hold daily converse with the dead; but far sweeter will it be to converse with the living, from whose intercourse, by a short and easy method, one may daily become more learned."

253

heartfelt sympathy to institutions of higher learning strug-
gling against the most adverse circumstances.

If parents could only understand, that, much as the par-
ish school deserves of their unflinching support, the College
and the University are even more deserving of their enthu-
siastic advocacy and utmost generosity. For the parish
school is destined to serve as a feeder to the college, just as
colleges are, in the mind of the Church, to serve as fruitful
nurseries to the University. And if the body of our people
only knew,—what the author can speak of from the most
certain knowledge,—how little the noble men who devote
their entire existence to the arduous functions of classical
instruction, receive of active, cheering sympathy and sadly
needed support from the community they serve so well!
No—there is no class of toilers for the public welfare, who
should be more cordially helped on in the divine life-work
they are doing, than those who rear our priests, our states-
men, our enlightened merchants and professional men.

The Divine Work done by our Colleges.

The sole aim and sole care of these devoted guides of
youth,—the very flower of our aristocracy of learning and
piety,—is to prepare for the Church and the country public
men whose example shall be a living lesson to all beneath
and around them, and whose salutary influence shall coun-
terbalance that of the unprincipled, the irreligious, the
selfish, and the sensual. Farther on in this book, we shall
speak of schools of science,—whether theoretical or applied.
We only wish at present to direct the parent in the choice
of a proper establishment of higher education, and to offer
to the educators themselves some practical suggestions that
may aid them not a little in their labors.

That in our establishments of higher Education we should
have men whose sole interest and sole avocation lie in their
doing thoroughly the work of rearing youth to the practice
of true piety as well as to solid learning, must be a subject
of congratulation to Christian parents. There is so much

heart-satisfaction for a father and a mother in the thought that the men and women to whom they intrust their dear ones, will make of their advancement in virtue a matter of even greater importance than their progress in knowledge!

The Catholic Ideal of Religious Teachers of Youth.

The ideal followed by such teachers of youth all through the middle ages is thus described by Digby:

"The care of religious men to educate the young was not confined to supplying them with oral or written instruction. It was for them especially that religion loved, under the form of the fine arts, to impress on the material elements around, the stamp of ideal humanity, that, as Fichte says, 'at their very awakening into life, they might be environed by noble objects, such as by a certain sympathetic power, would educate the outward senses, whereby the education of the inner man might be greatly facilitated.' It was the object of education not so much to impart a variety of knowledge, as to cultivate that mind which would be able either to reap the benefit of knowledge subsequently obtained, where an extraordinary degree of knowledge was required, or to discharge the ordinary duties of life with honesty and perseverance to the end, where there was no occasion for acquiring such a distinction.

"Agreeable to this plan, the young were to be thoroughly imbued with a delicate and profound sense of everything noble and gracious, which would be alike useful to all; that, to borrow a simile from Plato, as the young who inhabit a healthy spot are benefited by everything around them, so whatever was thrown before them from beautiful deeds, whether in the way of seeing or of hearing, like an air from pure places bearing health, might lead them to a resemblance, and friendship, and harmony, with what is good and fair."*

To his ideal of education in ages that must ever be dear to the Christian soul, let us only bring the living, practical

---

* "Mores Catholici; or, Ages of Faith," b. i., chap. vii.

spirit, the thorough intelligence of the needs of modern
society, and the hearty earnestness, which endeared to all
who knew him the great educator of our own times men-
tioned in the following passage. We submit it to the con-
sideration of all our great teaching bodies.

Earnest Workers doing Noble Work.

"The most remarkable thing which struck me at once on
joining the Laleham circle, was the wonderful healthiness
of tone and feeling which prevailed in it. Everything about
me I immediately found to be most real ; it was a place
where a new-comer at once felt that a great and earnest
work was going forward. Dr. Arnold's * great power as a
private tutor resided in this, *that he gave such an intense
earnestness to life.* Every pupil was made to feel that
there was a work for him to do—that his happiness as well
as his duty lay in doing that work well. Hence an inde-
scribable zest was communicated to a young man's feelings
about life ; a strange joy came over him on discovering that
he had the means of being useful, and thus of being happy ;
and a deep respect and ardent attachment sprang up to-
wards him who had taught him thus to value life and his
own self, and his work and mission in this world.

"All this was founded on the breadth and comprehensive-
ness of Arnold's character, as well as its striking truth and
reality ; on the unfeigned regard he had for work of all
kinds, and the sense he had of its value both for the com-
plex aggregate of society and the growth and perfection of
the individual.

"Thus pupils of the most different natures were keenly
stimulated ; none felt that he was left out, or that, because
he was not endowed with large powers of mind, there was
no sphere open to him in the honorable pursuits of useful-
ness. This wonderful power of making all the pupils re-

---

* Thomas Arnold, D.D., born in 1795, died in 1842. He was, successively, head
master of the Classical Schools of Laleham and Rugby,—preëminently success-
ful in each.

spect themselves, and in awakening in them a conscious-
ness of the duties that God has assigned to them person-
ally, and of the consequent reward each should have for his
labors, was one of Arnold's most characteristic features as
a trainer of youth. He possessed it eminently at Rugby ;
but, if I may trust my own vivid recollection, he had it
quite as remarkably at Laleham.

"His hold over all his pupils I know perfectly astonished
me. It was not so much an enthusiastic admiration for
his genius, or learning, or eloquence, which stirred within
them ; *it was a sympathetic thrill, caught from a spirit
that was earnestly at work in the world—whose work was
healthy, sustained, and constantly carried forward in the
fear of God*—a work which was founded on a deep sense
of its duty and its value ; and was coupled with such a true
humility, such an unaffected simplicity, that others could
not help being invigorated by the same feeling, and with
the belief that they too in their measure could go and do
likewise.

"In all this there was no excitement, no predilection for
one class of work above another ; no enthusiasm for any
one-sided object ; but a humble, profound, and most reli-
gious consciousness that work is the appointed calling of
man on earth, the end for which his various faculties were
given, the element in which his nature is ordained to de-
velop itself, and in which his progressive advance toward
heaven is to lie. Hence, each pupil felt assured of Arnold's
sympathy in his own particular growth and character of
talent ; *in striving to cultivate his own gifts, in whatever
direction they might lead him, he infallibly found Arnold
not only approving, but positively and sincerely valuing
for themselves the results he had arrived at ; and that ap-
probation and esteem gave a dignity and a worth both to
himself and to his labor.*"*

---

* Quoted from Knight, "Half Hours with the Best Authors." The italics are
our own.

17

The Presiding Spirit makes the School.

There is no doubt of it—the entire and most perfect suc-
cess of the work of education, carried on at any one mo-
ment by a great school or public establishment, depends on
the master spirit who presides over it, and who knows how
to infuse his own earnestness into his subordinates, to com-
municate to every one of his pupils something of the sacred
fire which burns within his own bosom. Where every pupil
is "made to feel that there is work for him to do,—that his
happiness as well as his duty lies in doing that work well,'
there will of a necessity be earnestness, not to say enthu
siasm, in the daily and hourly efforts of each student.

There is a way of making boys at college know and feel
that the study of Greek and Latin is only an introduction
to the whole of that ancient world and its civilization, with
which the world and civilization of to-day are so intimately
connected. We know,—and many among our readers, we
doubt not, have known, very young people, girls even of
tender age, who make it a delight to master the languages
of Greek and Rome, that they may thus be enabled to read
and appreciate the masterpieces of their great writers.

Let the men to whose lot it falls to teach boys the first
elements of the rich and beautiful tongues of Virgil and
Horace and Cicero,—of Xenophon, Plato, Demosthenes, and
Homer,—be the men they ought to be, full of the Christian
spirit,—thoroughly acquainted with the languages they un-
dertake to teach, thoroughly in love with their work, and
deeply interested in the advancement of each of their pu-
pils; knowing how to throw around their lessons and ex-
planations a little of that light of fancy which is so lovely
and attractive to young minds;—and they will find little
difficulty in communicating to these a love for their studies.

It is because the men who are charged with the task of
teaching Greek and Latin, are themselves but most imper-
fectly acquainted with the simplest elements of these lan-
guages (and we have known many such), that the labor of

learning, for boys full of life and naturally impatient of
dullness, becomes one of intolerable hardship.

A Bad Teacher is a cruel injustice to his Scholars.

We remember, in an institution for the highest and most
important of all human sciences,—to have seen a man in-
trusted with the duty of teaching a class of Hebrew to
young men who had been themselves, every one of them,
for years occupied in teaching the higher classes,—and this
Hebrew scholar had to spell most painfully every word and
syllable of the text (the Book of Psalms) he had under-
taken to explain. Of course he blundered even in the
spelling, confounding long vowels with short, and mixing
up in inextricable confusion the various consonants. Of
prosody, or harmony, or all the innate beauty and grace of
the language of the Royal Prophet,—there was not, could
not, be found a trace in these absurd readings. And yet for
a whole year this preposterous system of teaching Hebrew
was allowed to disgrace the institution and insult the intel-
ligence of the men on whom it was afflicted, and who could
not help themselves!

Not so had we been taught in our own dear Alma Mater,
where the most accomplished Rabbi to be had in the land
was called in and well paid to initiate us into the first ele-
ments of the inspired tongue. The very phrase as it flowed
from his lips impressed itself on our memory; its very har-
mony made us desirous of possessing the language and re-
solved to master all its difficulties.

Superiors of colleges, then, who are thoroughly in earnest
about having their work done and well done, will see to it
that those who coöperate with them in their most important
labors, shall be not only thoroughly in earnest, like them-
selves, but thoroughly competent, as well, to do the work
they take in hand.

They are aware that the mental education of every boy
intrusted to them, is like the planning and rearing of an
edifice destined to last forever: they know, therefore, that

the foundations must be carefully and solidly laid, if they would have the superstructure stand. For, in the name of common sense, what can you build on foundations which are themselves, without substance, solidity or cohesion?

Irreparable wrong of employing Incompetent Teachers for Beginners.

Hence, the absurdity, the crying injustice to both parents and pupils, of giving the charge of grammar schools or elementary schools in any educational establishment, to men who are not perfectly masters of the branches to be taught therein. An uncommonly clever boy will always manage, if he be at all intent on learning, to pick up from his own reading and reflections, enough to make up the deficiency in his master's knowledge or method. Indeed, such boys learn but little from any but the best masters; for they are pretty sure to be in advance of his lessons and of the majority of their fellow-students.

Here, however, our plea is in favor of the majority, or of the large minority in every large class of ordinary intellects. Their intellectual food has to be prepared for them with great skill and presented in form and quantity suited to their mental capacity and appetite.

This large minority is made up, most frequently, of the very men who will one day be the solid, influential men of every profession. They are not, while at school, the quick, the brilliant, or the clever men; they are, as experience shows, the men who are slow, serious, studious, and sure to succeed in the end. We have seen so many of these brilliant and dazzling college geniuses, come to nought in mature age, like these marvelous plants of Java and Sumatra which grow up to their full perfection in a single night, expand their bright flowers to the morning sun, and droop and wither before it has set. Their slower and less shining companions of the forest, are more timid in putting forth their early shoots, and less ambitious to display their rapid growth and flowering pride. The palms which furnish food to man, the oaks and other forest trees which go to build his home and his fleets, are the growth of years. All nature's most perfect and durable works are the slow and gradual produce of time.

Do not neglect the Slow Many for the Clever Few.

It would, then, be both want of wisdom and want of justice in any teacher to proportion his pains to the uncommon capacity of the few, while neglecting the need and claims of the many. And, surely, it can be neither wise, nor just, nor prudent in the faculty of any great institution to provide the more advanced pupils with skilled and experienced talent, while leaving the beginners to the mercy of mere tyros or blockheads.

It is, then, the interest and duty of the father to be most solicitous about the progress of his boy during this early stage of college study, and to inquire conscientiously into the quality of the instruction given him in every branch. Just as he would be most careful to watch over the moral purity of the young student and to inquire into his progress in self-restraint and self-denial, even so must he make sure that he is taught what is promised, that he learns thoroughly what he is taught, and that he does not acquire at the very beginning of his intellectual life, these habits of mental indolence and inaccuracy, which are scarcely less fatal to professional success, than the kindred moral habits are to solid virtue.

We repeat it, therefore: this thoroughness, earnestness, heartiness, are necessary in the men who take upon themselves the all-important task of guiding boys in the very first stages of classical education. The "indescribable zest" mentioned in the last extract, and the "strange joy" felt by children and youths who climb a high mountain for the first time, and look down from the summit on some glorious and untrodden region beyond, can never be the feeling of such as follow the guidance of those who cannot climb, and to whom the most modest literary eminence is as formidable a height as Mont Blanc or the Matter-horn.

Who of us, in boyhood and in early youth, had not experienced that same "indescribable zest" for facing impossible difficulties, as we ran along beside a loved master or parent over the broad sunny fields or up some wooded hill-side? Did not the spirit which gave buoyancy and strength to every limb come from the companionship and cheering words of the man we loved dearest on earth? And was not "the strange joy" of difficulty overcome and success accomplished begotten by his smile and his happiness in our efforts?

The Teacher's Enthusiasm, how Contagious!

Our readers will pardon us one reminiscence, all the more readily that no personal vanity mingles with the memories it calls up. In the ever-dear and venerable institution which opened its arms to us, a stranger and an orphan, nearly half a century ago, we found men the exact counterparts of Dr. Arnold, his equals, assuredly, if not his superiors, in disinterestedness and self-sacrificing devotion to their holy calling, and not his inferiors in secular or sacred knowledge ;— men, belonging by their birth to the first families in the land, and deeming it more than royal honor to serve God in their lowly and obscure labor of teaching youth, without other stipend than the roof above them and their humble garb of priestly poverty ; men whose heart and soul were in their work, and who knew how to kindle in our young hearts an ardent zeal for our own advancement, as well as a deep respect and lasting attachment toward themselves.

If, looking back now and comparing our own experiences and observations, we are forced to give to the great school to which we owe everything under God, the tribute of an admiration which only increases with each succeeding year, —it is because we recall how our dear masters labored to infuse into every student among their five hundred the hearty love of study and the no less hearty love of piety.

That there should be, in a school over which such men presided, whose whole life was the "Imitation of Christ" in practice, an atmosphere of genuine purity and piety, was natural; but there was, at the same time, an atmosphere of earnest emulation for study. In one other house—in France and beneath the very shadow of the ancient castle of the Laval-Montmorencys, did we see an equal zest for study, and, as should be expected, an incomparable fervor of piety,—as if the name of the great bishop who had founded the time-honored institution far away on the banks of the St. Lawrence, drew down a special and an equal blessing on it and on the great seminary that flourished beneath the shadow of his ancestral halls.

We cannot help, in reading the life of Dr. Arnold, and remembering the man who above all others crowned the work of Francis De Laval-Montmorency, * seeing in our own admired master every excellence set ,forth by the biographer in the renowned head-master of Laleham and Rugby. He was our companion in our studies, laboring continually with us, making the labor light not only by that high intelligence which could explain, simplify, and illumine what was most difficult and abstruse, but by making the labor joyous by his bright wit and sunny spirit.

Classical Studies a Training for the Public Man.

College or university education is, of course, specially designed to train men for every walk of professional and public life. It is not only churchmen, statesmen, and military men, but lawyers, physicians, great architects and engineers, great manufacturers and merchants, and men of independent wealth and position, who find in such schools the varied knowledge and ripe science they need,—but men of the most varied avocations, and of every social rank are fitted by such training,—when it really is what it professes to be,—to work successfully and attain eminence in any useful pursuit.

---

* The late Very Reverend Louis Jacques Casault, D.D., who obtained the erection of Laval University, Quebec.

A young man who has gone through a complete and serious college or university course, under masters who were, not shams, but thoroughly able to teach whatever they professed, is ready, on returning to his family, to enter upon any career that his talents, his inclination, may suit him for, or the will of his parents may open to him.

The Parents to blame for the Failure of their Sons.

That many do not bring from several years spent in college, the accomplishments and business aptitudes for which their parents were so anxious,—is due to a variety of causes, one of which, and not unfrequently the chief cause, is the parents' own want of consistency.

Let us explain this. As we have said above, the work of education is and ever should be,—in order to be successful, —the joint work of teachers and parents. This holds true of college training fully as much as of grammar-school learning. Indeed, we should rather say, that to make a college course perfectly successful there is need of a more watchful, more cordial, and more constant coöperation on the part of the father.

When you send your boy to the parish or the public school in order that he may get a thorough knowledge of what will fit him for a trade or for commercial business, both you and he, as well as his teachers, perfectly understand what the boy wants in the way of learning and what he is to do with it. He gets it within the expected time, and is forthwith apprenticed to his proper business.

This cannot be done with boys sent to college. You cannot determine beforehand, no more than the boy can himself, what profession he will embrace once his college course is completed. For a college course is by its nature intended to prepare young men for the learned professions, the priesthood, the law, and medicine.* Very, very rarely

---

* Hence the anomaly,—a most calamitous one,—of having a "Commercial course" in some of our colleges. Necessity alone,—the necessity of affording to children coming from Central and South America a school where they can be

does it happen that any one can predict of a boy who enters upon the long and important course of college education, that he will to a certainty become a priest,—and so of any of the other professions.

Besides, the Church, with the guidance of the Holy Spirit and the experience of eighteen centuries to enlighten her on the ways of men,—has ever had a most prudent care of college youth,—the flower of her children. She knows that, as it is for the sacred ministry,—so is it for each of the secular professions,—God must call to its duties those who are to fulfill them without deadly peril to themselves and with all usefulness to others. She has well-approved rules for the guidance of her ministers in determining who is called and who is not, as well as for the direction of the young men, who, at the close of their college studies, must elect what path they are to pursue in order to serve God in conformity with His will and their own intellectual and moral capacity.

When your Son can choose understandingly.

And it is only at the termination of these studies that such an election can be made with any degree of wisdom. Most unwise,—to say the least of it,—is the conduct of parents, who, having set their hearts upon having their son a priest, leave him no freedom in his own choice, and thus do him moral violence to impel him into a career for which he has neither vocation nor aptitude. What can they expect but misery to him and bitterness of heart for themselves, from a course so opposed to conscience and right reason ?

---

given a business education while having their faith protected,—can excuse the temporary existence of such a strange and baneful division of studies.

If our trained professional educators of the highest grade thus take on themselves to teach " book-keeping," etc., can they be justly surprised or offended, if men destined professedly, to give nothing but commercial or business training, should usurp the higher functions of classical and university education? It will not do to say *Ne sutor ultra crepidam.*. In truth the essentially important is that as in skilled mechanical labor, so in skilled intellectual labor and professioual training, every one should qualify himself to do thoroughly what he promises, and not undertake what he is not qualified to perform.

We are not, of course, denying that it is a most laudable desire in parents to have their sons advanced to the priestly office. Too many and too touching traditions connected with our native country and race, have cast a halo around fathers and mothers who sacrificed everything and endured the utmost of privation to see their child ministering at the dear altars of their faith. But we are only pleading here,— and in the interest of both the parents and their sons,—the necessity of not considering their becoming priests a fore-gone conclusion. The circumstances which made the desire of such parents not only heroic, but almost a sure sign of the divine will, have passed away with the secular persecu-tion that begat them. In the English-speaking world, there is now perfect freedom. Hence it is, that the will of God must have precedence of the desire of parents in a matter where the divine honor, and the dearest interests of religion are so nearly concerned.

How sacredly College Students should be Shielded from Evil.

What is most important for parents, who entertain such a praiseworthy ambition,—and what is to our immediate purpose at present,—is, that every father who sends his son to college with such a hope, should take especial care not to foster in his child's soul inclinations or habits that would render him unfit not only for the sacred ministry, but for any profession or public trust.

We must be pardoned, if we speak more plainly and say here how very little care certain parents take, during vaca-tions from college studies, to preserve their sons from amuse-ments and associations that are utterly irreconcilable with their avowed purpose. How often have not the heads of colleges to mourn over the total ruin of piety and innocence effected during a single vacation by the blind indifference or criminal indulgence of parents! The habits of self-de-nial and self-control contracted during ten months of severe discipline and courageous efforts at self-improvement, are lost in a single month, or a single week, and superseded by habits which we do not dare to describe. And yet, these very parents will be the first to cast on the college the blame which belongs solely to the parental home and its utter want of discipline!

Parents who have themselves had the benefit of a thorough university training understand all this well, and are careful to sustain the college authorities, even when everything does not please them in the way their boys are getting on. They are also most careful to encourage and direct the praiseworthy love of self-improvement in the latter,—feeling sure the while, that where a boy has talent and application, his college course will make a man of him, in spite of his professor's shortcomings.

Another cause of the baneful impatience of parents is the necessity which compels our colleges to admit, side by side with the undergraduates, very young boys, and, therefore, to have in a house professedly devoted to the higher classical and university studies,—not only grammar schools for teaching Greek and Latin, as preparatory to Humanities, Rhetoric, and Philosophy, — but an English elementary course preparatory to the grammar schools themselves. This gives the college a false position in the eyes of the parents, especially when these send their children very young, and when they are themselves uneducated, or, at any rate, unacquainted with the ancient classics.

Too much Demanded of our Colleges.

They see their next-door neighbor's boys, who are trained in the town school, not seldom more advanced in English, arithmetic, geography, reading, writing, etc., than their own boys of the same age at college; and then, at a time when the neighbor's boy has completed his course at the public school, and is entering on business, their boy is painfully toiling through elementary Latin, and later plodding still more laboriously through elementary Greek. They, judging things from their own standard, do not see and cannot appreciate the progress their son has made in all these years. They hear their illiterate acquaintance say— they, perhaps, hear their boy himself saying, "What is the use of Greek and Latin? Why spend so much time and spend so much money in learning, or trying to learn, *dead* languages, while the *living* English mother-tongue is (apparently) neglected?"

Reasoning thus, — they are tempted to take their boy away in the very middle of his studies, and then blame the college for their own fatal blundering. Now let us look at this in the light of common sense.

Folly of Interrupting College Studies.

There is no tradesman, no skilled mechanic knowing from his own experience how much time and labor it costs to become a first-rate worker in any craft, but would condemn such trifling with the work of a thorough education. A craftsman knows that a boy has to undergo his apprenticeship to the end in order to be thoroughly master of what he intends to learn. Nay,—you will find very few first-rate tradesmen who would not lengthen the term of apprenticeship rather than shorten it, so convinced are they of the necessity of long study and long practice to acquire consummate skill. They would think a man a fool who, having bound his son for seven years to a most important trade, would take him away at the end of three or five years under the pretext that, if the boy does not know his business by this time, he must be a blockhead or an idler, and his master not much better. The common sense of the average laboring man would condemn any parent for thus trifling with his boy's future.

Shall we set up a standard utterly opposed to this unerring common sense, when we have to judge of studies and training that are, in reality, an apprenticeship to the most important of all arts, the highest of all professions?

Let us go a step farther in this most practical subject.

The course of nature is, that, under ordinary circumstances, boys until their twelfth or thirteenth year should be prepared for college at home, under the eye of exemplary parents, enjoying all the blessed influences of the family circle. Nothing,—so God has ordained it,—can, in the ordinary course of life, take the place of a true Christian mother's love in forming within her home the mind and heart of her boys at this early age. The discipline established by her, supported by the father's whole authority, and perfected by his companionship with his sons,—is the most priceless of blessings for the future collegian,—the future public man.

It is, therefore,—speaking always with the same reservations,—an irreparable calamity for the boy, when he is taken prematurely from beneath his mother's wing to receive elsewhere the nurture which her love can alone bestow;—or when, deprived of a mother, or, again, when unblessed by a true Christian mother,—a boy is cast almost from childhood into the midst of a hundred or more other boys, like a blind puppy into a pond, to swim and scramble ever afterward for salvation and the life of heart and spirit.

Not all the supernatural devotedness of the best of masters can make up for this privation of maternal love and fostering tenderness.

When, however, a sad necessity imposes on our Catholic institutions these parental functions, it should not be forgotten that an immense debt of gratitude is contracted by the parents, and that abuse of our institutions is but an ungraceful way of discharging it.

If, therefore, you deem it imperative,—because you cannot obtain at home for your young boys the religious training which you desire,—to intrust them thus early to priestly hands, make up your mind at the same time to let the young tree grow through the remaining months of winter, through the slow spring and the stormy summer, watching and waiting patiently while the autumn of college-life is ripening and perfecting the fruits which are to reward your trustfulness, and your generous coöperation in this long husbandry.

It is important to Begin Well ; it is infinitely so to End Well.

It would be folly to place them in a college at so young an age, if you did not intend to keep them there to the end. It would be worse folly to take them out in the middle of their studies, in order to put them to business, or under the pretense that they have learned enough. The worst folly of all would be to interrupt the work of their thorough culture, just as the college course was near its close. You would thereby resemble the man who had watched his peach tree blossoming, and the fruit growing after the blossom ; and who, becoming weary of long waiting, would pluck the fruit while still green, and before the golden sun of autumn had matured and mellowed it. If you have but bitter and unsavory fruit on your table, after all your labor and waiting, who is to blame but yourself?

Think well, then, before you determine fully to give your child the benefit, the priceless benefit, of a college education ; think ten times more seriously before you determine to take him away in the middle of his course ; but let no consideration induce you to withdraw him when he is in the last crowning years of his intellectual and moral training.

The Distinction between a College Course and a University Course of Studies.

This is the proper place for pointing out the essential but little-understood difference between a complete college course and a university course proper. The former aims at giving such complete and thorough instruction in ancient and modern letters, in history, philosophy, and the sciences, as to enable the student at its close, to begin forthwith the special study of any of the great professions of theology, law, or medicine. This was formerly and is still characteristic of the colleges or college-schools founded and patronized by the Church,—the parent of university education.

The university, as distinguished from the college, gave instruction in these learned professions, enabling their respective students to become, successively and at determined stages of their course, bachelors, masters or licentiates, and doctors, in theology, ecclesiastical and civil law, or in medicine.

Thus, to borrow an illustration from the great Catholic Laval University, in Quebec;—the Seminary of Quebec, out of which the Laval University has grown, as the crown of ripe dates from the palm tree,—has its collegiate school which, at the end of the full course of literary and scientific instruction, qualifies the students by a searching oral and written examination to become bachelors of arts, or bachelors of letters, or bachelors of sciences, according to their proficiency in all the branches taught, or to their relative superiority in letters or in the sciences, while falling below the necessary degree of excellence in the other cognate branches.

The bachelor's degree confers on the graduate the right to have his name registered forthwith for any of the three university courses of theology, law, and medicine, which he elects to follow. Over each each of these courses presides a board of professors called, collectively, the faculty; each faculty confers degrees in its respective branch; and each has a special register on which is solemnly inscribed the name of each student duly qualified, this ceremony being called matriculation.

We should add, that the collegiate school (*Petit Seminaire*) is charged with the Department of Arts or that which, besides preparing, as above stated, all students for the university courses proper, perfects them in ancient and modern literature, and the mathematical and physical sciences, enabling them not only to acquire the degree of proficiency therein necessary for the bachelor's degree, but further perfecting them so as to become themselves masters in the great art of teaching and forming others in the professor's chair.

Parents, as well as all intelligent readers, will appreciate the exceeding care taken by the Church in past ages and at present, to prepare for their high and holy duties not only the priest who has to be the religious guide and teacher of others, but the lawyer and the magistrate who have to discuss and administer the laws of the State, and the physician in whose hands are placed the health, the life, the honor of families. We need not say that the legislator, the statesman and the publicist find also in the law school the science which can alone surely guide them in laboring by voice and pen for the dearest interests of their own nationality, and of the entire brotherhood of nations.

Fathers who think of all this in putting their sons to college, should, therefore, know that the college is itself in its most conscientious completeness, but a preparation for what is or must be, under one name or another, the university proper or its equivalent.

A Thorough Education fits one for Thorough Work.

You wish to see your son a priest ; but you would not have him other than a priest fit to teach all sacred science, and fit, as well, to appreciate the truth of all secular science. Do not say that the perspective of all these long years of study and of preparation after preparation, is only fit to discourage both parents and students. After having gone through the ordeal ourselves, and having had a long subsequent experience in the ministry,—we are forced to say most earnestly,—that our fear is not that the student of theology will become a priest too late or enter at too ripe an age on the awful duties of his new office ; our fear could only be to see him become too soon the teacher and guide of others, without having gathered the fruit of knowledge in its delicious maturity, when he could himself appreciate its qualities and commend them to the taste of his hearers.

A high-minded Christian father, who is guided in his desires and his judgments by such lofty views as these, will feel himself richly rewarded at seeing his son enter public life armed with that sure scientific knowledge, which is a mighty power to sway other men. This very knowledge will enable the priest, the lawyer, the physician, the scientist, the publicist, or the artist,—to make his mark at once. For, the amount of good done is not measured by time, but by the perfection with which it is accomplished.

It is not necessary that a priest should labor many years, but that he should labor well and to good purpose. Our Great High Priest lived thirty years in the obscurity, toil, and subjection of Nazareth ; He labored in public only three years ; and His praise in the Gospel is : "He hath done all things well ; He hath made both the deaf to hear, and the dumb to speak." *

For every son of yours, whether priest or layman, may your sweetest reward be to hear such praise from the lips of the good and the great !

The outcry against Greek and Latin.

If we have not wearied you outright, dear reader, we would fain add a few words in this place, and before concluding this chapter, on the opposition to the teaching of Greek and Latin in our modern colleges. Parents who hear the senseless outcry made on this subject, ought to know precisely both the motives of those who make it and the solid reasons on which is founded the universal practice of Christian schools for so many centuries.

When the opponents of classical education have asserted noisily, that Greek and Latin are "dead languages," and that the youth of the nineteenth century should not waste on studying the literary remains of dead nations so many precious years, which were more usefully bestowed in mastering living literatures,—they fancy that to this implied argument there is no possible answer.

It is, however, a manifest fallacy. The Greek and the Latin are not, and never have been, dead languages in the sense in which our opponents would have it understood. Till the downfall of the Greek Empire in 1453, both the classic

---

* St. Mark, vii. 37.

language of Demosthenes and Plato, and the local popular dialects, had never ceased to be in use,—the former in the numerous schools of the East, the latter among all classes in ordinary conversation. Even now, after more than four centuries of forced intellectual sterility much more than of religious intolerance, the vernacular Greek of Athens is nearer to the exquisite dialect of the Attic masters, than the vernacular Italian is to the tongue of Cicero. And yet, the very best modern scholars have good reason for affirming that the Italian spoken throughout the Peninsula is not a corruption of the Latin, but a living popular language coeval with the dialect of Latium, and ever spoken side by side with the latter, when it had become the polished and perfected idiom of the masters of Rome and of Italy. Wherefore it can be said, as a thing historically probable, if not certain, that, although since the downfall of Constantinople and of living Greek literature, the pure idiom of Attica ceased to be heard in the schools of oppressed Greece, still it continued to be spoken in its popular form everywhere, and to be understood by every educated person. Nor did all the learned men of Greece migrate to Western Europe after May the 29th, 1453.

How much more certain and undeniable is it that the Latin tongue, the official dialect of Rome and its government, the cherished idiom of its poets, its orators and its historians, never, for one year or one day, ceased,—even after the downfall of the Western Roman Empire,—to be the language of the schools, the law courts, the government, and, especially, of the Church in her liturgy and her official teachings and administration. Rome,—and the great intellectual centers created by Christian Rome throughout her vast empire,—have never at any time till now ceased to speak as a living language the tongue of Cicero, Livy, and Horace.

Thus, it is no exaggeration to say, that wide-spread as was the use of the Latin tongue in the days of Cicero, and apart from the mere perfection or elegance of form,—its use was even more general in Italy and throughout Western Europe in the days of Leo X.

Disuse of the Latin in Protestant Countries.

'Since the religious disruption caused, at that epoch, by Luther and his associates,—the Latin as the language of the schools and universities, as that of the great learned professions, and as the medium of official and epistolary intercourse, has been abandoned by Protestants, precisely because it was the language of Christian Rome. In our own day, moreover, rationalists and revolutionists have been unanimous in raising an outcry against the culture of the ancient literatures.

But the sounder public opinion of both Europe and America does not favor this sacrifice of the Greek and Latin to modern theories of progress and civilization. And we trust the day is far distant when the study of the classic masterpieces of Italian and Grecian genius shall cease to form the chief basis of high literary studies.

Indeed, in European countries that we need not name, one of the features of the recent wholesale persecutions against the Catholic Church, was the substitution of living languages for Latin and Greek, the compulsory education of clerical students in the State schools, and the consequent abolition of all special seminaries for the training of Catholic youth.

Efforts to destroy Priestly Vocations and Education.

Thereby the enemy showed that he understood the teaching of the Classics and the use of Latin and Greek to be one of the great instruments of the Church not only in her own special work of teaching and enlightening, but in the more general labor of promoting the true civilization of the race. We mean, of course, that in all Christian schools due prominence should be given to the Christian classics,—to the writings of the early Greek and Latin Fathers, whose beauties of thought and diction are all the more thoroughly enjoyed, when a thorough Christian and a thorough scholar fills the professor's chair, and guides the young minds he is training so as to see and admire only what is truly beautiful and admirable.

Let Catholic parents remember, that from the day which would see Latin and Greek banished from our colleges would date the ruin of all Christian education, the ruin of the priesthood, and the beginning for the Christian Church of a darker era than that of Julian the Apostate. For the intellectual darkness would not be measured by one man's life, nor limited to one generation.

What we need in our Colleges is,—not that the study of modern languages shall supersede that of the ancient Classics, and that the cultivation of mathematical and physical science shall take the place given hitherto to the teaching of ancient and ecclesiastical history,—but that extraordinary and united efforts shall be made to teach the Classics thoroughly, to throw such interest into the study of the ancient literatures and histories, that young men shall be able to master them, to get enamored of them, and to cherish the love of them ever afterward.

True Catholic Education combines the Ancient and the Modern.

Do we mean that thereby they shall neglect their own mother-tongue, or modern languages, or the mathematic and physical sciences, without which a scholar is only half a scholar? Most certainly not. We cannot forget that the training given in our own dear Alma Mater combined a thorough knowledge of both classical and scientific lore. And we are proud to see, that with the new responsibilities assumed by her in organizing a university course complete in every department, the old equal love for the culture of antiquity and that of the ripest science of our times still continues to burn with undiminished fervor.

It ought also to be well understood, that neither a thorough mastery of the ancient classics, nor the slight acquaintance with the Latin tongue required for the study of theology and the discharge of the priestly functions, has ever been, in the judgment of the Church, a sufficient intellectual education. The extraordinary sacrifices which she makes yearly in lands, where the revolution has stripped her of everything, to create or to sustain universities worthy of being in the foremost rank of true science, are a most eloquent proof of the desire she has that her priests shall be as superior in learning as she wills them to be superior in moral excellence.

The Clerical Standard of Science.

Surely a clergyman, mixing in daily intercourse with men of the world, with scholars and gentlemen in every walk of life, where all the living questions about society, religion, and science, about history and art in all its branches, come up for discussion,—must not feel that he is, in all these matters, treading upon unknown or uncertain ground. He must have already studied and discussed and mastered all these mighty problems. He must stand, in every company where the serious-minded and the cultivated meet, like one who is naturally looked up to for light, not as one who is compelled to be dumb through sheer ignorance, and therefore looked down upon. He will everywhere meet with conscientious and anxious inquirers after truth,—after the truth on these momentous issues between science and religion,— and must he perforce be silent? Has he no light in his lamp wherewith to guide the soul who is seeking the right road amid the surrounding darkness?

We need to have our clergymen leading the advance of intellect on every path of solid science. We need to have our young professional men in the world, after they come forth from our colleges, armed cap-à-pie with such armor that no assault shall pierce it, and with such victorious weapons, that no enemy shall stand before them.

The Classics are only Models of Literary Excellence.

The knowledge of Greek and Latin is only a small portion of the varied culture that fills a college course ; the study of the classical authors in these languages,—is for the intellect and the taste, a training and a molding similar to that, which the selected art - students from every country in Christendom have to undergo in Rome, while contemplating, studying, copying, and imitating the immortal works of pagan and Christian art collected there. Just as the painter or the architect in examining and analyzing the masterpieces left behind by the artists of Italy and Greece, finds daily new worlds of ideal perfection and beauty opened before him,—ideal forms and conceptions which he can make his own by study and imitation,—even so is it with the glorious forms of literary perfection bequeathed to us by antiquity. We can make them our own, copy them, endeavor to surpass them.

It is universally conceded, that to be a superior painter or sculptor, long years of study in Rome are an indispensable discipline. It ought to be,—indeed it is just as generally granted,—that to attain the first rank in literary excellence, the study of classical literature is a discipline none the less necessary.

Elizabeth Barrett Browning was almost as enthusiastic a student of Greek antiquity, as William Ewart Gladstone, or Guizot, or Wiseman. The writers, poets, orators, who might be mentioned as forming exceptions to this rule, are, in reality, no exceptions. The contemporary models on whom they formed their method and their diction, were, every one of them, the living copies of ancient excellence.

In one word, if you send your son to college, only keep him there when you find that he has both the talent and the love of study that will insure success. Then spare no encouragement to your boy, no help to his masters that can further and increase this success. Wait patiently for the end, and you will be surely rewarded.

If, on the contrary, you find, after necessary trial, that your boy has neither aptitude nor inclination for such studies,—you will do a prudent parent's part in withdrawing him and putting him elsewhere to studies proportioned to his talent and his bent, and under such discipline as may secure both his learning well what he is put to, and his cultivating his own heart by self-discipline.

CHAPTER XIV.

THE SECOND EDUCATION.

Man am I grown, a man's work must I do.

TENNYSON.

We are not here to promote incalculable quantities of law, physic, or manu-factured goods, BUT TO BECOME MEN : not narrow pedants, but wide-seeing, mind-traveled men. Who are the men of history to be admired most? Those whom most things became : who could be weighty in debate, of much device in council, considerate in a sick-room, genial at a feast, joyous at a festival, capa-ble of discourse with many minds, large-souled, not to be shriveled up into any one form, fashion, or temperament.--HELPS.*

THE public school, the college, and the university only prepare youth for the great school of the world. Academic training of every kind fit young men to educate themselves for the serious business of life. This second and decisive education should be kept in mind both by parents and by teachers, while a boy is undergoing in school the intellec-tual and moral discipline that is to form his character and to exercise on his future career so great an influence.

He must be told, while still amid the quiet shades of his Alma Mater, that he will have hard and noble work to do, and a long battle to fight. His educators only train him to familiarity with his workman's tools, and accustom him to bear and use his armor and weapons. On entering on his chosen professional sphere, he must prove that he is an

" Active doer, noble liver,
Strong to labor, sure to conquer."

We are anxious—in the first place—that the youth who

---

* "Friends in Council," i., p. 64; New York, 1861.

turns his back on school and his face toward the serious
and stern work before him, should show himself "a noble
liver," by the principles and virtues displayed in private
life, while proving himself, besides, in his professional
dealings, the "active doer, strong to labor, sure to con-
quer."

The "nobility of life," that all have a right to expect
from the long and carefully trained student, must manifest
itself in his duteous conduct toward his own family. Young
people returning home at the end of their academical edu-
cation, are, all too frequently, apt to fancy, that their
"good behavior" and their "accomplishments" are things
to be put by with their class-books and their diplomas, and
only to be brought forth from the closet for the admiration
and delight of strangers.

Be the Delight of your Home-Circle.

Have we not known young ladies, who charmed the large
audience assembled on the "graduating day" with their
musical and oratorical performances, and who could not be
induced to play, or sing, or recite one poetical passage in
order to gratify their home-circle, precisely because it was
but the home-circle? What perversity of temper, taste, and
judgment! Ah, young ladies, we were taught in our young
days—long ago—that every accomplishment brought from
school by the sons and daughters of any good family, were
to be chiefly and before all else, displayed for the pleasure
of father and mother and brothers and sisters. It was then
the rule and the fashion to delight the family circle each
evening with music and song and charade, brothers and sis-
ters all joining hand and heart and voice rapturously, pre-
cisely because father and mother were delighted lookers-
on, and all the more rapturously because they alone were
there to drink their fill of the deep delight. Has this rule
become "old fashioned"?

But our words are more for your brothers than for you.
Young men,—we happen to know it,—often toil heroically

to deserve their degree of bachelor or of master of arts.   It is most praiseworthy toil, assuredly ; and it should ever be an earnest to all who witness it of the still nobler qualities that are to mark the after-college life.

Do not forget, however, young laureates, that there are other arts, often harder to master, and not less necessary to you, which you are to study, to court, to possess, and to practice, if you would be the true men the world expects you to be.   There is a science, more needful even than those which enable one to read all the mysteries of earth and ocean and the starry heavens,—the science of living with others so as to contribute our utmost to their happiness.

Claim of Parents on their Educated Sons.

Before and above all others your parents have the first claim on you,—now that you are once more the inmates of their home.   Shall we consider together one or two points which are of most especial importance to you and to them at this critical period of life ?

Though you may be the most generous and devoted of sons, and most desirous of showing your parents how deeply you prize the self-sacrificing love that has been so long waiting for your return to the home, yet we venture to affirm that you are far from estimating that love at its real value.   Even where parents are so blessed with the goods of fortune, that the cost of the longest and most expensive education is to them a matter of no account, there are other sacrifices which a noble-hearted youth will consider to be infinitely greater.   There is the generosity of a mother's love, consenting to the long years of separation from her dear ones,—perhaps her only one.   This unsatisfied craving of a motherly heart is not one that dies out with time : it rather increases with each succeeding year.   For the love and pride of a true mother's heart look forward to the beautiful bloom of early manhood in her boy, with a yearning to which nothing can be compared in depth and intensity.

The father's patient waiting is often scarcely less deserving of filial gratitude and admiration. For, after all, it is to his sons that a father looks forward not only for the dear companionship which is a need of fatherly natures, but for the realization of the hope deposited in every father's heart by God's own hand,—of seeing himself living again and prospering in his sons. And how often does it not happen that a father's hopes and affections center in the son whose education and progress he watches with ever-increasing anxiety?

The Debt of Gratitude due to Poor Parents.

When the parents who thus "watch and wait" for the long-expected return of the absent one, are anything but favorites of fortune; when they have both toiled and suffered through the tedious college years, denying themselves everything, that the absent one should want for nothing; when they had set their hearts on seeing him combine in his own person, at the end of his studies, all literary accomplishment and moral excellence,—with what an unspeakable intensity of expectant love, do not these two fond, hungry hearts stretch forth to meet him on his coming home! Who can describe the mother's joy and triumph, when the boy she has parted with long ago returns a man, or almost a man,—every accomplishment and youthful grace exaggerated in the light of her motherly admiration?

Who can say, on the other hand, how much a son thus returning to the home of his childhood, has it in his power to do for the contentment, the perfect happiness of his parents? Sweet above all the rewards that mind could plan, or wealth purchase, sweet above all thought and beyond our power of expression, is the grateful devotion of such a son to such parents. . . .

A son blessed with such parents as are here described, must have brought away from their home—how lowly soever we may picture it—the undying memories of a love incomparable in sweetness and blissfulness. Whatever may

have been his experiences at college, as boyhood slowly
grew into youth and early manhood,—it is not likely that
the spectacle of others' wealth and home luxuries, could
have blotted away from his true heart the image of his
father's hearthstone and of her who kept ever burning
upon it the bright fire of her own womanly charities.

> "My own fireside! Those simple words
>   Can bid the sweetest dreams arise;
> Awaken feelings' tendcrest chords,
>   And fill with tears of joy mine eyes.
> What is there my wild heart can prize,
>   That doth not in thy sphere abide;
> Haunt of my home-bred sympathies,
>   My own—my own fireside!"

Yes—we have seen not only the young man, with all his
blushing honors thick upon him, find no repose, enjoy no
satisfaction, and apparently close his ears to the concert of
admiration and praise that greeted him inside and outside
the academic halls,—till he was fast clasped in his mother's
arms, and heard one word of simple congratulation from
her or from his father's lips. The added brightness and
warmth which his presence seemed to bring to the dear
hearth of his childhood, was more grateful to his inward
and outward sense than the rapturous applause of multi-
tudes. And, oh, how we have seen a happy mother's face
transformed by the sight of her returning boy, as if the
light of another world shone upon it, and her whole soul
beaming forth in the look of unutterable gratitude with
which she heard her darling's words and received his
caresses!

Loving to come back to the Old Nest.

We have seen sons, later in life, when they had homes of
their own,—homes, too, blessed with all a man's heart can
desire,—yet loving to fly back to the old nest where their in-
fancy had been sheltered, and coveting the sweet warmth
of their mother's wing, as eagerly as if the whole outside
world had not one other restful spot for them! Ah, true

men! to them shall be given, in their turn, sons and daughters who will love to make their father's home a paradise, and to crown his old age with the priceless love that he had lavished on his parents.

Do not be ashamed of being ever a little child when you seek the dear and holy atmosphere of a father's home and a mother's tenderness. It must be your praise in the eyes of all true men, ever to feel and to say of the roof beneath which you were reared—

> "My refuge ever from the storm
>   Of this world's passion, strife, and care;
> Though thunder-clouds the skies deform,
>   Their fury cannot reach me there:
> There all is cheerful, calm, and fair;
>   Wrath, envy, malice, strife, or pride,
> Hath never made its hated lair,
>   By thee—my own fireside!
>
> "Shrine of my household deities;
>   Bright scene of home's unsullied joys;
> To thee my burthened spirit flies,
>   When Fortune frowns, or Care annoys!
> Thine is the bliss that never cloys;
>   The smile whose truth hath oft been tried;—
> What, then, are this world's tinsel toys,
>   To thee—my own fireside!
>
> "Oh, may the yearnings, fond and sweet,
>   That bid my thoughts be all of thee,
> Thus ever guide my wandering feet
>   To thy heart-soothing sanctuary!
> Whate'er my future years may be,
>   Let joy or grief my fate betide,
> Be still an Eden bright to me,
>   My own—my own fireside!"*

You will say,—and most justly,—that a soul incapable of prizing the purest and dearest of all this world's joys,—a mother's proud affection and a father's manly love,—must be a soul afflicted with some moral deformity. Yet is it most true that there are many such.

---

* Alaric A. Watts.

If, in our long acquaintance with parents and their sons, we have been gladdened by seeing the former made happy by their children, by witnessing the fondest, proudest realization of a father and a mother's dreams,—we·have also known of more than one instance of bitter deception. Of the latter we only permit ourselves to speak here, in the hope that this page may attract the eye of advanced students, and warn them in time to prevent their incurring the guilt of the blackest human ingratitude and one of the most dreadful of possible misfortunes.

There have been sons, tenderly loved and cared for, educated at the cost of sacrifices known in their full extent to God alone, on whose future goodness and greatness both parents had built the dearest hope of their life, — and who, at the end of their college or university course, were ashamed to return to their paternal roof, as if to acknowledge poor father and mother were to them a degradation ! Ah, thrice unhappy parents who had conceived and nursed so long the fond, foolish, fatal ambition of devoting their substance and their lives to "making their son a gentleman"! As if anything but the gentle heart and the generous spirit could make the gentleman !

We glance rapidly at such moral monsters, both because we would be most unwilling to have our readers believe that they are anything else than rare monsters of ingratitude and baseness, and because we must hasten to say how common are the opposite examples of manly affection, and true nobleness of spirit.

To those who know the numbers of high-souled men sprung from the laborer's cabin, reared and educated at the expense of a whole life's toil and privation, and filling the most honorable stations in every rank of the community, we need not say that such perversity as we here hold up as a warning, can only be exceptional. Were the writing of this book to have no other effect than to spare, by prevention, a single motherly or fatherly heart such agony as we have beheld,—we should have good cause not to regret our labor.

Home-Treasures of Affection.

And so this much to remind young men, that their first duty, on their return home, is to their parents and their family. Within their home they should exert themselves not only to repay father and mother with unceasing love and reverence and devotion, but they should find especial delight in making up to their brothers and sisters for the manifold regrets of the long absence from home.

Friendships formed in college, we know it well, are often the purest and the most lasting ; still a friend's constant affection and support is rarely comparable to the treasure of a brother or a sister's love. Those only whose souls are guided in all things by principle and conscience, can appreciate what a noble brother's friendship is, or what is the treasure of a sister's undying fidelity.

Cultivate these home charities, these family affections, first of all and before everything else. And then persuade yourself that the first, and most frequently the best, school for studying the social virtues and social refinement,—is in the bosom of your own household.

As we are laying down a few practical rules to help young men in acquiring, together with the true graces of social manners, the true esteem of all who know them, let us begin by saying, that the solid foundation of all interior sweetness, outward gracefulness, and all real lovableness,—is God's grace in the soul's center, and the serenity which its presence produces.

You need a higher motive than ever not only for preserving undiminished the manly and unaffected piety of which you acquired the habit at school, but of increasing its vigorous growth in the sunlight of public life. You must not look for approval to those above, around, or beneath you : look to God alone ! Though but a layman and a young man,—you are now "God's man," bound to represent Him in the eyes of the world, bound to be His son in Godlike action, and destined to gain for Him many victories in the

battle of Truth against Error, of goodness against triumph-
ant depravity.   You are God's soldier and servant.   Look
to Him alone for strength, approval, and reward !

You are God's organ, in more ways than one ; you are
appointed by Him as a teacher to those "who sit in dark-
ness," who know your ancestral faith only through the
misrepresentations they have heard of it, who, perhaps,
know your God Himself only through the distorting haze
of a bad education and a false philosophy.

Mission of Educated Young Men.

You are to teach them.   This is so true, that hencefor-
ward, wherever you go and are known as a child of the
Great Mother, brought up in one of her privileged schools,
your life will be taken as a sample of her godliness, your
words will be repeated as the echo of her doctrines, and
your person, your manners, your very bearing in public
and in private, will be pointed out as the result of Catholic
culture.

Yes,—you are so truly a teacher, that your whole life
will be watched, scrutinized, recorded, and commented on,
—as a living lesson of Catholic enlightenment and morality.
In the schools which sprung up in the Spain of the sixteenth
century as well as in newly discovered America, the young
teachers—the saintly sons of the great St. Teresa—were
wont each morning to say, before beginning their lessons,
the following most beautiful prayer.   Do not fear to read
it, to make it your own.   A lovely flower is none the less
lovely or fragrant because it happens to bloom in a cathe-
dral close, and beneath the shadow of God's holy house.
So fear not to cull it and wear it near your heart.   Here
it is

"O most lowly-minded King of hearts Christ Jesus, by
the very heart of that merciful condescension which led
Thee, our Orient from on high, to visit us in our need, I
beseech Thee to create within me through the Spirit who
is Thy Gift, an humble and pure heart, all athirst for Thine

own secret teaching: in order that in this school of Thy
lowly followers, I may learn to guide, without leading
astray, the tender souls committed to me by Thy sweet
Mother." *

Wear near your heart, in an especial manner, the desire
to be Christ-like in your soul, and Christ-like in your life,
and the resolve to win to Him by the sweet fragrance of
your gentleness, your refinement, your modesty, your un-
blemished purity and honor,—the souls who know neither
Him nor your Great Mother!

You need only be true to the divine light and voice
within, in order to appear before others, in all the relations
of life, as God and men would have you. The conscious
possession of His grace, who is the deep ocean of peace,
sweetness, and love, will enable you, force you even, to
look with contentment and love on all persons and things
throughout His creation.

The spirit of true piety is not the sad, melancholy, brood-
ing, and bitter thing that a gloomy fanaticism would make
it. It is lightsome, joyous, loving, compassionate, and all-
embracing in its kindness. The Spirit of God in a youthful
soul, just beginning to run its race of usefulness in the
world, sheds abroad over earth and sky and ocean, over
the whole moral as well as the material world, the light of
deep and joyous contentment with which their Divine Author
uttered, in the beginning, the judgment, that "they were
very good."

It is sad enough to see old men, who have tasted of life's
bitterness and disappointments, without being chastened
by them or impelled to draw nearer to God,—who have
sate at the banquet of life without appreciating or enjoying
a single one of the delights spread out for them there by
the most bountiful hand of our God,—to go darkly and

* Humillime Rex cordium Jesu Christe, per viscera misericordiæ tuæ, in
quibus visitasti nos oriens ex alto, obsecro te, creare digneris in me cor humile
et purum, cupidissimum secretæ eruditionis tuæ: ut in schola humilium disci-
pulorum tuorum fiam dono tuo sapiens ad regendam sine deceptione novellam
prolem dulcissimæ Genetricis tuæ.

19

gloomily down to their grave abusing and cursing their fellow-men, and asserting that all is bad in this beautiful world of ours. They pass through life, like beasts of ill odor by night through the loveliest of gardens, without perceiving or having the capacity to perceive the varied wealth and beauty and magnificence of nature and art around them.

To the Pure of Heart the World is ever Beautiful.

Not so do the eyes of pure-hearted, noble-minded youth look out upon God's universe. They behold it overspread with the heavenly tints that clothed it at its prime, when God walked forth in visible form to enjoy the works of His own hands, "When the morning stars praised [Him] together, and all the sons of God made a joyful melody." * The divinely enlightened heart of the young and the pure is drawn instinctively toward what is good and lovely, not only in the society of men, but throughout every other walk of creation. And this lightsomeness and freshness of heart dies not away with youth, but lasts, in the true man, increased and intensified, through 'manhood and old age. The springtide of the pure heart is eternal. / The lamp of God which illuminates the soul-sanctuary never ceases to shed its golden splendors on the outside world. Its light only grows more vivid as the day of eternity draws near.

Oh, may that freshness of heart, that unfading youth of soul be ever yours, through all the vicissitudes of age, health, fortune, enjoyment, and suffering!

Let this interior peace, this deep contentment, this disposition to see in man and in nature the bright side only, save you, within your family circle, from the fatal faults of censoriousness and fault-finding. Have always words of praise for your dear ones.

> " Be to (their) virtues very kind ;
> Be to (their) faults a little blind." †

---

* Job, xxxviii. 7.   † Matthew Prior.

Carry with you the same rule into the outside world. Be prompt to see the good qualities of those with whom you have to associate; be slow to acknowledge their faults even to yourself; and be careful not to show one man in ten thousand that you have discovered in others or in himself anything you deem blameworthy.

Be, on the contrary, both prompt and generous in praising the good you see in others. Do not believe that all men are prone to evil and ever ready to do you a mischief. The longer you live, the greater and wider your experience of mankind, and the more will you have reason to bless God that there are so many noble and beautiful souls left on earth to prove the presence on it of good angels and of the God of angels.

Purity is always full of Reverence.

Never,—so long as He spares your mother's life,—fail to show her daily and hourly a love full of infinite reverence and tenderness. Let your love for your sisters be also most respectful and deferential. And should God send you, in His own good time, a woman who can be all in all to you let your love for her be distinguished by the same reverential feeling, and your life-long service to her be one of respectful and heartfelt devotion.

Reverence is to love, what a casing of purest gold and crystal, adorned with precious stones, is to the portrait of the one dearest to our heart: it preserves the loved image from soil and decay, while permitting us to gaze on the cherished features, and to wear it continually near our heart.

Think and speak of all women with something, at least, of the respect and the deference you are wont to show to your mother and your sisters; and never permit yourself anything approaching to disrespect toward the poorest, the lowliest, the most unworthy of their sex. If you would have a sure, an infallible sign marking out to you, in the intercourse of life, the man who should never be your friend, your companion, or your business associate, let it be disrespect to women. The man who forgets what is due to his mother's sex is neither a true gentleman, nor a true man · and he who habitually thinks and speaks evil of women, is. one who has long ago forfeited self-respect and is unworthy of the esteem of virtuous men. He is a moral leper to be shunned carefully and mercilessly.

Truth and Honor.

Be truthful,—truthful in thought, in intention, in word, and deed,—in the whole tenor of your life, as if. He who made your soul were visibly present to you in your studies, your conversations, your every daily act, standing—revealed to your eyes—by the side of every person you spoke to, and dealt with.

Be honorable.

> " Inform
> Thy thoughts with nobleness, that thou mayst prove
> To shame invulnerable, and stick i' the wars
> Like a great sea-mark standing every flaw,
> And saving those that eye thee."

He who has ever passed in Eastern lands for the wisest, if not the greatest, of men, said long, long ago : " A good name is better than great riches." * We must, however, hasten to warn you not to mistake false honor for the true, the shadow for the substance, the vain praise of men for the just judgment of God on the solid merits of His children ; the road of pride and self-worship, leading aloft and ending at an inevitable precipice, for the safe path in which the " noble liver" walks, while he seeks and sings praise to the Most High God.

The son, well-born and high-souled, has only one aim in doing, daring, and bearing great things,—to glorify his father, to reflect honor on the mother who bore him. The crown he wins he only values because he can lay it at their feet, the songs sung in his praise are only sweet to his ears. in so far as their music can reach and thrill the souls of his. parents.

---

* Proverbs of Solomon, xxii. 1.

This most true and lofty sentiment dictates also the care to be had of one's name and reputation. For the name one bears is the father's name, the family name ; and its honor belongs not to one's self exclusively, but rather to one's parents and kindred.

We know,—you, flower of our Christian youth, know it far better than the multitude,—that our dearest honor is that of the God who created and redeemed us, that of the Church, who, under Him, is the dear Mother of our souls. For them we stand or we fall ; on them is reflected alike our honor or our dishonor.

" The Pious and Just Honoring of Ourselves."

"The Catholic Church nourishes that 'ingenious and noble shame,' which Milton so extols, adding, ' or call it, if you will, that esteem, whereby men bear an inward reverence toward their own persons.' And if, as he continues, ' the love of God, as a fire sent from heaven ever to be kept alive upon the altars of our hearts, be the first principle of all godly and virtuous actions in men, and this pious and just honoring of ourselves the second, serving as the radical moisture and fountain-head, whence every laudable and worthy enterprise issues forth,'—where, except in the Catholic Church, can we find any security for its perpetual transmission? Where else can honor hope to find an inexhaustible source of that self-respect which makes man fear not so much the offense and reproach of others, as he dreads and would blush at the reflection of his own severe and modest eye upon himself, if it should see him doing or imagining, though in the deepest secrecy, that which is base.' " *

There lies the distinction between false honor,—the worship of self, accepted from the world for the sole sake of self, by the proud or vain man,—and true honor, the self-respect, the pious and just honoring of ourselves, for His

---

* Digby, "Compitum," b. i., ch. ix.

sake and His love, who is our Father in Heaven, and next for her sake, who is the Mother of His children here below.

We have a striking and memorable illustration of this in the conduct of St. Ignatius of Loyola. The once chivalrous and sensitive soldier, who shrank from the thought of worldly dishonor as from something a thousand times worse than death in its most appalling form, became, after his conversion, filled with an insatiable thirst for humiliations. So long as these only fell upon himself without involving his good name as connected with others, or with the honor of God and His Church, he would drink in and savor insult and scorn with more avidity, than the fainting traveler from across the burning wilderness, would drink of the first cool spring on his path. Thus, while pursuing under the guidance of the Holy Spirit, his first long course of moral discipline in the cavern near Manresa, Ignatius would sally forth occasionally from his retreat, dressed like the poorest of beggars, with matted hair, unshaven beard, sallow and sunken cheeks, and go limping slowly and painfully through the streets of the town to beg from door to door the bread needful to his sustenance. Little did the inhabitants, who gave or refused alms to the stranger, imagine that the sickly, emaciated, infirm young man, was one of their own proudest nobles, a soldier who had gloriously defended the honor of Spain. And as they watched him limping along the street on his shattered limb, the little boys, thinking him demented, would take pleasure in following him with jeer and scoff, as ill-bred children are apt to do. But whenever they did so, Ignatius would stand still, and with downcast eyes listen to their crys and abuse, as if their words of scorn and mockery were to him the most ravishing of earthly harmonies.

Where our Good Name involves God's Interests.

Many are the anecdotes told of this great-souled man, attesting his supernatural love of contempt and humiliation. When, however, he had begun to bind to himself, in the University of Paris, the chosen souls who, like Francis

Xavier and Peter Favre, were to be with himself the foun-
ders of the apostolic Society of Jesus, he was not willing
that any stain of dishonor should fall on his own name or
that of his companions,—because he knew that such dis-
grace would prevent the mighty good his associates were
destined of God to do in both hemispheres.

Thus having been once accused of some infraction of the
University rules, he was unjustly sentenced by the faculty
to undergo the shame of a public flagellation before the as-
sembled students and professors. He allowed the proceed-
ings against him to go on till the very moment came when
the punishment was to be inflicted, and then produced such
overwhelming proofs of his innocence, that he received the
compliments and congratulations of the very judges who
had so hastily condemned him.

This same zeal for the good name of his infant Society he
again and again displayed in Italy, and with such success
that the slanderers were silenced forever.

Thus is it with you, young men, who stand before the
world not only as the representatives of the families whose
names you bear, but also as the children of a Father and a
Mother, whose honor is in your keeping, and to whom your
honor, your good name and spotless reputation, are trea-
sures that you cannot compromise or barter away without
deepest guilt and undying infamy.

CHAPTER·XV.

BOYHOOD.

Ah, then how sweetly closed those crowded days !
The minutes parting one by one, like rays
  That fade upon a summer's eve.
  But, oh ! what charm, or magic numbers,
Can give me back the gentle slumbers
  Those weary, happy days did leave?
  When by my bed I saw my mother kneel,
And with her blessing took her nightly kiss ;
Whatever time destroys, he cannot this
  E'en now that nameless kiss I feel.
       ALLSTON.

How Boys look up to their Father.

IF fathers only knew the magic power they possess of fill-
ing the souls of their boys,—while boyhood's golden day is
still in its morning,—with sweet and holy memories that re-
main to embalm and sanctify a whole lifetime ! Somehow,
girls look to their mothers for all that makes the enchant-
ment of their earliest years ; but a boy, with the instincts
and yearnings of manhood strong within him, will look up
to his father as his ideal,—and to imitate him will as surely
be his first endeavor, as that of the bird impelled to leave
the nest, will be to try its wings in following the flight of
its parent. Girls are like sweet and delicate flowers that
need far more of shade than of sunshine, shedding their
fragrance and displaying their loveliness in the quiet nooks
of the garden, or along the shady borders of some lake in
the woods. Boys are like the trees in the forest ; they will

296

shoot up their slender stems alongside the parent trunk, stretching ever upward to spread their branches in the full light and heat of noonday.

Companionship with their father is the first great ambition of boys to whom God has given a true father, one worthy to be admired and imitated ; outside of school-hours, they yearn to spend with him every moment of re-creation and repose. From their mother they receive in the morning and evening, as it were, a double bath of life. A boy returns to his mother's arms and rests in the sweet glow of her affection at evening, when he has had his fill of lusty effort and outdoor exercise, as naturally as the lark, after sunset, descends from the purple clouds where he has been circling and carolling since early dawn, and seeks his nest in the flowering grasses. Her voice, the dear light of her eyes, her smile, and her caresses have on every faculty of a boy's soul the same effect that the subdued glow of twilight, the stillness, coolness, and dews of night have on growing shrub and tree after the parching day, the wind, and the storm.

The caresses of maternal love, the prayers murmured by her side, the kiss and the blessing with which she consigns her dear ones to sleep and to the keeping of their Guardian Angels,—are, in very truth, the sweetest image of God's infinite tenderness. The lessons of piety instilled into the willing heart of boyhood in these dear evening and morning hours, sink as naturally into its very substance and pene-trate to the inmost sources of spiritual life, as surely as the dew sinks into the thirsty soil and penetrates by every pore of tree and shrub and flower, of the grass on the meadow and the ripening corn, refreshing and invigorating their ex-hausted life-currents.

A Divine Work Divinely Performed.

Such is to boyhood, each morning and evening, the loving office of motherhood, the complement of the father's com-panionship throughout the day. Happy, most happy the

boys whose father's gentle and pious care lends itself with
devout and grateful eagerness to helping this office of
motherly love.   What may not be expected from boyhood
reared beneath the united influence of this twofold tender-
ness of a father and a mother whose affection is sanctified
by the divine blessing, and whose coöperation in training
their dear ones, is—they know and feel it—a divine work
divinely performed !

Let parents forgive us.   We are treating of sonship, its
duties, and its virtues.   What we have been just describing
lies at the very root of all filial virtue ; such nurture as we
here hint at disposes the soul to find the performance of all
duty sweet, as surely as the loving husbandry of the gar-
dener, aided by the late and the early rain, and all the gentle
influences of the heavens, prepares the fruit tree to bear in
autumn its most delicious fruit.

The Parents' Ideal in their Work.

One word, then, about that ideal which both parents
ought to keep before their eyes in forming the soul and the
exterior deportment of every one of their boys.   Of course,
in Catholic homes we suppose that every father, who has at
heart the preserving of his boy's soul in supernatural grace,
will make him familiar with the infancy and boyhood of
our divine Lord.   No Catholic home ought to be without
"The Life of Christ, by St. Bonaventura ;" and no father
ought to allow a single year to pass by without reading
this most beautiful book to all his children.   We suppose,
moreover, that they are made acquainted with such sweet
models of boyish innocence, grace, and heroism as are
found in the lives of St. Aloysius, St. Stanislaus Kostka,
Blessed John Berchmans, and others that we need not name
here.

What, however, it is imperative to set here before the
minds of parents and boys alike is some living exemplar of
lovely youth in boys brought up in the world and for the
world.   For in such we see more easily models that young

men of the world can imitate, models which will draw the eyes and the hearts of boyhood, and inflame them with a noble emulation.

Here, then, is the picture of a noble Christian youth from the pen of a woman of the late middle age:

"He was a vessel of all goodness, pitifulness, benignity, and sweetness. In his boyhood and early youth he was comely, cheerful, fond of pastime, and inclined to love all that was honorable and could be loved without sin: he was bright and gentle in his manner, having always kind words to say, open-handed, and so affable and gracious in his address that all who saw him were drawn to him, princes, princesses, knights, nobles, and folk of every sort. But when the good duke came to maturer years, all this joyous and innocent youth turned into sense and moderation, good counsel, devotion, and constancy; and though his conduct was ever deserving of all praise, yet he now seemed to advance still higher in the degrees of all virtues. He was a shining model of charity: he used to succor poor gentlemen, to bestow great gifts on poor monks and indigent clergymen; to poor scholars and to the needy of every condition he was a compassionate and bountiful almsgiver. He is also wont to dispense abundant alms in secret; he trusts in God with invincible faith, and turns to Him in all his necessities." *

This is the mirror we hold up to parents. For the guidance of mothers, while training their boys to all manliness, we have laid down rules in another work.† So now we address ourselves directly to the boy and the young man themselves.

The Two Things recommended to Boys.

We have lived all our lifetime among you, O you, who are so dear to us, that we should willingly give time, strength, life, and all to teach you the right road, as we

---

* Christine de Pisan, *Livre des Fais*, tome ii., ch. xiv.
† See "The Mirror of True Womanhood."

now see it ; to fill your minds with noble thoughts, noble
ideals, noble memories ; to inspire you with noble aims,
noble sentiments, and the courage that is equal to every
noble enterprise : we would fain fill your hearts, while pur-
suing all that is most elevating and ennobling, with joy so
bright and so overflowing, that your course should resemble
the clear, blue, full stream of the Rhone where it issues
purified from the Lake of Geneva, and prepares to be the
glory and wealth of Southern France.

"We have two qualities in our souls,"—wrote Plato long
ages ago,—"which we must preserve with equal solicitude ;
the one which prompts us to dare, and the other which con-
strains us to fear :—to be bold for virtue, and to be afraid
in respect to vice." *

We purpose to point out to you here in a few pregnant
words, what are the lawful objects on which boyhood and
youth may and should exercise that courage, daring, and
generosity of spirit,—that true chivalry which is innate in
them ; and what, on the other hand, are those enemies
which they have most to dread while running their race of
high-souled generosity.

Generosity of Spirit: its Object, DUTY.

Begin with your home-life. Learn early how to ennoble
every act of yours by acquiring, before and above all things,
to propose as the motive of your entire life, DUTY. Make
of the lofty sense of your duty to God the motive of your
duty to your parents ; and your early home-life having
been thus sanctified by perfect conformity to the Divine
Will, and to the will of your parents in view of the Divine
Majesty, this same elevation of purpose will follow you
through life outside of the paternal home, making your
whole career most pleasing in the sight of God and most
lovely before men.

Let us understand this well, without putting this vital
practical truth into a form that may at all savor of the pul-

---

* *De Legibus,* i.

pit, the catechism, or the school-room. We know that we hold our being throughout this life and the eternity of the life to come from Him whom we call God and Father. In the early chapters of this book is set forth the incomparable and incomprehensible generosity with which he so disposes all things in this life that we may be secure in serving Him while discharging all the offices of true manhoood, and that He prepares our magnificent reward in his own Eternal Home.

He is our God and our Father ;—owing everything to Him, our utmost reach of generosity in His service is rigorously *due* to Him. He alone has the supreme and indisputable right to oblige us, to bind the will of his creature, to dis-pose of our being, our time, our actions, or to communicate to others any share of that imprescriptible authority over us, that essentially belongs to Him as to the sole Author of all things.

The Glory of Life is the Discharge of Duty.

Just as a most generous and high-souled child in a family would deem it *due* to his best of parents ever to look up to him in order to ascertain his will and pleasure, making of the fulfillment of the paternal will and pleasure, the pride and joy and happiness of his own life ;—even so, O children of God, must you deem it your highest honor and make it your highest happiness to look up to that Father, most wor-thy of all love and praise and service, and to place in the discharge of your DUTY the pride and glory of your life.

He it is who places our parents over us in the home, and our superiors over us in Church and State. Their author-ity is derived from the Divine Author of our being. The reverence and obedience we pay to them is before all and above all due to Him. The fulfillment, therefore, of all duty in the home and outside of it is only the discharge of a most sacred obligation to Him who has the first right to command, and who knows how to reward with more than royal or imperial generosity the lowest duty as well as highest, the most obscure as well as the most public and glorious,—*because he looks to the heart with which we do it.*

Precisely because this loving and conscientious discharge of duty is so dear to God and so necessary and meritorious to us, He implanted in the very depths of our nature what philosophers and theologians call the moral sense, *the sense of duty.*

Do not turn away from this page with the notion, that we are entering upon a dull and dry discussion of a thing which is beyond the reach of most men. We shall endeavor to make this important matter both intelligible and interesting to you.

The Sense of Duty,—Man's Chief Character.

God gives to every living thing faculties, senses, instincts most admirably adapted to the kind of life they have to lead. The bee needs no education or training to prepare it to select the flowers from which it gathers its wax and its honey ; nor does it study the rules of geometry before setting about the construction of its hive ; nor has it to learn the topography of the neighboring country in order to make sure of finding its way to the sweetest flowers or the richest gardens, and then to retrace its path home to the hive. It has received from the All-Wise Creator the instinctive knowledge that enables it to construct its hive in the proper place, to fashion the powder it brings home so as to produce the best wax ; and it has a model in its mind of every cell that it builds, so that no architect's rule and compass are needed to correct its measurements or improve the exquisite regularity of the construction. The young bee as it first issues from its pupa state, is ready for its work, issues forth to gather wax and honey without a guide to lead it to its working grounds ;—and, no matter how far it wanders from the hive, it wings its way back with unerring instinct.

The notions of right and wrong, the sense of duty and obligation, are, within the human soul, instincts derived from nature, like the powers of the bee,—derived rather from the divine Author of nature, — with this difference, that whereas the bee is born perfect and able at once to fulfill the end of its existence, man is only born perfectible, capable of attaining by education, training, self-culture and meritorious effort the full moral and intellectual perfection of his being.

How this Sense must be Developed in Boyhood.

The sense of duty, with its corresponding inborn conception of obligation, of right and wrong, is like the natural gift of music and the vocal power of song. It has to be directed to its proper object, exercised, developed, and perfected.

Thrice happy the child, when the light of conscious reason first dawns upon his soul, whose parent is at hand to instruct him in the knowledge of his Almighty Creator, sweetly aiding mind and heart to find and grasp the supremely True and Good and Fair,—just as the first tendrils of the vine-plant are trained to grasp the oak on which it will soon hang its rich clusters, just as the acorn is planted where it finds a congenial soil and atmosphere, with sunlight and warmth to unfold all its mighty germs of strength and durability !

The man in whom this sense of duty was not thus early cultivated and developed, remains for ever stunted in his moral growth, incomplete in his manhood, a failure at best, and most frequently a bane to society and a curse to his fellow-men.

Where is the boy not deformed in intellect by a wrong culture, or depraved in heart by vicious association or self-indulgence, who does not yearn to become a perfect man, a true man,—a man great in knowledge, great in moral worth, great in his deeds, great in the eyes of God,—though he may not care to be great in the esteem and judgment of the world ? The aspirations of the heart of boyhood and youth, where the Christian faith is the light in which all things are viewed and judged, are not the promptings of pride, but the sense of responsibility, and the desire to be all that God wills each one to be. It is the fully grasped sense of that awful parable where the great King distributes talents to his servants ere he departs on some distant expedition. There are splendid rewards for those who double their gains; for the man who buries his gift, there is nothing but despair and gnashing of teeth.

Daring to be Great and Good for God's sake.

The child of Catholic parents with the deep and abiding sense of duty toward Him who is King, and Father, and Judge, will not be apt to think too highly of his own fidelity to the divine trust: he will rather, in that true humility inseparable from innocence and the presence of divine grace in the soul, feel disposed to see only his own shortcomings.

We would, therefore, where a boy's soul is noble and fired with a noble ambition, in which there mingles much more of the desire of doing God good service, than of gaining worldly praise, encourage him to aim high and do nobly,—to be a man among men, foremost among the best, like a tree of generous growth aspiring amid its fellows of the forest to rise ever higher toward the sunlight, the free air, and the broad, bright heavens, struggling to overtop them all,—and that, so as to be hindered of none from spreading its uplifted arms to the sun, the dew, and the breeze.

Provided the habitual thought and love of God with the living sense of duty be the motive power of your life, I bid you be generous and dare much.

The Love of Duty Tested.

This generous sense of duty, this chivalrous ambition of being foremost in all that is good and most pleasing to the Divine Majesty, must be proved and tested by loving, heart-felt, and constant service done to your parents. Unless your boyhood and youth bear these fruits of filial obedience and all most loving duty to father and mother, there is but little ground, if any, to hope that you may ever become a good or a great man. He never was a conscientious, faithful, meritorious servant of his country or fellow-citizens, who was a bad son or an unnatural brother.

If parents only follow the rules given above,* you will have in them such models as you will glory in imitating, such lofty and sweet authority as shall make obedience both easy and honorable. Still must you not fail either in reverence or in dutiful obedience even when they are not patterns of high virtue, or distinguished for culture, refinement, and amenity of disposition.

Obey, then, promptly, joyously, lovingly,—setting before your mind the Eternal Son of God made man, who so obeyed for thirty long years, thereby setting a pattern to the boyhood and youth of all time, whether living beneath the paternal roof, or reared outside of it under proper masters for the exercise of that profession, which they are in due time to honor by all the excellence of manly virtue.

Remember, that, in the old chivalrous ages, there was nothing to which boys and young men, who aspired to the rank of knighthood, applied themselves so readily, as to acquire the praise of obedience. For he alone was deemed worthy to lead, who had long learned to follow ; he alone was judged fit to command, who had learned to obey ; he alone could hope to attain supreme perfection in any craft or profession, who had sat for years under wise and skilled masters, till he 'had himself become a thorough master in what could alone raise him to the first rank.

Obedience is Heroic Love.

Beside the universally acknowledged necessity of this preparatory discipline to the young, there is in the happiness which such loving submission causes to parents, a something that must appeal powerfully to the frank and generous spirit of boyhood. How many noble boys have

---

* Chapters X., XI.

we not known who could not brook the thought of dis-
obeying even in the most trifling matters, because they felt
themselves how exquisite was the pleasure they gave their
parents by their constant and perfect obedience,—their true
love making them fear to cast the slightest shadow over this
happiness !

We who are grown old and look back with such mingled
feelings of regret and pleasure over the past years,—know
how sweet above all sweetness, is the memory of a parent's
delight, manifested by loving word or look or caress in ap-
proval of generous obedience or duty faithfully fulfilled.

Listen to what one who had searched all the ancient lit
erature of Christendom, as he had explored its castles,
palaces, and monasteries, in quest of the records of Chris
tian chivalry, says of this spirit of obedience as practiced
by our forefathers :

"The squire of chivalry had to perform the most 'labori-
ous offices, and the blow which he received on admission to
the order was to denote the sufferings for which he had
still to prepare himself. Büsching remarks that 'the habit
of obedience, the principle of which was derived from the
patriarchal ages, thus learned in youth, was a noble prepa-
ration for subsequent command. The progress to knight-
hood was long and gradual ; nothing sudden hurried the
boy from an unwarlike service to the life of peril. Every
one had to obey and learn, so that step by step he might
become familiar with the dangers and troubles of a chival-
rous life.' Equally admirable were the effects of this educa-
tion in regard to religion and the cultivation of the mind.
The saints have shown that the way of holiness lies in
obedience and observance of the most minute rules. That
furious ardor for bursting every restraint which possesses
so many of the moderns, ends, we find, in the subjection of
the soul to the passions, or in the loss of reason.

"No rank was then exempt from obedience. Von Gra-
venberg relates how his hero, Wigolais, though a king's
son, was bred up like other boys, to discharge every kind
of youthful service. The squire and the knight were able

to say, like the youth in Athenæus, 'If a ladder must be mounted, I am a goat; if a blow is to be endured, I am an anvil; for drinking water, I am a frog; for bearing the winter's cold without shelter, I am a blackbird,—the summer heat, a grasshopper; for walking barefoot any moment in the morning, a crane; for passing a sleepless night, a bat.' " *

So much on this divine generosity which boyhood can display in the loving obedience paid to parents or to all who hold their place.

The divine Strength and Joy springing from Obedience.

Boys do not always, indeed, only a small number do ever, appreciate or understand the force of soul derived from this habit of obedience, especially when it is founded on the supernatural motive mentioned,—imitation of the Incarnate God.

Persons who begin to practice what is known as "mountaineering,"—the climbing of the loftiest mountains and the most inaccessible peaks,—are at first conscious only of the fatigue and the danger accompanying their efforts. But, by degrees, to the sense of danger succeeds that of security, and fatigue diminishes with exercise, while success in ascending one elevation after another, imparts not only delight to the soul, but ever-increasing vigor and power of endurance to the limbs.

Even so has God, the author of our nature, so disposed things, that the discipline of obedience, when generously undergone, imparts to the will power to overcome difficulties seemingly insurmountable.

Dare to be obedient, then, and to emulate in this heroic discipline of self-subjection your Guide and Master, Christ!

Dare also to be temperate and self-denying. This, evidently, was understood to be an integral part of the hardy and wholesome discipline imposed on our forefathers in their boyhood and youth.

---

* Kenelm Henry Digby, " Orlandus," i., pp. 351, 352.

One unpracticed in husbandry might complain of the
skilled gardener who, when he has fruit trees of great pro-
mise, will set about pruning them, lopping off branches on
every side, and thereby destroying the grace and symme-
try of his favorites. Nay, he does more than that ; when
springtide calls forth all the loveliness of his garden, and
every tree is covered with its sweet blossoms, the gardener
will watch each blossom as it falls to give place to the pre-
cions fruit —mercilessly cutting away the flowers and fruits
that he deems superfluous or threaten to overload the
branches and overtax the vitality of the tree, sparing only
the fruit which promises to be excellent, and by its very
excellence to compensate for the loss of quantity.

The Pruned Tree bears the Richest Fruit.

Boyhood is the fruit tree, covered with the fair and exu-
beraut blossoms of promise. Who would bear fruits of un-
questioned excellence, must allow the wise and foreseeing
husbandry of a father, a mother, or a master's hand to
prune, and to graft, and to retrench even the sweetest flow-
ers of natural wealth.

A tree allowed to grow up in a rich soil, unpruned and
untrained, in its own wild luxuriance, will either run alto-
gether into barren leaf, or produce, year after year, a crop
of fruit of decreasing value in savor, in quality, in all real
excellence.

So is it with a boy who is allowed to indulge, unre-
strained, all his appetites, and to follow without hindrance
the bent of all his inclinations.

"The Spaniard"—says Landor—"has the qualities of
the cedar, patient of cold and heat, nourished on little, lofty
and dark, unbending and incorruptible." Prescott, in re-
counting the conquest of Mexico, sets forth the extraordi-
nary abstemiousness and power of endurance of Cortes and
his companions. A small ration of bread or Indian corn
distributed to each soldier once in the twenty-four hours,
was sufficient to sustain the heroic band amid the literally

unceasing attacks of the Mexicans who surrounded them
on every side ; and for months they had to subsist on this,
while performing feats of valor and undergoing fatigues
which appear incredible to modern readers. But no other
nation save one habitually temperate and abstemious to an
uncommon degree could have borne up against this accu-
mulation of labor and suffering. Nor has the Spaniard of
to-day degenerated from the lofty picture drawn of him by
Landor.

Such was also the ancient Republican Roman as painted
by Livy, "with a soul that nothing could conquer, an in-
tegrity that nothing could corrupt ; despising riches, absti-
nent and patient of labor, of an iron frame and will." *

Temperance and Piety go hand in hand.

In the heroic ballad poetry which describes the struggle
maintained for eight centuries by Christian Spain against
the Mohammedan,—the noblest national poetry in exist-
ence,—you have all the great virtues of the true man de-
scribed and illustrated in the lives of numberless warriors.
In the poem of the Cid a recreant knight is thus con-
demned :

> " You breakfast before mass,
> You drink before you pray ;
> There is no honor in your heart,
> Nor truth in what you say."

It was the custom for all,—for knights, particularly,—to
hear mass daily. As this was the commemoration of His
sacrifice who refused at the very moment of crucifixion and
at the height of his agony on the cross, to drink even the
wine and gall which would have made him insensible to
pain,—so men who professed to imitate Him in self-sacrifice
and denial deemed it monstrous to assist at the divine com-
memoration otherwise than fasting. Nor was it less incon-
sistent to assuage one's thirst before having offered up one's
morning adoration to God.

* History, xxxix. 40.

Would that such custom, together with the deep spirit of faith from which it sprung, was more general among us here in this New World!

In the life of Henry IV. of France, it is related that he was from infancy inured to all manner of hardship. He was made to go with boys of his own age, barefooted and bareheaded, to climb his native mountains. If he could only have retained these habits and all akin to these until his dying day, what a noble record had been his! The brave Du Guesclin, and Bayard, the model knight, were trained in the same healthful school of temperance.

St. Louis in his Boyhood, your Model.

These were all men of the world. Let us say one word of another who, while discharging all the duties of a sovereign, a soldier, a father, and a master, showed himself all through life, from earliest boyhood till his too early death, the most faultless and glorious model of every age.

St. Louis, King of France (Louis IX.), had for his companion, friend, and biographer, the Sire de Joinville, from whose life-like portraiture we borrow a few traits.

"The Saint," says he, "loved truth to such a degree, that even with the Saracens he would not draw back from what he had promised them. As to his appetite, he was so indifferent, that never in my life did I hear him ask for any particular dish, as many rich men do, but he ate contentedly of what the cooks served up to him. He was measured in his speech; for never in my life did I hear him speak ill of any one, nor did I ever hear him name the devil, a name widely spread through the realm, which cannot, I think, be pleasing to God. He diluted his wine by measure, according as he saw the wine could bear it. He asked me in Cyprus why I put no water into my wine; and I answered him the reason was because the physicians had told me that I had a large head and a cold stomach, and therefore need not fear becoming intoxicated. He replied that they deceived me; for if I did not learn in my youth to dilute my wine, and wished to do it in my old age, I should be attacked ‚with gout and pains in my stomach, so that‧ I should never have health ; and if in my old age I drank wine by itself, I should become intoxicated every evening, and it was a sorry thing for a man of worth to get drunk.'' *

The heroic king carried his abstemiousness much farther than is related of him here. He was only a boy—eleven years old—when he succeeded to the throne in 1226. Still, even at that age,—so carefully had he been brought up by his admirable mother, Blanche of Castile,—he showed himself endowed with the virtues of ripe manhood. He had learned under his mother's training "to be perfect master in the house of his own soul," that is, to hold under control his temper, his appetites, and his passions.

Let our young readers not turn away in dismay or discouragement from the perfect virtue of this gentle boy-king, as if it were an ideal too far above the reach of boyish imitation. Such virtue was not so very uncommon in the thirteenth century. Boys of all classes, in town and country, bore stamped upon their features something of the sweet supernatural piety, the modest, open air of unsuspecting innocence that we read of in Aloysius Gonzaga and Stanislaus Kostka. These were ages of faith, when childhood, boyhood, youth and early manhood were kept as free from the knowledge of all moral evil, as the heart of the rosebud is closed against the outside air till such time as it can unfold itself to the sunlight.

With that candor, simplicity, and childlike humility, were united robust health and a manly eagerness for all discipline that could enable the boy to become the accomplished youth, and the man to be fit for all the duties and responsibilities of his station in life

Dare to Excel in whatever you do.

Boys, moreover, were then trained in the notion that to excel in the avocation to which they were born and trained,—

---

* Hutton's translation.

though only that of the craftsman, the farmer, or the shepherd,—was to fulfill the Divine Will, and to render one's self deserving of the highest reward in the gift of the all-knowing and all-just. They were all taught that the poor carpenter Joseph and his humble companion Mary, though filling only obscure and lowly stations in the eyes of the world, were most dear to the heart of God and most exalted in the reverence of Christian ages. They knew, from the lives of the Saints familiar to them in the household teaching, and enshrined within their churches, or sculptured in stone on cathedral porch, or pictured in the lofty stained-glass windows,—that there were canonized gardeners like St. Isidore, the patron of Spain, canonized craftsmen like St. Eligius of Noyon, canonized shepherds like St. Genevieve, canonized servants like St. Zita and St. Margaret of Louvain, canonized slaves like St. Blandina, and so many others. The very apostles, who were universally revered as the spiritual parents of the Christian world, were fishermen who plied their trade on the Lake of Galilee,—and their Master was, in his day, held by his countrymen to be only a carpenter's son, and a carpenter himself, a near kinsman of these same Galileans, his first disciples and the apostles of his faith.

So, true manhood in the lowest ranks of Christian society was held to have its ideal perfection in being able to fulfill successfully the labors and duties of one's calling,—moral and spiritual excellence alone entitling either the peasant or the prince, the craftsman or the king to supreme glory in heaven or supreme honor on earth, to reign with Christ in eternity, or here below to occupy among the multitude of holy men and women a niche over altar or porch in God's earthly temple.

So, the pursuit of all intellectual and moral excellence necessary to one's condition and compatible with one's duties,—all in conformity with His will for whom alone all labored,—such was the conviction which regulated the aim and ambition of every man, woman, and child in these ages of faith, so little known by our modern world.

Why the Boy-King, St. Louis, is proposed as a Model.

Do not fancy, therefore, that the lovely figure of the boy-king, Louis IX., is that of one whom you may not and should not imitate. Even though a king in his own right at eleven, he continued to be in all things subject to his mother, the Regent, till his majority. But as he had been from childhood the most loving, tender, respectful, and obedient of sons, so he continued all through his youth and manhood, till that most admirable parent was taken from him.

She had taught him to be gentle, and temperate, and abstemious, and austere in his own private life ;—not only abstemious in the use of wine, from which he abstained altogether during entire seasons, and which he never used save in small quantities and mixed with water,—but in all other things. He never would allow himself to taste delicacies of any kind, such as very rare fruits, or fruits when they first began to be sold in the market and were very dear. He wore frequently, and for whole days together, a hair shirt beneath his robes or his heavy armor. King as he was, he was an enemy to extravagance or costliness in dress. On state occasions he appeared with becoming magnificence, just as his hospitality was always magnificent. But outside of such occasions, his dress was of the simplest kind, as his diet was ever of the plainest food.

With all that, he was every inch a king, a statesman, and a soldier, as all the world knows.

You also, who are of the boy-king's age, must dare to be, like him, most generous in dutiful respect and obedience to your parents and masters ; most generous in self-control and self-denial,—in temperance, meekness, modesty, in purity of soul and body, in studiousness, love of labor and self-cultivation, in ambition to be first in God's favor, and in accomplishing all that is most difficult and heroic in order to become His worthy servants and sons.

Of what you must fear and shun we make no special men-

tion at present.   By practicing the virtues above enume-
rated you will be sufficiently guarded against the evils most
to be feared at your age.   Besides, what is said in the chap-
ter immediately preceding this, and elsewhere throughout
this book, on the obstacles to true manliness of character,
will teach you what we would have you avoid and abhor.

We must not leave you, O children of God, without sub-
mitting to you, not for the mere purpose of admiration only,
but for that of imitation, one instance which you will your-
selves, we doubt it not, judge worthy of being honored by
a careful remembrance.

If you would look with veneration upon the heroic figures
of seven boys,—the sons of a sublime mother,—then turn
to what we have elsewhere written.*   Here we only relate
how a boy ten years old succeeded in a few weeks in conquer-
ing himself with a heroism that may well put to the blush
so many cowardly men of mature years, who remain the
slaves of their passions and evil habits till Death hands
them over, chained hand and foot, to the Eternal Judge.

A Lesson for every Generous Boy.

The child belonged to parents most gentle and most ex-
emplary in every way, who were sadly distressed by his
passionate temper, breaking out at the slightest provoca-
tion into fits of rage that bordered on downright insanity.
He had at one time very severely wounded his father's gar-
dener, striking him on the cheek with a pruning knife,
because he would not be allowed to mangle a beautiful
pear tree; and on another occasion, he well-nigh killed his
little sister because she would not give up to him some
favorite plaything.   At table the boy, if contradicted or
thwarted in his taste, would hurl plates and dishes to the
floor, or strike his brothers and sisters with whatever was
nearest to his hand.

Every imaginable remedy had been resorted to by his

---

* See the Story of the Suffering of the Seven Machabee Martyrs in "Heroic
Women of the Bible and the Church," chapter xix., p. 201.

parents,—the most loving arts of persuasion, severe bodily
punishment, confinement on bread and water; and all had
utterly failed to make the slightest impression on a na-
ture that no chastisement could frighten and no tenderness
soften. He was sent to school under masters who had had
wide experience in training youth both in the Old World
and in the New. It was hoped that contact with a large
number of other boys, the pious atmosphere of the school
itself, and the ascendency of renowned and exemplary mas-
ters, would call forth the latent germs of good qualities in
the soul of the hitherto incorrigible boy. Besides, he was
now of an age to prepare for first Communion, and this
religious event, his excellent parents fondly believed, would
induce him to practice self-repression and control.

They were sadly disappointed. The boy was exceedingly
clever, and outstripped in learning all his companions, when
he choose to apply himself. But his fits of application
were as irregular and as rare as his fits of outrageous vio-
lence were frequent and unaccountable. He could not be
admitted to first Communion when the appointed time had
arrived, and his masters, after exhausting every method and
experiment, sent him back to his parents before the end of
the term.

This was a great grief to both father and mother,—to the
latter most especially. She fancied that her child's evil
disposition was a secret judgment on herself, and searched
her conscience in vain for the dreadful sin that must have
drawn down this visitation on her home. She resolved,
with the advice of her spiritual guide, to try another year's
schooling under the same revered masters, and was sus-
tained in the eloquent appeal she made to them by the
highest religious authority in the diocese. The president
of the institution could not resist a mother's tears, the tears
especially of such a mother. And so another trial was
given to the froward boy, now beginning his eleventh year.

His parting with his mother was most touching. Folding
him again and again to her heart, and covering him with
tears and kisses, she told him, before his master, that she

prayed God to take him from her rather than allow him to continue obdurate to all teaching and good example. For the first time in his life the boy was seen to weep tears of genuine grief as he returned his mother's caresses.

There seemed to be, at first, some slight change for the better ; but the old temper soon broke forth, fiercer and uglier than ever. Still it was resolved to carry forbearance to its most extreme limits ; and things went on from bad to worse, till the time had come for the formation of the first Communion class.

The ungovernable child was then called to the room of the chaplain,—a holy man on whose gentle features holiness and goodness were stamped. "Charles," said he, addressing the little savage before him, "you have been more violent and insubordinate these last four weeks than we have ever before known you to be. Had there been amendment since school re-opened, you should be now admitted to the first Communion class. As it is, your dreadful violence has made you insupportable to your schoolmates, many of whom threaten to leave if you are allowed to remain here. Your masters say they can do nothing with you. So it has been resolved by the faculty that you shall be sent home to-morrow. . . . My dear boy, this will break your mother's heart.'

All of a sudden, at these last words, as if the grief-stricken mother had risen up to reproach him,—the boy fell on his knees in an agony of tears, weeping uncontrollably for several minutes, clinging to the knees of his venerable friend, and hiding his head on his bosom. At length he gasped out painfully, "Spare my mother ! spare my mother ! It will kill her. . . . I will change,—indeed I will. Only allow me to prepare for my first Communion ; and help me to overcome my temper." . . . Here the child broke down completely, and began to weep and sob convulsively. The good chaplain sent for the president and the infirmarian. For the little penitent, in the sudden extremity of his grief, had swooned away, and blood began to flow from mouth and nose. It was feared that he had

burst a blood-vessel. Happily this was not so, and a few
hours of repose in the infirmary restored the sufferer to his
equanimity. But there was a blessed and total change in
that ardent and passionate soul.

You, dear reader, who know how potent with God are a
mother's prayers, how irresistible the pleading of her tears,
will recall Monica and Augustine, and say that the Creator
of that young heart had, at a mother's supplication, touched
its springs of generosity, and awakened in it a new and
divine power,—that of self-repression.

From that day forth that boyish life became one uninter-
rupted series of heroic struggles with self, of heroic victo-
ries over self. This is no mere exaggerated assertion. It is
a lesson full of loftiest teaching for every one of us, no
matter what our age or station.

The chaplain, to help the boy as he had desired, gave
him a little note-book, on which he was to mark, twice each
day, on opposite pages, his "victories" over self by re-
pressing his outbursts of temper, or his "defeats" when-
ever he yielded to his passion. Charles was thoroughly and
terribly in earnest. The battle for him was during class
hours and play-time. He had few, if any, friends among
schoolmates or play-fellows. For, with all his ferocious
outbreaks of temper, he did not, till that time, give evi-
dence of a single generous quality. His hand and his
tongue had been against everybody in the school; and
everybody's tongue and hand seemed to be against him.

So, he was, at first, given but little credit for his earnest
desire to improve, and but little encouragement to do well.
There were many who had old scores to settle with him,
and not a few who were disposed to sneer at his real or as-
sumed self-restraint, and all too ready to sting him by jest
and scoff. Nevertheless, after the three first days,—as the
marks in his little note-book attested,—he was never once
known to give way to angry word or action! All the
marks, till the day of his death, were on the side of vic-
tory.

This result, however, was not achieved without fearful

struggles with his interior enemy. One day, during recreation hours, the chaplain was summoned to the infirmary, whither, it was said, Charles had been carried wounded and bleeding from some fray. Bleeding he was, it is true, but it was a self-inflicted wound. A larger boy had struck and beaten him cruelly for running across the cricket-field and tripping up one of the players, and the poor child had bitten his lip through and through in his desperate effort at self-control.

It was soon evident to all that the child was battling most manfully with his own tyrannical disposition, and to the general dislike succeeded an admiration quite as general. He was seen, before each recitation-hour and each recreation, to visit the Chapel and make a short and fervent prayer for increased strength to overcome himself. There was no affectation in the boy's piety. He was simple and straightforward in everything. His indomitable courage saved him from the temptation to as well as from the suspicion of hypocrisy.

The months preparatory to the day for first Communion soon passed. Charles, of course, was admitted, to the intense satisfaction of the whole school. His delighted parents had come to be present at the festival, and knelt beside their child at the altar. A happier mother could scarce be found on earth that day. Her face glowed like that of an angel as she received the Divine Gift, and tears of ineffable sweetness bedewed her cheeks ; nor was her boy less angelic in his rapt air and with his lively faith in the Great Presence.

It was a day long afterward remembered in the school. The happy parents asked and obtained permission to take their darling home for one week's rest. The weather was intensely cold, though in the first days of April. The boy caught cold on the way, and was laid up with pneumonia, which carried him away in a few days, preternaturally happy to die in his recovered innocence.

From the first appearance of serious symptoms, his mother felt instinctively that the seal of death was on him, and that the prayer she had made in bringing him back to school, had been answered most mercifully. She watched unweariedly near his bedside till the pure spirit had fled, and then lifting him up in presence of the weeping family and with the aid of the noble father, who at once understood what she would do, she offered him a willing sacrifice to the God of Angels. "Thou gavest him to us, O Father," she said; "Thou hast most lovingly prepared him for Thyself; accept him as a thanksgiving offering from the grateful hearts of his father and mother."

Well might the afflicted father often repeat the beautiful lines of a modern singer, as he remembered the bright close of that short life:

> "Thou wert a vision of delight, to bless us given;
> Beauty embodied to our sight, a type of heaven:
> So dear to us thou wert, thou art
> Even less thine ownself than a part
> Of mine and of thy mother's heart. . .
> Even to the last thy every word—to glad, to grieve—
> Was sweet as sweetest song of bird on summer's eve:
> In outward beauty undecayed,
> Death o'er thy spirit cast no shade,
> And like the rainbow thou didst fade." *

* David Macbeth Moir.

CHAPTER XVI.

MATRIMONY.

In the early education of youth, women were represented as the objects of respectful love, and the dispensers of happiness. The child was taught that, to be an honorable and happy man, he should prove himself worthy of the love of a virtuous woman. *This lesson* (says Uhlrich von Lichtenstein) *every boy sucked in with his mother's milk; so it was not wonderful that love and honor should become identified in his soul. When I was a child so young that I used to ride upon a stick, I was fully persuaded that I ought to honor women with all that I possessed,—love, goods, courage, and life.*—KENELM HENRY DIGBY.

She was high-minded in nothing but in aspiring to perfection, and in the disdain of vice : in other things covering her greatness with humility among her inferiors, and showing it with courtesy among her peers.—ROBERT SOUTH WELL, S. J. (The Martyr).

WE are writing for men of the world, advising them how to be good among the bad, and best among the good ; leading them by pleasant and devious paths to the contemplation of soul-stirring models of all human excellence ; and teaching where to find both true happiness and the surest means of attaining it.

One chief service that, as teacher and guide, we can render the young man about to enter upon the battle of life,—is to direct him in finding the woman whom God has chosen for him, to be his life-companion, his most faithful friend, his stay and counselor,—the joy of his heart, the queen and the light of his home. True Christian men, men who have had experience of life's bliss and life's bitterest sorrows, of its difficulties and disappointments, its disasters and its triumphs,—of all the sweets of a home made bright and sunny and blissful, or of a home made dark and dreary and desolate,—will say, on reading the title of this chapter, that its subject-matter is the most im-

portant in this book. They will also say, that a priest's
hand alone can trace out the rules which should guide
pure-hearted youth in finding the worthy object of love,
and point out the conditions on which the divine blessing
secures to spotless mutual love all the felicities of this life
and the next.

With such a purpose, and cherishing the hope that He
for whose glory we labor, will enable us to write what is
apposite to our purpose, we approach this portion of our
appointed task.

Christ's First Miracle wrought to Honor Matrimony.

Has it ever struck you, dear reader, that the first graceful
act recorded of the Lord, after he had quitted the privacy
of his mother's home at Nazareth, had been publicly bap-
tized in the Jordan, and had spent in the wilderness the
"forty days" so full of heroic abstinence and uninter-
rupted prayer,—was to go with his Blessed Mother and
his disciples to the marriage-feast at Cana, a little town
quite near Nazareth? His first stupendous miracle,—the
changing of the water into wine,—was performed there, at
the instance of that same Mother.

So, she who was the Mother of the New Life, the parent
of that regenerated humanity out of which Christ's Bride,
the Church immortal and unfailing, was to be formed, and
He the Bridegroom, the abiding Love and Worship of re-
deemed humanity, were both present at that marriage-feast.
It was fitting that she, the Eve of the new creation, should
urge the Second Adam to give a new wine to the hosts and
their guests. For was it not from the hearts of both these
true Parents of our race, that flowed the Blood given as the
price of our redemption, and applied in the Sacraments as
the sole means of our sanctification?

The Model of Wedded Love.

These Two, who loved each other as Mother and Son had
never loved before, and who loved us with an utter love,

were united in that great sacrificial oblation, which re-
paired the world ; the Son giving Himself for our ransom,
and the Mother giving herself in and with her Son, as she
stood sublime and unshrinking beneath that Tree of Life.
There must be, eternally, the exemplar of true love. For
love is the gift of self ; and these Parents of our souls,
loving us truly, loved us utterly, giving themselves to death
and shame and suffering unutterable, that we might live.

And so the new wine of Cana was the fit emblem of that
sanctifying blood, of that all - powerful grace of Christ,
which was to hallow anew the most ancient of God's or-
dinances, the matrimonial union. By the blood of Christ
was the mutual love of husband and wife to be consecrated,
and the whole stream of human existence to be purified. In
that love of Mother and Son, as afterward in the love of
Christ for his Church and of the Church for Him, were all
the children of both to find the model of chaste love.

Hence it is that he could say to his own, a few hours be-
fore he gave himself into the hands of his enemies : "This
is My Commandment, that you love one another. as I have
loved you. Greater love than this no man hath, that a man
lay down his life for his friends." *

If such be the divine model according to which we the
children of the Crucified have to practice toward each other,
in the intercourse of social life, all true love, all love that
God may bless,—how much more is that special love which
two souls who give themselves each to the other for the holy
and difficult companionship of a life-long existence, to be
molded on this eternal pattern of self-sacrificing charity !

Hence, also, is it that Christ's great Apostle has written
this complementary commandment : "Husbands, love your
wives, as Christ also loved the church, and delivered him-
self up for it, that he might sanctify it."†

Seek for your Bride the Purest and the Best.

It is the dearest interest of every young man seeking a

---

* St. John, xv. 12, 13.   † Ephesians, v.

companion, who is to be sun of his life, the honor and treasure of his home, that he should find the best, the purest, the most worthy in every way of the devotion of a whole lifetime, and that, having found her, he should not only keep her pure, stainless, and worthy of all love and honor, but that every day of his life he should labor to make her more so, and be himself before her eyes the living and ever-present copy of Christ's goodness and devotion.

The ideal of female loveliness, which is familiar to all pure Christian minds, is not so much one of bodily beauty as of that spiritual grace and attractiveness that arise from maturity of virtue superadded to baptismal innocence undefiled. It is extraordinary how deeply and widely the Lives of the Saints, the sweetness of woman's countenance in every Christian home, and the representations of Christian painting and sculpture even in the rudest periods of mediæval art, had impressed on the mind of Christendom the image of supernatural beauty.

Dante's portraitures, so heavenly in their grace and majesty, were exact pictures of living women he had seen in Italy, in his own native Florence. At the distance of six centuries, Tennyson only reproduces the ideal of Dante; for it existed in England as well as in Italy in the thirteenth and fourteenth centuries ; and, through God's good providence, it is still preserved in both countries in the lives and homes of millions.

Was it Isabella-the-Catholic, the worthy descendant of Elizabeth of Hungary, that the great modern poet had in his mind's eye when he drew the following likeness?

> " Eyes not down-dropped nor over bright, but fed
> With the clear-pointed flame of chastity,
> Clear without heat, undying, tended by
> Pure vestal thoughts in the translucent fane
> Of her still-spirit, locks not wide-dispread
> Madonna-wise on either side her head ;
> Sweet lips whereon perpetually did reign
> The summer calm of golden charity,

Were fixed shadows of thy fixed mood
Revered Isabel, the crown and head,
The stately flower of female fortitude,
Of perfect wifehood and pure lowlihead.

" The intuitive decision of a bright
And thorough-edged intellect to part
Error from crime ; a prudence to withhold ;
The laws of marriage charactered in gold
Upon the blanched tablets of her heart ;
A love still burning upward, giving light
To read these laws ; an accent very low
In blandishment, but a most silver flow
Of subtile-graced counsel in distress,
Right to the heart and brain, tho' undescried,
Winning its way with extreme gentleness
Through all the outworks of suspicious pride ;
A courage to endure and to obey,
A hate of gossip parlance, and of sway,
Crowned Isabel, thro' all her placid life,
The queen of marriage, a most perfect wife."

Wherever a Catholic mother,—even in the lowliest con-
dition of life,—is faithful to her conscience and observant
of the rules of her Religion in all that concerns the educa-
tion of her daughters, there is little danger of having these
grow up to anything but a most pure and lovely maiden-
hood. We have before us now families buried amid the
squalor of these groups of "shanties" which cover the
most uninviting portions of Manhattan Island, and in these
to all appearance most wretched abodes are to be found the
loveliest types of female innocence and beauty. Fathers
and mothers are there who prefer the comparative isolation
and greater domestic privacy of these cabins, because they
can there preserve their dear ones from the contamination
of a more crowded neighborhood and the dangers of swarm-
ing tenement-houses. In very truth, there are families who
thus cluster together on the barren rocks or in the fever-
generating swamps of Harlem, because they thus can form
associations of neighborhood that remind them of the vil-
lage community of the far-away fatherland

Whether in the cabin, therefore, or in the palace, it

depends upon the mother's training, watchfulness, and example, that her girl shall be or not an angel on earth, a beautiful soul shedding around the light of heaven and the perfume of paradise.

Be it your first and chief care to seek the beautiful soul much more than the beautiful body. There are comely and attractive women, who resemble exquisite vases of rich material and most classic form, but filled with a poisonous or loathsome liquor: woe to the imprudent man who should taste of the foul contents! The beautiful soul is a treasure beyond all price, placed sometimes in a homely vessel of unrefined material or rude workmanship, but whose value is altogether independent of either form or material. It is the most exquisite of perfumes given forth by the least brilliant of flowers; the water of life, of delight, and immortality, often gushing forth from a spring in some obscure or barren vale, or as often placed by the hand of the Creator in the lowliest and homeliest of vessels.

Young men who are themselves pure of heart will surely be directed by the secret and irresistible charm of true goodness toward a maidenly heart worthy of their affections.

That is the one supremely precious quality which a young man must find in the companion he would choose for life. There can be no love without it. For love is founded on esteem, and esteem can only rest on the certainty of innocence in the beloved object. One cannot love what one does not respect; but how can a young and pure heart respect a woman,—though divinely fair,—from whom the charm, the freshness, the fragrance of purity have departed, —like a beautiful flower rifled of its sweets and containing only the putrid corpses of the insects that have preyed upon it?

Be slow, therefore, in judging for yourself, even where, with the charm of personal beauty, you have found in a girl the outward signs of maidenly modesty. There is One who reads the heart and who will surely guide you in your choice, if you are only careful to consult His pleasure, much more than the inclination begotten by a fair face, a graceful person, and a modest bearing. It is all-important to you that you should be master of your own soul at this juncture, when a hasty choice might be a wrong choice, and when a wrong choice would make shipwreck of your whole future life. Lift up your soul to Him who is bound not to fail those who seek His light and strength in a choice so momentous.

There are other qualities beside maidenly innocence, even when it embellishes the highest beauty of form. We would say to you,—whether you be a prince or a peasant, the wealthiest of men or the poorest, depending only on your stout heart and strong arms,—Let the woman you would make your wife, *come from a well-regulated home, where the womanly virtues are carefully cultivated* Such homes are to be found in every class of society.

Though you feel drawn toward a maiden by the twofold attraction of beauty and apparent modesty and innocence, show not your interest, and give not your heart away, till you know more. Watch how she bears herself under the trials of home-life ; what respect she shows for her parents, what sympathy toward the suffering ; make sure that she is unselfish in all her conduct toward others, and especially in her sisterly devotion toward her younger brothers and sisters.

She who is ever mindful of the wants, the comforts, and happiness of others, and forgetful only of herself; who manifests that motherly devotion toward the younger members of the household, and tenderness toward every form of suffering,—will be sure to bring to your home the same wifely and motherly qualities. She will make the happiness of your life.

To learn what she really is, be not content with an acquaintance formed in the ball-room, or amid the crowd and glitter of a watering-place. Study her in her home-life. You need a wife who is to be your life-long companion, your most constant and trusted friend, your wisest and most disinterested counselor ; the dear sharer of all your holiest joys and deepest convictions ; the mother and educator of your children,—fitted by her enlightenment and solid piety, to bring the religion of your fathers home to their minds and their hearts,—who will not be satisfied with teaching them the great truths of Revelation, but show them these truths practiced and made lovely in her own daily life ; the prudent governor of your household, careful of every detail of domestic economy, knowing how to make her servants obey and work by love, charitable toward the poor, hospitable toward all, lovely and venerable in the eyes of your friends, your relatives, and acquaintance.

Together with innocence of life, solid piety, a good practical education, and the wifely and motherly qualities enumerated above,—is needed that sound sense, without which the most brilliant accomplishments only serve to make a young woman vain, idle, unreliable, and dangerous.

We have not mentioned truthfulness, because we suppose that there can be no true piety without it. We say to young men, Never give your heart or your hand to a woman who is capable of falsehood ; just as we should say to a young woman, Never accept the love or the friendship of a man whom you know to be addicted or inclined to intemperance.

In mentioning piety,—the enlightened and hearty practice of your own faith,—as an indispensable quality in the wife of your choice, we have sufficiently warned you against irreligious women, the worst curse of domestic life or public society.

Such, then, are the women—to omit the mention of other qualities, kindred to those which we have described,—who are alone worthy of a true man's love. They are the true women. Should Providence guide you to the possession of such, then are you most blessed. Your parents can give you education, position, wealth, an honored name and home ; society may bestow honor and trust ; but far above all that parents can bequeath and society can confer of what is conducive to happiness and honor, is a true woman, given to a man's heart by Him who knows the heart's needs, and wherein consist the felicity of a man's household and the glory of his life.

How to be Worthy of a True Woman.

But how are you to make yourself worthy of such a God-sent love? How are you to guard and cherish the treasure of a noble woman's heart? This is a most vital question.

Men are but too apt to think,—or to conduct themselves as if they thought,—that they had a right to expect a wife to bring them not only accomplishments and graces far superior to their own, but a soul unstained by sin, and a heart untouched by any other love. There are men,—very young men too,—who only think of the sacred and awful responsibilities of matrimony, when they have wasted their life on the worst pursuits and profaned their affections by the most criminal indulgence, and who believe that they honor a pure woman by offering her in exchange for the untouched and boundless wealth of her maidenly love, a heart utterly incapable of feeling, and a soul incapable of understanding, what love is.

It is, we fear, but a too frequent occurrence, that a bridegroom should bring to the matrimonial altar, manhood without the freshness, the innocence, and the vigor of youth, wealth without religion or piety or virtue, position without the honor and integrity which can alone adorn it, —while he expects and demands that the bride shall be as fair, as pure, as excelling in all natural and supernatural grace as Eve coming in her perfect womanhood from the hand of God. But we pause here, and leave what else might be said to the reflections of all good men.

You are, therefore, to be most earnest in keeping or in making yourself worthy, in the sight of the all-judging God, of the true love you are in quest of. A virginal heart with its perennial flow of deep, chaste, elevating love, is not unlike the San-Graal of our ancient Christian chivalry. Only the knight who had never stained his baptismal purity, or who had recovered his innocence by dint of heroic expiation, could possess or even behold from afar the sacred vessel in which had flowed the blood of the Lord. Even so, in those who seek the treasure of a pure womanly heart,—it is required that they should themselves be pure in order to appreciate it and to cherish its possession as dearer than life itself.

The holy flame and mighty power of true love which God the Creator would place in wedded hearts, is a something so divine, that he would have both man and maiden purify and prepare their souls by the two great Sacraments intended to bestow holiness where it is not and to increase it still more where it is. This wedded love and the special grace brought to the souls of worthy bride and bridegroom by that other Great Sacrament of Matrimony,—are the well-spring of all human happiness, the principle of domestic bliss,—the heart and center of all fatherly and motherly goodness. We know not how to convey the truth which is here before us,—and on which depends the existence of the Christian family and of human civilization itself.

Unspeakable Importance of the Sacrament of Matrimony received with Reverence.

The sacrament of Matrimony received with the deep reverence which its sanctity demands, is the consecration of human love in its highest form save one, that by which the heart dedicates its affections to God, to a life of contemplation, prayer and praise, or to the active service of Religion and Charity. We are, however, at present concerned with the no less vital subject of hallowed wedded love.

We would fain impress upon the minds of parents and of their marriageable sons and daughters, the necessity of treating this great sacrament of matrimony with the respect which is due to the most ancient ordinance of religion, which Christ so reverenced that He would have his own union with the Church serve as a model for the contract or covenant by which bride and bridegroom pledge themselves mutually to life-long devotion and self-sacrifice; and His own sacred love for the Church become the type of the incomparable and surpassing love which a true husband is to cherish toward his companion.

We would also impress this truth on those who are the teachers and guides of the Christian people. When they see, every day, human legislators casting aside, as useless or as restraints to individual right or civil authority, the sacred and time-honored marriage laws of the Catholic Church, and when non-Catholic denominations either concur with the civil magistrate in denying all sacramental character to the matrimonial rite, or strike at Christ's own legislation by countenancing or authorizing divorce,—it is high time that we should strengthen within our hearts and our homes the faith in the unity and divinity of Matrimony.

All possible persuasion should be used to make young people prepare their souls for this central act in their lives; and, therefore, all care should be taken to instruct both in public and in private, the faithful people on the nature of this sacrament, on the countless and priceless graces laid in store by God's fatherly providence in behalf of all who approach it reverently and worthily, and on the fatal and irreparable consequences of a marriage contracted without due deliberation or preparation.

All possible solemnity should be given to the marriage service. When we say "service," we do not mean the nuptial benediction given either in the church or elsewhere, without mass; but we mean the whole divine function as set forth in the Ritual, the nuptial benediction in the morning before God's altar, and followed immediately by the Nuptial Mass. The two together,—the sacrament and the sacrifice, the contract with the priest's blessing, and the oblation of the Divine Victim of Calvary, to call down all the graces and joys of Heaven on the union of two pure Christian hearts,—this alone is the Marriage Service.

Magnificent Ritual of the Nuptial Mass.

It is impossible to reflect seriously on the reality as we here present it, and impossible to read the sublime Nuptial Mass with the grand blessing after the *Pater Noster*, without feeling how solemn, how awful, and yet how joyous is this august function of the Church of our fathers. Is it not, therefore, sad,—nay, most deplorable,—to see it curtailed and degraded by the want of faith and want of reverence of so many Catholics, who make of the celebration of matrimony only a profane and empty form, into which no religious thought is allowed to enter?

"One of the most bitter griefs which God's ministers have to endure, is to be forced to witness or bless the union of persons who contract matrimony without being seemingly conscious of the sacredness of the rite, of the pure dispositions they are bound to bring to it, of the priceless graces attached to it, or of the terrible consequences of its profanation." *

To be sure, the marriage contract, for its validity in the eyes of the Church, needs only the presence of her authorized minister and that the contracting parties be perfectly free according to her laws. But what may satisfy the nude letter of the law ought not to satisfy the conscience of parents who fear God and of children brought up in His fear.

A marriage ceremony performed in the Church, at evening, with no matter what pomp, is not the marriage service as Catholics understand it. The altar may be aflame with lights and decked out with the loveliest flowers of spring; the organ may give forth the most triumphant of "Wedding Marches;" and the edifice itself be crowded with sympathetic friends or a throng of curious, idle sight-seers. All that is not the divinely beautiful Nuptial Mass,—the real marriage service performed at morning-tide; the prayerful assemblage of relatives and friends assembled round the altar on which He is present who died to win to Himself a spotless and immortal bride in our Mother the Church; the young lovers bringing to His feet their sinless hearts, that by His blessing their God-given love may be hallowed, deepened and elevated, and confirmed forever; and then the oblation of the unbloody sacrifice which commemorates and

---

* "The Golden Treasury of Prayer," p. 429.

continues that of Calvary, the sublime and prophetic bene-
diction of the *Propitiare*, uttered on these wedded souls
before the Holy Communion ;—the whole crowned by their
partaking together of that Bread which is the figure, fore-
taste, and pledge of the eternal possession ;—this, and this
only, is the Marriage Service of the Catholic Church,—a
rite appealing to all the most sublime beliefs, and stirring
the Christian heart to its inmost depths.

Yes, everything in the Catholic doctrine and practice
impresses on the souls of the young, that the love which
God hallows is a gift above all price, which can only be
worthily received in a sinless heart, and which it must be
the study and labor of a lifetime to cherish and to increase.

True Love ever Reverent.

On this last thought,—the duty and the necessity of
guarding, cherishing, and increasing this blessed mutual
affection,—we must insist a little further.

True love,—that is, God-given love,—fills the soul with
infinite reverence for the loved object,—else it will forth-
with degenerate into lust, which is the death of love and of
respect.   We cannot imagine the young Tobias and his
bride ever losing for each other a particle of that holy re-
spect and tender regard which God had planted in their
souls.   Even when the Archangel who had been sent to
preside over their union, had withdrawn his visible pres-
ence, his counsels, and his protection, we cannot help fol-
lowing the saintly exiles all through their life-journey as
walking ever hand in hand beneath the all-seeing Eye, and
encouraging each other to be daily and hourly more worthy
of Him in inward thought and outward deed.

Such were also Malcolm Canmore and his sainted wife,
Margaret, whose ardent love deepened and grew with every
successive year,—the soldier-king becoming ever more pene-
trated with reverence, gentleness and tenderness in presence
of his lovely wife, whom he could not think of without
tears, without wondering how such an angel was given to

him to love and keep. The very prayer-books she used were to him a something holy, which he would allow no one to carry but himself, kissing them devoutly as he gave them to her or received them from her, in presence of his rude Scottish chieftains, and till his dying day demeaning himself in public and in private, toward his spotless queen, as if he were her servant and bond-slave. How she must have loved him all the while,—how truly, how tenderly,—that she could thus inspire him with a devotion that never decreased and a reverence which ever grew with age!

So was it with another king,—a king too of the same old Gaelic race,—though separated from Scotland by a narrow sea,—Brian, King of Ireland. He is called the most kind-hearted of men by the author of the Nials-Saga, and regarded by the Norsemen of that and succeeding ages as the champion of the Christian faith against Scandinavian idolatry and barbarism, perishing like a martyr on Good Friday (April 18), 1014, because he would not himself draw the sword, shed blood, or defend his own life on the day when Christ died for us,—though he directed the battle against the enemies of his country and his faith. The Saga mentions his first wife, Kormlada, an inveterate heathen, put away by him, doubtless, because of her utter wickedness and sorcery. "She was the fairest of all women, and the best gifted in everything that was not in her own power, but it was the talk of men that she did all things ill over which she had any power."* That is, she coveted and possessed all the forbidden secrets of magic, and made the very worst use of her own splendid abilities. "Kormlada was not the mother of King Brian's children, and so grim was she against King Brian after their parting that she would gladly have him dead."†

This fury, if she did not cause the successful invasion of Ireland by the Vikings, was most certainly the soul of the mighty league formed against Brian and the Christians by the Norsemen, and in which the heroic old man lost his life.

---

* *Nials-Saga*, or "The Story of the Burnt Nial," Dasent's translation, vol. ii., p. 323. † Ibidem, p 324.

Far different must have been Brian's Christian wife, the mother of the three brave sons who fought with their father on that memorable day,—and the youngest of whom was miraculously cured by the blood which spurted from his father's death-wound.*

It was an age,—no matter what modern fanatics may affirm to the contrary,—when, in Ireland, overrun by the fierce worshipers of Thor and Odin, no Christian father of a family could tolerate within his own household treason to Christ in wife, or son, or daughter. The woman who was Brian's companion during all his long struggles against invasion from abroad and strife from within, was one worthy to rear such sons as those who fought Ireland's most glorious battle, and who won at the same time a decisive victory for the true faith. We mention these names and dates to stimulate our students of Irish History to complete the picture we have outlined, and thus to compare the practical faith of the court of Ireland in 1014 with that of Scotland half a century later.

Of the exquisite picture of true conjugal love presented by the life of St. Elizabeth of Hungary and her noble husband, the Landgrave Louis of Thuringia, we wish to say nothing here.† Their contemporaries on the throne, St. Louis of France, and his wife, Margaret of Provence, are no less admirable, and, perhaps, will appear more imitable to our readers. Louis brought to the bride chosen for him by his saintly mother a soul which still preserved its baptismal innocence unstained ; and she, on her side, had been reared with no less care in the refined court of her father, King René. When the young king bound himself by vow to rescue the Holy Land from Saracen rule, no persuasion could induce Queen Margaret to part from his side. Authentic history has preserved in all its touching details the story of her heroic magnanimity in the midst of the greatest sufferings and dangers, as well that of her royal hus-

---

* Ibidem, p. 337.

† See Montalembert's " Life of St. Elizabeth of Hungary ; " also " Heroic Women of the Bible and the Church," chap. xxxiii., p. 343.

band's infinite respect for "his Lady and Companion." The Mohammedans themselves were touched and surprised by the reverence in which she, a woman, was held by Louis and his warlike barons.

Indeed, domestic history,—the history of the Home,—in the Catholic ages, when all Western Europe was one in faith, is the history of man's reverence for woman, of the respectful, faithful, and often heroic service paid by lovers and husbands to the women of their choice. Woman, whether in the hut or in the palace,—was given by the Church to man to be loved, honored, reverenced, and served by him all his life long,—in memory of St. Joseph's loving service to Mary, and in imitation of Christ's constant love and care for His Spouse, the Mother of all Christians.

Such were the ideas and ideals of our fathers. Nor have these ideals yet ceased to govern hearts and homes in our midst.

CHAPTER XVII.

OBSTACLES TO TRUE MANLINESS.

I. *The Tyranny of Human Respect.*

Load me with irons, drive me from morn till night,
I am not the utter slave which that man is,
Whose sole word, thought, and deed, are built on what
The world may say of him.

In all things, a man must beware of so conforming himself, as to crush
his nature and forego the purpose of his being. We must look to other stan-
dards than what men may say or think. We must not abjectly bow down be-
fore rulers and usages ; but must refer to principles and purposes.—HELPS.

THERE is one enemy of true manhood, whether viewed in
the light of reason or of the Christian revelation, against
whose tyrannical and degrading influence the soul can only
be preserved by grounding it early in the fear of God, and
in that secure and lofty independence which springs from
conscientious, deep-seated attachment to Duty. The cow-
ardly fear of a false and depraved public opinion, as is but
too well known, is to-day and has ever been in the past, the
deadliest foe of truth and morality. The opinion, however,
of which we would speak here, is not that of the world in
the wide sense attached to the term "public opinion." It
is the judgment of a much narrower circle of men. We
might limit its meaning to the opinion prevalent in the im-
mediate society in which we live, to that of the men of our
own profession, nay, to the standard of thought and action
upheld by the persons with whom we daily come in contact,
even within our own home, or within the establishment to
which we happen to belong.

336

"Human respect" has, nevertheless, even a narrower sense than this; it is the fear entertained of what the low-lived or the low-bred, persons of low views or low tastes, but of determined will and character, may think or say of their betters. There are, among such people, in every social circle, in every walk of life, some who have the terrible faculty of sneering at whatever is superior to themselves or their own low standard of life. They make the lash of their ridicule more dreadful to the sense of their weaker and less cynical associates than any bodily torture or temporal loss.

"With some unfortunate people," says Sir Arthur Helps, —"the much dreaded *world* shrinks into one person of more mental power than their own, or, perhaps, merely of coarser nature; and the fancy as to what this person will say about anything they do, sits them like a nightmare."

It is against this abject and slavish fear of what others,— and these, too, men utterly unworthy of all respect,—may think, judge, say of us, that we wish to warn and arm our readers.

We have seen men led, step by step, to forego the fulfillment of the most urgent and sacred duties, and commit actions and contract habits most abhorrent to their nature,— lest they should be sneered at, or deemed unmanly by their acquaintance. This seems monstrous and incredible when considered by calm reason, or when mentioned to one who has had but little experience of men. To most of our readers,—of our young readers even,—it will recall the all too frequent realities of every-day life.

"There have been Catholics," says Digby, "who appear to take a pride in imitating the adversaries of their holy religion, and in being associated in friendship with them; no one so dear to them as he who had most daringly reviled their holy faith; men who were ashamed of everything but what they had solemnly renounced in their baptismal vows; ashamed of serving God only without regard to the opinion of the world; ashamed of the Cross; unwilling that a crucifix should be seen in their apartments; afraid to sign themselves like all faithful Christians at the accustomed

22

time ; and afraid or disdainful of all the exercises of a peni-
tential life ; as if they could gain anything by professing to
believe with Catholics, and living after the manner of the
Gentiles ; ashamed of some or all of the beautiful practices
prescribed by religion, which are dear to those who love the
Church of Jesus Christ : and harassed with continual fear,
lest they should not always be seen invested with the livery
of the world, and ready to concede to it the sentiments of a
Christian, and even the noble qualities of youth.

"The spirit of chivalry in religion would despise and
abhor this ungenerous and servile disposition, under what-
ever name it might be recommended, whether extolled as
liberality, moderation, or prudence : it is a disposition not
only essentially opposed to divine charity, but also to every
sentiment of human honor ; it denotes a want of faith ; it is
wholly of the world, and characteristic of those who are of
the world. It is deceived too in all its wisdom. It was
afraid of being despised, and lo ! its endeavor to avoid con-
tempt is the secret scorn of the very world that it would
propitiate ; whereas those who despised the ridicule or cen-
sure of the world while they were guided by the discipline
of the Church, who laughed at its charge of superstition or
idolatry, are seen invested with an heroic dignity that is
able to intimidate even the base assailants, whose front of
brass is never proof against the power of holy innocence." *

Who has not read of the great O'Connell's courageous
and uncompromising piety, when, at public dinners in Lon-
don, in presence of the most bitter assailants of his faith
and the mose irreconcilable enemies of Ireland, he would
stand up modestly and manfully to sign himself with the
cross before taking his place at table ?

We have not forgotten the example of the late Chief
Justice Morin of Quebec, who, while he was prime minister,
would go publicly every Friday to perform the Way of the
Cross at Notre Dame, Montreal, absolutely unconscious, in
his simple-minded piety, of the sneers and contemptuous

---

* " Godefridus," pp. 98, 99.

looks of the crowd of Protestant visitors who pushed their way rudely through the aisles, intent only on sight-seeing.

Noble Examples of Moral Courage.

And how can we ever forget the edifying and heart-stirring spectacle presented each morning by the Catholic churches of London, where renowned barristers ; members of Parliament, titled nobles, high officers of the army and navy, were to be seen not only hearing mass with rapt devotion, or receiving the Bread of Life with the adoring faith of seraphs, but serving the priest at the altar together with some little boy, whose soul was formed to Christian manliness and heroism by such examples? And what is not to be hoped for in a land where the highest, the most honored, the most learned, and the best, thus exalt themselves by honoring the faith of their fathers?

There, as the tide of a false liberalism or of avowed radical infidelity rises daily, threatening the institutions of the old Catholic ages,—shall still be found the chivalrous spirit of lofty faith embodied in the legends of King Arthur and his knights. Every true Christian youth treading in the footsteps of his generous father can say to his mother, in the words of the modern poet:

> "Man am I grown, a man's work must I do.
> Follow deer? Follow the Christ, the King,
> Live pure, speak true, right wrong, FOLLOW THE KING !
> Else, wherefore born?" *

This tyranny of human respect is to be found first at school and in college,—long before it has to be faced and beaten down in the walks of public life. The boy and the youth must be trained to trample under foot the despicable fear of the evil-minded and the evil-tongued, so as to be prepared to despise it in ripe manhood.

"The social spirit of a large school," says the Hon. and Rev. Mr. Petre, "is for the most part swayed by the

---

* Tennyson, "Gareth and Lynette."

crudest and baldest of boyish minds. At the period when muscle is strongest, what are the natural tastes, ideals, aspirations of the individual man? Are they not rather of the brutal kind, exhibiting themselves in a grossly physical standard of excellence, in feats of agility and strength, in the pleasures of a rude good-fellowship? It has been to us ever a pathetic spectacle to behold the struggles of minds sensitive and receptive by nature and early influence, struggling unconsciously against a power which they can not resist." *

None of our schools, we would fain believe, was ever subject to the despotic sway of such anti-christian, impious prejudices as governed the great French establishments since the suppression of the Jesuits (1764), and more especially since the great French Revolution (1789). Foremost in rampant intolerance was the Polytechnic School, which, since its foundation (1795), has been the nursery of the most distinguished men in military and civil professions. Down to a comparatively recent date, the pupils would barely lend themselves to a few occasional religious ceremonies that bore an official character. But woe to the man who dared in presence of his fellow-students to profess a cordial adherence to the tenets of Christianity, and still more to him who ventured to follow any of its practices within the walls of the institution!

An Heroic Student.

One day, however, the atrocious tyranny which prevented and mercilessly repressed any outward act of religious faith was heroically resisted and conquered by one true-hearted youth. He was preëminent for his talent as well as for his bravery, had brought with him from his admirable mother's home, enshrined in his heart of hearts, a love of purity which made him proof against all the awful temptations that surrounded his school-days, and a courageous piety derived from the examples much more than the teachings

---

* "Remarks on the Present Condition of Catholic Liberal Education," by Hon. and Rev. W. Petre, p. 16.

of both his parents. His talents, on his entrance into the Polytechnic School, won the admiration of his companions, while his frank, joyous, generous, and manly character, conciliated the affection of not a few.

He had made up his mind to do there openly what he had uniformly done at college, go to confession and communion. No student, since the memorable 25th of May, 1795, when the school was first inaugurated, had ever been seen at the Communion Table within their chapel. It was whispered that this proscriptive tradition was now about to be set aside, and the boldest and worst of the school conspired to prevent it. They resolved to stop at no excess either of outrage or of violence which might effectually deter any one from ever again following such an example.

Of this our young hero was perfectly aware. But he was determined to do quietly and publicly what he conceived to be his duty to God and to his misguided associates. So he went to confession, and, on the following morning,—some great yearly festival, when all were obliged to assist at mass,—he modestly and devoutly received the Holy Communion, and then withdrew to his place in the ranks, where he remained kneeling at the end of the service, while the students marched out past him.

The head conspirator, as he passed by the kneeling youth, whose eyes were cast on the ground and his arms folded across his breast,—spat on the face of the latter, who moved not, winced not under the insult. Another, and another, and yet another repeated the dastardly outrage ; but the kneeling youth contented himself with removing the filth from his face, without ever raising his eyes from the ground. The more generous of those who witnesed the scene murmured aloud at the indignity, and the murmur soon became pretty general, as one after the other of the many friends of the victim, remonstrated in no gentle terms. The climax came when the last of the unmanly crew, not content with spitting into the young man's face, struck him on the cheek.

There was forthwith an uproar, and more than one of those who had remonstrated, now took up the quarrel as a personal one. As everybody knows, the Polytechnic pupils are allowed to wear arms, and the law of dueling is rigidly enforced. One must either fight or leave the school. All admitted the bravery of our hero and his great superiority as a swordsman. Already, however, and before the latter had quitted the chapel, a large number had sided with him, not because they shared his convictions or his piety, but because they resented such a proceeding as an act of downright cowardice and unwarrantable intolerance. So, the authorities of the institution and the Minister of War himself peremptorily interfered to prevent any hostilities.

The noble youth himself, when he came forth from the chapel, professed himself ready to answer any one who should challenge his courage or impugn his honor, while many of his companions came forward to grasp his hand warmly, and to congratulate him on his manly assertion of independence.

It was a complete revolution. Our hero was not again molested when he deemed it proper to profess thus openly his reverence for the faith of his fathers; and more than one of his fellows took courage and imitated his example.

Since then the little band of Polytechnicians who practice their religion without disguise or reserve has been yearly on the increase, thanks to the numerous accessions of strength from the great Jesuit preparatory schools of St. Genevieve in Paris and St. Clement in Metz, as well as such other glorious schools as that of the late Monseigneur Cruice (*École des Carmes*).

Is this not,—only in a far higher form,—the heroic spirit which led the boy Gareth, in order to become one of Arthur's knights, to consent to serve a whole year as a scullion in Arthur's kitchen, concealing from all but his own mother, Queen Bellicent, his rank and his name, and subjecting himself to the brutalities heaped on him by the Seneschal Sir Kay,

> " A man of mien
> Wan-sallow as the plant that feels itself
> Root-bitten by white lichen."

Not so the bravest of all the Table Round, the peerless Lancelot : with the instinct with which brave hearts detect each other as surely as magnet draws magnet, Lancelot divines the boy's quality and worth, reproving the mean-spirited Kay.

> " Some young lad's mystery—.
> But, or from sheepcot or king's hall, the boy
> Is noble-natured.   Treat him with all grace,
> Lest he should come to shame thy judging of him.
> . . . So Gareth all for glory underwent
> The sooty yoke of kitchen vassalage ;
> Ate with young lads his portion by the door,
> And couched at night with grimy kitchen-knaves.
> And Lancelot ever spake him pleasantly,
> And Kay, the seneschal, who loved him not,
> Would hustle and harry him, and labor him
> Beyond his comrades of the hearth, and set
> To turn the broach, draw water, or hew wood,
> Or grosser tasks ; and Gareth bow'd himself
> With all obedience to the King, and wrought
> All kinds of service with a noble ease
> That graced the lowliest act in doing it."

This is the right-royal spirit of the children of God, who understand the priceless value of their birthright, who cherish that lofty spirit of freedom bestowed on them by their father, Christ, beyond and above all earthly honors, and whose soul can never stoop to be the slave of human opinion.

Not unfrequently in the little world of the school,—as in the broader and bolder world where Human Respect reigns supreme in court, and shop, in army and navy, by the fireside, in the ball-room, and reception-room, those who are bent on "following the KING," will hear themselves, in their most heroic hour, addressed as Gareth was by the Lady Lynette :

> " What dost thou, scullion, in my fellowship?
> Thou !—
> Dish-washer and broach-turner, loon !—to me
> Thou smellest all of kitchen as before."

And, what is to be the demeanor of the true knightly Christian under the outrage ?

> "Damsel," Sir Gareth answered gently,—"say
> Whate'er ye will, but whatsoe'er ye say,
> I leave not till I finish this fair quest,
> Or die therefor."

Even where Human Respect would damp the ardor of beginners by putting over them such tyrants as Kay, or giving them for guides in their quest of all true excellence purblind souls or unworthy models, whose lives, even more strongly than their words, would drive God's servant from the right road and all holy enterprise,—the spirit of God within boy and man would reply·

> "Say thou thy say, and I will do my deed !
> Lead, and I follow !"

And who can tell what may be, in God's purpose, the blessed, soul-saving influence of men who have,. like the mountain pine or oak or the cedars of Lebanon, grown up and waxed strong amid solitude, sterility, and storm?

Other Noble Examples.

We could, as we write these words, point to one man brought up amid the soul-struggles of that same Polytechnic School, become, as a soldier, the close companion of royalty itself on the battle-fields of Africa,—and now the head and the saintly guide of the chiefest training-school in America of one of our great religious orders.

We know of another, the near relative, almost the brother in age as he was in closest friendship, of Ireland's purest novelist, who living abroad in the world, while his uncle sought rest and refuge in the cloister, was always and everywhere, before and above all else, the professed and devoted Christian. Once called to the Capital on legislative business with a gentleman from Boston, a Unitarian, he charmed the other all along their journey by his bright joyous spirit and most interesting conversation. They shared the same room at the hotel, the Catholic gentleman before he retired, performing unobtrusively, but at full length, his customary devotions.

For weeks they continued to live and labor together, surrounded by an atmosphere which was anything but an atmosphere of purity and integrity, witnessing the sayings and doings of men,—and of Catholic men among these,—who were neither edifying, nor honorable, nor honest. Meanwhile, though forced to mix with persons of every official rank, it was the boast of the generous and candid-minded Unitarian that he had never seen anything in his companion's acts, or heard a single word from his lips, that was not most worthy of the thorough gentleman and the thorough Christian.

"I had never till then,—he afterward was wont to say —"seen any gentlemen kneel while saying his night prayers: indeed I had never known of an instance where a gentleman alone with another thought of saying any such prayers. So, what was my astonisment when I first saw my friend, whose learning, wisdom, and integrity I had learned to prize so highly, kneeling quietly down by his bedside, in the almost total darkness of the room, and when he thought me fast asleep, and pouring forth his soul in adoration and praise to God, with a fervor that struck on my interior sense like the first notes of a strange but most sweet music!

"I watched him thenceforward, night after night and day after day, to assure myself that all was consistent in his conduct, and my respect and admiration grew daily and hourly. For years our acquaintance continued, ripening at last into friendship. The lessons I learned in his life and in his home, were to me lessons of a new religion,—which I was impelled to study, to admire, and to embrace.

"If I am a Catholic to-day with all my family, we owe that inestimable grace, under God, to the light of my dear friend's example."

How many others in our day, as in the first ages of the Church, have been led into the household of the faith by the irresistible example of Catholics who knew not Human Respect, showed themselves openly, in public and in private, what they were, true to God and fearless of human

opinion ? We heard from the Lady Lothian, whose saintly
life was a blessing to all London, and whose saintly death
filled all Rome with its fragrance,—the touching story of
her own conversion ; how curiosity or a kindly interest in
her Catholic servants induced her to visit the place where
they went to worship on Sundays ; how she found a poor gar-
ret in a private house thronged with a promiscuous crowd,
among whom a priest busied himself in hearing confessions.
Then came the mass, celebrated on a poor temporary altar,
while the rapt devotion of the kneeling crowd of worshipers,
and all the poverty and nakedness of the place, reminded
the high-born lady of the Stable of Bethlehem and the
throng of Shepherds bidden to adore the new-born Messiah.

The example which we are about to adduce, if it have its
consoling, its heroic, its most glorious side, teaches also this
lesson, that the Divine Majesty exacts from highly privi-
leged souls a terrible expiation for yielding even a mo-
mentary and secret consent to some one of those public sins
which are the ruin of the proud and the rash.

At the head of the Young Men's Sodality, attached to the
church and college of St. Francis Xavier, Saint Louis, was,
just when our great civil war broke out, an officer of the
United States army, distinguished alike for his birth, his
talents and bravery, and still more for his enlightened and
active piety. He was the pride and the model of the Catho-
lic youth of his native city.

Unfortunately, as it ever happens in civil contests, the
question of allegiance to the Federal Government as against
the rights of the individual States, was discussed with fierce
passionateness, neighbor taking part against neighbor,
friend against friend, and brother against brother within
the bosom of families hitherto most united. It so happened
that a brother officer, a former schoolmate at the Military
Academy, took openly sides with the seceding States, en-
tering into a warm controversy with our friend, who as
openly professed himself bound by his oath of allegiance
to the flag of the Union. The dispute found its way into
the public prints, and the former friend deeming that an

imputation had been cast upon his honor, sent his adversary a challenge.

The terms in which it was conveyed, the taunt of disloyalty to the South, and the imputation of unworthy motives were such as must gall beyond endurance even the most phlegmatic. Colonel G—— was, like all his family, a man of proud, sensitive, and wrathful temper. Much as he had learned to conquer himself, the reception and reading of the missive found nature off its guard. He resolved to accept the challenge thus cast in his teeth. It was but the act of a moment, known only to Him who reads the secrets of hearts,—and disclosed to no human being save his confessor. It was,—we have said,—only a momentary consent yielded by natural passion, but recalled the next moment under the impulse of divine grace with heartfelt sorrow.

The noble and pure soul could not brook that even this secret stain should long remain upon it; so Colonel G—— sought his confessor, and implored the divine forgiveness on his sin. The next morning he knelt contrite and purified at the Table of the Lamb, pouring forth his grief at the feet of his divine Guest, and making there heroic resolves for the future.

Just as he rose from the audience with the King of Kings, and was about leaving the church, he was met by a member of the Ladies' Sodality, a woman of humble station but revered as a Saint by all who knew her. "I have a message for you, Colonel," she said, in her gentle tones, while her face shone with a light that was not of earth. "Our Lord has been deeply offended that one so dear to His heart as you are, so favored by Him, and bound by your place to give such high example to others, should have consented, even for a moment, to risk your own life or take that of another in a duel. God, however, has accepted your sincere sorrow; your sin is forgiven. But I am bidden to tell you, that, in expiation of your guilt, you shall forfeit your life in the first great battle in which you are engaged."

The Christian gentleman bowed down every power of his soul before this manifestation of that adorable Will so merciful and tender even in the decrees of its justice. He could have no doubt, he had none, as to the awful truth of the communication thus made to him. To his brother only did he, on the eve of his departure for active warfare, disclose his impending fate, and its cause. The certainty of the event gave to his whole conduct thenceforward a character of unspeakable moral beauty. With his whole heart and soul he devoted himself to the cause of the Union, watching over his every thought, and word, and deed, as one should who had already half entered beyond the veil, and on whom the light of the Divine Judgment had already fallen. There was in his whole bearing a calm, unruffled serenity, a firm and steady gentleness, a charity and forbearance toward others, a helpful and brotherly kindness toward his subordinates, an unwearied devotion to the sick, the suffering, and the wounded, that were only half understood and appreciated when he was no more. A thousand graceful acts were then told of him by the men who had witnessed his chivalrous bearing in life, and wept at the remembrance of his glorious death.

He was made chief of staff to his friend, General Rosecranz. They were of the same religious faith ; indeed, if we remember aright, the General owed his conversion in great part to the beautiful life of his loved companion in arms. Side by side throughout the autumn of 1862, the two soldier-friends labored to organize a large and effective army. The very last day of the year found them before Murfreesborough at the head of about 50,000, and confronted by a force equal in numbers and in bravery. Rosecranz as well as his chief of staff knew that on the battle to be fought on that memorable 31st of December, depended in a great measure the success of the cause to which both his friend and himself had devoted their lives.

Long before the dawn the general-in-chief had the Holy Sacrifice celebrated in his tent, Catholic officers and men devoutly assisting thereat, and Colonel G—— taking to himself the honor of serving the priest. The two friends received with touching fervor the divine Gift,—the bond of that most sacred union of souls, which the impending death of one of them could not interrupt. Many a brave man knelt at that tent-door, in the cold and gloom of the December morning, or partook of that Bread of the Strong, who beheld not the dawn of the new year.

Throughout the first part of that eventful day, Colonel G—— displayed a calm joyousness which his chief alone could perfectly understand. He seemed to multiply his presence over the vast field of action as his horse bore him like the wind to communicate orders to the various divisional commanders. And, it is said, when the worsted Union forces paused to reform their line and renew the struggle, he profited by the lull to withdraw to a quiet corner near a fence, and there to kneel unobserved,—as he thought himself,—to renew the offering of his life.

He had passed unharmed through the terrible scenes of the morning and the early afternoon. As the victorious enemy were concentrating all their strength for the final shock, he knew with unquestioning certainty that his last hour was come. Again and again as the Federal right were driven from position to position, General Rosecranz had cheered his brave men with the assurance that "this battle must and shall be won!" Did his generous chief of staff, as he made his last prayer, offer up his young life to the God of battles for the triumph of the Union arms? ·We know not.

But when he rose, a new light was on his face, as he took his place by the side of his commander; his voice had a tone of triumph as he bore the final orders along the line. And when the advance sounded, his sword leaped from its scabbard, as he prepared to quit the side of Rosecranz and lead the charge in person. At that moment, and while waving his sword, a cannon ball struck off his head, the blood covering the person of his devoted friend and general.

Yes,—the fortune of battle was retrieved; but in the deep sadness which tempered the joy of generals and soldiers, all recalled the chivalrous figure of G—— as it had shone over that bloody field and had been stricken down with the cheer of victory ringing from his lips.

They only knew and admired the blameless life, the unshaken attachment to duty, the heroic devotion to principle, the untiring and ingenious charity —the accomplished gentleman and the dauntless soldier. God and His angels alone knew of the one momentary stain on the beautiful soul atoned for by this early and tragic death,—as that purified Spirit was greeted on high with the " Well done!" from His lips who is the sole Lord of Eternity. In him was what we commend to the study of our cultivated youth, the *Altum quiddam et excelsum, nihil timens, nemini cedens, semper invictum.* *

---

* " A something (heart) elevated and sublime, which feared nothing, yielded to no (wicked) one, evermore unconquered."—CICERO, *De Finibus*, ii. 14.

CHAPTER XVIII.

OBSTACLES TO MANLINESS (CONTINUED).

II. *The Seduction of Evil Example.*

But if their talk were foul,
Then would he whistle rapid as any lark,
Or carol some old roundelay, and so loud
That first they mocked, but, after, reverenced him.
                                          TENNYSON.

IT were hard to show which is more baneful to the health
and growth of all true manliness, the influence of human
respect or that of evil example. The sneer or scoff of the
base or the perverse, acts through fear of ridicule, on the
soul like the chilly atmosphere or late frosts of springtide,
preventing the fair buds from bursting their sheaths, or
blighting, as by one breath, the opening flowers, and thus
marring all the promise of the year. Evil example, on
the other hand, is like the sickly atmosphere that broods
over some marsh-covered region, converting the very bounty
of the soil into a rank luxuriance that is worse than barren-
ness, and slowly but surely poisoning in man all the springs
of health and bodily vigor.

Nothing can be more lovely to the beholder than **the**
Italian regions known as the Maremma and the Roman
Campagna at the springtide of the year,—or the plains and
forests of Guiana, when the rainy season is past, and the
earth clothes itself with the incomparable magnificence of
its tropical vegetation.

If, while visiting, near Ostia, the scenes where Augustine
and Monica conversed at eventide fifteen hundred years

351

ago,—just when the malarial fever was draining in the heroic mother the last sources of life,—you should be tempted to repose at evening beneath the wide-spreading ilexes or pines, or to spend the night beneath the clear, calm sky, with the mingled fragrance of a thousand wild flowers around you,—we bid you beware! There is death in that balmy air, death in the grateful coolness and serenity of the treacherous atmosphere. It is not an unapt picture of the scenes where evil example is all-powerful. Let us pause awhile, and take in the salutary truth gently and pleasantly.

> " About your feet the myrtles will be set,
>   Gray rosemary, and thyme, and tender blue
> Of love-pale labyrinthine violet ;
>   Flame-born anemones will glitter through
>   Dark aisles of roofing pine-trees ; and for you
> The golden jonquil and starred asphodel
> And hyacinth their speechless tale will tell.

> " The nightingales for you their tremulous song
>   Shall pour amid the snowy scented bloom
> Of wild acacia bowers, and all night long
>   Through starlight-flooded spheres of purple gloom
>   Still lemon-boughs shall spread their faint perfume,
> Soothing your sense with odors sweet as sleep,
> While wind-stirred cypresses low music keep."

The cities which once studded that shore have long ago ceased to be inhabited. The shepherds and swineherds forsake the lowlands at sunset and betake themselves to their villages among the surrounding hills, for they know that Fever is king on the plain.

Universal Sway of Evil Example.

Such is the silent, pestilential, irresistible power of evil example in the world.

Example is potent in the home,—from the court of the sovereign or the mansion of the chief magistrate, to the hut of the backwoodsman, or the most wretched lodgings of our laboring poor. Example is all-powerful of father over sons, of the mother over her daughters, of elder brother over his younger, of prince or magistrate over their subject people, of priest over his flock, of every man placed in authority over those beneath him.

Need we describe the baneful effects over the minds and hearts of children of the evil example of their parents? There is not one of us who cannot daily convince himself of it by observing near his own home how the evil life of a father or a mother slowly but surely perverts the happiest dispositions in their children.

It is, nevertheless, of the utmost importance that we should take a few lessons from the history of the past as well as the experience of our own time.

Jeroboam, a descendant of that Joseph who had been the second parent of Israel, as well as the savior and ruler of the Egyptian empire, was forced to take refuge there from the jealousy of Solomon. There, however, he imbibed a great admiration of the barbaric civilization of the people, sought an alliance with the reigning family, allowed the sensuous worship of the Egyptians to captivate him, returned to his home in the mountains of Ephraim with a heathen wife,—and, when chosen king of the new kingdom of Israel, erected, in opposition to the Temple of Jerusalem, two places of worship in which he installed the statues of Mnevis, the god-calf, so well known to Moses and his contemporaries during the captivity in the land of the Pharaohs. He consecrated a priesthood of his own, flattering the rebellious Ten Tribes with the declaration that the deities which had made Egypt so prosperous and so powerful would now secure their own national supremacy : he was the first on that same revered site of Bethel so dear to Jacob and hallowed by so many traditions, to offer incense to Mnevis with his own hand, forbidding thenceforth any of his subjects to go to worship in Jerusalem.

They were but too faithful imitators of his apostasy, induced to forsake or blaspheme the God of their fathers, not so much by the edicts of their chosen ruler, as by the seduction of his example. And thus we find in Jeroboam the pattern of more than one Christian king.

23

Achab, Jeroboam's successor at the distance of half a century, knew well what ascendency royal example had in swaying the conduct of court and kingdom. He married a Phenician princess, Jezabel, and with her brought into his realm the abominations of the Phenician idolatry, and into every family almost the added pollution of his wife's morality. Achab, though believing in the God of his fathers, was seduced by his wife's example to bend the knee to Baal and to erect to him a magnificent temple with a retinue of thousands of ministers in his own capital. And so, to please Jezabel and Achab, all Israel worshiped Baal.

Fatal Weakness of the good King Joshaphat.

There was worse than this. Contemporary with Achab at Samaria, reigned the good King Joshaphat in Jerusalem. There was nothing he could think of for the glory of the true living God, for the extirpation of idolatry, the education and welfare of his people, that Joshaphat did not undertake with his whole heart. Nevertheless, the necessity of uniting against common foes having forced him into an alliance with Achab, he and his son were thus brought within the fatal influence of Jezabel and her court, so full of superstition and sensuous enchantments.

The pious King of Juda was induced by the wiles of the enchantress to seek the hand of Athalia, Jezabel's daughter, for his son and heir. Athalia's seduction made a Baal-worshiper of her husband, induced him, when he ascended the throne, to cut off his brothers and their offspring, and to have Baal proclaimed in Jerusalem as the national god.

Was it not by flattering, in a like manner, the national vanity of the English, by nursing the natural hatred of foreigners and foreign domination, even in things spiritual, —that Henry VIII. separated England from the Holy See? He could not obtain from the Sovereign Pontiff a decree divorcing Queen Catharine, and the faculty of raising Anna Boleyn to his bed and throne, nor persuade his people to countenance his adulterous hypocrisy. But he did succeed

in making the national anti-Roman prejudice favor his crea-
tion of an independent national church, with a schismatical
Archbishop of Canterbury, who soon granted the divorce
sought for, and the faculty of having as many wives as
Henry chose.

And so was verified the saying as old as the world:

Regis in exemplum totus componitur orbis.
" The King's example sways each subject's home."

In all this Henry had only followed the example of the
Archbishop of Constantinople, Photius, and his Greek Em-
peror.   They nursed and fanned into a fatal blaze the in-
veterate jealousy entertained by Greeks against Latins, by
Constantinople against Rome,—severing from union with
the See of Peter the whole of Eastern Christendom for up-
ward of a thousand years!   And in the footsteps of Pho-
tius walked every Greek bishop, in the footsteps of the
bishops walked the priests,—just as the princes and nobles
followed the example of their emperor!

Is not this the history of the English Reformation?

Still nearer our own times we have in the personal exam-
ples of two kings of France, the direct cause of the down-
fall of the monarchy, of the ruin of morality and of religion
itself.   The uncommonly long reign of Louis XIV. and of
his immediate successor and great-grandson, Louis XV.,
were one unbroken series of the most shameless scandals.
The palaces of these descendants of St. Louis had become,
in the eyes of all Europe, the abode of openly avowed and
almost legalized adultery,—the fearful scandal of the sove-
reign's private life and the open immoralities of his home
setting a pattern to be imitated by every one of his nobles.
And thus, for upward of a century, corruption and licen-
tiousness in the home-life of the leading nation of Christen-
dom spread from above downward, from royalty and no-
bility, to the wealthy middle classes, and from these to the
laboring masses in city and country.

With licentiousness spread extravagance, and with ex-
travagance grew the oppression of the poor by the govern-

ing classes. Step by step with immorality, venality, and oppression, progressed distrust in religion; in the French society of the 18th century, the gay vices of the court of the regent D'Orleans and of his pupil the fifteenth Louis were in fashion, and equally fashionable were the infidel and skeptical opinions of Voltaire and his Encyclopedists, —the example of the high-born loosening in the bourgeoisie beneath them all belief in royalty, in virtue, in morality, in religion, all respect for everything till then held most sacred by the nation. And so the popular masses, having lost all respect for those above them, for laws, legislators, and magistrates, and having been moreover systematically trained for several generations to connect religion with all the vices and oppressions of royalty and nobility,—rose at length, in a moment of deep and general distress, and were let loose by their wily leaders upon the governing classes,—sweeping away in a deluge of blood every institution in Church and State.

Evil Example at Our Own Doors.

Have we not warning examples nearer still to our own day, to our own homes? Suppose,—in the freest country under the sun, and amid all the mineral and agricultural wealth, all the most splendid industrial and commercial resources that God's fatherly providence can bestow as a heritage on a people,—suppose that the sole purpose of gaining sudden wealth becomes the mainspring of action in the men who monopolize the nomination of candidates for every office, national, State, municipal; that the amassing of wealth by the use of official patronage and legislative action becomes the darling aim of office-holders and legislators;—suppose that corruption on the one hand, and venality on the other, in a great State, is carried on so scientifically and successfully as a trade by one bold bad man, that the entire administration, legislature, and judiciary seem devised to secure immunity in plundering the public,—and that this systematic plunder is carried on for years, while the paralyzed arm of the law is powerless to arrest the malefactor, and a depraved public opinion only feebly denounces the enormity,—will the evil, think you, stop with one man, or be confined to one locality, or to one department only of the public business, or one sphere of private enterprise?

Peculation carried on in the halls of legislation or in the departments of government whenever vast commercial or industrial enterprise call for the highest legislative or administrative action,—will, if unvisited with condign punishment, be imitated in every corporation throughout the land.

Let one public officer trusted for years with the custody of large funds or the management of vast moneyed interests, betray his trust, and be only so feebly punished by the law or so lightly whipped by public opinion,—and you will find the example presently imitated all over the land. If the municipality that should guard sacredly and vigorously economize the interests and moneys of a city, prove faithless to their trust, will the bank in which the poor man deposits the savings of his hard-earned wages, be more faithful, more conscientious?

And if the clerk who keeps the books, or the agent who collects the funds of any one private merchant, sees men, placed above him in the hierarchy of official trustworthiness, shameless and secure in their peculations,—will he not be tempted by these examples, to go and do likewise?

No! there is no hope for public morality, where the highest personages in the community show by their conduct that they take no account of honor, of principle, of conscience,—of the fear of God and the dearest rights of others, when they have the hope and the means of gratifying their cupidity.

And one of the most deplorable results of the unrestricted freedom of the public press, is to make these instances of dishonesty and triumphant fraud familiar to every home, to every child in the land,—thereby taking away from the innocent mind of childhood the impression that dishonor is a something rare and frightful, and that the men who hold the place and fulfill the functions of the fathers of their country, are untainted with the sordid vices of the thief and the low cheat.

It is a sad day for any people, when the divine precept "Honor thy father and thy mother,"—becomes one of practical impossibility, because those on whom its obligation falls, as they look inside their home and abroad throughout the land, find it difficult to reverence those, who, while bearing the responsibilities of fatherhood, bear also stamped on their brows and their lives the brand of indelible dishonor.

How many children do we not see in the homes made wealthy by the plunder of the public treasury, or the betrayal of private trust, who, instead of holding down their heads in shame, or deeming it imperative not to enjoy or retain a shilling of the ill-gotten gain of a father,—will continue to brazen it out, to marry and give in marriage, to consort on a footing of equality with their former acquaintance,—as if the wealthy classes of the community were the immediate descendants of a penal colony of thieves, swindlers, forgers, and pickpockets, with whom the "professional cleverness" of their fathers was rather a thing to be cherished and honored in the possessor, than a title to dishonor and exclusion?

Debasement of Public Character.

It is not to the praise of a nation when it ceases "to visit the iniquity of the fathers upon the children, upon the third and fourth generation." It would be a false and fatal mercy, a most baneful liberality, that would set up in the lowliest or in the highest home in the land, any other ideal of ancestral honor or of the priceless inheritance of an unspotted name, than that which has been revered before us, since the world was a world.

"When Don Beltram * inquires respecting the character of his son Don Garcia, on returning from the university,

---

* In *La Verdad Sospechosa* of Alascon;—quoted by Digby, "Compitum," book i., ch. ix.

and hears that he has no evil quality, but that of not always speaking the truth, he exclaims : *I would pardon him for everything but for that. I should prefer his being dead. What! he utters what is not true! O honor! O ancestors! How am I fallen!*

" 'Garcia, art thou noble?' 'I am your son,' replies the young man.—'Is that sufficient?'—'I think so.'—'Absurd thought! To act nobly, is to be noble. Such is the beginning of noble houses. But thou, if infamous by thy habits, art no longer noble. Paternal escutcheons, ancient descent—of what avail? *Thou noble! Thou art nothing! Thou noble, who utterest an untruth! Thou art nothing. Whether noble or plebeian, no one can lie without being the scorn of the people.*"

What dishonor and infamy would such men have deemed it in their sons to add to falsehood, dishonesty, betrayal of the most sacred trusts, the appropriation to one's private uses of the moneys confided to one's keeping by clients, by widows, by orphans, by the poor laborer seeking to provide an independent home for his dear ones? Alas! alas! is it so uncommon in these calamitous times, that even members of the most honored of all secular professions,—the law,— should forget what they owe to it and to themselves, and betray the trust of even the widow and the orphan? And has not the abasement of professional honor, this deadening of private and public conscience, not been the consequence of evil example, set, at first, by one placed high in public esteem and public trust, and acting downward and around on others, like leprosy communicated to companies of the noblest and the best, by drinking out of the cup of some secret leper who had long sat, unknown, at the common board, and grasped their hands in brotherly friendship, and poisoned the atmosphere with his very breath?

Should the close of the nineteenth century bring no change for the better to the courses pursued in public life by the men whose example is authority, the next century shall see but little of the manhood which founded the Republic and first administered its government.

" Weakness to resist gold
   If weakness may excuse,
What murderer, what traitor, parricide,
Incestuous, sacrilegious, but may plead it ?
All wickedness is weakness."

The Remedy in the Eloquence of Good Example.

Religion, love of country and kind, the noble ambition to transmit to one's children the inheritance of an honored name still further increased by one's own blameless life, and the still more noble ambition of making an obscure name glorious by true merit, of founding by one's own exertions the imperishable nobility of public virtue and private worth,—all these motives, and many more than these, some even loftier than these (did we dare to express our thought fully) impel the true man to make it the aim of his life to be to others, with the assistance of divine grace, a shining light in his own generation.

Those who have traveled through Belgium and Holland, — known formerly as the Low Countries,— cannot have helped admiring the indomitable perseverance and wonderful ingenuity with which, during the lapse of so many centuries, an entire people has labored to win and to preserve their native land from the inroads of the adjacent ocean. At the beginning of the Christian era it was little better than a vast morass, but the untiring labors of so many generations have now made it one vast garden. Need we say that there was a period when the Republic was the first maritime and commercial power in the world ?

But there is the sleepless and relentless ocean ever thundering at the gates of this people ; for their country is, in reality, like a mighty fortress evermore beleaguered by a still mightier foe. The slightest breach in the gigantic walls would at once admit the resistless waters, and the labor and sacrifices of ages would go for nothing.

In such a country, then, it is the duty and the interest of every man to see to it that the stupendous embankments which keep out the sea shall be kept in constant repair ; it would be the duty of every man, woman, and child almost, if there was a single breach apparent in their wide extent, to rush to the spot and help repair the ruins and stop the inflow of the devastating tide.

Is not this also the case in our own Louisiana, where the most precious portions of the low-lying country have been only saved from the ravages of the Mississippi by the persistent labor of man? When some breach has been made by the swollen river in the dikes or embankments that guard the lowlands from inundation,—where is the true man who does not hasten to the scene of danger, to aid with main and might in repairing the evil?

Surely, there are contagious moral disorders as resistless in their spread as the swollen river in its flow, as blind and unsparing in their destruction as the ocean waves impelled headlong by the utmost fury of the tempest. We have described two of them in these chapters, and to the ravages of the last and most destructive, the only preservative lies in the withstanding force of good example.

Let us begin with the family circle. Just as a parent's evil life is most baneful within the home, as well as outside of it in proportion to its social standing and influence, even so and exactly in the same proportion, is a father's good example helpful toward every noble aim and deed. Had Providence permitted the virtuous and accomplished son of Louis XIV. to live and reign in his father's stead, there can be little doubt but that his pure life and generous spirit of self-denial would have gone far to repair the scandals of his father's reign. The economy which his example would have made popular, would have become a rule in every noble household, and from private life it would have passed into the public administration, thereby saving France from ruin and her people from despair and the hatred of all authority.

Even when the Great Dauphin was prematurely cut off, and his royal father continued his career of self-indulgence and ruinous extravagance,—the Dauphin's worthy son, the saintly pupil of Fénelon, would have become the savior of the monarchy and his home the model of every household within the kingdom, had not he and his young wife been poisoned by members of their own family.*

As it was, the regency of Philippe d'Orléans surpassed in profligacy the preceding reign, and the tide of corruption held on its course, ever increasing in volume and velocity, till the throne and Church of France went down in the deluge.

Would you see how the example and devotion of one man can rouse an entire people to withstand and shake off the tyranny of a degrading and inveterate vice? Then you have only to recall the life and services of Theobald Mathew.

In the home itself nothing can be more familiar as well as consoling than to remember how the life of a father in every way worthy of the position and character of a Christian parent and true man, will continue to be for generations the living law and practical ideal of his descendants. Even when these depart momentarily from the right road, they can easily be recalled to it by the memory of their ancestor's goodness, and the authority of his lofty example.

This nobility of virtue, so honored, exalted, and praised by the Church in all ages, is transmitted by a true father to his sons with the name that he bears. Thereby to bear that honored name,—honored even among a race of peasants and borne by them with a pride that shrinks from a stain as from a something worse than death,—is to feel one's self bound to nobleness of sentiment, of aim, and deed. This, in the old Catholic lands, was the foundation of the popular saying, *Noblesse oblige* ('Nobility obliges'). Not alone in the ancient provinces of Spain, inhabited by the Basques, could every husbandman in the country hamlets, like every denizen of the cities, proudly recall his lineage and point to the escutcheon over his door, but even in other lands where families occupied for centuries the same homesteads, though far removed from the pretensions of modern wealthy abodes, the nobility of a good name filled and surrounded every

---

* See the article *Marie Adelaide de Savoie, Duchesse de Bourgogne*, in *Le Correspondant* of the 10th and 25th March, 1878.

home like an atmosphere, and neighbors far and wide saw above each door,—though no escutcheon was emblazoned there,—the spotless family name inscribed ; while every man and woman and child who bore it knew that it obliged them to be true to the blood in their veins. You have only to recall the example of the Rechabites, quoted above, to understand what we would here inculcate. Doubtless, this glorious race of true men, during all the centuries that they have been faithful to the obligations of their ancestral nobility of virtue, bore on their banners no emblazoned shield. Houses they have never built, and, therefore, their dwellings had neither sculptured doorway, nor escutcheon of marble or bronze to tell the traveler of the possessors' lineage. All knew them to be the sons of Rechab. That unsullied name was a prouder patent of nobility than that of baron, or count, or duke.

Not undeserving of serious consideration are the words of one who knew the Rechabites well and could appreciate, in a degenerate age, their shining example of inviolable fidelity and unshaken constancy.

"Woe to them that are faint-hearted, who believe not God ; and therefore they shall not be protected by Him. Woe to them, that have lost patience, and that have forsaken the right ways, and have gone aside into crooked ways. And what will they do when the Lord shall begin to examine ?" *

We can never forget the noble examples set by the gentlemen of the Society of St. Vincent of Paul in Paris. Not content with mapping out the whole of that vast capital, and distributing it to the conferences or district committees, in order that not one street should be left unvisited by these apostles of charity, and not one needy home should escape their active beneficence,—they studied the science of edifying by good example much more than the delicate art of bestowing relief without distressing or humiliating its recipient.

---

* Ecclesiasticus, ii. 15, 16, 17.

The civilized world knows how fatally the skepticism of Voltaire, aided by the evil life of the governing classes, had blighted the growth òf faith in the souls of the laboring population in Paris and in the surrounding provinces. Then came the fearful excesses of the French Revolution, in which these classes actively participated, leaving the stain of blood on so many fathers and mothers of the existing generation. Of course, undying hatred of the Christian name and of all that related to religion became a household worship with these parents and their children. How could they ever become reconciled to Religion, to her worship, and her sacraments ? Not by the voice or the ministrations of the priest. Him they would not listen to. By the examples of the noble men, men of the world, soldiers, lawyers, magistrates, men of illustrious birth, or rendered illustrious by their talents and public services,—whom they saw daily seeking out every form of obscure or secret privation and suffering, and ministering to the poor and sick with supreme devotedness and supreme delicacy. When they saw these men on Sundays devoutly assisting at Mass, or reverently approaching the Holy Communion, their hearts began to soften toward the religion of 'their fathers. The eloquence of true charity set forth beneath their eyes in so many touching deeds of beneficence, self-denial, and self-sacrifice, won their hearts, first, and thus opened the avenue of their minds to the knowledge of the true faith. For,—such has been the invincible logic of all ages. True Charity is the divinest form of True Religion.

In the churches of Paris, as well as of those in the neigh boring dioceses, but very few men comparatively, at the fall of Napoleon I., had courage enough to be seen at confession or communion. The force of human respect was so great that such as dared to profess and practice what they believed, had to do so with more or less of secrecy. The yearly lectures in Notre Dame given by the two apostolic men Lacordaire and De Ravignan, broke the force of antichristian opinion and custom. The latter it was who made the happy innovation of closing his Lenten course of sermons by the solemn exercises of a retreat of eight days in favor of men exclusively, and closing on Easter Sunday by a general communion. Then it was that revolutionary and skeptical Paris was given the extraordinary and edifying spectacle of beholding the thousands of men,—the élite of French manhood,—who filled the vast Cathedral, pressing forward rank after rank, to partake of the Bread of Life, and to glorify the God of their fathers by receiving adoringly the divinest of His gifts.

Thenceforward it became the custom of the generous members of that advance-guard of Faith and Charity, the Society of St. Vincent of Paul, to send some of their members, every Sunday in the year, to receive Holy Communion publicly in the various churches of the capital and in those of the surrounding cities and villages, far and near. General officers of the army and navy, the foremost members of the learned professions, officials of high rank, and men who bore the proudest historic names in Europe, were thus to be seen giving forth the light and warmth of their pious examples in those centers of Voltairian unbelief and revolutionary impiety, where all faith had been utterly killed in souls by the evil examples and teachings of the preceding age.

And thus do they continue to edify and build up in the France of to-day the ruin on which desolation and despair seemed to have settled as utterly as on Thebes and Memphis, and Babylon and Nineveh.

A Sublime Instance of Self-Sacrifice.

One instance taken from the history of a man whose air of childlike simplicity and innocence remains impressed on the soul of the author, and whose fame as a mathematician is only inferior to his generosity as a Christian, must find place here. It will tell our readers, that, whereas France is still fruitful in such heroic souls, there is sure ground to hope for a revival at some future day of the living and chivalrous faith of St. Louis.

Baron Augustin Louis Cauchy had been preceptor to the Comte de Chambord, or Henri V., as he is called by the French Royalists, and had ever remained as loyal to the cause of legitimate monarchy as he was to his baptismal faith. No promise of advancement, no prospect of emolument or honor could ever induce him to swear allegiance to any form of government that was not administered or sanctioned by the lawful princes. Nevertheless, and while winning the admiration of the whole scientific world, he remained the most simple-hearted and amiable of men, the most fervent and charitable of Christians. Of course his whole life was devoted to good works. After 1830 he was never seen at the courts of the sovereigns elected by the French people, and he was but ill at ease in the receptions of the legitimist nobility to which he belonged and where his virtues and talents were fully appreciated. Every leisure hour was given to Christ in the persons of His poor, or in the performance of the most heroic works of charity.

As he was daily thrown into the society of the most learned men in France, being himself a member of the Institute and having filled the highest professorships in the University, his heart was continually saddened by the practical unbelief of so many of his colleagues, the victims of a godless and anti-Christian system of education. More than one of these had been induced to study the Christian religion, and to embrace it heartily, by the pure life and ever-active charity of Baron Cauchy.

One young Academician, in particular, had won the Baron's sympathy. He had been from childhood exposed to the worst influences of French infidelity, and had not the remotest idea that the Catholic Religion or Christianity itself could be anything else than the worst enemy of science and civilization.

It so happened that in the summer of 1857 the young Academician fell sick of the small-pox, the case presenting such virulent symptoms that all the friends and acquaintance of the young man fled from him, leaving him to such care as hirelings could give him. Baron Cauchy thereupon resolved to win that dear soul to God at the risk of his own life. So, he became his friend's nurse, never leaving him for a moment, and lavishing on him all the loving and gentle care which was to be expected from one so naturally noble and tender, but who seemed transformed into an angel of God in the sick-room.

The patient recovered, gaining health of soul with that of the body. But his savior died, having caught the malignant disease, and rejoicing with unspeakable delight to see his friend a true believer. The spirit of the illustrious dead seems to have passed into his convert; for, ever since he stood over the grave of his benefactor, he has taken up the apostleship bequeathed to him by the departed.

All Paris heard the story of that heroic death and of the conversion which was its consequence. No city in the world witnesses more of such examples of all-sacrificng charity, of angelic piety than Paris the Magnificent, where the two ex tremes of Goodness and Wickedness are found side by side at every step, where the two great armies of Catholic charity and anti-social Hatred confront each other in every street. Which is to be victorious,—the Love ever ready to give its all and to lay down its life for the suffering and the needy, or that Hatred that would sacrifice all to its unreasoning fury or its insatiable thirst of enjoyment?

> " What might be done if men were wise—
>   What glorious deeds, my suffering brother,
> Would they unite in love and right,
>   And cease their scorn for one another!
> Oppression's heart might be imbued
>   With kindling drops of loving kindness,
> And knowledge pour, from shore to shore,
>   Light on the eyes of mental blindness.
> All slavery, warfare, lies, and wrongs,
>   All vice and crime, might die together,
> And wine and corn, to each man born,
>   Be free as warmth in sunny weather.
> The meanest wretch that ever trod
>   The deepest sunk in guilt and sorrow,
> Might stand erect in self-respect,
>   And share the teeming world to-morrow.

> WHAT MIGHT BE DONE ? *This* might be done,
>   And more than this, my suffering brother,—
> More than the tongue e'er said or sung,
>   If men were wise and loved each other."*

This is the mission of laymen, of men of the world. We need not tell the true Christian man that the wisdom which can alone avail to light one forward on the path of such urgent and arduous duty, is that which borrows her lamp from Faith, and that the only love capable of triumphing over the armed battalions of Hate, is the charity born of the Crucified.

But in order to recruit and warm with a divine enthusiasm these armies of the God of Charity, we priests must fire our own souls with that flame which is more penetrating, far-reaching, and irresistible than the fire from heaven which the winds bear about in the thunder-cloud. Its overwhelming suddenness and energy must tell the nations that God is in the cloud, the whirlwind, and the fire.

Oh ! that all the children of God in this age of reasoning unreason, unbrotherly humanity, intolerant liberty, and most destructive progress, were vessels filled with the fervent spirit of the Gospel and the sweet odor of Christ,— how resistless would be their every word and example ! If only all of us who have at heart the cause of Christ, and with it the cause of humanity, and the dearest interests of country,—would only proclaim aloud in our heart and life as well as by our lips, that the Cross is our banner and the Crucified our sole chief, how the ideal of true manhood and true manliness would soon be gloriously realized in our homes, our associations, and the whole outside world !

> " Who shall be nearest, noblest, and dearest,
>   Named but with honor and pride evermore?
> He, the undaunted, whose banner is planted
>   On glory's high ramparts and battlements hoar,
> Fearless of danger, to falsehood a stranger,
>   Looking not back when there's duty before !
> He shall be nearest, he shall be dearest,
>   He shall be first in our hearts evermore ! "

---

* Charles Mackay.

" Your work may be to bring considerate thought
  To humbler toilers in the hive of men :
Yet take refreshing draughts to brains o'erwrought,
  To careworn, heart-sick soldiers of the pen.
A mother mourning o'er a child departed:
  Or worse, pursuing evil ways in life :
You may take comfort to the broken-hearted,
  And rescue the weak struggler in the strife.
To the repenting, or repentant, sinner
  You may bring light, and bid his terror cease ;
Some fallen sister you may seek, and win her
  Into the pleasant paths of hope and peace.
You may dispel from shallow doubters doubt,
  Chaos, to which is said, ' Let there be light !'
And guide the skeptic as he gropes about
  In darkness, dreaming of an endless night,
Where poverty and want are tempters : where
  Vice hath no check from Comfort ; none to teach ;
Where self-inflicted sorrows bring despair—
  Your Lord may let your soothing influence reach
Where more resistless tempters triumph—worse
  Than want and poverty—you may be nigh
When plethora of gold creates a curse,
  And wealth demands what riches cannot buy.
You may help those who help themselves—whose **prayer**
  Is for GOD-AIDED efforts ; who, believing
In SELF-HELP, greatly think, and grandly dare,
  And those more blest in giving than receiving :
Whose charity revives like sun-lit dew :
  And adds to bread the health-boon of the leaven ;
Happy in making happy ; ah ! how few
  Enjoy on earth the chiefest joy in Heaven !
Your task it is to lead the soul to God !
  Teaching to bless His staff and kiss His rod !" *

    * Samuel Carter Hall, " The Trial of Sir Jasper."
24

CHAPTER XIX.

THE PROFESSIONAL MAN.

Here were men devoted to a supernatural end, even in the legal profession ;men, consequently, like Sir Thomas More, ready to mount the scaffold rather :than contradict it by denying the Spiritual Supremacy of the Pope, or assenting .to any heresy which a tyrant or an absurd people might propose—men like ¦Felix, the great magistrate, described by Sidonius Apollinaris, . . . "a man of ,constant friendship, and who exalted his rank by his humility"—men such as D'Agnesseau not only imagined, but knew, named, pointed out. *What a broad spirit was his* (he says ; speaking of Langlois), *what precision of thought, what justness—we might almost dare to say, what infallibility of reason! There was nothing to exceed the soundness of his mind, unless it was his heart. His house had become a happy asylum for learning, experience, wisdom, and truth ; a kind .of temple, where sometimes the most important affairs of religion used to be treated, and where the ministers of the altar were surprised to find in a man of the world, not only more light and knowledge, but even more zeal for the purity of discipline, more ardor for the glory of the Church, than in some who approached the nearest to the sanctuary.*—DIGBY, *Compitum,* b. iv., ch. i.

WE feel, in beginning this chapter, as if we were about to enter some holy place consecrated to Him to whom alone belongs the perfection of all Holiness, Truth, and Justice ;— a place hallowed not only by the immemorial reverence of past ages, but by the immediate presence of the Godhead Himself. There are mighty interests of a threefold nature, of which God, the creator of man, the author of society ,and the protector of social order and happiness, intrusts the administration to a chosen few, and in favor of their kind the sacred interests of the soul and the spiritual life, the august interests of justice, law, and order, and the scarcely less important interests of bodily health and life to be pre- served and promoted.

Of the priesthood and its duties we are precluded from

370

treating by the very scope of our work; of the high and important professions of the Lawyer, and the Physician, we proceed to speak, reserving to the next chapter what relates to other public avocations.

I. *The Lawyer.*

We need scarcely recall to Catholics the doctrine of all our schools of theology on the nature and origin of law in general. They teach that "law is the divine will made known to rational creatures, and imposing on them the obligation of doing certain things and avoiding others, under pain of punishment." This same will of the Author of our being imposes on us in like manner the obligation of obeying the laws enacted by the human legislator, who borrows his authority from God, in whom resides the supreme right of compelling the wills of His creatures.

Hence the fundamental principle admitted in all moral theology, that just laws are binding on the conscience on account of their conformity to the divine eternal law. Nor will it be out of place to recall here the words pronounced in our own legislative halls by one whose memory must be ever dear to Americans,* and while contending for the religious freedom guaranteed by our Constitution:

"You make laws in this hall of supreme temporal power; but then, can you make them binding on the consciences of men? Yes, with one condition. If men, before your laws are enacted, have, as a principle in their hearts, the belief that God sanctions authority—that there is a higher and holier Law-maker who gives sanction to your laws. Where will you place the security and sacredness of legislation, but in this principle of the necessity of an account where deception will be impossible?"

Hence, also, in the thought and language of Christian Europe the close alliance between religion and justice, between the priest and the lawyer, and the parallels continu-

---

* Archbishop Hughes of New York.

ally drawn between their respective offices,—the one having to minister at the altar of the Living God and to sit in His place as the judge of consciences, while the other was said to minister in the sanctuary of justice.

"Our old and beautiful French language,"—says the Count de Montalembert,—"immortal and intelligent, true representative of the good sense of our fathers, knew by a wonderful instinct to assimilate religion to justice. · It was always said ' the temple of law,' ' the sanctuary of justice,' ' the priesthood of the magistracy.' We ought to accept and respect this synonym, and to take it for our guide, in legislation ; preserving the ·dignity of what is most august in the secular government of the State, which is certainly the administration of justice ; maintaining inviolable the temple of law and the temple of God, the sanctuary of justice and the sanctuary of truth, the sacerdotal character of the priest, and the priesthood of the judge." *

It is a well-known matter of history, that the Church from the earliest ages not only penetrated with her spirit of freedom, enlightenment, and mercy the legislation of both the Eastern and Western Empires, but, at the downfall of the latter, established, encouraged, and supported throughout Christendom the great law-schools which have been the fountains of modern legal science. She watched with equal solicitude over the serious special studies necessary, respectively, to the lawyer and the theologian. The same may be said of her schools of medicine.

Solicitude of the Church for the Legal Profession.

In her motherly anxiety for the reign of justice and equity as distinguished technically from law, she enacted, whenever she could, rigorous statutes against the abuses of law-courts and the chicanery of practitioners. Her constant endeavor,—it will be found, on studying carefully the annals of the Christian ages,—was to elevate the legal profession, to glorify it in the opinion of the people, and to inspire

---

* Quoted by Digby.

its members with a deep sense of religious self-respect and responsibility. The Emperor Justinian made a special edict, by which all advocates in the imperial courts of law were forced to swear on the Gospels, at the beginning of every trial, that they would not plead a cause they knew to be a bad one, and that they would withdraw from it the moment they discovered its injustice. The laws of Spain enjoined a like oath. In 1274, Philip III., the son of St. Louis, issued an ordinance to the same effect. But—what may prove of more interest to our readers—in 1237 the English bishops assembled in council at London decreed thus:

"We order that whoever desires to obtain the office of a lawyer, ought to present himself to the diocesan, and to take oath before him that in all causes in which he is employed he will exercise a faithful ministry, not delaying or destroying the action of justice toward the opposite party, but in defending his client by the laws and solid reasons." *

"We see proof," says Digby, "of the prodigious action of Catholicity in rendering strict, virtuous, and holy the character of the advocate. When secular honors were attached to the profession in France, the knight of laws was required to swear that he would never use his insignia in profane occupations, but in maintaining the rights of the Church and the Christian faith, and in the service of learning. The French lawyer, on being inscribed on the roll of advocates, engaged never to undertake just and unjust causes alike, without distinction, nor to maintain any with tricks, fallacies, and misquotations; he was not to set too high a price upon his services; he was not to lead a dissipated life, or one contrary to the modesty and gravity of his calling. He was not, under pain of being disbarred, to refuse his services to the indigent and oppressed. In the *Mirroir des Justices,* written in the reign of Edward II., it is laid down that a pleader or lawyer must be a person 'receivable in judgment, no heretic, nor excommunicate man. He is to be charged by oath that he will not maintain nor defend what is wrong or false to his knowledge; he is to

---

* Matthieu Paris, *ad annum* 1237,—quoted by Digby.

put in before the court no delays nor false evidence, nor move nor offer any corruptions, deceits, nor consent to any such.' " *

This much will suffice to show the aim of the Great Mother of nations both in so guarding against abuses the profession of the law, that its administration should ever result in upholding right and righting wrong, and in directing the ministers of justice with such jealous care, that no stain could fall on their ermine.

The present Need of a thorough Legal Training.

At an epoch when there is a general tendency toward lowering the traditional sacredness of the administration of justice, and of substituting a hasty and superficial legal education for the long and thorough preparation required in the days of our fathers,—it may not be inopportune to say a few words of encouragement to such as refuse to follow the short and easy path to the place and profits of the jurisconsult, the magistrate, or the pleader. With the same earnestness with which we should urge thoroughness in the education of the priest, we now plead for it in the training of the lawyer. And just as we are thrilled with gratitude and delight when we hear of our venerable ecclesiastical superiors' conscientious efforts to raise higher and still higher the standard of excellence in their preparatory seminaries and schools of theology, even so do we bless God when we learn of the establishment and success of Law Schools where professors and pupils vie with each other in conscientious zeal to make of the noble science they aim at mastering, a something divine to be worshiped and honored by life-long devotion. †

---

* "Compitum," b. iv., ch. i.

† We know the distinguished and devoted men who have given such fame to the Law-School of Laval University, Quebec, and have seen several of the eminent lawyers who have honored their masters by their incorruptible integrity more even than by their legal knowledge and forensic eloquence. We pray that in the Montreal Law-School, the same excellence may ever reign, and the same success attend the graduates! The noble rivalry which should exist between the parent university and its offshoot, should only produce a higher common

The Lawyer's Ideal.

It cannot be too lofty. The science which is necessary both to the advocate and the judge,—to say nothing of the legislator,—is not only exalted in its nature, but vast in its extent, and as exact in its every detail as its matters are most perplexing in their multitude and variety. Much more even than priestly science,—comprising the reasoned knowledge of dogmatic and moral theology, of canon law, conciliary jurisprudence, and ecclesiastical history, of the Sacred Scriptures and the languages which serve as a key to their study ;—the science of jurisprudence not only borrows much from theology and its cognate branches, but it ranges over the entire framework of society, the relation of man toward man in the city, and the nation,—and those of each nation toward the entire human race. There is no science comparable to that of the accomplished lawyer—the jurist—in the vast and complex range of its subject-matter ; none superior to it, save theology alone, in the sacredness and vital importance of the interests with which it deals in practice.

We cannot, then, be surprised that the Catholic Church which had received from the expiring Roman civilization

---

ideal and a more triumphant result,—just as the commingling of the mighty waters of the Ottawa with those of the St. Lawrence forms a deeper, wider, and nobler stream, enriching, adorning, and glorifying a land so full of the noblest promise for all future time.

Just as we write,—to our unspeakable satisfaction,—come the tidings that Georgetown College is about to crown all its past priceless services to our Catholic youth by perfecting its Law-School and Medical School, and taking measures to secure to our country the advantages of a great university complete in its every department. So the Society of Jesus in the United States, the illustrious Society of Saint Sulpice in Montreal, and that noble band of devoted priests, revered throughout Canada as the " Seminary of Quebec,"—join hands and hearts to endow the youth of America with schools worthy of the brightest ages of Christian civilization. Who can doubt of God's blessing on them ?

" Walk in joy . . .
    Made free by love ; a mighty brotherhood
    Linked by a jealous interchange of good.
A glorious pageant more magnificent than conqueror's return. "

the inheritance of its grand system of legislation and jurisprudence, should have cherished this heirloom with a religious care, and deemed the knowledge of law and the administration of justice second only in dignity and importance to the guardianship of the divine Deposit of Revelation and the sacred functions of the Christian priesthood.

In France, where all that pertained to the study of law and the administration of justice was ever held in singular honor,—the "worship of Justice," its "temples," and its "priesthood," were not empty words : the popular language expressed notions, convictions, and sentiments deeply rooted in the souls of the people. Not even the wholesale ruin wrought in all the ancient institutions of Christian France,—and in the constitution of her law-courts, parliaments, and magistracy, more than in any other,—has been able to obliterate from the minds of her people the idea that Justice is a something divine, and that her ministers are specially consecrated and separated by their character and functions from the lay multitude. Besides, the sacredness of their functions and the eminence of the dignity they held in the estimation of all classes, caused the members of the judiciary to be accounted noble: hence the distinction of *noblesse d'épée* (nobility or aristocracy of the sword) and *noblesse de robe* (nobility of the judicial robes or ermine).

We must not pursue this analogy beyond the limits of France and into the constitutions and customs of other countries. Even to the present day England rejoices in raising to the peerage the most eminent among her judges ; and of those who have honored the high office once graced by the martyred Sir Thomas More, several within the century had been born in the lowliest station. It is old Catholic tradition holding on its steady course in spite of religious and political changes,—like the White Nile above Fachoda, disappearing, to the eye of the careless observer, beneath a dense and impenetrable growth of papyrus and other aquatic plants, but pursuing still its way to the ocean.*

* See Schweinfurth, "The Heart of Africa," i., chap. iii.; and Sir Samuel W. Baker, "Ismailia," chap. iii. 54 (New York ed.).

The Church herself more than once manifested the high esteem in which she held lawyers, one of them, Guy Fouquet, being elected to the chair of St. Peter, in 1265, under the name of Clement IV.

For the instruction of lawyers themselves this much may be deemed more than sufficient on the high dignity of their profession. Less we could not say for the interest of the general reader. What shall we say of the mighty issues that depend on their professional skill, their uprightness, and conscientious devotion to their clients?

Interests Intrusted to Lawyers.

Lawyers are intrusted with the fortunes and the honor of families, as well as with the liberty and life of individuals. On the professional virtues of no one class in the community does so much of its temporal happiness depend as on the men who undertake to defend and vindicate right against wrong before the august tribunals of justice. On no class does it depend so largely, so exclusively even, to bring justice, law, authority into contempt, or to make these venerable names still more sacred in the esteem of all classes.

The profound respect which the writer has ever entertained both for the bench and the bar, induces him to hold up here to the entire legal body,—to such at least as share his own religious faith,—the mirror of one noble life, that of a man whose memory is still fondly cherished in his native country, and who deserved to be the parent of one of Spain's most saintly and accomplished daughters.*

Diego de Escobar was an advocate in the royal court of chancery at Valladolid, and professor of civil and canon law in the University of Salamanca. His extreme delicacy of conscience, however, caused him to give up practicing in the law-courts after a brief career of extraordinary brilliancy. Thenceforward he devoted himself to the duties of his professorship, charming and edifying the numerous youth of the university by his gentleness, his childlike sim-

---

* The venerable Marina de Escobar.

plicity, and spotless purity of life much more even than by his uncommon learning and eloquence. In the Latin 'biography of his daughter is contained a brief 'Rule of Life' which this exemplary Christian had drawn up for himself, and which is here submitted to the reader. "My first care shall be, when I rise in the morning, to say my prayers and invoke the Blessed Virgin, then go to hear Mass, and, on festivals, to the Sermon, which I shall listen to attentively and devoutly, beseeching our Lord to give me grace to serve Him. I am resolved, wherever I may be, not to assent to or countenance murmuring, to prevent and reprove swearing, to give good advice, to pardon offenses, and above all to suffer and bear with unruffled soul insults, afflictions, and ill fortune; also daily to visit some sick person, consoling and assisting him to the best of my power; also to visit those in affliction, in order to comfort them; to follow the dead to their last resting-place; to give alms cheerfully to every one who asks from me; to entertain hospitably the homeless poor whom I may meet on the roads or public places, and to give them food and drink and clothing, considering that in their persons I receive into my house Christ, who is present in the poor—to take care that no one leaves me sad and desolate, but rather joyful and refreshed; to wear sackcloth or a rope next my flesh, to take the discipline once a week, to fast not only on the prescribed days, but also on the vigil of every feast of the Blessed Virgin, and, if I can, on the Fridays; to endeavor as far as I can to hinder litigation, and to apply myself diligently to this purpose; not to act tyrannically with persons going to law, but to speak to them courteously and in a friendly manner; to dictate lectures to my pupils for their especial benefit; in fine to meditate on the life and passion of our Lord Jesus Christ; to be grateful to God for the benefits I receive from Him, and to love Him for His goodness." *

Do not say that the mirror of such a life reflects an ideal

---

* *Vita Venerabilis Virginis Marina de Escobar,* lib. i., c. 1.

too superhuman, too far above the low level of what modern society esteems as excellent and exemplary. You, men of the world, are still Christian men, men who believe in supernatural virtue and supernatural grace as a help toward such virtue ; you believe also in the necessity for all who would have a share with Christ to be Christlike, and, therefore, supernatural. Would you forgive a priestly teacher, writing on such deeply practical matters, to address you as men who only believed in naturalism,—the worship of mere natural excellence, to the exclusion of all the divine forms of goodness and greatness so familiar to our fathers ?

Why the Lawyer's Ideal must be Supernatural.

No! In the consciousness of our own innate weakness amid the general abasement of morals and manners around us, we must not drift unresistingly downward with the current, but lift our eyes and hands and hearts upward to the eternal hills where is our Hope and Helper,—as well as our Model. The vision of One thorn-crowned and treading the steep road of Calvary beneath His heavy cross, is never to be lost sight of. We are His disciples and followers. Hence it is that in all Catholic countries,—all throughout Christendom, indeed, before the middle of the sixteenth century,—the image of Christ crucified was hung up on the wall full in view of the judges' bench,—as if He it was who presided at the administration of justice, as if lawyers and judges felt bound to be guided in the practice of their noble profession by His spirit and His maxims, tempering all human justice and law with His Mercy and Charity.

We remember, in visiting the *Palais de Justice* at Paris, to have seen, in the magnificent hall called *Salle des Pas Perdus* a large crucifix suspended from the wall. Palace, hall, and crucifix have since been swept away by the drunken fanatics of the Commune,—the worthy representatives of our modern naturalists and levelers.

Our lawyers and our judges, however, will only be all the more worthy of the name they bear, all the more honored and blessed of those who need impartial human justice,—if they bear with them, impressed on their hearts and their lives the likeness of Christ crucified. They must follow Him! And we should fail in our assumed duty did we not tell them so.

> " The bird hath not known the path,
> Neither hath the eye of the vulture beheld it.
> The children of the merchants have not trodden it,
> Neither hath the lioness passed by it." *

We have been privileged to know and to live with some of the best, the saintliest, the most lovable, and the most accomplished of Christian men ; but none of the dear and venerable forms so familiar to us in youth and mature life ever effaced the sweet images of these two ornaments of the Bar and Bench of Lower Canada, Justices Panet and Morin, to each of whom every word written for his own guidance by Diego de Escobar might be literally applied.

Of this Royal Way of the Cross, followed by all such true men, we can say with one who was in his day the wonder of the Roman world, the master and guide of great lawyers and illustrious orators : "This is the religion which possesses the universal way for delivering the soul ; for, except by this way, none can be delivered. This is a kind of royal way, which alone leads to a kingdom which does not totter like all temporal dignities, but stands firm on eternal foundations." †

This Royal Road is the Highway of Honor.

One word to all members of the Bar on this right-royal highway of Christian honor, and on the dishonorable and

---

* Job, xxviii. 7, 8.

† St. Augustine, *De Civitate Dei*, l. x., c. 32 : *Haec est religio quae universalem continet viam animae liberandae ; quoniam nulla nisi hac liberari potest. Haec est enim quodammodo Regalis Via, quae una ducit ad regnum, non temporali fastigio nutabundum, sed aeternitatis firmitate securum.*

degrading tendencies from which it is the deep interest of all that the profession of the law should be "delivered" and preserved. St. Louis, King of France, was, among other mighty cares, so anxious that no suspicion of wrong-doing should attach itself to the administration of justice within his kingdom, that he built what is known as *La Sainte Chapelle* ("The Holy Chapel"), by the side of the central court of justice in Paris, placing within this most exquisite of all existing church edifices the Crown of Thorns worn by our Lord, and which the holy king had brought with him from Palestine. There, daily, judges and advocates were wont to assist devoutly at the Holy Sacrifice, before proceeding to their usual avocations,—the presence of the diadem of shame worn by the King of Kings in His passion, and the celebration of the most august of their religion's mysteries serving as an eloquent exhortation to the conscientious discharge of their august office.

In this same sanctuary all the members of the Bar formed a pious brotherhood, bound together, not by the common purpose of promoting their own worldly or pecuniary interests, or of protecting prevarication or wrong-doing or incompetence, against those above or below themselves, but by the sincere and firm design of saving their professional robes from even the slightest stain of dishonesty, of guarding their clients from the possibility of wrong, and of furthering to the best of their power the interests of their dependents and the cause of impartial justice. Their model was a Frenchman, Sulpicius Severus (died 410), held as a saint in some parts of France, and who was equally studious of the interests of justice and of the science of law, and as zealous in putting a stop to lawsuits as he was to urge forward those he had undertaken.* It was, however, then, as it has been ever since, a hard struggle for high-souled lawyers against the custom which prevailed among their false brethren; and France has had her canonized

---

* *Neque enim ille magis juris consultus quam justitiæ fuit ; neque instituere litium actiones malebat, quam controversias tollere ;* applied by Cicero to a contemporary of the same name as the Christian advocate.

Advocate, Ivo de Kaermartin, of whom is sung on his feast-day ·

> *Advocatus, non latro,*
> *Res miranda populo.*

"An advocate, yet not a thief,—a thing transcending all belief."

Ancient and Modern "Picklocks."

The opposite character, the unprincipled or half-educated pettifogger,—the man of greed and gold,—is no new character in the world. The portrait made of him in the days of Queen Elizabeth is that of many a man in the days of Queen Victoria, and those who might sit for it abound on both sides of the Atlantic :

> "Here is Domine Picklock,
> My man of law, solicits all my causes,
> Follows my business, makes and compounds any quarrels
> Between my tenants and me ; sows all my strifes
> And reaps them too ; troubles the country for me,
> And vexes any neighbor that I please." *

Of course, the men whose ignorance, incapacity, and bad actions dishonor a noble profession, should never be cited or accepted by any enlightened or impartial person as the fair representatives of that profession. It is both illogical and unjust to argue from the exceptional guilty few to the innocent and upright many. The majority, however, in any profession would seem, in the judgment of the public, to become responsible for the conduct of a dishonest minority, when they neither protest in a body against open and crying wrong, or when they neglect to stop the abuse by stringent enactments and exemplary punishment.

There are two classes of persons toward whom members of the Bar may display the disinterestedness and devotion worthy of their calling, or that spirit of peculation which is now the bane of so many courts of law : the poor and the upper classes. So far as the poor are concerned, it may suffice to hold up to all the mirror of the Christian generosity and charity practiced by lawyers in some Catholic lands.

---

* Ben Johnson.

We have spoken of St. Ivo, as the acknowledged patron of the legal profession. Perhaps the reader may wish to know on what grounds this Saint merited such a distinction. Ivo Hélori de Kaermartin, was born of an illustrious family near Tréguier in Lower Brittany in the year 1253. He was thus a contemporary of St. Thomas Aquinas, Dante, and Petrarch, living in an age of great intellectual activity and culture,—when the study of law was held in extraordinary honor. He completed his philosophical and theological course in the University of Paris, and his course of canon and civil law at Orleans,—the former under the celebrated canonist William de Blaye, who afterward became bishop of Angoulême, and the latter under Peter de la Chapelle, an eminent lawyer, who became bishop of Toulouse and a cardinal. This elevation is one fact among thousands to show in what esteem superiority in legal lore was held by the Church in that age.

Home Education of the Christian Lawyer.

Ivo was blessed in having a mother whose accomplishments and piety enabled her to mold her boy's soul to the pursuit of the noblest aims and the practice of the most generous virtue. She labored early and successfully in impressing him with the conviction that he must become a supernatural man and a saint. This high purpose gave a direction to all his youthful studies and to his career in ripe manhood. At Paris and Orleans he shone among the numerous youth of each university with the twofold splendor of his uncommon talent and unearthly purity of life. Not that men of saintly lives were then rare in the great schools of France, Germany, and Italy,—for history attests the contrary; but, as these belonged for the most part to the great religious orders of St. Dominick and St. Francis, then in the early summer of their glorious prosperity, the union in a young layman and a law student of the highest gifts of intellect and the most exalted piety was a thing even then deserving of admiration.

Both in Paris and in Orleans the noble youth was remark-able for· his rigorous abstemiousness, never tasting wine or anything intoxicating, abstaining even from the use of flesh meat, strictly observant of the fasts of the Church, and giving to sleep the shortest space he could. But he gave most of his spare time to visiting the poor and sick in the hospitals, where his presence was ever like a sunbeam.

The Advocate of the Poor.

He had made a secret vow of perpetual virginity; and this, while disposing him to enter the service of the Church at a later date, made him refuse the most tempting offers of mar-·riage. Indeed, the birth, the surpassing talent and elo-·quence of the young lawyer, as well as his growing reputa-·tion, opened to him the doors of the best families and the avenue to the highest dignities in the State. He was, how-ever, wholly devoted to his profession, devoted especially to the poor and defenseless. These soon found out their friend and protector; and even during this first period of his career, Ivo was known as "the Advocate of the Poor," —a most glorious distinction.

The appellation became more especially his, when at length he was induced to receive holy orders. As, in every diocese in France,—and indeed of all Western Christendom,—the bishop's court was the one to which the laboring poor loved to appeal for justice, Ivo was, immediately after his ordina-tion, appointed "official," or presiding officer at the ecclesi-astical court of Rennes. Here he was not permitted to remain long; for the Bishop of Tréguier, who claimed him as his diocesan, forced him to accept the position of ecclesi-astical judge in his own native city. He made of his court a model, reformed the entire administration of justice, and became the idol of the people far and near. For, not satis-fied with fulfilling his own duties as judge, he held himself ever in readiness to go to other courts to plead the cause of the needy and the oppressed.

Revered as he was by high and low, this readiness to.

advocate the rights of the widow and the orphan, of the husbandman and the day-laborer, seemed to create neither jealousy nor unworthy rivalry among his brother lawyers. On the contrary, his deep knowledge not only of law but of human nature, his almost preternatural sagacity in detecting guilt and following it through all its dark windings, and the eloquence which he displayed in favor of the innocent,—made him a welcome favorite everywhere.

When his bishop forced him to accept a pastoral charge, he displayed in his parish of Tresdretz the apostolic virtues of which he had already given the promise while a layman. He was a true father and protector to his people, to the poor in particular. He built near his own residence an hospital and asylum for the sick and the poor, in which he lavished daily on them all the care of the most tender charity. He died at the age of fifty in 1303, mourned by all Brittany, and, indeed, by all France, so universally was he beloved and revered. John de Montfort, Duke of Brittany, went himself to Rome to solicit his canonization, solemnly affirming on oath that he had been cured by the prayers of the man of God of a sickness pronounced by the best physicians to be incurable. The examination into the heroicity of his life and virtues was begun in 1337, and completed ten years afterward, when the name of Ivo was placed on the list of God's most glorious servants, and the 19th of May, the day of his death, was appointed as his feast, thenceforward to be the great feast-day of Christian lawyers.

Even in England the great Breton "Advocate of the Poor" was revered by the people as well as by the members of the profession he had so highly honored; his name was given to churches and to institutions, and still survives in more than one place.

We are only solicitous in thus glancing at so holy a life, that every true-hearted lawyer should be,—the advocate, the defender, the devoted and disinterested counselor of the poor.

25

Compare this Picture with That.

As to rich and powerful clients, what can we say here, while the daily press is full of the most disheartening and disgraceful tales of peculation, fraud, and even forgery committed by men,—whose profession gives them the rank of gentlemen, but whose deeds show them to be worse than the felons they defend or help in bringing to punishment?

Is it not a terrible arraignment of so noble a profession to hear it daily said, by the organs of public opinion, in a free country, that some of our courts of justice seem only to be organized for the purpose of permitting lawyers to absorb the entire fortune of their ill-starred clients during the slow process of a suit? that neither the judges on the bench, nor the Bar as a body, will dare or care to interfere to prevent the enormous and ruinous fees levied on the wretched contestants? that men standing high in their profession are almost weekly discovered to have betrayed the trust of the widow, the orphan, the minor, or the too-confiding client, by using the property of the latter for their own personal profit?

And then, the odious spectacle presented in certain criminal as well as in certain civil suits, where the life and reputation of the living,—even when compelled to give their testimony as witnesses, are searched and held up to the prurient curiosity of the sight-seers in the court and of the expectant millions outside! the souls of the innocent and the sensitive, because they are forced to testify, being put to tortures that would shame all the judges and satellites of the most barbarous inquisitions of bygone ages! crimes and hideous details of secret and most loathsome guilt rehearsed again and again before judge and jury and listening public, and borne by the press all over the land like the seeds of the most destructive pestilence, to fall on the minds and hearts of all-reading youth and childhood? And we wonder at the alarming growth of precocious depravity and premature crime,—as if any other reaping could be expected from such sowing! Even in the age of Cicero, as the great

lawyer and orator tells us, to good men like Piso, the atmosphere of law-courts became intolerable because unwholesome to the moral sense. *Hominum ineptias ac stultitias, quæ devorandæ nobis sunt, non ferebat:* "He (Piso) could not endure the improprieties and follies committed by the men of our profession, and which we had to swallow patiently." *
What would both Piso and Cicero have thought of the degrading and corrupting spectacle offered by our law-courts daily for months and months in succession, as certain infamous trials dragged their loathsome length along, or, as at this moment, a certain contestation over a wretched millionaire's will enables the lawyers of his unnatural sons to exhibit to the foul taste of reporters and readers every hideous detail of their dead parent's moral, mental, and bodily infirmities!

We heard a lawyer express his conviction that such trials with their protracted displays of moral turpitude were as useful and as necessary to the young practitioner as the lessons and exercises of the anatomical amphitheater were to the surgeon and physician. We beg to differ with him, knowing that we have on our side the ripest talent and most honored names of the American Bar. Of the courts of justice dishonored by such practice, and of the wisdom therein acquired, we think with the illustrious Roman orator, "that it were hard to say whether such a school for legal training, or the men who go thither to learn, or the odious nature of the lessons there taught, contributes most to pervert and corrupt the mind of youth." †

The Judiciary.

It is to the upright and eminent men who grace the judgment-seat as well as their high calling, that we must look for a remedy.

"Nino, thou courteous judge, what joy I felt
When I perceived thou wert not with the bad!" ‡

* Cicero, "Brutus," n. 67.
† *Non facile dixerim; utrumne locus ipse, an condiscipuli, an genus studiorum plus mali ingeniis adferant.—De Officiis,* ii. xiv.
‡ Dante, "Purgatorio," viii.

Passing over the necessities or political expediences: which have led to making the judiciary elective in so many of our States,—lest we should for a moment allow the suspicion of partisan prejudice to rest on our teaching,—we hasten to say, that it is in the power of our judges to do much, very much, to purify their own profession from these increasing abuses, and to promote the most vital interests of the nation by guarding carefully the sacredness of the legislator's trust and of their own office.

In the examples quoted in this chapter,—in the lives especially of such men as St. Ivo and President Langlois, every true man, who has at heart the immaculate honor of his place and the purest interests of justice, will find an ideal,—the loftiest and the most ennobling.

There are, we would fain believe, few, if any, among our judges, who are not thoroughly acquainted with the life and writings of the great magistrates who shed such immortal luster on the ancient administration of justice in France, and did such glorious service in promoting various important legal reforms as well as in withstanding the arbitrary acts of those in power. Think of the great Chancellor D'Aguesseau (died 1751), who was, according to Voltaire himself, "the most learned magistrate that France ever possessed;" and who, "independently of his thorough acquaintance with the laws of his country, understood Greek, Latin, Hebrew, Italian, Spanish, Portuguese, etc." But far more precious to his memory and important for our purpose, is the fact that, according to the Duke de St. Simon, his moral character was a happy blending into one harmonious whole of "gravity, justice, piety, and purity of manners." Would you hear what he did or attempted to do in the cause of justice and good government? "He employed his authority as *Procureur Général* in most cases wisely and honestly. He reformed the system of the management of public hospitals; improved the discipline of courts of justice; and instituted a quicker mode in the investigation of criminal cases previous to their being brought to judgment. D'Aguesseau aspired through life to the high but difficult reputation of a legal reformer;—and it is in this particular that his reputation has the greatest claim upon our respect.˙ . . . *His praiseworthy attempts were resisted, no doubt, by all those whose mistaken interests suggested to them that the attainment of justice ought to be kept expensive and uncertain, instead of being rendered cheap and secure.* He is said to have confessed that he did not go so far as he wished, *because he did not like to reduce the profits of his professional brethren.* This was a mistake even in mere worldly policy ; for when law, as well as any other article of exchange, is dear and worthless, the purchasers will be few." .

˴ This fault he nobly redeemed when raised to the office of Chancellor of France, in 1717. He opposed with inflexible firmness the schemes introduced by the political economist Law "for substituting fictitious wealth for real capital." As this fatal financial policy prevailed at court, the Chancellor who opposed it was dismissed and exiled. Two years afterward, when the bubble had burst, the Chancellor was recalled. "His high sense of integrity and justice would not allow him to hear of a national bankruptcy : he insisted on making good the government obligations, or at least allow-, ing those who held its paper to lose only a proportionate part ; and, by thus preventing a bankruptcy, he contributed in some degree toward restoring general confidence." *

Surely here is a noble model for our most enlightened and most exalted magistrates. And yet France can boast of still loftier instances of learning and virtue in her chancellors. The family of Séguier alone from 1460 to 1789 could boast of sixty-eight of its members filling the highest dignities in the magistracy,—a glory within their profession to which nothing similar is found in history. Ah, would to God that distinguished lawyers among us could inspire their sons with such an admiration of their own calling and a devotion to it, that every succeeding generation of their descendants would aim solely at surpassing their parents

---

* See biographical article in "Penny Cyclopædia."

in eminence of ability and integrity of life. Pierre Séguier, who held the office of Chancellor in 1635, seemed to unite in his person every merit. He braved Richelieu when that minister was all-powerful, and resisted alternately, during the long minority of Louis XIV., the power of every faction that swayed either the court, the nobles, or the popular masses. It was only when such incorruptible magistrates were no longer found to oppose the progress of absolute power, that the will of such men as Louis XIV., the Regent D'Orleans, and Louis XV., became the supreme law in the State. Séguier, however, was so much above court and nobility, army and politicians, that he was sent alone and unarmed to quell a formidable insurrection in Normandy, and succeeded in bringing back the rebels to obedience by the sheer ascendency of his "sacerdotal gravity and fervor." In an age preëminent for its intellectual culture, the Chancellor was so distinguished for learning and devotion to letters, that he not only had a principal part in organizing the French Academy, but he was chosen to be its president, and declared its protector, while in his house, for thirty years, were held the sittings of that celebrated body. Need we remind our readers that, from these great and proud families devoted from father to son to the profession of the law, have sprung most of the men who have shed on French letters such transcendent glory?

We shall hope that our lawyers and magistrates, by cherishing such ideals as these, and by loving to walk in these ancient paths of learning, honor, and integrity, may be ever able to say to their descendants :

> "The good and mighty of departed ages
> Are in their graves : the innocent and free,
> Heroes and poets, and prevailing sages,
> Who leave the virtue of their majesty
> To adorn and clothe this naked world. And we
> Are like to them—such perish, but they leave
> All hope, or love, or truth, or liberty,
> Whose forms their mighty spirits could conceive,
> To be a rule and law to ages that survive."

II. *The Physician.*

It was Homer who sang of the Physician so many ages before the Christian era,

'Ιητρὸς γαρ ανὴρ πολλῶν ἀντάξιος ἄλλων.

" A wise physician, skilled our wounds to heal,
Is more than armies to the public weal." *

Machaon, of whom the poet here speaks, and his brother Podaleirios, were reputed to be sons of Esculapius,—and therefore held to be demi-gods,—on account of their admirable skill in the healing art, much more than by their rank among the Grecian princes. " In Herodotus we see how the physician Democedes was honored by kings and nations. . . . The Thracian physician in the army, who told Socrates what he had learned from Zamolxis, seems to have had a profound sense of the dignity of his art when he said, that as you cannot cure the eyes without curing the head, nor the head without healing the body ; so neither can you cure the body without curing the soul. Another of these wise physicians, unlike the wretched impostors from the Jewish university of Salerno, was the sage who recalled St. Augustine from the vain study of astrology. Tertullian called medicine " the sister of philosophy." In the eighth century a school of philosophy was opened in the monastery of Monte Cassino. In the early ages, the monks and hermits practiced through charity the cure of diseases. They were our first and best physicians well skilled

' In every virtuous plant and healing herb
That spreads her verdant leaf to the morning ray."

The Benedictine monks had always schools of medicine. They studied Hippocrates, Celsus, and Galen, whose science is the astonishment even of our age. Saints Cosmas and Damian, who are daily commemorated by the Church,†

---

* Iliad, xi. 514 : the English translation is Pope's.
† In the Canon of the Mass,—a most extraordinary distinction.

TRUE MEN AS WE NEED THEM.

were eminent physicians, who suffered martyrdom about the year 303. Never taking any fee, they were styled by the Greeks Anargyri (from the Greek ἀνάργυρος, costing no money)." *

The Church's Equal Love for both Professions.

It were hard to say which of these two great professions Law and Medicine—was held in greatest estimation by the Church, so carefully did she from the very beginning train both lawyer and physician to the highest skill in their calling and the most scrupulous discharge of their duties. St. Luke was by profession a physician, the favorite companion of the great St. Paul in his apostolic labors, one of the four inspired historians of our Lord, besides being the author of the only inspired history of the infant Church (the "Acts of the Apostles"). The traditions of these first ages affirm that he was also a painter of more than ordinary skill, and hence he has been chosen by Christian artists as their protector and special patron. That this accomplished man—a converted Gentile—should have been chosen by St. Paul to be his associate in the apostolic ministry, laboring with the great founder of the Grecian and Macedonian churches during so many years, would prove that his heart was as pure and beautiful as his mind was cultivated.

Ever since his day the great schools of medicine, placed under the immediate control of the Church, have aimed at fostering in the souls of their pupils that deep spirit of faith and piety, that innocence of soul and purity of life,—which can alone enable the physician to be what he ought ever to be,—the second minister of God's mercy and healing power at the sick-bed and in the bosom of Christian families. Hence the Christian religion has ever labored to impress on the minds both of physicians and surgeons that they are the custodians of the bodily health and temporal honor of individuals and families, just as the priest is the guardian of the soul's welfare, the healer of its wounds, its divinely

* Digby, "Orlandus," ii. 259, 260.

appointed guide in the paths of spiritual health and perfection.

The physician, in all Catholic countries, is considered to be the conscientious assistant of the priest by the sick-bed and in the hour of mortal danger, prompting the patient to be reconciled with God, and—in urgent cases—refusing the ministry of his profession to the sick or dying person till the latter had complied with the divine commands and placed the soul's interests in perfect security. In thus aiding the priest in his most sacred functions, and helping the operation of God's most merciful ordinances for the soul's salvation,—the physician also finds, by experience, that he is mightily furthering the success of his own salutary art, and promoting the cure of the body. For beside the natural connection between peace of conscience and the subsidence of physical pain and irritation,—there is a special promise annexed to the reception of the last sacraments of alleviation from suffering and restoration to health, when God's fatherly providence deems it best for the sufferer.

The Physician's Angelic Model and Patron.

Before the age in which Christ and His apostles lived, there had been, in the annals of God's people, a most memorable example of the union of this twofold healing power, in the person of the Archangel Raphael ("The divine healer"). One of the most beautiful, touching, and instructive books of the Old Testament,—that of Tobias,—relates how God sent from on high His messenger to bestow the rarest blessings on two widely separated branches of a Hebrew family living in exile, and distinguished for exalted virtue. To the head of one household eyesight is restored, and to the other the grace of being freed from the obsession of an evil spirit, while both are bound more firmly together in living faith and fruitful charity by the nuptials of their children, brought about by their angelic benefactor.

Thus Raphael became to the early Christians what he had been for the Jewish people in exile and since their restoration,—the ideal of the true physician, acting under the divine guidance, and seeking the cure of the sick soul while laboring to heal the body.   How many imitators of Raphael and Luke, and Cosmas and Damian, have not the Christian ages beheld since the beginning!   The history of every country in Christendom, during the middle ages, is filled with the most instructive and edifying anecdotes concerning the devotion of physicians to their twofold task of promoting every good work, while laboring constantly for the advancement of the sciences pertaining to their own calling. The Church showed her care for this professional excellence by founding central schools of medicine and raising some of them to the rank of a university, as well as by her liberality in promoting the splendor and efficiency of the medical schools existing in such great centers of learning as Paris, Montpellier, Bologna, Pavia, Padua, Venice, Florence, and Rome.

The honor too in which she held physicians soon led to their rising in popular estimation.   In the Italian Republics they formed a most honorable class, whose members not only attained great wealth, but very often wielded the highest offices in the State.   Just as, all through these ages of faith, the lawyers were encouraged to form separate guilds and confraternities devoted not only to self-protection and mutual encouragement, but to all sorts of works of charity, even so and much more so did the members of the medical profession unite for the like purpose.   The deep and sudden changes effected in Catholic countries by modern revolutions have not altogether blotted out these admirable unions. Even where they have fallen asunder, the best elements of them have gone over to other newer and more active bodies, —like that of St. Vincent of Paul in France.

Apostolic Spirit of Modern Physicians.

And this must remind our readers of some of the most glorious and touching incidents connected with the revival of faith and charity in the France of our day.   Foremost among the noble men whose deeds of piety and beneficence have contributed so much to preserve and propagate religion in the Kingdom of St. Louis, are to be found physicians. The long stuggle they had undergone to rise to distinction in their profession, and the manifold opportunities furnished by it for mixing with all classes of men and women poisoned with the Voltairian unbelief,—they only considered to be the providential means of doing their duty by the sick souls brought under their influence.

During the months of March and April, 1862, the author had been sent by his ecclesiastical superiors to preach the Lenten Station in Coulommiers, some fifty miles to the east of Paris, in the diocese of Meaux. This portion of Bossuet's ancient diocese, as well as the entire territory surrounding the capital of France, is a moral waste over which the skepticism of the eighteenth century had first swept like a terrible frost over an orchard in full bloom, killing not only the fair blossoms but the trees themselves to the heart's core : and then to the blight had succeeded the earthquake convulsing the entire region and upsetting all the mighty monuments of existing civilization.

The city itself was filled with a hard-working population, doubly wretched in that they wrought unceasingly for insufficient wages, and had lost all their ancestral faith, having ceased to look forward to the eternal rest and bliss as a compensation for present ills.

Noble Christian men resided in their midst who made continual efforts to relieve both their moral and corporeal distress, such as their Mayor,—a most admirable man,—and the Chevalier des Mousseaux, so well known for his writings on Spiritualism. But local prejudices and bitter political antagonisms marred all the good work done by such as they. And bad as was the city folk, the surrounding peasantry were even worse. Their religion was a blind hatred of all religion, superadded to their inveterate envy of all wealth and superiority. The few churches which the Revolution had spared were left free to the women, very many, if not most, of whom did not dare to go to confession or communion through fear of their husbands. Indeed the men, as a general rule, only appeared in church twice a year, at Christmas and on Palm Sunday,—impelled thereto by some traditional custom or some strange superstition.

How Magistrate and Physician can Work Together.

Every Sunday, however, the members of the Society of St. Vincent of Paul in Paris, sent some of their associates, to go publicly to confession and communion at Coulommiers, in order to encourage the lukewarm and vacillating Christians among the *bourgeoisie* and the laboring classes to imitate their example and practice openly the religion of their fathers.

Among those who came thus weekly to fulfill their share of this apostolate of good example, we remember a magistrate, still young, but much admired for his learning and eloquence. He was wont to go quietly on these errands of truest charity, at great inconvenience to himself, and at the sacrifice of his home-comforts with wife and children on his only day of rest. But he knew for WHOM he was making the sacrifice, and deemed it of little account in the great crusade which he and his associates were thus silently carrying on. There was a young physician also,—though it may be that some of our readers will not deem a man of near forty young ; and his was a most beautiful and most heroic soul. From him we learned many most interesting details about the share which physicians and medical students had in bringing home to the needy and suffering poor as well as to their wealthy, enlightened, and aristocratic neighbors,—the sweet light of faith and charity,—and, with these, the long-vanished hope of another and a better life.

Since then, as the whole world knows, what heroic examples of patriotic devotion and Christian charity did these same men,—lawyers and physicians and students, members of the Societies of St. Vincent of Paul, of St. Francis Xavier, and St. Francis Regis,—display on the field of battle, in the crowded hospitals, during the horrors of more than one siege, and while their country was at the darkest hour of its destiny!

Of the like services rendered to Religion by English Irish, and Scotch medical men, we can make but brief mention. Everybody knows how high is their standard of professional knowledge, and how well merited the elevated social position ever held by physicians in all the three kingdoms. Our own personal memories recall, among other pleasant and edifying things, the modest figure of more than one distinguished London physician coming daily into the Sacristy of Farm Street church to serve Holy Mass, and, not unfrequently, serving several in succession. We know them, to be, on both sides of the Irish Channel, not only foremost in the ranks of modern science as well as in all that pertains to their own calling, but foremost also in every association and good work aiming to elevate the laboring man, or to promote education and charity. In furthering all these great social and religious objects physicians and lawyers go hand in hand with the priest.

Most happy should we be to cite instances of professional excellence and devotion. But obedience to religious authority only permitted us a brief glance at the dear old land of our birth, leaving behind a craving which we still hope may be satisfied ere we die. And, besides, it is beyond our purpose and scope to recite the many glorious examples of indomitable courage and professional faithfulness to duty recorded of physicians and surgeons in the dark, trying days of famine and pestilence, on the battle-fields of Europe, Asia, and Africa, during the last fifty years. Our own Civil War,—were we to enter into such details,—would furnish us materials for an entire volume, if we would recount the merits of American surgeons; while the terrible scourge, the Yellow Fever, now desolating our fairest Southern cities, places once more in conspicuous light the heroism of our physicians, our priests, and our Sisters of Charity.

It is heroism displayed in the performance of DUTY; and duty is to God. He alone can praise and reward it fitly.

We can only show how glorious and praiseworthy it is to live and die faithful to it. And this brings us to our concluding observation.

Why the Physician should be thoroughly Skilled in his Profession, and thoroughly Conscientious.

Men of the highest culture and widest experience will bear us out in the assertion, that no professional man should possess in a superior degree to the physician absolute thoroughness in theoretic and practical knowledge, a deep devotion to his calling, a living faith, and unblemished reputation.

His scientific acquirements are needful to the firm confidence which he must have in himself and in his ability to deal with the most serious dangers to the health and life of his patients; his reputation for solid piety, high principle, and conscientious devotion to duty, is needful to the absolute confidence which his patients must repose in him.

Consequences of a Surgeon's Intemperance.

We can never forget one tragic occurrence of very many years ago, that may serve to point our meaning here. A clergyman had been summoned in haste at midnight to the bedside of a young lady in imminent danger of death. During nearly forty-eight hours, previously, the utmost skill of two good physicians had been unavailing to give her relief, and a third,—an eminent practitioner, but a man, unhappily, of dissipated habits,—had been sought in vain, and came in while the priest was preparing the sufferer for the worst. His arrival inspired all present with new hope and gave courage to the exhausted young mother. The priest withdrew to allow the three physicians to hold a hurried consultation. Presently the young lady's husband came to say that his wife was dying. She was in a death-like swoon, from which she was only recalled by the most powerful restoratives. When the soul thus fluttering be-

tween life and death was able to address both her tearful
husband and the physician of the soul,—she motioned to
all but them to leave the sick-room ; and then addressing
the priest, " Oh, Father," said she—" Doctor —— is not
sober, and I must die." . . It was even so, the surgeon
so superior in skill to all his peers, far and near, had been
for several days in a deep debauch, and was still under its
influence. The poor sufferer, who had looked forward to
his coming as to her only chance of life, had no sooner per-
ceived from his appearance, his trembling hands, and foul
breath, that he was not master of himself,—then she felt,
all hope forsaking her and swooned away. In vain did the
priest, as briefly and eloquently as the urgency of the case
demanded, endeavor to raise her courage and exhort her to
put her trust in the Great Giver of life and strength,—she
begged to be allowed to retain the Crucifix that he presented
to her lips, and with that in her clasped hands, she expired,
while the priest and the household were praying together
in an adjoining room. The shock received by the refined,
gentle, sensitive, young creature after all her terrible suffer-
ing, prostrated her utterly ; and with her perished her babe.

It was hard to persuade the young husband 'whose heart
was thus crushed and whose beautiful home was left deso-
late and childless, that Doctor —— had not killed both his
wife and his child, by presuming to show himself to her in
a state bordering on *delirium tremens.* Nor did the other
physicians attempt to palliate what was utterly inexcusable.
How far this sad case injured the reputation and practice
of the offender himself, or whether the indignation of the
public and of his medical brethren induced him to change
his ways, we cannot say, nor would it further our purpose
to make it known to the reader.

The case,—an exceptional one,—is mentioned to show
how much above these low habits and degrading excesses
should be physicians, clergymen, and lawyers,—all men
who are liable to be called at any hour of the night or day
to the sick-bed, to save from the most serious peril the life
of the body or the life of the soul, or to settle,—in presence

of a near Eternity and of the God who dispenses its re-
wards and punishments,—the most momentous questions of
worldly interest, involving the peace and welfare of families.
We who are expected and bound to be the light and guides
of others, should ever be ready to render them the full ben-
efit of our ministry,—and, at what time soever we are sum-
moued to the bed of sickness, it should truly be said that,
on our appearance,

> " Abashed the devil stood,
> And felt how awful goodness is, and saw
> Virtue in her shape, how lovely."

To the worth of medical men we bear a willing and well-
deserved testimony of respect and affection, founded on long
acquaintance and the experience of uniform professional
skill and personal virtues.   In how many of them,—as we
now look back and recall their manifold merits,—did we not
find verified every word of the beautiful eulogy passed on
a saint by a mediæval writer?

> Fide, vita, verbo, signis,
> Doctor pius et insignis
> Cor informat populi.
> Mens secura, mens virilis
> Cui præsens vita vilis
> Viget patientia.

> " Pious and distinguished doctor,
> Whom faith, word, and signs instructor
> Fashioned for the people's heart.
> Mind secure, of manly power,
> Through the present fleeting hour
> Patience, virtue doth impart." *

The true Christian who feels himself honored in filling the
office of God's instrument for the preservation of life, the
increase of health, the happiness of families, and the wel-
fare of the whole community,—will ever bear it in mind,
especially where there is danger of death,—that the inter-
ests of the soul are dearer to God than bodily life or
health.

* The translation is from Digby as well as the Latin quotation.

CHAPTER XX.

THE STATESMAN.

> With grave
> Aspect he rose, and in his rising seemed
> A pillar of State ; deep on his front engraven
> Deliberation sat, and public care ;
> And princely counsel in his face yet shone,
> Majestic, though in ruin : sage he stood
> With Atlantean shoulders fit to bear
> The weight of mightiest monarchies ; his look
> Drew audience and attention still as night
> Or summer's noontide air.
> MILTON.

> Keep us in safety, and the chairs of justice
> Supplied with worthy men ! Plant love among us.
> Throng our large temples with the shows of peace ;
> And not our streets with war !

OF politics, in the odious sense given to the word by
modern morality, we wish to say nothing ; of politicians —
that is, men who trade or gamble in the distribution of
public office and patronage,—we have no word to say. Nor
would any enlightened reader desire that the priest should
soil his robe or busy his pen with concerns which to men of
his calling must ever happily remain a mystery,—a land
unknown and untrodden.

With men who are intrusted with public office in the
State, and have it in their power to serve the best interests
of their fellow-citizens and thus advance on earth the cause
of justice and right order,—that is, the cause of God,—we
have much to say which may be deemed both timely and
needful.

We understand by a statesman, one thoroughly trained

to the knowledge and administration of public affairs, and thoroughly able to govern the State wisely. The knowledge and management of public business, in any department, requires one to be educated thereto. The science or art of governing large bodies of men,—of governing a whole people, especially,—is of all arts the most difficult, of all sciences that which presupposes the most consummate wisdom and prudence. It requires, therefore, a most careful education, a long and patient training, a mind well stored with the clearest and most varied knowledge of men and things, a judgment well balanced, a will of indomitable firmness, and a virtue superior to all self-seeking.

How a Statesman should be Trained.

This much we say of what a statesman is and how he should be formed and endowed,—because of the belief which is daily gaining ground, that in order to govern well one only needs good sense, intregrity, and the choice of the people. The choice of an entire people would not enable the most sensible and trustworthy person among your acquaintance to sail a ship round Cape Horn, with a crew of honest and sensible men like himself,—but also, like him, utterly ignorant of the laws of navigation, unacquainted with the ocean, its currents and its winds, and unacquainted, as well, with the simple structure, equipment, and management of any vessel, great or small.

And this much we say, even at the risk of uttering commonplaces,—in order to satisfy the plainest understanding that we are not all fit, at any moment, to take in hand the helm of the ship of State.

The good sense of the most illiterate,—which is nothing more than the instinct of propriety,—tells them that as no calling requires in a man so vast an amount of knowledge and experience as that of the statesman and ruler,—so none should have a more careful apprenticeship. We have seen, in the preceding chapters, that the accomplished lawyer, the accomplished physician, the accomplished clergyman, the accomplished professor of any science, must have, —just like the accomplished artisan and artist,—a long, long course of special study and practice. But the statesman is bound to have,—if he would not continually blunder on the gravest practical matters,—the science of the profoundest jurist, with a thorough knowledge of political economy, of all past history, of the condition and resources of other States; and to this must be added no slight acquaintance with theology and canon law. For to the statesman belongs not only to regulate the enactment of wise and just laws on all public matters, but to superintend and direct their administration.

Hence it is that in all great governments young men destined to serve the State as ambassadors or administrators were trained in a special school at the end of their ordinary college or university course. It has ever been the case in modern Rome,—and it is so, as any one may see, in the great European and Asiatic monarchies. And, be it said here without any other purpose than that of further elucidating our meaning,—such appears to have been the object of the "Civil Service" law recently passed by Congress, and which has not yet had any general or serious application. Just as our Navy and Army form special services under Government, requiring a long and careful education,—even so should the civil service of the Federal Government or of the several State Governments only admit such as have been most carefully prepared and trained for the discharge of their weighty duties. This alone can secure us a succession of enlightened and able statesmen, and of efficient civil servants, such as a great civilized community requires. For, we Americans must not flatter ourselves that we are as naturally born with ability to rule the State and direct the mighty and complex machinery of government, as the duck is to swim as soon as it has broken its shell.

What is the State?

One of the first things the statesman ought to know before entering into the public service, is who and what is the master he has to serve. The word "State" is made use of at the present moment to offset the word "Church."   Indeed, it is the avowed purpose of modern governments to invest the abstraction called State with an omnipotence never at any period of her history claimed by the Church of Christ as one of her attributes. For, whereas the Church expressly disclaims supremacy or even direct power in matters pertaining to civil government, our statesmen of the Bismark and the Cavour school, will have the laws of the State not only supreme but practically infallible, to be set above the laws of the Church, the laws of God, and the dictates of conscience.

Even in other countries, where the constitution and the innate sense of the people, guarantee a real and full liberty of conscience, there is a growing tendency to invest the State with this same odious attribute of omnipotence and infallibility. Under the pretense of effecting a complete separation between the religious or ecclesiastical and the civil or political power, they have gone a step farther and claimed for the latter "absolute independence and supremacy in its own sphere." This favorite phrase, however, is made to cover a fallacy. The Christian religion, from the beginning, has consistently asserted not only the clear distinction of the spiritual and the temporal authorities, but the independence and supremacy of the civil authority within its own proper domain. It was the will of the divine Author of Christianity that men should render unto Cæsar the things that are Cæsar's while giving to God what exclusively belongs to Him. It was the injunction of His Apostles that all who bore the name of Christian should obey the civil power in all things that were not manifestly in opposition to the law of God and to the dictates of conscience; and this full and conscientious obedience to the constituted authorities, has ever been understood by Christians as a real though indirect compliance with the Divine Will itself. For God's majesty is seen by the eye of faith behind the temporal ruler; and in fulfilling the lawful ordinances of the latter we only submit to the divine ordinance itself.

We cannot remind the men of our day either too seriously or too frequently of the fact, that it is God who commands us to serve our country, and that we only serve it more efficiently and gloriously by looking up to Him, as to the Almighty Master who gives to such service its dignity, and promises to the faithful servant the only true and abiding reward that devotion and self-sacrifice deserve.

He would take but a low view of his own public func-, tions, who would consider the choice of his constituents as the only source of the high obligations he assumes, their will as the rule by which he is to direct his aims and his policy, and their approval or their blame as the end toward which he must direct his efforts.

Public men who set their hearts on mere popularity,— though the greatest possible and the most lasting,—as their sweetest recompense, are like adventurers in a balloon seeking to soar high and go far, favored by the calm and regular currents of the atmosphere. There are but few who ever arrive at the goal they promised themselves, or who descend to their original level with sound limbs and contented minds.

The public service,—that of the statesman particularly,— is anything but plain sailing. It is troubled by treacherous shoals and storms that no wisdom can forecast, and no skill can control. Supposing the fairest prospect to be yours, and that success beyond your expectations has crowned your every measure,—do not be intoxicated with the applause you receive. The most glorious servants of Republican Rome were conducted through a double line of the most splendid edifices ever erected, to the temple of Jove on the Capitoline Hill, while all Rome strewed their path with flowers, while young men and maidens sang triumphal hymns in their honor, and incense fumed all along the streets to intoxicate the sense even in the intervals of shout and song. But within a few feet of the temple of Jove in which they were crowned and might deem themselves demigods,—was the dreadful Tarpeian Rock down which the hands of that same people might dash them on the morrow.

We have seen in our day these terrible alternations of popular enthusiasm and frenzied ingratitude. We have seen mighty monarchs crowned amid the peans of the popular millions, and driven from their capitals like malefactors in disguise fleeing before the hounds of justice ; we have witnessed in the midst of modern Rome, the delirious demonstrations of a people's gratitude and veneration toward the most fatherly of sovereigns, the most single-hearted and generous of benefactors ; and, a few months later, that whole people, headed by its own army, besieged that noble Parent and Prince in his own palace, after murdering his servants. Have we not also seen our own statesmen and chief magistrates entering upon their high office amid the loud acclaim of a whole people, and descend from their station unblessed, unloved, uncared for? Are there not, among kindred peoples, contemporary instances of prime ministers who were but yesterday the idols of the worshiping multitude, and whose very residence may be to-night sacked by these same worshipers? "Honors and dignities are benefices which fortune and the world have charged with such great pensions, and the reserve of so many troubles, that in the end men are glad to escape from them."

Serve God in serving the State.

Why do we insist on this? Solely for the purpose of inducing our statesmen and public servants to be high-souled, to have from the beginning of their career these lofty views of duty which shall preserve them, in the inevitable day of disfavor and disappointment, from feeling that their life has been wrecked and wasted, and that they have served only an impotent or an ungrateful master. To Catholics, who understand what "purity of intention," working for God solely or principally in all that one undertakes and accomplishes,—there will be but little difficulty in understanding how soul-stirring is the *Sursum Corda !* not only in setting one's foot on the steep and icy path of public duty, but in the middle way when difficulties crowd upon one, and there is none to cheer by kind word or deed, and above all in the disastrous ending, when cast down by utter defeat and disappointment. Where you labor for His service, and seek His honor and glory, who cherishes only the pure and ardent desire of your sonly heart, and esteems the generosity that no difficulty dispirits and no defeat discourages, as far more praiseworthy than the most glorious success,—you shall never be cast down by adversity nor lifted up into pride or self-laudation by prosperity. So, to the statesman, much more than to the citizen in any walk of private life,— we must say : O brave heart, you have a dangerous road to travel ; see to it, then, that God the all-powerful, and the ever-helpful, be first, and middlemost, and last in your aims, in your hopes, in all your labors !

This consideration will enable you to appreciate the wise counsels delivered in the following passage by one who had forgotten conscience for ambition and the fear of God for his sovereign's favor, at the very crisis of his country's fate, and winked at a despotic king's unholy passions, when the latter, to gratify them, was ready to create a schism, and, like Lucifer in Heaven, to break up by rebellion the divine unity established by Christ.

> "Mark but my fall, and that that ruined me.
> . . . I charge thee, fling away ambition ;
> By that sin fell the angels ; how can man then,
> The image of his Maker, hope to win by it?
> Love thyself last : cherish those hearts that hate thee ;
> Corruption wins not more than honesty.
> Still in thy right hand carry gentle peace,
> To silence envious tongues. Be just, and fear not:
> Let all the ends thou aim'st at, be thy country's,
> Thy God's, and Truth's ; then, if thou fall'st,
> Thou fall'st a blessed martyr. . . .
> Had I but served my God with half the zeal
> I served my king, He would not in mine age
> Have left me naked to mine enemies." *

Governments for the People, not for the Governing Class.

The great mistake of statesmen is either to fancy that the

* Shakspeare, "King Henry VIII.," act iii., scene ii.

service of their country has nothing to do with the service of their God, or to make of the acquisition of place and power the sole end of their efforts, or to sacrifice conscience, justice, truth, and religion to policy and party. The theories of government that would tend to make of the people a flock of sheep to be shorn for the sole benefit of their rulers has found no countenance from the pontiffs and doctors of Holy Church. Again and again have her most eloquent and most authorized writers proclaimed that God deposited with the body of the people the authority necessary for all the ends of social life, and that it is from the people that magistrates and rulers derive their legitimate powers. But the exercise of that authority, in God's design and in accordance with the nature of things, should ever be for the benefit of the people, and regulated according to the express will of the divine Creator and Governor of the moral world, so as to secure to the members of the community peace, plenty, and prosperity,—all the ends of order and justice.

Moreover,—as revealed religion is a fact admitted by peoples and governments still calling themselves Christian, they are bound, if they would be consistent in their belief and profession, to square their own lives as well as the principles of their polity,—their laws, their administration, and intercourses with other peoples,—in conformity with the Divine Will as revealed by Christ. Hence, there should be nothing in their legislation or their policy to contradict the sublime doctrine of the unity and brotherhood of the race, of their common reciprocal duties here and their common destiny hereafter. The charity that binds brother to brother, under the law of love of the One Almighty Father, should be at the bottom of all public duties and obligations, as at the bottom of all private virtues and neighborly offices.

Every form of selfishness both in the public magistrate and in the private citizen conflicts with that divine charity which is the very life-breath of Christian society, and which ought to be the animating spirit of all nations who claim to be the offspring of Christian civilization. Indeed, the true Christian statesman, acting up to the principles of his faith, must look upon himself as a public servant,—doing service to God while serving the interests of the commonwealth.

The Christian Statesman is Gloriously Singular.

These principles and practical rules of conduct may not be, indeed we know are not,—those which guide the generality of public men. Perhaps it might be said, that to be guided by such supernatural truths would only render one singular, or expose one to be excluded altogether from public life. We do not think that the Christian spirit of Alfred the Great hindered him in overcoming his enemies, or in pacifying his kingdom and giving to it these very laws which are to-day the vital principles of the American Constitution. We do not think that the child-like innocence, the constant desire of seeking the divine pleasure and glory in every measure of his government, in every law that he passed, in the wise and impartial judgments he rendered, and in his successful efforts to reconcile the rights of his civil government with those of the Church within his kingdom,—rendered St. Louis pusillanimous, or lowered him in the esteem of his contemporaries or the admiration of posterity. And so with his great kinsman St. Ferdinand III., King of Castile, the wise legislator, the brave and heroic soldier, the model man and Christian in every relation of life.

These true statesmen were, to be sure, SINGULAR ; that is, they stand out alone before the mind's eye, amid the multitude of really good and great man who lived in the same age, like those Round Towers of Ireland rising above the ruins of the past and the desolation of the present, a wonder and a mystery to the artist as well as to the historian. St. Bernard says somewhere *nihil sanctum nisi singulare*, —"every true saint is a something singular,"—in the perfection which raises him above the multitude. Be not afraid to be singular and surpassing in your uprightness,

your integrity, your firmness in resisting the torrent of cus
tom and the degrading influences of the surrounding atmo-
sphere.

And this brings us back to the extract which heads this
chapter. He surely was singular, that Seraph Abdiel, who,
amid the countless host of angels who followed Lucifer in
his revolt, was

> "Faithful found
> Among the faithless, faithful only he ;
> Among innumerable false, unmoved,
> Unshaken, unseduced, unterrified,
> His loyalty he kept, his love, his zeal ;
> Nor number, nor example, with him wrought
> To swerve from truth, or change his constant mind,
> Though single." *

This glorious singularity was never more needed than
amid the universal disposition toward social change and
the consequent general confusion of ideas, which mark our
times.

Even the best statesmen of the epoch, iu the wish to con-
ciliate the antichristian principles which tend more and
more to prevail in the policy of modern governments, with
the august and venerable notions and maxims that were
once accepted by all Christendom,—resemble not a little the
astute leader described by the poet in the heading of this
chapter.

The masterpieces of the Creator, even when fallen and
degraded by rebellion against Him, preserve the outlines of
their primitive grandeur. God does not take away from
His worst enemies either native wisdom, or superior knowl-
edge, either the genius to plan great things or the fortitude
necessary to their execution. The minister of state who
enlists whole senates in the unholy crusade which he un-
dertakes against liberty and religion, will not be deprived
either of his gift of "princely counsel," or of the ruined
majesty of presence which still awes the vulgar, or of the

---

* "Paradise Lost," book v., near the end.

golden flow of eloquence and the facinating look, which can hold an audience spell-bound, and command

"attention still as night
Or summer's noontide air."

We are contemplating here the statesman, minister, ruler, who is a man "according to God's own heart," like the great poet and warrior-king of Israel ; a man who seeks to make the interests of the Eternal Majesty first, middlemost, and last in all his policy.   Such a man, though he may not perhaps ever be the popular idol of the hour, will be sure to draw the attention and to deserve the respect of the solid men of principle and conscience, of the enlightened and far-seeing who are not dazzled by newborn and brilliant theories, but who are ever anxious that the present of nations should be made up of all the elements of greatness of the past, so that the growth of national prosperity shall be like that of the giant trees of California,—increase of strength, vitality, and beauty in every portion of the mighty frame, from the earth-roots that buttress up the towering trunk to the extremity of the wide-spread arms, and the topmost bud of this year,—the latest addition to the height of the lordly tree. Not so, with most of the statesmen whom erratic public opinion so loudly bepraises. The to-day of the constitutions they create or patch up hastily is not the legitimate growth of the national life of yesterday. It is fictitious, not natural ; it is not the production of nature, and is therefore doomed to have neither duration, nor salutary influence.

The work and the fame of the workman are also doomed to be short-lived.   "For behold they that go far from Thee shall perish : Thou hast destroyed all them that are disloyal to Thee." *

Not so the good and great name of the statesman, who, convinced that the constitution of a nation, with its laws, its time-honored customs, and its institutions, are its natural, God-given, and God-directed social growth,—only aims

* Psalm lxxii. 27.

at helping and perfecting the work of the all-wise and all-mighty hand.   His glory shall be like these stupendous monuments of Egypt, which survive the peoples who witnessed their erection.   From amid the undistinguished graves of millions buried beneath the invading desert around, the pyramid stands sublime, as immovable and as durable as the solid earth.   The traveler from afar sees it in the morning air like a point scarcely visible on the level rim of the eastern horizon.   But as he journeys across the sandy waste, what was only a speck increases in magnitude, growing, growing upon the sense, till a nearer approach lifts up the stupendous mass into the sky, dwarfing into insignificance the other mighty monuments of departed ambition or genius.

The Fruits of True Statesmanship.

From a statesman entertaining these sound principles and supernatural views, what should the community expect?

To answer this question we have only to ask ourselves what are the most urgent needs so often set forth in the public press,—not under the influence of political passion, or when pleading for some partisan purpose; but when agreed upon a generally felt want.

We need reforms in legislation, and in the halls of legislation.   We need to reconstruct (if that indeed be possible), in this country at least, the very machinery of the ballot-box, and the mode of nomination and election for every public office.   We put it to the enlightened men of every political party, who are not office-holders, or candidates for office, whether the constitutional liberty of the American citizen, in its most sacred and important exercise,—that of the suffrage,—is not so shackled by traditional custom, by the tyranny of party, that its exercise is only a mockery of freedom.   Neither in the choice of Federal, State, or municipal officers,—are the mass of the citizens consulted about the selection of candidates; nor in the form of voting for them are the electors allowed much more freedom than a regiment in the front rank of battle is given to advance or to retreat. They have to choose from lists made up by two or three men without any regard to their wishes ; and they have to choose between candidates imposed upon them,— or to throw their vote away.

Thus are the people not left free to place in the highest and most important offices in the State the men whom they know to be most worthy. The exercise of their sovereignty in its most august function is thus defeated of its purpose, and made a delusion and a mockery.

We pause, and hasten to pass on. For the ground beneath us is like the scarcely cooled lava within the crater of Vesuvius; it is scorching hot, and the hidden fires are heard to mutter and felt to rise and fall threateningly beneath the feet of the venturesome intruder.

We need radical reform in the exercise of our most sacred liberties. We need a remedy against corruption in the very sanctuary where our law-makers meet. We need an immediate preventive against privileged and partisan legislation. For Venality has long been the bane and the shame of more than one legislative assembly ; and the question is, "Who will dare to exorcise the Evil Spirit from its usurped and accustomed place of power?"

We need laws to repress rampant crime. Who is safe in his own house, either in the most peaceful country place, or in the most public street of the crowded city? There was a time when the midnight robber fled in haste when discovered in his unholy work ; but now every burglar is a murderer, and every murderer can promise himself almost certain or comparative impunity! Why, robberies are committed in our most frequented thoroughfares, in our crowded street-cars, and not a soul will care or dare to interfere! And robbers daily conspire to assail citizens on the open street, and in the full blaze of noonday, plunder them and almost murder them in sight of hundreds, and escape all detection! Ladies, refined, well-born, highly connected, cannot venture to travel in one of our "palace cars," without being spirited away by villians, while vainly appealing for protection to the descendants of the men who colonized New York and New England, and founded the glorious edifice of American freedom ! And with all this,—in a country blessed with such varied wealth and magnificent agricultural and commercial resources, as country never enjoyed since the world was a world, we here in New York are so loaded and borne down by taxation, that property is not worth the holding, and that universal bankruptcy is staring us in the face !

Surely we need reforms,—and need statesmen who will save the State from ruin in the midst of overflowing plenty save the sacred name of law and justice from the sacrilegious hands of their makers and guardians, save the divine character of authority from the contempt and hatred of the people, and save society, — become like a ship with a drunken, quarreling crew, driven headlong before the storm —from going to pieces.

Yes, the words of the poet sound like the command of an inspired prophet :

> " Keep us in safety, and the chairs of justice
> Supplied with worthy men !   Plant love among us.
> Throng our large temples with the shows of peace,
> And not our streets with war ! "

CHAPTER XXI.

THE TOILERS OF THE PEN.

No : Captain Sword a sword was still,
He could not unteach his lordly will ;
He could not attemper his single thought ;
It might not be bent, nor newly wrought :
And so, like the tool of a disused art,
He stood at his wall, and rusted apart.
'Twas only for many-souled Captain Pen
To make a world of swordless men.

LEIGH HUNT.

The most obstinate beliefs that men entertain about themselves are such as
they have no evidence for beyond a constant spontaneous pulsing of their self-
satisfaction—as it were, a hidden seed of madness, a confidence that they can
move the wor'd without precise notion of standing-place or lever.

Two armies of toilers stand before us,—mighty armies
both of them,—the army of Men of Letters, and the vast
hosts of Industry ; the former aiming at exploring all the
mysteries of knowledge, at enlightening the intelligence of
men and swaying their souls ; the latter, in manifold de-
pendence of them, conquering the material world, forcing
the earth and all its elements to yield up their treasures
to industry, and thereby to minister to all the wants and
pleasures of mankind.

We purpose to speak lovingly of these two hosts of toil-
ers,—of men of letters in this chapter ; of industry and
labor in the next.

It is no exaggeration to say, that, under God, and directed
aright by reason and conscience, Literature is the greatest
force of the moral world,—it is not only the force which
represents Mind in its conflict with rebellious Matter,—but

415

that which enables knowledge to mold and control immortal mind itself.

Knowledge has been the mistress of the world from the beginning. Let us not be too proud of the superior enlightenment of our age. Were it ever to come into the mind of influential persons to create a Universal Exposition of the Ancient and Modern Literatures, together with the productions of high art collected from all ages and countries,—we should not be tempted to be so over-boastful as some of our writers would make us.

Are we, then, disposed to glorify the past at the expense of the present? No, assuredly. We only wish to profit by all the glories of the mighty past so as to make the present greater, more glorious still, more enlightened, more prosperous, peaceful, and heaven-like. The past, for the man who reflects, grasps the full reality of things, and expresses it to himself or others,—is the entire human family toiling through the uncounted ages to make this fair world of God's more beautiful and blissful for us, their posterity.

A sweet modern singer * has painted this past as a dead king, who lies crowned, but cold, in his sepulcher, while the present, his daughter, reigns over us and claims our homage.

> " She inherits all his treasures,
>   She is heir to all his fame,
> And the light that lightens round her
>   Is the luster of his name :
> She is wise with all his wisdom,
>   Living on his grave she stands,
> On her brow she bears his laurels,
>   And his harvests in her hands.
>
> " Noble things the great Past promised,
>   Holy dreams, both strange and new :
> But the Present shall fulfill them,
>   What he promised, she shall do."

High Mission of Men of Letters.

There, precisely, lies the difficulty, to make **the present**

---

* Adelaide Anne Procter.

realize what the past had conceived of, and to leave no one of its glorious promises unfulfilled. The man who would do his whole duty to God and his own kind, by making the very best use he can of his gifts and his opportunities, does not stop to compare the merits of his own generation with those of the men who have gone before him. He looks up to the God who has placed him on the present point of space and time, and labors here and now with his whole heart to do all the good he can, and in the best way he can. This is what every conscientious man of letters will do.

For, writers who are worthy of their high calling know that they have a mission to fill ; they feel the dignity of it. They honor the great minds iu the past who have toiled to fulfill a similar duty in their own day. It is even remarkable that the writers who declaim continually against what they call " the worship of the dead past," are, every one of them, mediocrities, whose works are foredoomed not to survive their authors. We doubt if there ever lived a man of genius who was not a most reverent worshiper of departed excellence, an ardent imitator of the deathless masterpieces bequeathed to us by the mighty dead.

Nay, they are not dead voices which speak to us in these same masterpieces of wisdom, eloquence, and poetry. They thrill every pulse of our living hearts, as they have thrilled those of a hundred generations before us. We believe in the divinity of genius. God endows a human spirit with a share of His own creative might ; gives to the pen of the writer or the voice of the speaker somewhat of the power of the Almighty Word when it said, " Be light made ! And light was made ; " and " Let the earth bring forth ! And the earth brought forth."

If the mighty host of the glorious toilers of the pen could only understand Who it is that sends them to cast over every region of earth the seeds of that Tree of Knowledge and Life,—TRUTH ! If, going forth early to the divine work of this husbandry of souls, writers would lift their hearts to Him from whom alone all true inspiration descendeth, and then prepare their furrows beneath His eye, and cast

27

in the immortal seed while calling upon His Name,—how rich and blessed would the harvest be! To such toilers, in every walk of the world of letters, we could lovingly say ·

" Sow with a generous hand ;
    Pause not for toil or pain ;
Weary not through the heat of summer,
    Weary not through the cold spring rain ;   ·
But wait till the autumn comes
    For the sheaves of golden grain.

" Scatter the seed, and fear not,
    A table will be spread ;
What matter if you are too weary
    To eat your hard-earned bread :
Sow while the earth is broken,
    For the hungry must be fed.

" Sow ;—while the seeds are lying
    In the warm earth's bosom deep,
And your warm tears fall upon it—
    They will stir in their quiet sleep ;
And the green blades rise the quicker,
    Perchance, for the tears you weep.

" Sow : and look onward, upward,
    Where the starry light appears—
Where, in spite of the coward's doubting,
    Or your own heart's trembling fears,
You shall reap in joy the harvest
    You have sown to-day in tears." *

A Noble Literary Worker.

Not without a purpose have we called up from the past the figure of this angelic woman, to utter words of cheer and exhortation that we all need,—we who labor obscurely, untiringly in the field of Truth. Her heroic example may well fire the hearts both of those who lead and of those who follow in the serried ranks of literary workers. No less a man than Charles Dickens has deemed it a privilege to sketch a life which, short as it was (she died in her thirty-ninth year), was wholly devoted to making her parents'

* Miss Procter.

home delightful, and the homes of the poor bright and con-
tented. Her beautiful poems seemed only the natural out-
pourings of a soul full of all the divinest harmonies of
earth and heaven, and given forth while concealing her
name from the public,—just as the sweetest strains of the
nightingale are uttered within the darkest recesses of the
grove.

"She was exceedingly humorous (Dickens tells us), and
had a great delight in humor. Cheerfulness was habitual
with her, she was very ready at a sally or a reply, and in
her laugh (as I remember well) there was an unusual viva-
city, enjoyment, and sense of drollery. She was perfectly
unconstrained and unaffected ; as modestly silent about her
productions, as she was generous with their pecuniary re-
sults. She was a friend who inspired the strongest attach-
ments ; she was a finely sympathetic woman, with a great
accordant heart and a sterling noble nature. No claim can
be set up for her, thank God, to the possession of any of
the conventional poetical qualities. She never by any
means held the opinion that she was among the greatest of
human beings ; she never suspected the existence of a con-
spiracy on the part of mankind against her ; she never re-
cognized in her best friends her worst enemies ; she never
cultivated the luxury of being misunderstood and unap-
preciated ; she would far rather have died without seeing
a line of her composition in print, than that I should
have maundered about her, here, as "the Poet," or "the
Poetess." . . .

"Always impelled by an intense conviction that her life
must not be dreamed away, and that her indulgence in her
favorite pursuits must be balanced by action in the real
world around her, she was indefatigable in her endeavors
to do some good. Naturally enthusiastic, and conscien-
tiously impressed with a deep sense of her Christian duty
to her neighbor, she devoted herself to a variety of benevo-
lent objects. Now, it was the visitation of the sick, that had
possession of her ; now, it was the sheltering of the house-
less ; now, it was the elementary teaching of the densely

ignorant; now, it was the raising up of those who had wandered and got trodden under foot; now, it was the wider employment of her own sex in the general business of life; now, it was all these things at once. Perfectly unselfish, swift to sympathize and eager to relieve, she wrought at such designs with a flushed earnestness that disregarded season, weather, time of day or night, food, rest. Under such a hurry of the spirits, and such incessant occupation the strongest constitution will commonly go down. Hers, neither of the strongest nor the weakest, yielded to the burden, and began to sink.

"To have saved her life, then, by taking action on the warning that shone in her eyes and sounded in her voice, would have been impossible, without changing her nature. As long as the power of moving about in the old way was left to her, she must exercise it, or be killed by the restraint. And so the time came when she could move about no longer, and took to her bed.

"All the restlessness gone then, and all the sweet patience of her natural disposition purified by the resignation of her soul, she lay upon her bed through the whole round of changes of the seasons. She lay upon her bed through fifteen months. In all that time her old cheerfulness never quitted her. In all that time, not an impatient or querulous minute can be remembered.

"At length, at midnight of the second of February, 1864, she turned down a leaf of a little book * she was reading, and shut it up.

"The ministering hand that had copied the verses into the tiny album was soon around her neck, and she quietly asked, as the clock was on the stroke of one·

"'Do you think I am dying, mamma?'

"'I think you are very, very ill to-night, my dear.'

"'Send for my sister. My feet are so cold. Lift me up.'

"Her sister entering as they raised her, she said: 'It has come at last!' And with a bright and happy smile, looked upward and departed.

---

* "The Imitation of Christ."

"Well had she written:

> ' Why shouldst thou fear the beautiful angel, Death,
> Who waits thee at the portal of the skies,
> Ready to kiss away thy struggling breath,
> Ready with gentle hand to close thine eyes?

> ' Oh, what were life, if life were all? Thine eyes
> Are blinded by their tears, or thou wouldst see
> Thy treasures wait thee in the far-off skies,
> And Death, thy friend, will give them all to thee.*' "

We have given this long extract from the pen of one who liked not Catholics,—blinded as he was by the prejudices of early education and of the great English world around him,—because it is a heartfelt tribute to the worth of a Catholic lady, whose pure fame as a writer is but the least of her merits.

She had followed to the letter, from her earliest girlhood and her first contributions to literature, the lesson conveyed in her own poem, "Sowing and Reaping":

> " Sow ; and look onward, upward,
> Where the starry light appears—
> Where, in spite of the coward's doubting,
> Or your own heart's trembling fears,
> You shall reap in joy the harvest
> You have sown to-day in tears.'

No more pregnant lesson can be learned and practiced by every one of us, O dearest brothers of the pen!

And now what shall we say to each battalion in this vast array,—as you pass in review before our mind's eye,—oh, you who ought to be the invincible army here below of Him who is called the Lord of Hosts, but who is the Eternal Truth, the Light Uncreated, "a God of all knowledge,"— *Deus Scientiarum Dominus?*

Theological Writers.

At the head of the magnificent procession advance those

---

* From the Biography by Charles Dickens, serving as an introduction to " Legends and Lyrics," London, ed. 1866.

who have devoted their lives to the study of their Divine Author Himself, and of the relations which bind Him to man and the universe,—and who consecrate their pens to setting forth and vindicating Truth in its fountain-head. Foremost among the resplendent throng is he, the great Prophet-Legislator, whose books head the divinest of all books,— the Bible. With his head encircled with the intolerable light which he drew from intimate converse with the Holy One of Israel, he passes before us, followed by Josue, Samuel, David, and the majestic figures of the Prophets. And then comes the vision of the Mount of Transfiguration, where Moses and Elias do homage to the Word Incarnate, and beneath are Peter and James and John,—the eye of faith grouping around the representatives of the Old and the New Testaments, the august succession of apostolic men, who have continued, age after age, to show forth to the nations Christ, the Way, the Truth and the Life. Oh, what a glorious company of divine men extend their ranks from the illuminated summit of Thabor, along the pathway of humanity down to our own day! Paul and his great convert, the Areopagite, Justin-the-Martyr, Cyprian, Basil and Gregory Nazianzen, Athanasius and Chrysostom and Ambrose, Jerome and Augustine, Gregory and Leo, Bernard and Innocent III., Anselm and Aquinas and Bonaventure, Suarez and Francis of Sales and Liguori! What names! And yet, as the ages go slowly by before us, how many others no less great in intellect and holy in life, stand forth grouped around these their illustrious contemporaries and coadjutors in the cause of sacred truth!

But from out the saintly ranks, as they pass, voices proceed full of eloquent teaching for the soldiers of Truth in our own time. Let us hearken to a few.

"The words of a priest are either true or sacrilegious:" *Verba sacerdotis aut vera, aut sacrilega."* *

Why is the Catholic priest detested? Why is he who announces truth deemed an enemy? *It is*—replies St. Augustine—*that they love truth so well, that all who have another*

---

* Fulbert of Chartres.

*love wish that the object of that love should be truth; and,
unwilling to be deceived, they are not willing to be con-
vinced of their error; therefore they hate him by whom the
falsehood of what they love is made manifest.*[*]

"But you, chosen generation, you weak things of the
world who have forsaken all things that you might follow
the Lord, go after Him, and confound the things which are
mighty; go after Him, ye beautiful feet, and shine in the
firmament, that the heavens may declare His glory. .
Shine over all the earth, and let the day, lightened by the
sun, utter unto day the word of wisdom; and let night,
shining by the moon, utter unto night the word of knowl-
edge. . . . Run ye to and fro everywhere, ye holy fires,
ye beautiful fires; for ye are the light of the world; nor are
ye put under a bushel. He to whom ye cleave is exalted,
and hath exalted you. Run ye to and fro, and be known
unto all nations!"[†]

How the Light and Fire from Above are Obtained.

Would you learn the secret of this supernatural inspira-
tion, the source of this all-consuming fire which burned
within the Doctors of the Holy Church, and enabled them
to illumine and inflame the world? Take from the hand of
yonder figure[‡] who steps forth from the crowd, the tablet
he offers you, and read:

Marianus, an Irish monk, who founded a monastery at
Ratisbonne, described as surpassing most men in beauty
of countenance and simplicity of manners, was so venerated
in the school, that every one felt assured he was inspired in
all his works by the Holy Ghost. "He was most remarka-
ble for his diligence in writing on parchment, both for his
own brethren and for others. Many large volumes were the
fruit of his holy zeal and hope for an eternal recompense.
Repeatedly with his own hand he wrote out the whole of
the Bible, with its commentaries. He also wrote many little

---

[*] "Confessions," x. 23.   [†] Ibidem, xx. 25; translated by Dods.
[‡] Raderus, *Bavaria Sanata*, ii.,—quoted by Digby, "Compitum," i., ch. x.

books and psalters and manuals for poor widows and poor
clerks and scholars of the same city, for the remedy of his
own soul; and these he gave them gratis.

"It is said that one night the guardian forgot to give him
sufficient candles when he was writing some divine volume,
and that he did not hesitate to continue writing without
material light, the three fingers of his left hand, by divine
mercy, appearing to serve him for lamps.   The sacristan,
when in bed, recollected his omission, and rose up to carry
candles to his cell, when through the chinks of the door he
beheld him writing with the aid of this celestial light.
Aventinus styles him a poet and a theologian, second to
none of his age."

This anecdote comes to us from the mountains of Bavaria
like the odor of violets culled along the head-waters of the
Inn, the Isar, and the Lech long centuries ago, and serving
to embalm a holy memory.   One or two more fragrant flow-
erets from saintly hands, and we shall fix our attention on
the next band in the procession.

Quid est victoria veritatis, nisi charitas ? asks the same
great son of Monica, as he disappears amid the starry mul-
titude of his fellows.   "For what do the soldiers of Truth
do battle, if it be not to secure the triumph of Charity?"
Hear you this, O brethren, who strive so heroically to make
Truth victorious? And, you who are so anxious to heal the
wounds of Christendom, to reunite all minds and hearts be-
neath the sway of the Great Mother, lay up these words in
your memory, and with them treasure this saying of the
latest and most loving soul among that shining galaxy of
Doctors: "Truth that is not charitable, comes from a cha-
rity that is not veritable." *

And now comes Philosophy, the venerable parent of all
true science.

We do not mean to separate true philosophy, from true
science.   The philosopher professes to explain all things by
means of their deepest and most hidden causes.   He, there-

* St. Francis of Sales : *La vérité qui n'est pas charitable vient d'une charité qui
n'est pas véritable.*

fore, endeavors to push his analysis of the universe to its very center,—to pluck out the heart of Knowledge and lay its secrets bare to the eye of all. Three mighty mysteries invite his speculations,—God, man, and the material world. He would fain say on each of these all that can be said,—so that the veil should be lifted forever on the nature of the Infinite Godhead, on that of man, half-spiritual, half-animal as it is, and on that of matter in its intimate constitution, its forces, and its duration.

Thus Philosophy professes to expose to its pupils the constitutive principles or elements of all existing things, their relations toward each other, the laws which mind has to follow in acquiring this knowledge, and the tests by which it may discern certainty from uncertainty, truth from its counterfeit, error.

Before Christ the schools of Eastern Europe, of Africa, and Asia, sought, century after century, to disclose to the world the secret of the Divine Nature, its existence, and its attributes,—the nature, origin, and powers of the soul of man,—and the origin and destiny of the visible universe. They were earnest men, these seekers after the highest truth, and generation after generation of them applied themselves to their laborious quest with an ardor and a perseverance in keeping with their lofty purpose, and deserving of more satisfactory results. Like our Western miners,—they knew from the fragments of gold at the surface or those borne down from the uplands in the river courses,—that there was beneath them somewhere an exhaustless vein of the precious ore. And so, they sought, and explored, and tormented the surface of the earth on every side, by night as well as by day, band of resolute workers succeeding wearied band,—till they concluded that gold there was none.

Christian Philosophy, the Parent of True Science.

We know how fragmentary were the truths discovered or held by these indefatigable investigators of old. At length Christianity arose, completing the divine knowledge contained in the books of Moses on the origin of the material universe, on man's beginning and final destinies, and on that Eternal and Uncreated Being, the sole author of all created things.

The long-sought truth was thus disclosed in its deep native bed, and the lamp of Revelation shed a clear and steady light on the magnificent realities, so dimly perceived and obscurely spoken of by Greeks, Egyptians, Persians, and Brahmins.

In the light of the Christian Philosophy,—that is, of Reason guided and illumined by Faith,—man was told what satisfied his innate curiosity to know clearly whence he came and whither he tends, and who is the mighty First Cause of the existence of this vast universe.

Thereby was a firm basis given for all further investigation of nature and its Divine Author. To measure the immense progress made by philosophical truth since the dawn of Christianity, as compared with the most complete results reached in the pagan-world, one has only to compare Plato and Aristotle,—prodigies both of them,—with the majestic theological and philosophical edifices reared by Thomas Aquinas in the thirteenth century, and by Francisco Suarez in the sixteenth.

The ripest scholar who cannot find on the lofty subjects most deserving of man's study, knowledge enough to satisfy his understanding or to guide and help him surely toward still greater heights,—must have a mind ill-constituted or ill-disciplined. Even Leibnitz,—the greatest and most accomplished genius among Protestants,—declared at the end of his life, and after having devoted his great powers to the exhaustive study of the subject,—that he could not help considering the principles of the Mediæval Scholastics on matter, its forces, and forms, as the most satisfactory to his mind. And in our own day, scientists the most opposed not only to Catholic teaching, but even to the very existence of immaterial spirits in the universe, are forced to uphold, though in a different terminology, the once derided scholastic systems on matter and its properties.

We are in presence of these great geniuses of the Catholie, the Christian world,—men of angelic life, in whom was verified the saying of the Master : "Blessed are the clean of heart, for they shall see God." Men of the world immersed in the pleasures of sense, Christian men, even, who do not habituate themselves to self-denial, cannot know—though they may understand—how immensely abstinence from sensual gratification and purity of soul dispose the mind to see clearly and to see far into those luminous depths where Truth abides, and where the chaste eye of the soul is given to behold so much of the great Primal Cause and in Him, of the causal relation He holds to the entire world of mind and matter! Are we venturing too high above the common ken? Let us come back to earth, then.

Science should not play Phaeton.

Only,—to writers on intellectual philosophy, almost as much as to scientists dealing with matter and its evolutions,—we would say one warning word. In metaphysical investigations, as in those of the geologist or biologist, there are broad pathways along which all the great minds of the past have traveled, not blindly and without thoroughly exploring for themselves every stage of their progress, and accounting for all the phenomena observed at every step. There is a "common sense" which must guide the greatest genius as he advances in any field of observation or research, and which he cannot set aside without exposing himself to the risk of straying from the truth—the right direction,—and of leading others, who follow him astray. Let us illustrate our meaning.

Philosophical Formulas, Snares for the Philosopher.

We, Americans here in this New World, as Europeans in the most civilized lands of ancient Christendom,—have followed with mixed curiosity and amazement certain famous disquisitions about the origin in the mind and the real value in the world of experience of intuitive notions and primary principles of knowledge. Gioberti mixed up his metaphysics with his religion and his politics,—formulated his views in a few brief and pregnant apothegms, which, he said, contained as certainly the scientific equation of all philosophy, religion, and history,—as the algebraic formula $S = gt^2$ expresses the laws of velocity in falling bodies. His formulas, however, which were pressed for adoption upon American scholars as earnestly and persistently as if they defined unquestionable dogmas of philosophical faith, were either radically modified or altogether abandoned by the author himself in his last writing.*

Even so, the various hypotheses, which were adopted, at different successive epochs, to explain the motions of the heavenly bodies, were advocated as so many scientific truths by their authors, and successively modified or abandoned. At the present moment, science proposes, uses, adopts, or abandons many such hypotheses in stellar and physical astronomy,—showing by her cautious use of formulas and general conclusions, that in all fields of observation inductions must not be broader than the phenomena observed.

Would that our ideologists, our geologists and our evolutionists were equally cautious, reserved, and rational in the conclusions they draw from imperfectly observed phenomena, or in the hypotheses they press upon us as demonstrated certainties!

When a child follows a trusted guide away from the broad highway and the light of the sun to explore some marvelous underground cave, child though he be, his instinctive good sense warns him to go no farther, when he finds the air of the cave become unfit to breathe as they advance; —or when the lamp in the hand of his guide goes out,— both man and boy will deem it high time to retrace their steps back to God's pure vital air and the light of day.

So it is with your theories, or your inductive systems; when you find that they lead you to results that are as dangerous to faith and morality as mephitic air is to the lungs, —then be sure you have gone too far in the wrong direc-

* See Mr. Botta's analysis of Gioberti's Philosophy in " Ueberweg's History of Philosophy," vol. ii. page 502.

tion. Or when the lamp of reason and common sense re-
fuses to shed further light on the darkness before you, go
back to the broad sunlight of true science.

O most unwise Philosophy, O most unreasoning Science,
why so impatient of that Revealed Truth which has been
the sun of the civilized world for so many pregnant cen-
turies, which has been the chaste light of the homes of our
fathers, and warmed their hearts to deeds of divinest cha-
rity and heroic self-denial? And do you wish us to prefer
the feeble, uncertain, short-lived glimmer of your two-penny
candle to God's unquenchable sun in the firmament?

> " And delving in the outworks of this world,
>   And little crevices that it could reach,
> Discovered certain bones laid up, and furled
>   Under an ancient beach,
> And other waifs that lay to its young mind
>   Some fathoms lower than they ought to lie,
> By gain whereof it could not fail to find
>   Much proof of ancientry,
> Hints at a pedigree withdrawn and vast,
>   Terrible deeps, and old obscurities.
> Or soulless origin, and twilight passed
>   In the primeval seas,
> Whereof it tells, as thinking it hath been
>   Of truth not meant for man inheritor ;
> As if this knowledge Heaven had ne'er foreseen
>   And not provided for !
> Knowledge ordained to live ! although the fate
>   Of much that went before it was—to die,
> And be called ignorance by such as wait
>   Till the next drift comes by.
> O marvelous credulity of man !
>   If God indeed kept secret, couldst thou know
> Or follow up the mighty Artisan
>   Unless he willed it so ? . . .
> But if He keeps not secret—if thine eyes
>   He openeth to His wondrous work of late—
> Think how in soberness thy wisdom lies,
>   And have the grace to wait.
> Wait,—nor against the half-learned lesson fret,
>   Nor chide at old belief as if it erred,
> Because thou canst not reconcile as yet
>   The Worker and the word." *

---

* Jean Ingelow.

Journalists.

It is but truth to say that journalism is the mightiest force of the moral world,—always, of course, leaving out of comparison that Almighty Power, which allows human liberty and human intelligence free scope for their action, just as it allows the ocean currents to play within their deep and wide bed, and the winds to come and go in their courses, subject only to the Sovereign Will whose control all must obey.

We speak, in the first place, of secular journalism, compared with which, as a power, that of religious journalism is what the mass and influence of the least satellite of Saturn are to the mighty globe of the Sun.

Yes, secular journalism is the mightiest of moral forces outside of the incomparable power for good of the Church of the Living God. Compared with the attraction which she exercises, to her civilizing, sanctifying, and creative influence during her existence of more than eighteen centuries,—every moral force mentioned in the records of humanity appears trifling and short-lived.

The journalist by profession is, therefore, among the toilers of the pen, he who can do most good or most evil, according as he makes a right or a wrong use of his power and opportunities. And, assuredly, the profession is among the most laborious in the whole range of literature.

We would fain say a heartfelt word of appreciation and sympathy to those knights of the daily press, whose untiring devotion and unflagging industry are as little known to the public they serve as the results of their labor are applauded.

Need we mention the men who, single-handed, and obscure, have succeeded in founding some of our foremost daily newspapers ? How many among these have been inspired by the example of Benjamin Franklin, editing, at the age of sixteen and while still an apprentice, "The New England Courant," instead of his brother James, and founding in his own name and at his own risk the "Pennsylvania Gazette," at the age of twenty-two ! Assuredly, if it is honorable by life-long thrift, energy, honesty, and sagacity, to be able to amass a fortune counted by millions, and to establish a great commercial or industrial business that is the admiration of the whole civilized world,—it is no less so, nay, it is, in our judgment, much more so to create a great daily journal and to make it not only a pecuniary success, but a national institution, a mighty vehicle for the communication of true enlightenment.

It was deemed a gigantic and almost a visionary scheme to tunnel the Alps beneath Mount Cenis, and to attempt to open a ship-canal across the Isthmus of Suez, thus emptying the waters of the Mediterranean into the Red Sea, and opening a new, shorter, and safer highway to commerce between Europe and Farther Asia. Surely a great journal that serves as the daily vehicle of news and interchange of thought between widely separated divisions of the human family, is a something equally glorious to the man who conceived and achieved its establishment. An accident may block up to-morrow the tunnel between France and Italy, or the desert sands may render the great ship-canal unnavigable. But no earthquake, no power of wind or waves or moving sands, can mar a great and successful newspaper.

Its prosperity and ever-growing usefulness depend solely on the talent, the sagacity, the indomitable application of the little army of literary men who carry it on. And it is for the encouragement and direction of these that we are desirous of making a few timely remarks.

The Noble Aims and Uses of Journalism.

We are perfectly aware that we cannot, in justice to our own definite purpose, here discuss the various classes of daily and periodical journalism. We are concerned solely with the great daily secular newspaper, which not only furnishes to its reader the most recent and trustworthy information on every possible topic of interest, but reviews all the important events in the world of politics, science, literature, art, and commerce.

The great daily newspaper, then, is in itself an abridged history of the world's life for each day. The question, therefore, is for a true man having the control of this daily record of the world around him, whether he shall, like the conscientious painter, present to the public only such matters and aspects of real life as are calculated to instruct and to improve, or, like the worst school of Realists, depict indiscriminately the good and the evil, virtue and vice, heroism and depravity, the most ennobling deeds and recitals, or the most loathsome and defiling scenes from human nature fallen and hideous in its moral ugliness.

We suppose the ideal journalist whom we have now here before us, to have been blessed with a mother as careful of his purity of soul, while yet under her care, as of her own hopes of eternal salvation,—as watchful to keep away from the eyes and ears of her boys and girls every book, publication, picture, sight, or conversation, that could make their unsullied minds suspect the existence of moral evil,— as she would have been watchful to keep the deadliest poison from their food, or fire and flame from the white curtains of the crib or the bed in which her darlings reposed. What journalist, what noble-souled man could wish his mother to have been other than this in her loving and jealous care of his childhood and boyhood's innocence?

We suppose, further, that this boy, so tenderly cared for, and become, perhaps, a journalist and a true man through this very nurture, has now a wife and children infinitely dear to him. He has chosen his wife because he thought he had discovered in her the living image of his mother,— who, in her turn, would be sure to do for his children what had been done for himself,—keep their souls and their lives from the thought or the approach of evil as long as they remained in her Home-Paradise.

Have you not still, after so many years of married life, so tender, so jealous a care of your wife's innocence and of her absolute ignorance of the evil world you know of,—that nothing could induce you to break in upon her happy dream of ignorance, or to lift the veil that covers from her pure eyes the dark depths of that same outside world with their hideous forms of sin and shame? Is it not one of the deepest joys of your life to keep ever before the minds of your children that other serene, lightsome, angelic world, which is only a distant vision, beheld through the mists of sense, of that world of purity, peace, imperishable beauty, and glory unfading that we were all created for? Have you never told your own heart, or told wife and children, during your brief intervals of heart-rest at home,—that the unseen world is the only real world,—the world of unchangeable and eternal realities?

What your Wife and Children should not read.

And now take up one of the great daily journals in a vast metropolis either of the Western or the Eastern hemisphere. Here is one before us,—let us look at it calmly, being both men who have had a most varied experience of human vicissitudes. Well, here, in one sheet of this morning paper, thrown into our homes before the breakfast hour, is an entire page,—containing in print matter sufficient for one hundred pages of this book,—filled, two-thirds of it, with details of the most revolting immorality, and the remainder pertaining to the drama and the stage, reciting what is scarcely, if at all, less objectionable to the pureminded.

Would you read .to your wife, at table and during the meal on which you both with your children invoked the blessing of the Most Holy God,—this dreadful tale of wife-murder and suicide committed in presence of the three hapless children of such parents, and committed through jealousy? And would you allow your innocents to hear the shocking details of the immorality with which the murderer had accused his victim, and with which she in her turn had taunted the fiend she called husband? Would you, after exhausting this dreadful tale, continue to depict murder after murder, one more odious crime succeeding another, till the very atmosphere of your breakfast-room seemed

28

tainted with the odor of the charnel-house or the Pit, and the very bread and tea on your table seemed to savor of human blood ?

You may belong to the Realistic School in art,—but such realities, you must confess, are not such as you would willingly submit to the eye of mother or sister, of wife or children ;—nay, you would blush to read them to your father, your brother, or your friend.

What your Wife and Children should never see.

But from this perversion of one of the most sacred offices of journalism,—turn we to the remainder of the page before us. Its matter relates to an art, scarcely less noble,—if faithful to its original destination,—than that of the journalist. See how the reviews and notices here presented of the drama and the stage, are as unfit for the eye of your wife and your daughter, as were the dark deeds of the murderer, the suicide, the highwayman, the forger, or the absconding cashier.

The dramatic art like that of the journalist aims, in its sole legitimate and praiseworthy sphere, to make men good, and to make the good better by setting forth ennobling examples and heroic deeds, by inspiring respect for religion and virtue, much more than by creating a hatred and horror of vice.

Here is a theatrical manger whose only care is to fill his house daily, and who cares nothing about the means of attraction, provided the public are enticed to fill his seats and his boxes from floor to ceiling. He finds that the latest productions of the French dramatists have for the sensualist, the pleasure-seeker, the man whose mind is skeptical and whose heart is loveless,—for the woman who is without conscience, principle, or virtue, the same flavor that highly-spiced meats have for the depraved palate ;—and so, they get some venal pen,—a pen that would write for Beelzebub, if Beelzebub paid for it in gold or in honest "greenbacks," and this pen does the devil's work of transforming a bad

French play into a worse English one. Hence your "New Magdalen's" *et toute cette inondation de fange d'outre-mer!*

We must not, however, be too hard on the French. Low as French dramatic art is fallen, Satanic as its ideal seems so often to be,—there is still art in the conception and treatment of each unworthy subject, and very often exquisite art in the diction. And, besides, the French drama may be a truthful picture of French society,—though not, assuredly, of that noble French society we have known, loved, and admired ; and, most assuredly, is French drama no real picture at all of any one class or phase of American or English society.

But here,—among criticisms of other dramatic patchwork, —is the elaborate review of a society-play modeled on the objectionable French pattern, which is condemned by good critics as irredeemably bad,—not pretending to any high moral purpose, but pandering to the lowest appetites of the most abandoned sight-seers, and, confessedly, without the slightest claim to artistic merit or literary excellence in plot, execution, or style,—its only charm in this respect being the incessant play of double meaning,—tickling the prurient fancy, as continual bubbles of mephitic gas from a stagnant pool offend the sense of the passers-by.

And yet this production, so devoid of every one of the qualities of true art, so contrary to all the ideals of art that is purifying and elevating,—is praised by the journalist before us and his critic, and thus recommended as a legitimate amusement to the pure-minded wives and innocent daughters of our American homes !

Which of these departures from the duty and office of the true journalist, deserves the severest animadversion,—the revealing to the mind of the sinless, unsuspecting young reader of all these horrible mysteries of crime? or the inviting (by implication) the mothers and children of our hitherto simple and pure American homes, to admire on the stage men and women belonging to the *demi-monde*, or to a world and a society which are not the abode of truth, purity, domestic virtue, or public worth?

Treat Religion most Reverently.

Then, take the matter of Religion, so dear to all American homes, in spite of their deep differences of belief, and of the entire freedom guaranteed by law and granted by the temper of our people on religious questions. Where a secular journal speaks of such matters, one expects that it shall be done calmly and respectfully, without entering into the merits of doctrines, or pronouncing judicially on points which cannot be fully known to the writer.

It is bad policy as well as bad taste to sadden or irritate thousands upon thousands of homes, where time-honored doctrines are still held dearer than life, and where venerable religious authorities, held up by the journalist to ridicule or contempt or hatred, are still regarded with deep and conscientious reverence. It cannot be well, under plea of liberality, or freedom of opinion and judgment, to wound daily millions of your fellow-citizens in their most tender part, because the wrong done thereby to one great religious body may make your paper more acceptable to all the hostile denominations.

There is a loftier principle involved here than your pretended freedom of thought and judgment, albeit no one asks you to communicate to the world in oracular form the opinions you have formed and the judgments you have arrived at ; you are perfectly free to form and entertain them, but it were wise not to be so free in giving them publicity. This sacred principle is,—not to make Religion less holy, less worshipful, less dear to your own children by placing prominently before them the dissensions that reign between churches or between the members of the same church, the failings and faults of this prominent minister of a certain church to-day, and to-morrow, as an offset, the weaknesses and guilt of ministers of a rival creed. Thereby you impress the minds of the young with the conviction that there is "no balm in Gilead," no virtue in Religion itself to make men good and keep them good,—and so, Religion is brought into contempt. For, it is the logic of human

nature to identify the minister with the creed that he ex-
pounds, and to extend to the altars at which he sacrifices
the odium begotten by his own unworthiness. It is an in-
justice, moreover, to the majority of edifying, self-sacri-
ficing, exemplary men who belong to the sacred ministry to
cast on their unstained robes the deep soil that has fallen
on the vestments of the few.

Hide your Criminals : Deify your Heroes.

For the one unfortunate whose sad death and downward
career you chronicled yesterday and held up as a warning,
—not to his brethren, who do not need it,—but to your own
children and to the entire reading public, who are disedified
by it,—you might point to-day to those devoted bands of
priests who replace each other near the plague-stricken citi-
zens of New Orleans, Vicksburg, Memphis, and Grenada,
—brother taking the place of dead brother in the foremost
post of danger and duty. Were our own city—which God
forbid—to be visited to-morrow by the dread southern
scourge, you who have penned these offensive, injurious,
and unjust articles, would be the first to laud to the skies
the courage and heroism of the ministers of Religion in the
hour of man's sorest need. Were the Angel of Death to
knock suddenly at your own door, whose hand would you
grasp more lovingly and gratefully, as you felt life and
this fair earth withdrawn suddenly from you, and stood on
the brink of the dark abyss of eternity ? Whose voice
would be most welcome to your ear ? or wake more surely
in your soul the pulses of immortal hope in the God of your
childhood ?

No ! You should never tolerate that any one of those who
coöperate with you in your mighty labors, should directly
or indirectly throw suspicion or disrespect on what is and
must ever be the dearest treasure of our hearts and homes,
—the Religion of our Fathers.

This may suffice. There are so many rich and vast fields
of knowledge and varied interest open to journalism, such

deep mines of useful and delightful information that re-
main to be discovered or thoroughly explored, and from
which you can daily draw an exhaustless supply for your
readers! To the generous enterprise of our great journals,
to their splendid achievements in more than one depart-
ment of science and literature, we are proud and happy to
bear our humble tribute of praise and gratitude. It is mar-
velous to see what a feat is accomplished by the journalist
in every one of his issues,—and what a boundless store of
information is placed at the disposal of every reader for the
merest trifle! Are we insensible to the prodigious amount
of labor that the collecting of such a store required? No,
indeed. Nor do we belong in mind or heart to any other
world than the beautiful world which is our own, or repine
for past ages because the present contains ills that we de-
plore. We are of our age and country. We would fain
make the country the most glorious that ever the sun shone
upon, and the age the most fruitful in Godlike deeds and
heroic manhood.

To this result the true journalist can contribute im-
mensely ;—and, in all that we have presumed to suggest
here, we have been only endeavoring to assist him to be
true to his mission and his conscience.

The Religious Journalist.

Si quando in dubiis nutabant pectora rebus,
Ipse erat interpres ducens mortalia corda
De tenebris ad lumen; uti solet ignea lampas,
Longinqua de turre micans, adducere noctu
Turbine jactatos secura ad littora nautas.

" Whene'er men's souls on Doubt's black waves were tossed,
His voice amid the gloom was wont to cheer
The wavering ;—like a light-house near the coast
Which high above the raging surge doth rear
Its far-seen beacon to benighted sailors dear." *

We would speak of the Catholic journalist with the re-
spect, the admiration, the deep and grateful affection due

---

* Baptist of Mantua, *De Sacris Diebus Augusti.*

to him for the life-long services done to ourselves, due still more for the priceless benefits conferred on the community at large.

Few seem to suspect how delicate, how difficult, how painful, and how ill-requited are the functions of the Catholic journalist. Fewer still, perhaps, know how much of varied learning, of abnegation, of deep humiliation, not unfrequently, and of heroic perseverance is displayed in the lowly editorial rooms of so many Catholic weeklies that we could name. There are men, whom we know and love well, who show in the disinterestedness, the single-mindedness, the absorbing devotion to their ungrateful task very much of if not all the devotion to supernatural duty shown by the lonely missionary of some obscure Rocky Mountain tribe of Indians, or by the Jesuit among the perennial plagues of French Guiana.

They do not desire or need our praise ; but it is for us an imperative need and duty to send this heart-cry of ours to these noble and heroic toilers in their chosen post of labor. Are there not among them so many who have, at the sacrifice of all earthly wealth and honor, at the cost as well of health and all comfort or consolation,—toiled on uncheered, unappreciated, unrewarded by gratitude or emolument,—year after year for almost a lifetime, and who, looking back through the dismal prospect of these long years, can say, "We have labored all the night and have taken nothing"? And yet, looking up to the Master for whom they work and in Whom alone they trust, they are ready to begin again every week, every day, repeating cheerfully to Him and to their own brave heart: "But at Thy word I will let down the net." *

Such men can appreciate, and more than appreciate, the lofty sentiment conveyed in the following lines of the blind poet :

"When I consider how my life is spent
Ere half my days in this dark world and wide,
And that one talent which is death to hide
Lodg'd with me useless, though my soul more bent

* St. Luke, v. 5.

> To serve therewith my Maker, and present
>   My true account, lest He returning chide;
>   Does God exact day-labor, light denied,
> I fondly ask? but patience to prevent
>   That murmur, soon replies : God doth not need
> Either man's work or His own gifts; who best
>   Bear His mild yoke, they serve Him best : His state
>   Is kingly; thousands at His bidding speed,
> And post o'er land and ocean without rest;
>   They also serve who only stand and wait."

But we must hasten by our own united efforts the coming of God's good time,—of a day when religious journalism shall no longer be condemned to thrive or pine away in obscure corners, like certain illicit or unavowable trades, or to be thrust far away from the sunlight into some darksome angle of the conservatory, or neglected nook of the garden, like some plant of ill name or some flowering shrub of unpleasant odor, little beauty, and very questionable utility.

There are rumors of a convention of Catholic journalists. We hope that the rumor may be true, and pray that the proposed convention be held before the autumn of 1878 pass into winter.   Nor should the promoters of this project be in the least concerned at the unkind or unjust things said of them by a small portion of the religious press, or by the illiberal innuendoes and silly sneers of a few secular journals.   There are so many precious advantages to be derived from a cordial union among Catholic journalists, and by a steady coöperation toward the same grand purposes, that hasty blame from friends, or undeserved imputations from outsiders may be passed by without a word or thought, seeing how much is to be gained by coming to a definite understanding on the work to be done by our press and on the means to secure its being well and thoroughly done.

Union for Domestic Progress, not for Aggression.

The Catholic Congresses held in Europe have been of immense benefit to journalism,—not only by their bringing about perfect unity of views and unanimity of action, but by elevating journalists in their own estimation, by bringing together accomplished and distinguished men enlisted in the same cause, by enabling them to count their numbers and estimate their own power, by determining the centers where Catholic journalism needs to be supported, and by giving such support liberally. . . . We have here no political parties to favor or to oppose; we have no crusade to make either against the secular press or against other religious denominations. We have enough to do to second by every means of publicity, by the united labors of our best literary talent, the efforts of the Hierarchy and clergy to make truth shine forth in its own native splendor, to bring truth in action,—the lives of the great and the good in every past age,—home to every family and individual in the land. We shall have glorious labor enough to do to make the House of our Great Mother known to those of the household itself in all its length and breadth and height, inside and outside, with its untold and incomparable wealth of holiness, of beauty, of loveliness. The Catholic journalist will ever find enough to do in helping to make the children of the faith worthy in every way of their birthright of grace and greatness,—without exciting the groundless alarms or provoking the hostility of any portion of the press or the public.

To the noble men who fulfill this blessed mission of expounding and spreading the truth,—we have only one more word to say: Let them, in all circumstances and under the most trying provocation, observe the rule of charity and moderation recommended, almost with his dying breath, by Pius IX. Therein they will also be carrying out the beautiful sentiment quoted above from St. Francis of Sales, whom the same ever dear and venerated pontiff gave to journalists as their special patron. It is well for all of us to learn and to ponder how

> "The highest good
> Unlimited, ineffable, doth so speed
> To love, as beam to lucid body dark,
> Giving as much of ardor as it finds.
> The sempiternal effluence streams abroad,
> Spreading, wherever charity extends." *

---

* Cary's Dante, " Purgatory " xv

CHAPTER XXII.

THE BUSINESS MAN.

If you will cry out upon idleness, I am not disposed to dispute about words. It is certain that labor was not in the middle ages considered the end and sole business of life. It was thought that man, even earthly man, liveth not by bread alone, and that he requires other enjoyments than those of the body. Labor was regarded as the penalty of sin, and, as such, man desired to endure as little of it as possible. But things are now greatly changed, and do not say for the worse. God, who in the chastisements of this world provides for the good of man, permits that when nations lose sight of Heaven, avidity should impel them to " hard labor " in the strict judicial sense of the word, to which human justice forces dangerous criminals. So while passions are unchained in men's hearts, self-interest forges fetters for them, and leisure decreases in proportion to the increase of evil desires. This is the case with nations as it is with individuals ; and it is providential as well as severe.*

In the modern world,—at least where there is nothing like nobility of birth,—men will seek to rise, in proportion as they are free to rise, by steady application to business. Thus, they will first rise to wealth, and through wealth to social distinction. Even in democratic communities the learned professions lead of themselves to social position and to political power. But the power which wealth of itself bestows on its owner, is entirely independent of political party and distinct from the influence attached to what is known as social position or respectability.

Of this power, or—as we shall call it—extensive ability of doing good, we shall speak presently when treating of the manufacturer and the merchant prince. For the moment, we shall speak of the qualities and virtues that make the man of business.

* Reverend Father Cahier, *Vitraux peints de Saint Etienne de Bourges*, imperial folio, Paris, 1842-44.

We shall say little, however, of mere industry, of steady application to one's pursuit, and of that indomitable perseverance without which the most feverish activity would be like the waters of Niagara, a mighty power wasted in noise and display. Besides, in our introductory chapter we have insisted at length and repeatedly on the absolute necessity of having a definite purpose in life, of setting one's heart wholly on carrying out that purpose, and of never ceasing to pursue it to the end.

This is to be, in your own chosen sphere, "the active doer." But you have, besides, to be in every sphere, no matter how high or how lowly, "the noble liver;" and it is this nobility of life in the business man of every class that we must now urge upon the reader's consideration.

The first requisite toward this nobleness is to make sure that you work for Him to whom belong both the day and the night, and whom all things are bound to serve. You,— whoever you are, or what path soever you follow in this rushing world of activity,—are by baptism the son of the Great King, living in His house, subsisting on His bread, aiming in all things to please that most loving Parent and most magnificent Master. Whatever your occupation, then, whatever you have to do or to suffer, seek only to please Him. This constant tending in all our aims, sentiments, actions, sufferings, to do solely the most righteous will of the Most High God,—is what is called "a right or pure intention." Without this you cannot please God or serve Him or have any claim to reward from Him.

This is the meaning of the pregnant passage in Christ's earliest recorded teaching: "Where thy treasure is, there is thy heart also. The light [lamp] of thy body is thy eye. If thy eye be single, thy whole body shall be lightsome. But if thy eye be evil, thy whole body shall be darksome."* Make God and His eternal possession your chief treasure: set your heart upon never losing that, whatever else in life you may lose or you may gain. Look ever up to Him in

---

* St. Matthew, vi. 21, 22.

the beginning of all your ways, and let your heart go with your eye : thereby His will shall be like an unquenchable lamp shedding its light upon your road through life,—or, if you prefer to view this fundamental truth otherwise, the love of Him within your heart will be like an unfailing light which you bear ever with you, making every path you walk in lightsome,—full of pleasantness, and peace, full of the unalterable joy of a conscience at rest, to which self-seeking, deceit, or dishonesty, are things unknown and impossible.

This is the fundamental principle of active Christian piety,—the very first letter of the alphabet of practical holiness so familiar to our forefathers, so universally familiar still among their faithful descendants. The following passage of the great St. Bonaventure expressed this perpetual yearning of the heart of the Christian man for God and His eternity :

"The first stage of our journey toward eternity is the right intention of eternal things. The soul of man through this aspiration toward what is everlasting, is borne upward, urged onward, and given strength to proceed on its early journey. It aims, first, at possessing the One Eternal Reality, fixing its attention upon it, reaching forward to it, persisting in its quest of it, making of it the chief motive of its life,—because that one eternal thing is the one thing necessary, which consummates by possession all the soul's desires, and fixes them on the One treasure, which shall not be taken from it forever. Our reason tells us that we must fix our aim on this, before directing our views to aught else : for our highest and most honorable achievements must prove unavailing, when the eye of the heart is turned aside from its Eternal Object." *

Yes, surely, this is the lamp of right intention, of living active faith by which all Christian men of business must direct their steps every day they rise. And one cannot but perceive, on the simple enunciation of this most rational

---

* Sanctus Bonaventura, *De Septem Itineribus.*

and most beautiful doctrine,—that fidelity to this practice of purity of intention must make life a success, while the forgetfulness of·God and eternity leads to utter failure, ruin, and despair.

In looking at the many and most melancholy wrecks that daily strew the shores of the great stream of active life,—how many a man can say, as he sits and meditates over the causes of his own ruin,—just what the poet says of his own misapplied gifts and wasted life?

> "I have been cunning in mine overthrow,
>   The careful pilot of my proper woe.
>   Mine were my faults, and mine be their reward.
>   My whole life was a contest, since the day
>   That gave me being, gave me that which marred
>   The gift,—a fate or will that walked astray.
>   Had I but sooner learnt the crowd to shun,
>   I had been better than I now can be;
>   The passions which have torn me would have slept;
>   *I* had not suffered, and *thou* hadst not wept.
>   With false Ambition what had I to do?
>   Little with Love, and least of all with Fame.
>   . This was not the end I did pursue;
>   Surely, I once beheld a nobler aim.
>   But all is over—I am one the more
>   To baffled millions which have gone before." *

The mere human sentiments,—without a thought of God or of one's accountability to Him,—which are expressed in this long wail of Vanity foiled and finding itself face to face with Self, ruined and dishonored, are pitiful enough, and all the more so that the suffering spirit had never sought God, and in its agony, has no thought of seeking Him.

Let us learn wisdom betimes, and trim the lamp of conscience by the light of these lurid fires of Despair. We have uttered the word "Conscience:" it is or should be for the busy man of the world,—the merchant, the banker, the broker, the manufacturer,—what a mighty spell-word was ever conceived to be among the Eastern nations, all powerful to guard from ill, to release from difficulty and danger,

---

* Byron, "Epistle to his Sister Augusta."

and to obtain in need the most precious boons from a super-
natural power.

The reality of conscience is more than all that for you,
if you can only apprehend its meaning aright, and be
guided by its teachings.

Conscience is God's own light and voice in our inmost
soul telling us, at every step of our journey through life,—
and telling us, with unmistakable clearness and unerring
certainty,—that we must be true to the Light within us and
walk according to its guidance; true to our own soul's con-
victions, spiritual aspirations, and tendencies; true to our
fellow-men, whoever or whatever they may be,—true to
them in our words and actions, as if God were immediately
to judge us after each action and each word; true to God
Himself,—honoring Him, our acknowledged Master and
Parent, by never allowing stain or suspicion of stain to fall
on our personal honor, on our truthfulness, our honesty,
our integrity, our faithfulness to given word or plighted
promise;—so true to God and to ourselves as His sons, that
to us falsehood, deception, betrayal of trust, dishonest deed
or thought or aim, must be an utter impossibility.

Have they not banished conscience, in our days, from
many walks of the business world? Have they not quenched
the divine lamp in the soul's sanctuary, and derided (for
they cannot silence) the incorruptible voice within them?
And with conscience have not trustfulness, and good faith
and security, and uprightness, and immaculate honor dis-
appeared from all the great marts and centers of commer-
cial life?

Will you help to bring back the Divine Presence, the
ever-burning Light, and the Voice that cannot be bought
or silenced,—to the counting-house, the exchange, the fac-
tory? Let the writer point out the way, as he has learned
it, not only from the experiences of modern times, but from
the teachings of by-gone generations. He will hold up the
mirror, and you will find those whom to copy and to follow.

You will hear around you daily voices saying: "Catho-
licism is pernicious; it is best not to meddle with it. It

makes a man a coward; he cannot sin but it accuseth him; he cannot swear but it checks him; he cannot sophisticate but it detects him. 'Tis a spirit that mutinies in a man's bosom; it fills one full of obstacles; it is turned out of towns and cities for a dangerous thing; and every man that means to live as he pleaseth, endeavors to trust to himself and live without it? They are right. The confessional, the advice, or even implied judgment of holy persons, who with the firmness of their souls by reasons guide us, may, and will, form a hinderance to many undertakings. The Marquis of Tabara, being engaged in an arduous affair, applied to Marina de Escobar, begging her to commend it to God. He seemed already on the point of succeeding in it, when the venerable Marina told him that it was not expedient, and sent Father Luis de Ponte to announce to him the result of her prayers. Though it required a hard sacrifice, the Marquis received her counsel as from God, and relinquished the pursuit of his project. He acted like the pilot in a storm, who being directed by the young St. Catherine of Sienna to turn his vessel to the wind, obeyed her, and in consequence came to the desired port in safety.

" Catholicity beholds in many things familiar on the road of human industry, the tree of prohibition, and forbids the sweetness, though it promise that knowledge which made Eve address the apple in the words,

> ——' Experience, next, to thee I owe,
> Best guide ; not following thee, I had remained
> In ignorance.' " *

Modern industry, modern business, like Eve, when the forbidden fruit has been plucked and tasted, finds that the sweet savor lasts but a moment, leaving behind the bitterness of death. Even before the poison has wrought its worst on heart and brain, the sinner discovers that conscience, not gain is the "best guide," and would give worlds to recall his past "ignorance," and forget the pangs and terrors of the guilty knowledge he has acquired.

---

* Digby, "Compitum," iii., ch. v.

As we pen these lines, in the last days of August,* the great daily papers are filled with lists of men, "business men" all of them, who rush to the courts to profit by the expiring bankrupt law, and no one offers the pretense that these same bankrupts are acting in good faith: No, the whole public of this great commercial metroplis acknowledges without a pang of remorse or a blush of shame,—that the expiring law favored fraud and dishonesty, and that these rushing crowds who throng all the avenues of the courts of law, are acting fraudulently, dishonorably,—robbing their creditors and perjuring themselves in the very oath they dare to take!

Are matters carried on more honestly, more conscientiously on the Stock Exchange, in our numerous Savings Banks, by our great railroad corporations in city and country, by the great merchants who are not ashamed to defraud the revenue whenever they can purchase impunity, by our manufacturers who set aside all the laws of natural equity and—too often, alas,—of humanity itself in their dealings with the laboring millions ? And shall we go out, like our scientific exploring expeditions, with sounding-rod and drag-net, and measure these depths of iniquity and shame one after the other? or shall we draw up to the light of day from the slime of their native beds the dark mysteries, and the dishonored names that it were better to leave buried there forever?

"It may be indeed an unworthy consideration," says Digby, "but the fact is, that the mere desire of promoting their own success in their respective employments can direct practical men to desire an extension of the influence of the Catholic faith, which affords the best securities against the calamities, disgrace, and ruin to which they are exposed by the dishonesty of others, of their rivals, of their assistants, and perhaps even of their own children. *For the effects of such instruction, if unimpeded, would be a deep sense of responsibility, and a delicacy of conscience on the least as well as on the greatest occasions !*"

---

* 1878.

We might take the most Catholic of the great continental nations at the very period when Western Christendom was not broken asunder, and Spain was at the very height of her industrial and military greatness,—and show what unbending integrity and inviolable honor presided over every industrial enterprise and commercial transaction. Take this "photograph" of one city of Northern Spain,—as a sample of every other city throughout the Peninsula and including the then glorious and thrifty Portugal,—and judge of the tree of Catholic conscience by its fruits.

"At Burgos the inhabitants are not idle or strayers abroad; but all, not only men but women, seek to gain their bread by the labor of their hands, exercising virtuously all kinds of liberal and mechanical arts. The merchants who enrich the city are full of faith and liberality. The priests are most studious of the divine worship and diligent in application to learning as well as to their sacred offices. The magistrates regard the public welfare with prudence and integrity. In fine, men of all orders and professions are exact in the performance of their respective duties; so that the city daily increases in prosperity and fame." *

You have, we presume, traveled in Italy, as well as through the countries of Northern Europe. You are therefore not unacquainted with the style in which Christian Europe, before the middle of the sixteenth century, decorated the places of public business,—the Town Hall, the Exchange or Merchants' Hall, and the Guild Hall. Passing over the magnificent municipal and civic edifices of the Low Countries, France, Germany, and Northern Italy,—we shall mention one easily accessible to the religious pilgrim or the pleasure-seeker on his way through Etruria to Rome. Stop at Perugia for a day,—and visit the Exchange (*Sala del Cambio*), to admire the immortal creations of Perugino, the beautiful city's noblest son. The whole place is filled with divine and graceful forms in keeping with the lovely coun-

---

* Marinæi Siculi, *De Rebus Hispanicis*, lib. iii.

try and with the pious spirit of its people. One feels even now on entering the place,—desecrated though everything has been by a spirit far from Christian,—as if one entered a sanctuary of religion, instead of the hall where Perugia's men of business met in times when conscience reigned supreme, and honor was the soul of commercial activity. Indeed, the contemporaries of Pietro Perugino did want to make of their Exchange a sort of sanctuary blessed by religion, where every glorious figure on walls and ceiling should recall to them their accountability to the God who is infinitely just and infinitely faithful and true.

The painting of this superb monument of commercial honor was done at the expense of the Guild of Woollen Drapers. Are we suggesting? No, indeed. Nor are we preaching. We deposit a few germs of deep and salutary thoughts in generous hearts, and pass on.

We exhorted the business man, at the beginning of each day,—to trim his lamp at God's own altar; and then to be guided by conscience during the varied labors that awaited him.

What is more important still, is that you should in the steady and truthful light of your conscience, examine the transactions of the last twenty-four hours.

Examine, O merchant, how you have dealt with your associates, with your debtors and with your creditors. God has prospered you, and increased your substance tenfold and a hundredfold. All the fruits of industry have increased and multiplied in your hands. Have you grown more conscientious,—more scrupulous about truth, about your plighted faith, about even the minutest detail of your business, according as you grew in wealth? Has prosperity bound your heart more lovingly, gratefully, firmly to Him from whom every blessing comes down on men and the work of their hands?

But,—above all,—how do you treat your dependants? They are many,—a host in themselves, perhaps. Do you treat them, every one of them, *justly*,—as man is strictly bound to treat the veriest savage, who labors for him or who exchanges his furs or his simple wares for their lawful and fair equivalent in money? Do you treat them *generously,*— as brother should treat brother for whose life-blood and soul he is to account to their common Father and Judge? Or do you exact from those beneath you the very utmost their strength at its greatest pitch of exertion can produce for a stipend that barely suffices to keep body and soul together? And if so, how do you expect to fare at that dread Judgment Seat, whither not one minutest fraction of your wealth will follow you, but where a kind word to the sinking heart of your poor toilers, or a merciful alleviation of their intolerable load of labor, or a timely addition to the pittance of the over-worked mother, or daughter, or sister, or of the father borne down by the care of the dear ones he can neither feed, nor clothe, nor warm—*would plead for your soul more powerfully* than the hundreds of thousands you have squandered in ostentatious charity,—the very worst form of heartless vanity?

Charity? Ah, we go often far away from our own door to seek objects of so-called charity,—while those who look up to us for the bread of to-day or for the brotherly sympathy often more needful than bread to the famished heart, —are allowed to go the whole night and day, and weary week after week, unpitied, uncared for, unthought of!

Look well into your conscience, O brother! God has given you much: from our heart we pray Him to give you still more. But bethink you, while it is yet time, that your responsibility is in precise proportion to the unbounded liberality of Providence in your regard.

To manufacturers of every class,—these great princes of our industry,—of whom their country is so justly proud,— what shall we say, in addition to this adjuration? Shall we add our voice to the many warring voices that now resound throughout both hemispheres stirring up Labor against Capital, or steeling capitalists to the sad needs of those dependent on them? God forbid! The ministry of the priest to-day must be what it has always been, one of mediation and conciliation between brothers at variance,—

trusting himself to both in his efforts at pacification, and trusted by both as true love and true charity ever is.

We see, however, the mighty tide of popular discontent rising higher day by day, and lashed into greater fury by. the breath of passions that are not of Heaven, and of an eloquence that is not fired by true love of the brotherhood.

We all remember how a great English chancellor, nearly half a century ago, pleaded the cause of timely reform before the House of Peers. In his prophetic dread of the evils which were sure to arise from acknowledged wrongs, left so long unremedied, and from inveterate abuses crying out for reform, he cast himself on his knees before the lordly assembly and besought them with tears to have pity on their country, and to spare their order and themselves the fearful consequences of popular revenge. He was heard, and the reforms were granted.

We could kneel to you, O you on whose generosity and intelligence depends so much of the welfare of your country, and beseech you with a voice that would borrow its tones from no venal interest or unworthy passion,—to consider how much you can do to better the condition of millions of working men and women within the land.

But were it given us to be in spirit or in the body by your side, when, at the end of your day's manifold cares, and before you commit yourself to that sleep which is the image of the eternal repose,—we should lovingly whisper in your ear to open the book of your conscience there, beneath the eye of the all-seeing God, and to examine yourselves as to how you stand,—in strict justice, in brotherly charity, in the claims of common humanity,—toward each one of the families who toil for you, who labor to build up your fortune and your fame.

You stand for them in the place of God,—representing His fatherly care, His tenderness, His justice, His generosity,—the wise love that cares for the souls and bodies, for the health, the hearts, the homes of the many who look up to you to make life bearable, health robust and flourishing, hearts grateful and happy, homes bright and blessed by all the sanctities of Christian and family life. Is this your care? Assuredly, it is your interest; most assuredly it is your duty; and your duty is to your GOD!

Read the following anecdote carefully, and we then leave you to the inspiration of that Mercy who is the great Healer of all our wounds in this life, and the advocate in the great Judgment of all who have been merciful.

"Gregorius Tilianus, a most learned youth, being found in sickness lying on a poor bed, which he had chosen expressly for its wretchedness, the visitor said, 'I am ashamed to see you lying like a needy beggar.' 'Say, rather, like a king or emperor,' he replied cheerfully. 'Do they not in time of war lie as roughly?'

"In his last hour he ordered the poor to be convoked and admitted. These were already in the vestibule, and so eager to enter, it was difficult to keep them back. 'Let them enter,' he says, 'and not suffer Christ to wait before the door; and distribute my alms to them in my presence, and say to each not to return thanks, as it is in payment of what I owe to them, and not a gift. Then dismiss them, and invite them to return to supper.'

"It was a touching sight to observe the grief of the poor as they pressed in to their friend. The blind, the lame, orphans, widows, the aged, epileptics, and lepers, and those suffering from all sorts of maladies and calamities,—all wept but Gregory, who had a smiling countenance as he spoke to console them, adding, 'Not alone to the poor does God show mercy, but also to those who do good to the poor?'

"In disposing of his property he ordered that even his books should be sold and the price given to the poor. 'Sell it,' he says, 'either in whole or in parts, and spare not the nobility of books. For there is nothing on earth so noble and precious that it ought not to be employed to the glory of Christ. . . . I wish we had the gold of Arabia, that we might distribute it with the books!" *

---

* De Richebourcq, *Ultima Verba Factaque.*

CHAPTER XXIII.

THE LABORING MAN.

It is a common sentence that knowledge is power; but who hath duly considered or set forth the power of ignorance? Knowledge slowly builds up what ignorance in an hour pulls down. Knowledge, through patient and frugal centuries, enlarges discovery and makes record of it; ignorance, wanting its day's dinner, lights a fire with the record, and gives a flavor to its one roast with the burned souls of many generations. Knowledge, instructing the sense, refining and multiplying needs, transforms itself into skill, and makes life various with a new Six Days' Work; comes ignorance drunk, on the seventh, with a firkin of oil and a match and an easy "Let there be,"—and the many-colored creation is shriveled up in blackness. Of a truth, knowledge is power, but it is a power reined by scruple, having a conscience of what must be and may be; whereas ignorance is a blind giant who, let him but wax unbound, would make it a sport to seize the pillars that hold up the long-wrought fabric of human good, and turn all the places of joy dark as a buried Babylon.

IF we have reserved the laborer for our last chapter and the crown of our work, it is not that we love him less or hold him of less account than the professional man or the man of letters. On the contrary, in every one of the preceding chapters, the great virtues inculcated had for one of their chief purposes to bring the rich, the learned, the powerful, and the influential into more brotherly sympathy with the working-man.

We are poor ourselves, and of the poor; our life has been spent in laboring among them, and we consider that the sweetest reward of our present toil shall be in having our books find their way to the home of the laboring man in city and country.

It is no new gospel that a priestly hand could hold out to the sons of toil the whole world over. We cannot

454

promise to make this earth a fool's paradise where dream-
ers, idlers, and schemers might dawdle away, in all the
ignoble vices that idleness and knavery beget, the golden
years given us to merit eternity. Nor may we hold out to
those who are not the heirs of great wealth or high rank
any other Heaven hereafter than that purchased and prom-
ised by the Redeemer of mankind.

Redeemer! Saviour! God of our souls! Comforter of
our homes,—the Friend and treasure of the poor,—a laborer
Himself, while living among us, to sanctify and sweeten
labor; we know that Jesus of Nazareth is all our own,—
ALL, even with the glory and bliss of His eternal kingdom!
What other gospel, then, do we, can we desire, than that
which the sweet and patient Son of Mary, the pupil and
adopted child of Joseph the Carpenter, presents to us?

"Come to Me, all you that labor, and are burdened, and
I will refresh you. Take up My yoke upon you, and learn
of Me, because I am meek, and humble of heart: and you
shall find rest for your souls." *

Yes,—He presents Himself to you, O toilers of the field,
the factory, and the city,—you whose sweat and whose
tears fall upon the hard earth or into the salt sea; He comes
to you, in His boyhood and early manhood, with His hands
hardened from the carpenter's toil,—long before He stretched
them forth on the bitter wood of the cross to be pierced and
torn with the nails; He comes to you, as that Jesus the
Good Shepherd whose feet wearied not in traveling again
and again and again from one end of His native land to the
other in quest of the suffering poor or the over-burdened
workmen, to cheer them at their toil, to lighten their mis-
ery; and how often, in His own sweet seasons of visitation
and needful comfort, has not that same Good Shepherd
knocked at your door, His head wet with the dews of the
night, and His blessed feet torn and bleeding from the road?

O brothers,—it is in the vesture of His love that we
all wish Him to come to us,—with "the purple garment'

* St. Matthew, xi. 28, 29.

showing through its rents where whip and scourge have ploughed the flesh, His head encircled with piercing thorns, His meek face bruised with buffets and soiled with dust and spittle, and tears and blood, the strong hands grasping and the mangled shoulders bearing the Cross, and the deep eyes looking into the soul of every one of us to say: "I am the Good Shepherd." "Behold I have graven thee in My hands;" * "Yea, I have loved thee with an everlasting love, therefore have I drawn thee [to Myself], taking pity on thee;"† "It is I, fear ye not!"‡ "I, I Myself will comfort you!" § Ah, dear above all that earth and sky contain that is most dear, is to the manly, grateful heart of the laborer, the poor, the suffering, this God of our hearts, this God of our fathers coming to us in our daily need clad in the livery of His love, bearing on hands and feet, on head and heart the glorious wounds inflicted for our sake!

And what does he preach? Patience, purity of heart, contempt of earthly riches, a noble ardor, an insatiable hunger and thirst for all Godlike virtue; fortitude under suffering and trial; unwearied and unfaltering trust in His own ever-present aid; an ambition to be so like Himself in thought and word and deed that all men may see in you the living image of Jesus mighty in loving,—that is, in laboring, suffering, and accomplishing great things for His love; a heart too great for this world and all the things of time, and to be filled only by the Infinite God and the Charity of His everlasting kingdom.

But this is too high a flight. Let us see, more calmly and with the sights and sounds of our daily toil around us —what He, our model, wishes every laboring man to be.

Would you contemplate for a moment the army of workmen who have practiced the most heroic virtues in following Christ, and whom the Church has placed among her canonized saints? The Apostles were fishermen by occupation,—and St. Paul, the most eloquent of them all, was by

* Isaias, xlix. 16.   † Jeremias, xxxi. 3.
‡ St. Matthew, xiv. 27.   § Isaias, li. 12.

trade a tentmaker, and like his brothers in the Apostleship, earned his own bread while laboring to spread the faith of Christ. The men and women who were first drawn to Him by the preaching and the lowly laborious lives of these Apostles were from the laboring classes,—becoming, in their turn, the ardent propagators of the Gospel specially destined for the lowly and the poor. Thus Onesimus,—the fugitive slave, whom St. Paul converted while imprisoned at Rome, became to the captive Apostle an energetic helper. As Christianity spread, and with its extension persecution waxed fiercer, the laboring classes everywhere furnished their glorious contingent to the host of confessors and martyrs. In every city of the Roman Empire, the common laborer, the tradesman, the liberated slaves of both sexes stood forth before the tribunals beside their masters to confess Jesus Christ, and died with them in the most fearful tortures to confirm this courageous testimony. What need of these details?

We have at this moment,—among many other venerable names which we omit,—St. Patrick, a slave and shepherd, as the apostle and patron of Ireland, St. Isidore, a farmer, as one of the chief protectors of Spain; St. Genevieve, a poor shepherdess, the honored protectress of Paris; and among the most recently canonized French saints, Germaine Cousin, another poor shepherd-girl, and Benedict Labre, a man who devoted himself to even worse poverty and hardship. Then, as we glance over Christian Europe, we meet here and there with SS. Crispin and Crispinian, martyrs, the patrons of shoemakers, and shoemakers themselves · St. Theodotus, an innkeeper, and also a martyr; St. Homobonus, St. Maximus, and St. Justus, tradesmen and shopkeepers; St. Phocas and St. Serenus, gardeners; St. Galmier, a locksmith; St. Margaret of Louvain, a servant-maid in a tavern, under a master and mistress who died victims to their charity, and in the hour when they had given up all things to follow Christ. The Blessed Peter of Sienna was a combmaker; St. Zita of Lucca, a servant-maid; St. Justa and St. Rufina, of Seville, were workers in earthenware, which they sold themselves. St. Fazio of Verona was a silversmith; St. Thibaud was an apprentice shoemaker. And have we not among the recently beatified of the Society of Jesus Alfonso Rodriguez, a lay-brother and a porter, —a man so divinely wise that he was the spiritual guide of Peter Claver, the apostle of New Grenada,—one of the most heroic souls that ever honored any country?

Can you not hear, as the saintly host of glorified working men and women pass before you in the train of the Lamb, the beatitudes pronounced by the Master, reëchoed triumphantly by these, His faithful disciples: Blessed are ye poor! . . . Blessed are ye that hunger now! Blessed are the meek. . . .

Will you learn what the holiest men known in the history of the Church thought, under divine teaching, of the exalted sanctity to which every laborer, every working man and woman, every tiller of the soil the whole world over can be, by cultivating their hearts aright and making them like the heart of the Master, meek and humble, patient and charitable?

"When Blessed Anthony," says the historian of the fathers, "prayed in his cell, he heard a voice, saying, 'Anthony, you have not yet reached the measure of a tanner in Alexandria.' The next day, taking up his staff, the old man set out for the city, and having come to the tanner's house, he entered and asked him to describe his manner of life, as he had left the desert to learn it from him. The tanner replied that he was not aware of his doing any good. *Therefore,—he added,—when I rise in the morning, before I sit down to work, I say that all this city, from the youngest to the oldest, will enter the kingdom of Heaven, while I, for my sins, deserve eternal punishment; and I say the same thing in the evening before I lie down, and I believe from my heart what I say.* 'It is enough,' said Blessed Anthony, 'I understand my vision.'" *

Would you have the priest enter your homes and preach you another gospel than this? or propose to you a dearer,

* De Vita Sanctorum Patrum, in Migne's collection.

safer model than your own Jesus? or say to you that you must take up a gospel of hate, and strife, and violence, and bloodshed,—instead of His sweet Gospel of patience, meekness, humility, love, and peace?

He who writes these lines, while he was a poor missionary in the backwoods of Canada thirty years ago (in the autumn of 1847), and while sharing with the poorest settlers among his widely-scattered flock the comforts piety provided for the priest even out of extreme poverty,—set himself about devising many schemes for the improvement of these hardy settlers' lot, and for the greater good of their brethren both in Canada and in the old country. The government, the Canadian bishops and clergy, and all the most enlightened men in the country united, at the missionary's voice, to open the waste forest-lands to colonization, and to aid every farmer and his sons toward possessing independent and comfortable homes, and toward securing them many other helps and advantages. The missionary's voice found thus a ready echo in generous hearts: his sole merit was in having uttered a timely word of exhortation; to others belongs the praise of having made of his dream a great and living reality.

And this we say here,—not through egotism,—but to tell the reader that the priestly heart which speaks in these pages, is one that has ever been devoted to the laboring-man and his best interests. Yes,—the writer knows what noble souls are those of the toiling millions when not led astray by that fell "power of ignorance," mentioned in the extract heading of this chapter, or fascinated by the ungodly and unmanly theories of "Ignorance drunk," who, blind, blasphemous, and brutal giant as he is, would this very day,—if the spirit of Christianity were not there to prevent him, pull down the whole edifice of civilization over our heads, even though he should himself perish in the ruin.

We happen to know, also, the brave, warm, true heart that beats beneath the rude exterior and homespun of the working-man. We have so often shared the hospitality of his roof, and have admired the native delicacy and refinement, the gentle courtesy, the unbought and unbounded generosity,—and all the other virtues that lie beneath that homespun,—like purest gold or rarest gems in their native mine.

What then ? Do we not wish to improve these virtues ? Most assuredly. But we would have them grow in the sunlight of Christ's truth and teaching ; we would have the rich soil of these brave hearts made fruitful by the grace of Him who is, for the peasant as for the prince, for the working-man as for his employer,—"the Way, the Truth, and the Life."

We would have pure gold remain gold ; only we would refine it, fashion it into vessels fit for God's own altar in Heaven.

And you, O dearest brothers, do not give your ear or your heart to this new gospel of hate they would have you believe in. In a country such as this in which you have cast your lot, you are free to rise,—you see so many rise every day from your own level to sit, in Church and in State, with the princes of the people. Be conscientious, God-fearing, sober, steady, persevering, lovers of truth, of honor, of honesty, and all true manliness,—and God will surely prosper you.

Do not believe in the raving of a few madmen, about the abolition of wealth, and all such idle, destructive fancies. Do your best, honestly and honorably, to become independent, to become wealthy. What you get is your own: God grant you to make a right use of it, and with it to help others around you to rise.

Look at our magnificent American forests,—see how by the side and beneath the shade of these lordly trees, that are the admiration of the whole earth, their juniors and successors shoot up, straight, vigorous, and aiming at being one day the equals in height and stateliness of their elders. But cut down that glorious forest or set fire to it, and never again until the end of time will such a magnificent growth arise from the ashes.

PUBLICATIONS

OF

P. J. KENEDY,

Excelsior Catholic Publishing House,

5 BARCLAY ST., NEAR BROADWAY, NEW YORK,

Opposite the Astor House

Adventures of Michael Dwyer...................	**$1 00**
Adelmar the Templar. A Tale................	**40**
Ballads, Poems, and Songs of William Collins......................................	**1 00**
Blanche. A Tale from the French..................	**40**
Battle of Ventry Harbor.........................	**20**
Bibles, from $2 50 to.............................	**15 00**
Brooks and Hughes Controversy...............	**75**
Butler's Feasts and Fasts......................	**1 25**
Blind Agnese. A Tale........................	**50**
Butler's Catechism.............................	**8**
" " with Mass Prayers.............	**30**
Bible History. Challoner......................	**50**
Christian Virtues. By St. Liguori..............	**1 00**
Christian's Rule of Life. By St. Liguori.........	**30**
Christmas Night's Entertainments.........	**60**
Conversion of Ratisbonne..................	**50**
Clifton Tracts. 4 vols...........................	**3 00**
Catholic Offering. By Bishop Walsh.............	**1 50**
Christian Perfection. Rodriguez. 3 vols. *Only complete edition*..............................	**4 00**
Catholic Church in the United States. By J. G. Shea. Illustrated...........................	**2 00**
Catholic Missions among the Indians........	**2 50**
Chateau Lescure. A Tale.......................	**50**
Conscience; or, May Brooke. A Tale..............	**1 00**
Catholic Hymn-Book..........................	**15**
Christian Brothers' 1st Book..................	**13**

Catholic Prayer-Books, 25c., 50c., up to **12 00**
☞ Any of above books sent free by mail on receipt of price. Agents wanted everywhere to sell above books, to whom liberal terms will be given. Address

P. J. KENEDY, Excelsior Catholic Publishing House,
5 Barclay Street, New York.

1

Christian Brothers' 2d Book....................	*$0 25*
" " *3d*	*63*
" " *4th*	*88*
Catholic Primer................................	*6*
Catholic School-Book.........................	*25*
Cannon's Practical Speller....................	*25*
Carpenter's Speller............................	*25*
Dick Massey. An Irish Story..................	*1 00*
Doctrine of Miracles Explained...............	*1 00*
Doctrinal Catechism...........................	*50*
Douay "	*25*
Diploma of Children of Mary.................	*20*
Erin go Bragh. (Sentimental Songster.).........	*25*
El Nuevo Testamento. (Spanish.)...............	*1 50*
Elevation of the Soul to God..................	*75*
Epistles and Gospels. (Goffine.)...............	*2 00*
Eucharistica ; or, Holy Eucharist.............	*1 00*
End of Controversy. (Milner.).................	*75*
El Nuevo Catecismo. (Spanish.)...............	*15*
El Catecismo de la Doctrina Christiana. (Spanish Catechism)........................	*15*
El Catecismo Ripalda. (Spanish).............	*12*
Furniss' Tracts for Spiritual Reading.	*1 00*
Faugh a Ballagh Comic Songster............	*25*
Fifty Reasons.................................	*25*
Following of Christ............................	*50*
Fashion. A Tale. 35 Illustrations.............	*50*
Faith and Fancy. Poems. Savage..............	*75*
Glories of Mary. (St. Liguori.)...............	*1 25*
Golden Book of Confraternities...............	*50*
Grounds of Catholic Doctrine.................	*25*
Grace's Outlines of History...................	*50*
Holy Eucharist................................	*1 00*
Hours before the Altar. Red edges..............	*50*
History of Ireland. Moore. 2 vols.............	*5 00*
" O'Mahoney's Keating.......	*4 00*
Hay on Miracles	*1 00*
Hamiltons. A Tale............................	*50*
History of Modern Europe. Shea..............	*1 25*
Hours with the Sacred Heart..................	*50*
Irish National Songster.......................	*1 00*
Imitation of Christ............................	*40*

Catholic Prayer-Books, 25c., 50c., *up to* 12 00
  ☞ Any of above books sent free by mail on receipt of price. Agents wanted everywhere to sell above books, to whom liberal terms will be given. Address

    P. J. KENEDY, Excelsior Catholic Publishing House,
      5 Barclay Street, New York.

Irish Fireside Stories, Tales, and Legends.
(Magnificent new book just out.) About 400 pages
large 12mo, containing about 40 humorous and pa-
thetic sketches.   12 fine full-page Illustrations.
Sold only by subscription.   Only...................... **$1 00**
Keeper of the Lazaretto. A Tale.............. **40**
Kirwan Unmasked. By Archbishop Hughes..... **12**
King's Daughters. An Allegory................. **75**
Life and Legends of St. Patrick.......... ...... **1 00**
Life of St. Mary of Egypt... .... **60**
" " *Winefride............................* **60**
" " *Louis........ ....* **40**
" " *Alphonsus M. Liguori............* **75**
" " *Ignatius Loyola.* 2 vols. **3 00**
Life of Blessed Virgin.................... **75**
Life of Madame de la Peltrie................. **50**
Lily of Israel. 22 Engravings.................... **75**
Life Stories of Dying Penitents................ **75**
Love of Mary **50**
Love of Christ........................ **50**
Life of Pope Pius IX....................... **1 00**
Lenten Manual........ .... **50**
Lizzie Maitland. A Tale....................... **75**
Little Frank. A Tale...................... **50**
Little Catholic Hymn-Book..................... **10**
Lyra Catholica (large Hymn-Book)................ **75**
Mission and Duties of Young Women........ **60**
Maltese Cross. A Tale....................... **40**
Manual of Children of Mary.................. **50**
Mater Admirabilis........................ **1 50**
Mysteries of the Incarnation. (St. Liguori.)... **75**
Month of November.......................... **40**
Month of Sacred Heart of Jesus.............. **50**
" " *Mary........................* **50**
Manual of Controversy..................... **75**
Michael Dwyer. An Irish Story of 1798........... **1 00**
Milner's End of Controversy.................. **75**
May Brooke ; or, Conscience. A Tale............ **1 00**
New Testament........................ **50**
Oramaika. An Indian Story................. **75**
Old Andrew the Weaver..................... **50**
Preparation for Death.   St. Liguori.......... **75**

Catholic Prayer-Books, 25c., 50c., *up to . . . . .* **12 00**
☞ Any of above books sent free by mail on receipt of price. Agents
wanted everywhere to sell above books, to whom liberal terms will be given.
Address

P. J. KENEDY, Excelsior Catholic Publishing House,
5 Barclay Street, New York.

Prayer. By St. Liguori.......................... $0 50
Papist Misrepresented..................... 25
Poor Man's Catechism...................... 75
Rosary Book. 15 Illustrations.............. 10
Rome: Its Churches, Charities, and Schools. By Rev.
   Wm. H. Neligan, LL.D...................... 1 00
Rodriguez's Christian Perfection. 3 vols.
   Only complete edition...................... 4 00
Rule of Life. St. Liguori................... 40
Sure Way; or, Father and Son............ 25
Scapular Book................................ 10
Spirit of St. Liguori........................ 75
Stations of the Cross. 14 Illustrations........ 10
Spiritual Maxims. (St. Vincent de Paul)........ 40
Saintly Characters. By Rev. Wm. H. Neligan,
   LL.D...................................... 1 00
Seraphic Staff................................. 25
"   *Manual,* 75 cts. to................. 3 00
Sermons of Father Burke, plain................ 2 00
   "   "   gilt edges............ 3 00
Schmid's Exquisite Tales. 6 vols............. 3 00
Shipwreck. A Tale........................... 50
Savage's Poems............................... 2 00
Sybil: A Drama. By John Savage.............. 75
Treatise on Sixteen Names of Ireland. By
   Rev. J. O'Leary, D.D...................... 50
Two Cottages. By Lady Fullerton........... 50
Think Well On't. Large type................ 40
Thornberry Abbey. A Tale.................. 50
Three Eleanors. A Tale.................... 75
Trip to France. Rev. J. Donelan............ 1 00
Three Kings of Cologne..................... 30
Universal Reader............................ 50
Vision of Old Andrew the Weaver........... 50
Visits to the Blessed Sacrament............. 40
Willy Reilly. Paper cover.................. 50
Way of the Cross. 14 Illustrations........... 5
Western Missions and Missionaries......... 2 00
Walker's Dictionary........................ 75
Young Captives. A Tale.................... 50
Youth's Director............................ 50
Young Crusaders. A Tale................... 50

Catholic Prayer-Books, 25c., 50c., *up to* 12 00
 Any of above books sent free by mail on receipt of price. Agents wanted everywhere to sell above books, to whom liberal terms will be given. Address

   P. J. KENEDY, Excelsior Catholic Publishing House,
       5 Barclay Street, New York.